STRAND PRICE

D1174417

Law and Order

COLUMBIA STUDIES IN AMERICAN HISTORY

Alan Brinkley, General Editor

COLUMBIA STUDIES IN CONTEMPORARY AMERICAN HISTORY

Alan Brinkley, General Editor

See p. 295 for a complete list of titles in this series

Law and Order

STREET CRIME, CIVIL UNREST,
AND THE CRISIS OF LIBERALISM
IN THE 1960S

Michael W. Flamm

COLUMBIA UNIVERSITY PRESS NEW YORK

Columbia University Press
Publishers Since 1893
New York, Chichester, West Sussex

Library of Congress Cataloging-in-Publication Data
Flamm, Michael W.
Law and order : street crime, civil unrest, and the crisis of liberalism in the 1960's / Michael W. Flamm
p. cm. (Columbia studies in contemporary American history)
Includes bibliographical references and index.
ISBN 0-231-11512-1 (cloth : alk. paper)
ISBN 0-231-50972-3 (electronic)
1. Crime—United States. 2. Demonstrations—United States.
3. Riots—United States. 4. Liberalism—United States.
5. Conservatism—United States. 6. United States—Politics and government—1963-1969.
(Columbia studies in contemporary American history)

HV6789 .F573 2005
364.97/09/046 22 2004061853

Columbia University Press books are printed on permanent and durable acid-free paper

Printed in the United States of America
c 10 9 8 7 6 5 4 3 2 1

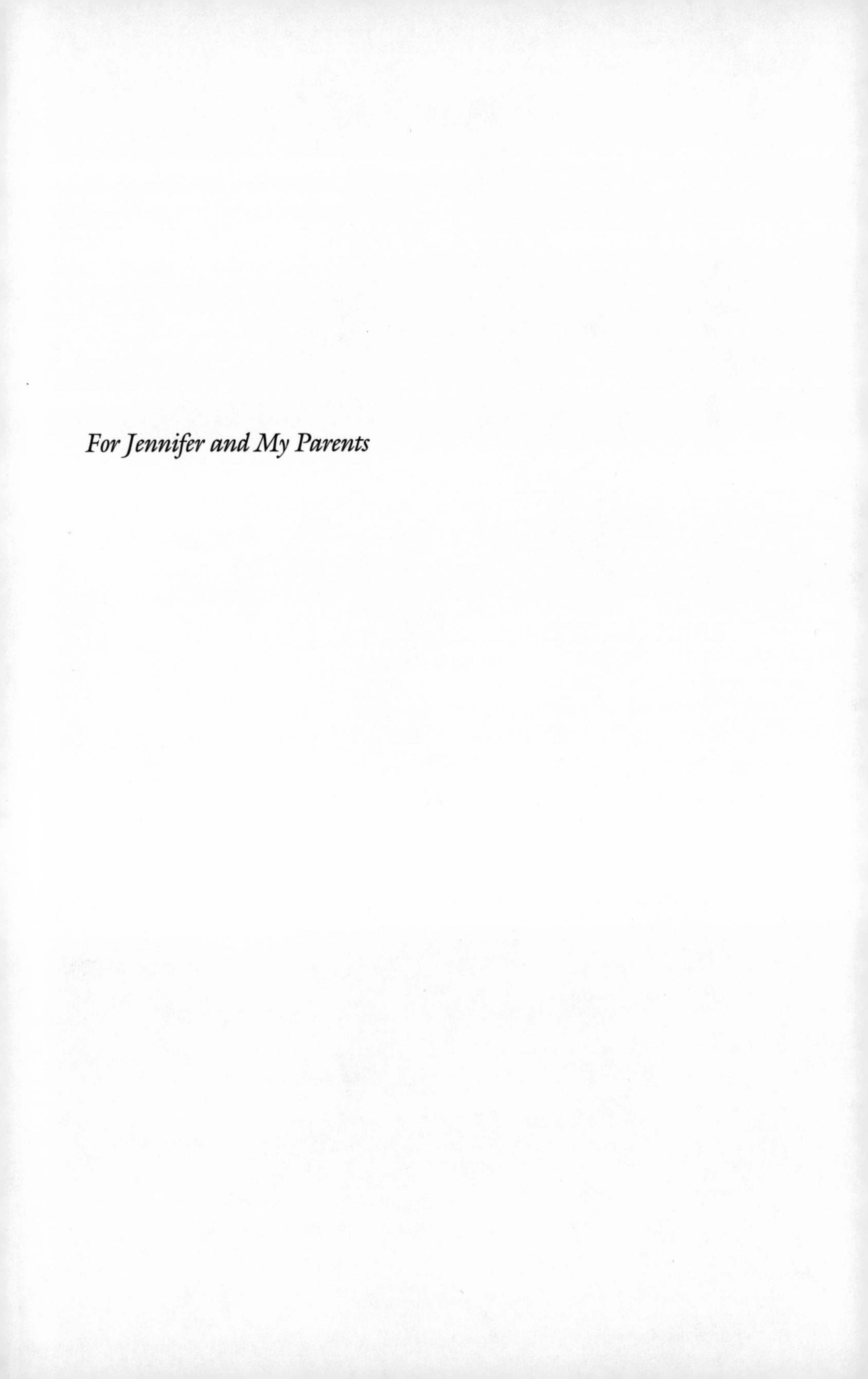

For Jennifer and My Parents

Contents

Illustrations

Illustrations appear as a group after page 82

Acknowledgments

In the course of researching and writing this book, I have accumulated many personal and professional debts—far too many, in fact, to ever repay properly. Nevertheless, I would like to make a partial and belated effort to thank at least some of those to whom I am grateful, beginning with those professors at Harvard who inspired my love of history: Bernard Bailyn, David Donald, Bradford Lee, Drew McCoy, and, above all, Alan Brinkley.

I first met Alan in my senior year of college. Although I had never taken a course with him, he readily agreed to serve as my thesis advisor. Since then he has taught me virtually everything I know about history and the historical profession. As a teacher and mentor, first at Harvard and then at Columbia, he has shown me that it is possible to balance a commitment to scholarship with a commitment to students. As a friend and colleague, he has demonstrated loyalty and generosity, kindness and consideration. I could not have completed this book without his intellectual guidance and personal support.

Graduate school is often a lonely and frustrating experience. But at Columbia I had the benefit of an extraordinarily supportive group of friends and teachers. In workshops, my fellow graduate students challenged me to develop and clarify my ideas. In seminars, Elizabeth Blackmar, Richard Bushman, David Cannadine, Eric Foner, and Kenneth Jackson taught me to appreciate the myriad ironies and complexities of history. Special thanks must also go to Ira Katznelson and Daryl Scott, whose comments and criticisms vastly improved sections of this work. And I owe a huge debt of gratitude to the members of the Probability Seminar, particularly Aaron Brenner, Eric Wakin, and Michael Zakim, whose good fellowship, intellectual insight, and generous collegiality led me to look forward with great anticipation to Thursday evenings in Fayerweather Hall.

Over the years, other friends have nurtured this author and sustained this project by offering kind thoughts and critical comments. Among those to whom I am especially grateful are Vincent Cannato, Matthew Dallek, Jonathan Engel, Charles Forcey, James Mabry, Tom Maguire, Lisa McGirr, Francesca Morgan, Wif Petersberger, Phil Prince, Jeff Roche, Jon Schoenwald, John Stoner, and Margaret Usdansky. I am also indebted to Eric Rothschild, the former chair of the Social Studies Department at Scarsdale High School. As a mentor and colleague, he taught me by example most of what I know about the teaching of history. As a friend, he encouraged me to pursue graduate studies even though it meant leaving a world that I knew and loved.

The collaborative nature of the historical profession has significantly improved this work. David Farber, Laura Kalman, and Michael Kazin generously offered perceptive criticisms of all or part of the manuscript. At various conferences, Robert Goldberg, David Greenberg, Leo Ribuffo, and Bruce Schulman also commented extensively on papers which emerged from this project. And at various times, Rick Perlstein graciously shared his thoughts and insights. In addition, this book has benefited greatly from the careful critiques of anonymous reviewers as well as the astute analysis of David Stebenne, whose friendship I treasure.

Research assistance came from many quarters, including the Arizona Historical Foundation, the Minnesota Historical Society, the Herbert Hoover Institution, the George Meany Memorial Archives, the Rockefeller Archive Center, the Museum of Television and Radio, the Television News Archive, the Political Commercial Archive, the New York Municipal Reference Library, the National Archives, the Library of Congress, and the Richard M. Nixon Library, where Susan Naulty was extremely helpful and courteous. Financial support came from Columbia University as well as the John Fitzgerald Kennedy Presidential Library and the Lyndon Baines Johnson Presidential Library, whose wonderful staff merits special praise. In particular, I want to thank Claudia Anderson, Allen Fisher, and Michael Parrish, whose invaluable suggestions led me to a wealth of materials that I might otherwise have overlooked. Their professionalism made it a pleasure to visit Austin and is a tribute to archivists everywhere. Thanks are also due to those individuals who allowed me to conduct interviews with them: Joseph Califano, Douglass Cater, Lloyd Cutler, James Gaither, Nicholas Katzenbach, Matthew Nimetz, Norbert Schlei, James Vorenberg, Ben Wattenberg, Lee White, and Adam Yarmolinsky. I only regret that I could not complete this book in time for all of them to read it.

I feel honored to be a member of the faculty at Ohio Wesleyan University, where my colleagues have provided a supportive and congenial environment. I also feel fortunate to have had two gifted editors at Columbia University Press in Peter Dimock and Anne Routon. Their good sense and wise contributions—as well as the keen eye of copy editor Leslie Bialler—have made this book far better than it was when it first arrived in their capable hands. Of course, any and all mistakes or omissions remain entirely my own.

Lastly, I am profoundly grateful for the love and support of my parents and my wife. As a child, my mother and father filled me with a respect for, and devotion to, knowledge and learning. As an adult, they provided encouragement and reassurance when I most needed it. For her part, Jennifer McNally has brought more joy and happiness to my life than any person could possibly expect. At times words are inadequate. This is one of those times.

Law and Order

Introduction

In June 1968 a white father of five from North Carolina expressed his view of the state of the nation with these words:

> I'm sick of crime everywhere. I'm sick of riots. I'm sick of "poor" people demonstrations (black, white, red, yellow, purple, green or any other color!) I'm sick of the U.S. Supreme Court ruling for the good of a very small part rather than the whole of our society. . . . I'm sick of the lack of law enforcement. . . . I'm sick of Vietnam. . . . I'm sick of hippies, LSD, drugs, and all the promotion the news media give them. . . . But most of all, I'm sick of constantly being kicked in the teeth for staying home, minding my own business, working steadily, paying my bills and taxes, raising my children to be decent citizens, managing my financial affairs so I will not become a ward of the City, County, or State, and footing the bill for all the minuses mentioned herein.[1]

By the late 1960s, many whites, affluent and nonaffluent, liberal and conservative, urban and nonurban, had already experienced similar sentiments. Their fear, anger, resentment, and disgust, while genuine, was also part of a complicated nexus of racial, gender, class, and generational anxieties. Amid a pervasive sense that American society was coming apart at the seams, a new issue known as law and order emerged at the forefront of political discourse.[2] The issue first moved from the margins to the mainstream of national politics in 1964, when Barry Goldwater made it a central campaign theme in his challenge to Lyndon Johnson. As street crime, urban riots, and political demonstrations mounted over the next four years, it grew in intensity despite the desperate—and, in the end, doomed—efforts of the Johnson administration to contain it. By 1968 law and order was the most important domestic issue in the presidential election and arguably the decisive factor in Richard Nixon's narrow triumph over Hubert Humphrey. Almost 12 million voters had deserted the Democratic banner since the Johnson landslide four years earlier, many because they had come to believe that personal safety was now of necessity a political priority.

Anxious whites received little solace from liberals, who failed to take the matter seriously until it was too late.[3] In the face of the rise in crime (the murder rate alone almost doubled between 1963 and 1968), they initially maintained that the statistics were faulty—a response that if not incorrect was insensitive to the victims of crime as well as their friends and family, co-workers and neighbors.[4] They also tended to dismiss those who pleaded for law and order as racists, ignoring blacks who were victimized more often than any other group and insulting Jews who had steadfastly supported the civil rights movement. Finally, liberals insisted with some merit that the only truly effective way to fight crime was through an attack on root causes like poverty and unemployment. The argument helped to justify the War on Poverty in 1964, but soon left the Johnson administration vulnerable to conservative claims that the Great Society had worsened the epidemic of urban violence.

Above all, liberals routinely and consistently defined crime control as a local problem. Constitutionally and logistically, it was—in 1968 state and municipal governments still employed more than ten times as many full-time law enforcement officers as the federal government.[5] But the definition seemed rather convenient when liberals had already classified virtually every other social ill, most notably public education, as a national imperative. "Somehow, in the minds of most Americans the breakdown of local authority became the fault of the federal government," wrote a somewhat baffled Johnson in his memoirs.[6] Implicit in the statement was his rueful acknowledgment that after four years in office, his administration had failed to convince many whites, particularly urban ethnic Democrats, that it understood their fears and frustrations.[7] The loss of law and order eroded faith in government, leaving liberals unable to find a compelling "moral voice" on the issue.

By contrast, conservatives spoke with a cogent "moral voice" on law and order. In the wake of the Goldwater debacle, the issue helped to unify them. In constructing a popular message with visceral appeal, conservatives maintained that the breakdown in public order was the result of three developments aided and abetted by liberals. First, the civil rights movement had popularized the doctrine of civil disobedience, which promoted disrespect for law and authority. To make matters worse, President Johnson, in a crass and cynical bid for African-American votes, had condoned and even applauded demonstrators when they violated what they viewed as unjust and immoral laws. Second, the Supreme Court, in a series of decisions such as *Escobedo* and *Miranda*, had enhanced the rights of criminal defendants at the expense of law enforcement.[8] Finally, the Great Society trumpeted by the White House had directly or indirectly rewarded undeserving minorities for their criminal behavior during urban riots.

Conservatives also offered a positive program for the restoration of what they saw as a society of decency and security. Inverting their traditional stance on federalism, they maintained that the national government should assume a major role in the local fight against violence and disorder. The president should exert moral leadership from Washington, reinforcing respect for the law and promoting contempt for those who violated it. The Congress should curtail the liberal welfare state, which promoted paternalism and dependency at the expense of opportunity and responsibility. The Supreme Court should overturn recent rulings and ease excessive restraints on the police, allowing them to collect evidence and conduct interrogations as they saw fit within broad limits. And the federal courts should set a positive example by imposing harsher sentences on convicted criminals. In short, extremism in pursuit of law and order was no vice.

At a theoretical level, conservatives presented a dual vision of order. On the one hand, they repudiated the progressive ideal of a planned society administered by distant experts. Reasserting a conservative variant of American populism, they expressed hostility to social engineering as practiced by Supreme Court justices and Great Society bureaucrats who represented disembodied authority. Defending local institutions and individuals, conservatives praised in particular the neighborhood policeman who protected local values—political, moral, and property—and kept the civil peace despite outside interference. On the other hand, they contended that the community's right to order—to public safety as they saw it—took precedence over the individual's right to freedom. Rejecting the claim of radicals that public space was where demonstrators could assert such rights as free speech and free assembly, conservatives maintained that it was where izens with a legitimate stake in the community could enjoy themselves if ey complied with the legitimate demands of legitimate authority.[9]

At a popular level, law and order resonated both as a social ideal and political slogan because it combined an understandable concern over the rising number of traditional crimes—robberies and rapes, muggings and murders—with implicit and explicit unease about civil rights, civil liberties, urban riots, antiwar protests, moral values, and drug use. Of course, street crime differed in important ways from the other causes of civil unrest, but politicians, pundits, and propagandists across the political spectrum hastened to blur this distinction. In the process, they loaded law and order with layers of meaning virtually impossible to disentangle and turned it into a Rorschach test of public anxiety.[10]

What ultimately gave law and order such potency, then, was precisely its amorphous quality, its ability to represent different concerns to different people at different moments. To be sure, the issue often rested on deliberate omissions, such as the reality that civil disobedience was often the only recourse left to demonstrators denied fundamental freedoms and confronted by officials who themselves repeatedly defied the law. But at the same time, it clarified (or simplified) a confusing image of danger and disorder. Law and order identified a clear cast of violent villains (protesters, rioters, and criminals), explained the causes for their actions (above all the doctrine of civil disobedience and the paternalism of the welfare state), and implied a ready response (limited government, moral leadership, and judicial firmness).

Yet law and order was more than the sum of its parts. Conservatives charged that the loss of it was the most visible sign and symbol of the perceived failure of activist government and of liberalism itself. In their view the welfare state had squandered the hard-earned taxes of the deserving middle class on wasteful programs for the undeserving poor. It had also failed to ensure the safety and security of the citizenry—the primary duty of any government. The charge posed a quandary for liberals. How could advocates of civil liberties and civil rights effectively differentiate between criminal behavior and civil disobedience, between lawful demonstrations and unlawful riots, between actual crime and irrational fear, without appearing to side with the supposed villains rather than their victims? A domestic credibility gap had emerged that liberals would find virtually impossible to close.

■■■

This book is a work of political culture.[11] By weaving an analytical narrative around selected events, campaigns, and legislation of the 1960s, it examines the impact that law and order had on an ideological watershed in American history. The methodology employed explicitly privileges the importance of political history and the role played by individuals, namely an elite class of political experts. This study draws heavily—though by no means exclusively—on traditional archival sources, on the public records and private papers of administration officials and campaign advisers. In a decade generally defined by social movements—and historians of social movements—it contends that political elites often defined how ordinary people viewed and interpreted the events that shaped their lives. In turn, the reactions of average Americans affected the decisions of the political actors and policymakers themselves. The argument advanced implicitly is that a "feedback loop" existed between political action and public opinion even as immediate events and long-term developments exerted influence.[12]

Among those developments which provided fertile soil for law and order, three were particularly important. The first was the Great Migration, which in the first half of the twentieth century changed the complexion and dynamic of northern cities. But the exodus of millions of blacks from the rural South coincided with industrial decline in the urban North, which accelerated in the late 1950s and drained the inner-city pool of good jobs for unskilled workers.[13] Disproportionately young and poor, the new arrivals and their children consequently contributed disproportionately—as both victim and perpetrator—to the postwar crime wave that gathered force in the 1950s and swept across America's cities in the 1960s. In New York, for example, robberies—the truest indicator of unsafe streets—rose from 6,600 in 1962 to more than 78,000 by 1972.[14]

In the late 1950s, black men displaced white ethnics as the new face of urban violence. By the late 1960s, white Americans overwhelmingly associated street crime with African Americans, who were more than seventeen times as likely as white men to be arrested for robbery.[15] That association, along with the reaction to urban riots, would lay the foundation for law and order. For many whites, the appeal of the issue was undoubtedly a reflection at least in part of racial prejudice and historical anxieties.[16] But for most whites the appeal of law and order was due primarily to genuine fear, a sentiment shared by many blacks. As the long-time labor leader and civil rights activist A. Philip Randolph observed in September 1964, "[W]hile there may be law and order without freedom, there can be no freedom without law and order."[17]

A second factor was the Cold War and the long shadow it cast over domestic politics. During the 1950s, conservatives used the language of anti-communism to challenge liberalism. By the 1960s, moderate liberals like John Kennedy had inoculated themselves against the charge that they were "soft" on communism. Now conservatives had to articulate a new vocabulary. The language they chose was law and order.[18] It thus became a mutation of anti-communism, with "peace through strength" serving in both cases as the watchword. More extreme conservatives even contended that communist agitators had sparked the riots. If communists directed by Moscow were the agents of international disorder, they maintained, then rioters directed by communists were the agents of internal disorder.

Mainstream conservatives distanced themselves from this argument. Their target was liberalism, which they blamed for the loss of public order.[19] Liberals tried to respond, contending that a society of law and order was a harbinger of fascism or communism.[20] But their efforts fell on deaf ears, in large part because personal security had become as legitimate and potent a political issue as national security. By 1968, the situation bore striking parallels to 1948. Then Harry Truman had faced a challenge from the left (Henry Wallace) which threatened to splinter the Democratic coalition. Now Hubert Humphrey faced a challenge from the right (George Wallace) which posed a similar threat.

Economic conditions constituted a third, somewhat contradictory, context. On the one hand, the abundance of the postwar era permitted both liberals and conservatives to shift the plane of political debate away from economic policy.[21] The affluence of the 1960s also fed what one historian has called the "hope and hubris" of officials in the Kennedy and Johnson administrations.[22] Confident that they had discovered how to assure perpetual economic growth, they launched the War on Poverty and the Great Society with enormous expectations, promising that they would cure both social distress and social disorder. But when street crime increased and urban riots erupted, conservatives pounced. Poverty was not the reason for the breakdown of law and order, they insisted, because the United States was a wealthy nation, more prosperous than ever both in historic terms and in comparison to the rest of the industrialized world, where crime rates on the whole were much lower. Moreover, conservatives added, most poor people were not criminals—a line of reasoning that liberals themselves frequently invoked when defending minorities against charges that they were criminal by nature. Thus liberalism found itself ensnared in a trap of its own design.

On the other hand, the economic stagnation of the late 1960s, which had reached the high-wage manufacturing sector a decade earlier, reinforced the frustration of white workers and made them more receptive to messages that blamed others—especially minorities—for their predicament. Between 1965 and 1969, higher taxes and rising inflation led to a noticeable decline in real wages for working-class whites.[23] Anxious about the economic competition blacks seemed to pose at work and the physical threat they seemed to pose at home, many whites felt besieged.[24] The home now assumed a dual significance. It was a material investment which neighborhood decline, real or imagined, could wash away in a moment; it was also a symbolic place where masculine identity rested in large measure on the ability to shelter and protect the women of the family—wives, mothers, and daughters—from outside harm.[25]

The Great Migration, the Cold War, and the economic climate were necessary preconditions for the emergence of law and order. Changing patterns of gender relations and family structure, which eroded traditional forms of patriarchy and authority, also created sources of tension for many Americans, particularly white males. And the "Baby Boom" ensured that generational tensions would come of age in the 1960s. But none of these long-term trends preordained the arrival or impact of law and order. Of equal importance were immediate events, ideological imperatives, and political tactics. Only they can fully account for the issue's rapid rise to—and equally rapid fade from—national prominence.

■ ■ ■

A few words on the historiography of the 1960s—and the place of this book—are in order here. Although the historiography of the decade has made great strides in recent years, it remains relatively underdeveloped. The scholarly debates thus far lack the richness and complexity of those of earlier eras, such as the evolution of the New Deal and the origins of the Cold War. Where they do exist, they often tend to marginalize conservative developments and rehash the radical-liberal clashes of the period, such as whether the demise of the New Left was due mainly to official repression, internal conflict, or public apathy.[26] The situation is understandable, given the considerable influence still exerted by prominent scholars who were directly engaged in the liberal or radical struggles of the decade and for whom it marked a formative moment in their lives.[27] But the result is unfortunate, for it has meant that the conservative side of the 1960s has received little attention until recently.[28]

This account restores a conservative perspective to the conventional political narrative of the 1960s. It presents the decade as a time of countervailing tendencies in which liberalism, radicalism, and conservatism clashed in ideological combat for the hearts and minds of American voters. And it amplifies the lost voices of what Richard Nixon would term "the silent majority." Finally, it contextualizes the successes, failures, and limits of liberalism. By taking stock of the conservative constraints that existed at the time, it may prove possible in hindsight to arrive at a more balanced appraisal of the liberal record.

This account also supplements rather than supplants existing interpretations. With regard to the origins of the War on Poverty, for example, it suggests that the debate over the motivations of Kennedy and Johnson administration officials is incomplete. Whether their intent was only to secure the votes of African Americans—as some have suggested and others have vehemently disputed—remains unclear and, in all likelihood, unknowable since the dispute rests largely on assumptions of human behavior rather than concrete evidence. But what seems plausible is that urban peace was also in the minds of administration officials in late 1963 and early 1964 because they already associated delinquency and crime with poverty and race. Thus the Johnson administration's subsequent and fateful decision in October 1964 to bill the War on Poverty as in part an anti-crime measure was at least somewhat in keeping with the program's original intent.

Unlike the debate over the origins of the War on Poverty, the demise of the New Deal order has attracted considerable popular and scholarly interest. Not surprisingly, historians and commentators disagree on this critical issue. In particular, they differ on when precisely and why exactly urban white voters began to desert the Democratic Party and embrace the Republican Party—or abandon electoral politics altogether. Thomas and Mary Edsall, authors of *Chain Reaction*, identify the critical moment as the 1960s and the main cause as the reaction against the Great Society and the excesses of the black power movement. The Democratic Party, they and others contend, then compounded the crisis by responding to the grievances and demands of a militant minority while ignoring the fears and desires of a "silent majority."[29]

But in *The Origins of the Urban Crisis*, his prizewinning book on postwar Detroit, historian Thomas Sugrue has argued that urban antiliberalism predated the Johnson administration and determined the "politics of race and neighborhood" in the North in the 1940s and 1950s. Opposition to racial integration and miscegenation dominated local elections even in the

"Motor City," where liberal organizations like the United Auto Workers presumably held sway. Therefore, the conservative backlash of the 1960s was not, according to Sugrue, "the unique product of the white rejection of the Great Society. Instead it was the culmination of more than two decades of simmering white discontent and extensive antiliberal political organization."[30]

Sugrue has convincingly documented the existence and virulence of northern racism at the municipal level. He has also made the case, albeit implicitly, that the New Deal order was inherently unstable almost from the start. But the disintegration of the New Deal coalition at the national level was not inevitable. Prior to the early 1960s, many urban whites in effect split their ballots. They balanced support for conservative local candidates opposed to residential integration with support for liberal national candidates committed to civil rights.[31] By the mid-1960s, however, the balancing act had become untenable in large part because a local issue—"crime in the streets"—had brought "simmering white discontent" to a boil and become conflated with a national debate over the collapse of law and order. Put another way, the willingness of local Democrats to accept the racial liberalism of the national party had grown smaller as the costs of doing so had grown larger.

More importantly, both the Edsalls and Sugrue place too much emphasis on the role of racism and too little on the role of security. After 1964 the distance between voters and issues narrowed as anxiety over the loss of public safety widened.[32] The unraveling of liberalism was therefore not simply the result of racism *per se*. It was, rather, due also to the widespread loss of popular faith in liberalism's ability to ensure personal security. The reaction against the Great Society was, likewise, rooted significantly in the perception that it had failed to curb social unrest—and may even have contributed to it.

Crime and disorder were the fulcrum points at which the local and the national intersected. Anxious whites now saw how national policies affected their neighborhoods; eager conservatives discovered how to exploit local fears. Law and order thus became the vehicle by which urban whites transmitted their antipathy to neighborhood integration and fear of racial violence from the municipal to the presidential arena. The Johnson administration had no illusions about this development. In November 1967, aide Ben Wattenberg reported to the president that "whites will vote readily for a Negro for Congress or Senate, but not for City Hall—not when the Police Department and/or the Board of Education may be at stake. That is where the backlash is; that is where the fear is."[33] And that was where the White House was largely powerless to act, given constitutional restraints, limited resources, and the nature of the Democratic coalition.

By November 1968, the conservative fears reflected by the demand for law and order outweighed the liberal hopes raised by the promise of the Great Society. In that critical presidential election, which in retrospect marked the end of the liberal ascendancy in national politics, many accounts have emphasized the importance of the Vietnam War, a subject on which most voters saw little difference between Democrat Hubert Humphrey and Republican Richard Nixon, who won narrowly. By contrast, they saw a significant difference between the candidates on law and order—and by a decisive margin favored the conservative position.

In ideological terms, Nixon's triumph was more complete than his slim popular margin (less than one percent) would suggest. Using dubious but persuasive logic, he repeatedly cited the simultaneous rise in street crime and social spending as proof that both of Johnson's domestic wars—his War on Crime and his War on Poverty—were costly failures. The conservative argument trumped the liberal position, which maintained that the Great Society had limited the growth of the crime rate. Nixon also asserted without irony that the first civil right of all Americans was freedom from violence. In the debate over law and order, conservatives had thus inverted the arguments and appropriated the language of liberals, who could not construct a plausible counter-narrative. In the process, the right had reshaped national politics and transformed the personal security crisis of the late 1960s into the equivalent of the national security scare of the late 1940s.[34]

During the 1970s, law and order faded from the national limelight. The issue's loss of salience suggests three important points. First, although law and order had always rested on a base of social factors—urban migration, rising crime, racial unrest, and economic stagnation—it had also depended heavily on the political climate and tactics that had propelled it into the center of the debate. With a Republican in the White House, conservatives lost interest in portraying local safety as a national responsibility, particularly when the crime rate rose steadily from 1969 to 1971. Then the Watergate Crisis severely tarnished the law-and-order credentials of the Nixon administration while attention shifted to the weakening U.S. economy. Second, the failure of the Humphrey campaign effectively demolished the liberal view of crime as a viable political stance, making it impossible for presidential candidates to identify themselves with the idea that social inequality was the main cause of street crime. As a result, conservatives rarely had either cause to trumpet law and order or a target against which to aim it. Finally, the issue had always depended to a certain extent upon the conflation of violent crime and urban disorder. When the riots diminished in the 1970s—for which the Nixon administration took full credit—the politics of crime reverted to traditional arenas like mayoral and gubernatorial contests, where it continued to resonate.

Law and order nonetheless had a number of important and lasting consequences for national politics. It contributed to the crisis of liberalism and aided the growth of conservatism. It eroded the appeal of liberal leaders like Hubert Humphrey and enhanced the appeal of conservative figures like Ronald Reagan, who in 1966 launched his political career by riding the issue to victory in the race for governor of California. Law and order helped to expose fissures within the Democratic Party and bridge divisions within the Republican Party. And it left shrewd, intelligent politicians like Lyndon Johnson groping for alternatives. Above all, it enabled many white Americans to make sense of a chaotic world filled with street crime, urban riots, and campus demonstrations. The legacy of law and order was a political atmosphere in which grim expectations displaced grand ambitions.

1.

Delinquency and Opportunity

In 1958, a white woman in Chicago wrote to Roy Wilkins, the president of the National Association for the Advancement of Colored People (NAACP), to express her outrage at the rape and mutilation of a white girl by five black teens armed with broken bottles and switchblades. "All you are interested in is getting seats in trains and restaurants ..." she asserted. "You never tell your people to be decent and honest when they are among decent white people." In his careful reply, Wilkins first expressed remorse and regret. But then he added that it was not "fair that every Negro should feel personally hurt when some misguided member of his race commits a crime.... I know of no disposition on the part of our Association or of Negro citizens generally to excuse crime and violence. What we do resent is the smearing of a whole race because of the bad deeds of a few."[1]

The exchange highlighted two important developments that were taking place during the 1950s. The first was the growing fear of a nationwide rise in the rate and severity of juvenile delinquency.[2] By the middle of the decade, youth crime had claimed the top spot in public opinion polls of pressing national issues. To many anxious adults, America now appeared on the verge of a clash between generations, between authority and anarchy, respect and rebellion.[3] The second development was the increasingly racial cast that juvenile delinquency had assumed by the end of the decade. This trend concerned blacks like Wilkins, who worried that more and more whites might start to perceive a connection between civil rights and urban violence.

During the 1950s, the public perception of youth crime shifted in subtle but significant ways. In the first half of the decade, as prosperity cushioned the social impact of the Great Migration, the national media tended to portray juvenile delinquency as a universal problem with psychological roots. In the second half of the decade, as de-industrialization eroded the economic base of the Great Migration, the national media started to depict juvenile delinquency as an urban problem with racial overtones. As a result, black and white liberals began to debate quietly the explosive equation of race and crime while conservatives moved to take advantage of it.

Amid the growing sense that a racial crisis loomed in America's cities, the Kennedy administration entered office determined to reverse the seeming passivity of the Eisenhower era. With the critical support of nonprofit institutions like the Ford Foundation, ambitious policymakers in the White House launched a campaign against delinquency that eventually escalated into the War on Poverty, which deployed many of the same soldiers and strategies as the earlier skirmish.[4] The War on Poverty also led to the War on Crime, which President Lyndon Johnson declared in early 1965. Thus the Kennedy administration's anti-delinquency mission laid the groundwork for the liberal intervention in the domestic quagmire of law and order.

I

Juvenile delinquency became a pressing problem during World War II. In the first six months of 1943, youth crime jumped by more than 40 percent according to an FBI survey of major cities.[5] The cause seemed obvious to most commentators. With the Great Migration an unacknowledged reality amid wartime dislocation, race was not a prime suspect. With the Great Depression a fading memory amid wartime prosperity, poverty was not either. The convenient and comforting culprit was the war itself, which seemed to have insidious but temporary effects.

The negative impact most often cited by observers was the wartime disruption of families—and the lack of parental supervision that resulted from it. With fathers at war and mothers at work, older children were now exposed to the temptations of war. "Every day," reported *Newsweek*, "more teenage-girls, deprived by the draft and industrial needs of parental guidance, are drawn to the side-street shadows and park benches of the nation lured by the glamour of uniforms."[6] Younger siblings were also at risk. According to the president of the American Legion Auxiliary, American "latch-key children" had the potential to "make the Russian wolfpacks look like kittens." She and other conservatives were quick to accuse working mothers of neglect—a charge liberals were equally quick to reject. Women in the paid workforce remained, however, a popular target of blame, particularly when youth crime and divorce rates rose again in the early 1950s.[7]

Despite the return of many fathers from the military and mothers from the factory, juvenile delinquency worsened after the war, particularly in working-class neighborhoods like the Brownsville section of Brooklyn, where economic decline both hastened and reflected demographic shifts. As the number of white ethnics (especially Jews) declined in absolute and relative terms, the Puerto Rican and African American population expanded dramatically.[8] According to official figures, the new arrivals provided a disproportionate number of perpetrators as well as their victims.[9] In response, the New York Police Department (NYPD) began in 1948 to target selected neighborhoods for additional patrols by special units. But the effort was unsuccessful in Brownsville, where the delinquency rate rose by 400 percent between 1951 to 1958. Over that same period, it rose by 100 percent in the city as a whole.[10]

Liberals contested the validity of the statistics, as they would in the 1960s. Sociologist Daniel Bell of Columbia University contended that the crime rate as calculated by the FBI was of dubious value because it was based on outdated census data. It also relied on local crime figures, which were manipulated by individual police departments or compiled by new reporting systems whose surprising results cast doubt on earlier tabulations.[11] The academic critique gained anecdotal support from some officers, who claimed that "as far as general delinquency on the part of the kids committing more crime, or offenses, it isn't any greater than it was 20 years ago."[12] But professional reservations could not alter the public perception that delinquency was escalating beyond control.

The perception drew strength from two main sources. The first was the emergence of black and Latino youth gangs, whose racial identity added a troubling dimension for ethnic whites.[13] The second was the growth of a popular media dedicated to the graphic depiction of violent crime and the cultural blurring of class lines in films and on television. According to Bell, the convergence of mass media and mass audience had combined to open "windows" into areas of human behavior heretofore unseen by middle-class Americans. "Hence if violence, once bounded, has flowed over the walls," he wrote, "it is not true that the amount of violence has increased." Drawing on a historical perspective, he further contended that urbanites in the 1950s faced less violence than a century ago.[14] The point had merit. But it was also irrelevant, for it failed to address the real fear many felt.

Bell was nonetheless correct to stress the impact of the media, which reflected and reinforced public unease over the direction and pace of cultural and social change. "Youths more than adults bore the imprint of these changes," suggests one historian. "They were the harbingers of a new society, and adults were prepared to punish the messengers so much did they wish to avoid the message that the family was rapidly changing, that affluence was undercutting old mores, that working women were altering the sexual politics of the home and workplace, and that the media were transforming American culture into a homogenized mass that disguised local distinctions and prepared the way for a new social order."[15] Public reaction to the delinquency scare of the 1950s thus coincided with shifting attitudes toward the place of youth culture in American society.[16]

II

At the national level, the media treatment of juvenile delinquency went through two stages. In the early to mid-1950s, the emphasis was on the universality of the problem, which affected every community and all teens regardless of race, class, and locale. By the late 1950s, the changing face of America's cities, coupled with the emergence of the civil rights movement, led to a greater focus on the racial composition of youth crime. No longer could liberals, black or white, ignore the perception that race and crime seemed intertwined. Now the difficult and delicate task was to explain how discrimination contributed to lawlessness—without appearing to deny or condone it.

In the decades after World War II, the demographic landscape underwent a tectonic shift. As the suburbs boomed, doubling in population between 1950 and 1970, the central cities stagnated, losing millions of residents.[17] At the same time, the complexion of urban life changed. As millions of middle-class whites moved to suburbia in pursuit of the ranch home and picket fence of their dreams, millions of working-class blacks migrated to the urban North in search of work and a better life after the collapse of the sharecropping system in the rural South.[18] It was a dramatic development. But in the early 1950s it was invisible to most Americans—especially the new suburbanites.

Accordingly, the media concentrated on the universal nature of the delinquency crisis. In the popular press, troubled teens came from all walks of life, all types of communities, and all parts of the country. Most articles were careful to cite examples from large cities, affluent suburbs, and small towns. Poverty and race were rarely mentioned. The focus instead was on the decreasing age and increasing violence of the offenders. A 1952 incident in Arkansas in which two boys, ages seven and nine, looted a gas station while their parents were at a night club attracted national attention. The press also publicized the 1953 case of a female teenager in Utah who, after exchanging gunfire with police, reportedly said, "I hate cops; I wish I had got me one."[19]

The universalist interpretation received intellectual support from Benjamin Fine, education editor of the *New York Times*. In *1,000,000 Delinquents*, a nonfiction best-seller in 1955, he used the Cold War and a disease metaphor to emphasize how delinquency, like cancer, was a serious threat that could easily spread and infect all of society. In particular, it could warp young minds, threatening the "American way of life," weakening democracy, and aiding the spread of communism. But despite the sometimes overheated rhetoric, Fine offered on the whole a restrained, thoughtful, and balanced critique.[20] A supporter of slum clearance, he nonetheless stressed that no direct correlation existed between youth crime and urban poverty or poor housing—witness the explosive growth in suburban delinquency. In more than 350 pages of anecdote and analysis, he also mentioned race only once—as an identifying adjective.

Fine advocated an expanded role for government, with political control at the local level, expert guidance and financial assistance at the federal level. Above all, he sought more spending on public schools, "the first line of defense," including improved teacher education and expanded psychological services. But for the most part Fine accepted the findings of Professor Sheldon Glueck and Dr. Eleanor Glueck, authors of *Unraveling Juvenile Delinquency*, who placed primary emphasis on family cohesiveness and effective parenting. The Gluecks acknowledged that physical poverty, coupled with job insecurity and residential instability, imposed severe strains. They placed greater weight, however, on emotional deprivation. "In almost every respect," wrote Fine in agreement, "the delinquent is an unhappy and dissatisfied person; he is emotionally disturbed."[21]

Hollywood lent popular support to this interpretation with a pair of films. *Blackboard Jungle* was a box office success when released in 1955, even though it was banned in Memphis, reviewed harshly by many critics, and condemned by numerous organizations (including the Parent-Teachers

Association, the Daughters of the American Revolution, the Girl Scouts, and the American Legion).[22] The film also launched Sidney Poitier's career and broadened the appeal of rock music (through the soundtrack's use of "Rock around the Clock" by Bill Haley and the Comets). Most important, it provided implicit support for the idea that delinquency was primarily a product of the home, not of poverty or race.

Blackboard Jungle opens on a note of somber realism, with a written disclaimer expressing support for America's schools and youth. The first scene displays the entrance to North Manual High School, a run-down vocation school in New York City where a new and idealistic young teacher named Richard Dadier (Glenn Ford) confronts a class of demographically diverse delinquents led by Gregory Miller (Poitier) and Artie West (Vic Morrow).[23] But the film does not portray the two in equal terms. West is a one-dimensional figure whose sociopathic behavior stems from his fear of military service and an early death. By contrast, Miller is a multidimensional character whose love of spirituals (he sings in the Christmas Pageant) and dedication to work (he is a mechanic after school) counterbalance his delinquency. Not surprisingly, it is Miller who sides with Dadier in the final showdown with West. His change of heart inspires the other students, including a Latino named Pete Morales (Rafael Campos), who symbolically breaks the blade of West's knife. Ultimately, only another ethnic white, an Italian-American named Belazi (Dan Terranova), remains loyal to West.[24]

The motivation of the delinquents is unclear until a world-weary detective offers an explanation. "They were five or six years old in the last war," he tells Dadier and a fellow teacher (Richard Kiley) after West and his gang have mugged them. "Father in the army. Mother in the defense plant. No home life. No church life. No place to go." Gangs, the officer adds, are taking the place of parents. But the critical speech, which reinforces the film's true message about delinquency, comes from Dadier's wife (Anne Francis), who urges him to remain at North Manual rather than transfer to a better school. "Most people are worthwhile," she says, "We all need the same thing. Patience. Love. Understanding." The film then closes with Dadier and Miller leaving school together, each pledging to return and finish what they have started.[25] Although the idea of the "redeemable" black youth has always had some appeal, it is hard to imagine a film with a similar message being as successful, or even being made, a decade later, when the perception of black teens had shifted significantly in the wake of Harlem, Watts, and other riots.[26]

In the spring of 1955, shortly after the success of *Blackboard Jungle*, production began on *Rebel Without a Cause*. It made no effort to duplicate the urban reality of the earlier film. Instead, it depicted suburban delinquency from the perspective of alienated and affluent (or at least comfortable) white teens, absorbed in their own lifestyle and isolated from the values of the authority figures (parents, teachers, police) around them. But in other respects it imitated and duplicated the success of *Blackboard Jungle*. Politically, *Rebel Without a Cause* generated similar controversy because of the negative influence it allegedly had on impressionable youths. Artistically, the film made James Dean a star and outlined the essential teen-movie archetypes, including the alienated yet sensitive loner, the "good girl" who loves him, and the distant adults who are uncaring or hostile. Financially, *Rebel Without a Cause* firmly established the commercial viability of the youth genre.[27] But perhaps as significant was the way it, like *Blackboard Jungle*, offered an image of juvenile delinquency increasingly at odds with the reality of youth crime in urban America.

The national media was slow to take notice at first, perhaps because it in general reflected the liberal faith in integration, probably because most reporters and editors were not residents of the neighborhoods most affected. But by the late 1950s articles began to appear that explicitly depicted, at times in alarmist tones, urban delinquency in racial terms. *Newsweek* reported how a pack of more than ten black youths had attacked two white teens mistakenly thought to belong to a rival gang. One white died—and his assailant later explained how, while the unconscious victim lay face down, "I took my butcher knife and jabbed it into him. I struck it into him real good until I felt the bone." *Time* declared that the situation in those New York public schools with sizable minority populations was grimmer than in *Blackboard Jungle*, with teachers terrorized and classrooms trashed. A white cab driver from Brooklyn recalled how he used to play with blacks as a child. "But now [they] are fighting and making trouble all the time."[28]

Of course, trouble also came from racist whites. Some of it was relatively random, as when fifteen white teenagers in Chicago decided one evening to "beat a nigger" and then watched as one of them crushed the skull of a black youth with a ball-peen hammer.[29] But much of the violence and vandalism attributed to casual delinquency was in fact deliberately aimed at blacks trying to integrate previously all-white projects and neighborhoods. One study of postwar Detroit suggests that white adults involved in demonstrations and protests often condoned incidents of assault and arson by juveniles. Frequently, the racist activities of white teens were what one historian has termed "a sanctioned expression of communal sentiment," supported and even protected by sympathetic parents.[30]

Despite the continued prevalence of such violence, the dominant perception of the "typical" urban delinquent started to shift from the white ethnic to the African American. As anxiety over street crime grew, more whites—even some liberals—were willing to discuss openly the nexus between race and violence, while fewer were willing to see black teens as equally deserving of understanding, sympathy, and a second chance.[31] The national media contributed in important ways to this new and implicit image of juvenile delinquents. In 1958, *Time* reported that "many of the North's big-city mayors groan in private that their biggest and most worrisome problem is the crime rate among Negroes." For crimes involving violence or the threat of violence—murder, manslaughter, rape, robbery, and aggravated assault—arrest figures from New York, Chicago, and Detroit indicated that black males were overwhelmingly overrepresented. Calling it a "shocking pattern," *Time* contended that liberal discomfort and lobbying by the NAACP had fostered a code of silence among prominent politicians, public officials, and metropolitan newspapers, which typically would not print a criminal's race unless he was at large and his race would help identify him.[32]

In a gesture at balance, *Time* cited a prominent black journalist from Detroit, who contended that the statistics in large part reflected both police persecution of African Americans and police neglect of ghetto crime. But the magazine contended that better policing might actually lead to even more one-sided arrest figures. Nor would *Time* accept the argument that migration, overcrowding, and poverty were the main causes of black criminality. Foreign-born whites had suffered from dislocation, density, and deprivation, the magazine observed, but had low crime rates relative to both African Americans and native whites. *Time* also rejected, however, the conservative assertion that black criminality was the result of inherent immorality. The main problem was white prejudice. "Negro leadership could make a start toward lowering Negro crime rates by abandoning the conspiracy of concealment," the magazine suggested, but the primary need was to end segregation, which "breeds resentment and tension, feelings of alienation and inferiority." The article concluded by urging liberal whites to fight "discrimination in the North with the same fervor they show in arguing for civil rights in the South."[33]

What *Time* thus highlighted was a feeling of optimism among white liberals, a sense that the civil rights struggle might lead to social peace as well as social justice. During the Montgomery Bus Boycott in 1954, for instance, crime and delinquency had declined. "Thousands of people had been given a sense of purpose, of their own worth and dignity," concluded author and activist Michael Harrington, ignoring the possibility that the police had shifted enforcement patterns or that more people had remained at home. "On their own, and without any special urging, they began to change their personal lives; they became a different people."[34] That hope, that faith in integration and the transformative power of the movement, was both ironic and short-lived, because most liberals would soon strain to deny any connection between black crime and civil rights—a connection that segregationists already alleged explicitly and bluntly. In Mississippi, for example, the Citizens Council of Greenwood prepared a lurid pamphlet entitled "Crime Report Reveals Menace of Integration."[35] By the early 1960s, conservatives would reframe that linkage, asserting that the doctrine of civil disobedience had undermined respect for the law and fostered criminal behavior.

But in the late 1950s it was the coupling of crime and integration that most troubled the NAACP, which tried to break the causal chain. In response to a request for a strong stand against minority disorder in the New York public schools, the executive director wrote that the association was "greatly troubled both about the juvenile delinquency problem itself and about the way in which it has been used by our opponents as a propaganda weapon against us." He added that the NAACP, while denying that it had any special responsibility for black crime, would advocate community cooperation as a way to address matters without "giving the opposition added grounds for saying that crime is a Negro problem."[36] NAACP President Roy Wilkins expressed similar sentiments. He asserted that the United States needed law and order because "many of our enemies are using incidents of juvenile delinquency to buttress their fight against us and against desegregation of the schools."[37]

The troubling issue sparked a vigorous debate within the NAACP, which in 1958 reached an internal consensus. Publicly, it would stress that the black community stood ready to combat crime but would not accept sole responsibility for the fight. Nor would it accept that criminal behavior was a racial characteristic. As Wilkins noted, all ethnic groups produced their share of criminals, and white embezzlers stole far more than black thieves did, with far less publicity.[38] Crime was, rather, the predictable outgrowth of "economically-disadvantaged and culturally-limited migrant populations" adjusting to urban life.[39] Privately, the association committed itself to a politically risky and potentially untenable course of action: deny that blacks committed a disproportionate number of crimes by citing police and media bias; or, if pressed, concede the point but state that it was because of "the continued failure to admit them to equal opportunity with the rest of the nation."[40]

The racial dimension of urban crime and juvenile delinquency would pose a serious dilemma to the NAACP in the years to come. But for others it presented a considerable opportunity. For conservatives, black crime would become the means by which to mount a flank attack on the civil rights movement when it was too popular to assault directly. For liberals, the issue would point the way to a new item on their social agenda, a War on Delinquency that would naturally transmute into a War on Poverty. The wars synchronized smoothly, offering important benefits to two critical constituencies, black Americans filled with hope and expectation by the civil rights movement and urban whites imbued with fear and insecurity by rising lawlessness. For a new Democratic administration determined to make its mark through activism, the challenge and the risk were great—but so too seemed the potential rewards.

III

Juvenile delinquency was near the bottom of the Eisenhower administration's domestic agenda. But in 1960 the election of John Kennedy brought a renewed commitment to urban policy. Within months of assuming office, he had formed a presidential commission to study juvenile delinquency and sent legislation to Congress to support youth programs. Ultimately, neither the commission nor the legislation would have immediate impact, as juvenile crime continued to rise. The initiatives were, however, significant in two respects. First, they signaled a new willingness to explore delinquency in the ghetto. Second, they contributed many of the personnel, laid the tactical and intellectual groundwork, and bequeathed a climate of concern about race and crime that was, if largely unstated and overlooked, nonetheless an important part of the background for the much broader and more significant War on Poverty. It in turn would attract considerable conservative criticism—and become one of the pillars of the Johnson administration's War on Crime. Thus it was a liberal Democrat, Kennedy, who took the first steps into the political minefield of urban crime and disorder, poverty and race—a minefield that would subsequently explode many of the liberal hopes and aspirations of the early 1960s.

The Eisenhower administration took little action in response to the public outcry over juvenile delinquency. Committed for ideological and fiscal reasons to the principle of limited government and the promise of a balanced budget, it authorized in 1954 only a token expenditure to study the issue.[41] Following a national conference on youth crime, however, the president in 1955 recommended (without great enthusiasm) an annual program of state grants. Six years of political and jurisdictional debates followed.[42] In the meantime, street gangs proliferated, a development dramatized by the hit Broadway musical *West Side Story*.[43] Alarmed, Democratic Senator Hubert Humphrey of Minnesota proposed a Youth Conservation Corps modeled on the Civilian Conservation Corps, which in the 1930s had built character as well as trails and parks. But the proposal languished in Congress, ignored by the administration and attacked by conservatives opposed to the cost and liberals worried that the boot camps would become alternative detention facilities while the structural causes of juvenile delinquency remained untouched.[44]

During the 1960 campaign, Kennedy devoted little attention to juvenile delinquency, even though polls showed that most Americans felt the Democrats could handle the issue better than the Republicans.[45] But shortly after the election it gained momentum. First, Attorney General Robert Kennedy named his old friend David Hackett as special assistant to coordinate the Justice Department's anti-delinquency program.[46] Then the House narrowly voted to enlarge the Rules Committee, giving moderates a slight majority and enabling liberal legislation to escape the stranglehold of conservative Chairman Howard Smith of Virginia. In May 1961, the president established the President's Commission on Juvenile Delinquency and Youth Crime (hereafter the Delinquency Commission). Four months later, he signed into law the Juvenile Delinquency and Youth Offenses Control Act.[47]

The Delinquency Commission prepared a report that predicted a coming juvenile crime wave. Declaring a state of "national emergency," it depicted a nation locked in "domestic war" and faced with imminent defeat from the dual threat of a growing youth population and a growing delinquency rate. The report identified a wide range of environmental or structural causes, including substandard housing, cultural deprivation, family disintegration, racial discrimination, high unemployment, and poor education. It also insisted that federal planning, coordination, and prevention were required because at the moment no major city was successfully coping with delinquency on its own.[48]

To promote those objectives, the Delinquency Commission directed federal grants to experimental programs like the Gray Areas Project in New Haven and the Mobilization for Youth (MFY) in New York. The latter was the epitome of what the administration hoped to replicate across the country.[49] A multifaceted community organization, it served the ethnically diverse, economically marginal Lower East Side, where delinquency rates were higher than in the city as a whole.[50] Offering facilities and resources for community organizing, welfare assistance, and family counseling, MFY relied on a mix of public and private support.[51] Above all, it was committed to providing delinquents with the tools to realize their middle-class (in theory) ambitions, an analysis and approach championed by Lloyd Ohlin, a professor at the Columbia School of Social Work and an MFY board member.

Ohlin and his colleague Richard Cloward systematically outlined this approach, which became known as "opportunity theory," in their influential 1960 work, *Delinquency and Opportunity*. Although the authors maintained that delinquency was a subculture, they posited that delinquents held mainstream values and aspirations but lacked the means to achieve them. Frustration and despair mounted, Ohlin and Cloward argued, when the decline of urban institutions like the public schools, political machines, and organized crime eroded social controls and blocked legitimate as well as illegitimate avenues of advancement. Violence and delinquency thus resulted when middle-class goals collided with lower-class reality. Downplaying the role of the family (the book contains virtually no references to it), the authors promoted instead the need to restore order and opportunity in slum communities.[52]

The Delinquency Commission employed both scholars as consultants. It also made opportunity theory its guiding intellectual premise, although it altered the structural emphasis, retaining the focus on opportunity but concentrating on empowering individuals rather than transforming institutions. "We cannot control delinquency by building new institutions," the Delinquency Commission contended, "we must prevent it by building new opportunities for underprivileged young people to find a useful place in the mainstream of American life." The compromise left many dissatisfied. "In the end," recalled a staffer who also served in the War on Poverty, "much of the [commission's] philosophy was watered down, distorted beyond recognition, or abandoned completely."[53]

Although amorphous in theory and experimental in practice, the antidelinquency program proved an influential foray by the federal government into the complicated and controversial area of crime control. The grant-in-aid features in particular would provide a model for important legislation to come, including the Law Enforcement Assistance Act of 1965 and the Safe Streets Act of 1968. But the political costs of appearing to provide sympathy to minority youths at the expense of security to middle-class whites were high. As one writer has observed, "Here was a Democratic administration, understandably heedless of the full consequences, embarking on the disastrous course of allowing itself to be identified with efforts to 'understand' the urban street criminal, and helping to fund organizations that opened fissures in the urban political coalitions on which the Democratic Party completely depended."[54] The Delinquency Commission also attracted criticism from friend and foe alike for its lack of intellectual rigor and substantive achievements—criticism that foreshadowed what the War on Poverty would face.

From the start, opportunity theory had numerous detractors—a fact Hackett well knew when he hired Ohlin, who eventually became the head of the Justice Department's Office of Delinquency.[55] "At any time from 1961 to 1964," observed Daniel Patrick Moynihan, then at the Labor Department, "an afternoon of library research would have established that the Cloward-Ohlin thesis of opportunity, though eminently respectable, was nonetheless a minority position, with the bulk of delinquency theory pointed in quite a different direction." Most research in fact pointed to the importance of family socialization, not neighborhood institutions. That finding conflicted with the Kennedy administration's desire for dramatic and immediate solutions to the delinquency problem. But to conservatives more interested in moral indictments of wayward youth than social programs for troubled youths or structural critiques of urban society, the family model proved useful. The similar backgrounds of former Governor Al Smith and famous gangster Al Capone, wrote one columnist, suggested that it was "high time that foundations, political office holders, and others concerned with crime abandoned the fallacious concentration on what is outside and looked inside these young hoodlums."[56]

MFY came under fire for what it did and did not do. On the one hand, it failed to curb juvenile crime, although it may have slowed the rate of growth. On the other, it generated controversy when it became involved with rent strikes, school boycotts, voter registration drives, and civil rights demonstrations. "What this has to do with curbing juvenile delinquency," declared the *New York Herald Tribune*, "or why public funds should be used, is a cause for bafflement." The *National Review* even contended, dubiously, that MFY was communist-infiltrated.[57] By 1964, the War on Delinquency was so controversial that it barely won renewal despite a strong administration defense predicated on the belief that the poverty bill (facing House consideration shortly) would otherwise meet almost certain defeat.[58]

That belief was not unfounded, because the anti-delinquency campaign functioned in large measure as a blueprint for the War on Poverty, which inherited from the Delinquency Commission a common set of personnel, a common enemy (deprivation), and a common tactic (community action).[59] Above all, the War on Delinquency bequeathed to Sargent Shriver and the Office of Economic Opportunity a common set of unstated assumptions about the growing menace of juvenile crime, increasingly associated with African Americans. That perception would serve as an ominous backdrop to the deliberations and negotiations which led to the declaration of the War on Poverty.

The continuity in personnel and web of connections between the two "wars" are noteworthy.[60] The Poverty Task Force received critical input from Hackett, Ohlin, and Richard Boone, Hackett's deputy and a captain in the Chicago Police Department, who had previously worked with Ohlin for the Illinois Parole Board and the Ford Foundation. Shriver had met his future wife, Eunice Kennedy, in 1946 when both were on the staff of the National Conference on Juvenile Delinquency; it was Eunice, in turn, who persuaded her brothers to form the Delinquency Commission in 1961.[61] Officials from the Ford Foundation, the National Institute for Mental Health, and the Labor Department also had a foot in both camps.

Although it was John Kennedy who lent the power and prestige of his office to the Delinquency Commission, it was Robert Kennedy who displayed a personal commitment to it.[62] "The juvenile delinquency committee," one scholar has noted, "was the passageway that led Kennedy from his background as a conservative lawman into the political persona for which he is remembered, as the soulful champion of the downtrodden—it connected the two versions of himself. Delinquency was at first blush a law enforcement issue, so attending to it was consistent with the main thrust of Kennedy's career thus far; it didn't have the soft, abstract quality that he associated with most of the leading liberal issues and personalities."[63]

The attorney general at first tried to build political support for the Delinquency Commission by depicting urban delinquency as a serious threat to the entire nation.[64] Not surprisingly, given his pursuit of Jimmy Hoffa and labor corruption, he also depicted delinquency as in part an outgrowth of organized crime and the public cynicism it bred, which "contributes to the confusion of the young."[65] But he soon accepted the intellectual rationale behind opportunity theory and described the Delinquency Commission as a model for the Office of Economic Opportunity and an attack on the roots of crime, poverty in particular.[66]

The transition from delinquency to poverty was virtually seamless. No paradigm shift was required, for Ohlin and Hackett had already begun to view delinquency as shorthand or code for urban poverty and, by extension, racial discrimination.[67] Equally seamless was the decision to make community action—and its corollary, the maximum feasible participation of the poor—the tactic of choice. In November 1963, Hackett suggested that the poverty program should build on the policy precedents set by the Delinquency Commission to attract bureaucratic support. Hackett also recommended that the poverty planners use MFY as a spearhead and maximum feasible participation as a mantra.[68] The idea spread like wildfire. By mid-December, community action was, in the words of one historian, "transformed from an incidental weapon in the war on poverty into the entire arsenal."[69]

That the origins of the War on Poverty lay in the fight against delinquency is not particularly controversial. Nor are several other issues associated with the poverty program.[70] One, however, remains sensitive: the extent to which the poverty program was aimed at securing the votes of African Americans. Cloward and Frances Fox Piven contend that patronage politics dictated the creation of the Office of Economic Opportunity.[71] At an urban policy conference years later, Kennedy and Johnson administration veterans voiced divergent opinions of the Piven and Cloward thesis, with Hackett expressing vehement disagreement.[72] Scholars of the poverty program have subsequently and naturally differed as well.[73] Yet essentially the debate seems beyond resolution because it rests largely on an assumption about human—and official—behavior, rather than on any real or persuasive evidence.[74]

More importantly, what both critics and supporters of Piven and Cloward tend to overlook is the possibility that urban peace, not patronage, was also a serious, albeit implicit and unstated, goal for the War on Poverty, even before the large-scale riots of the mid-1960s.[75] By 1963 federal policymakers and ordinary citizens saw disorder and delinquency as real and racial threats in America's cities, both to white ethnics and African Americans, the most common victims of black crime. Given the close ties between the Delinquency Commission and the poverty planners, it seems unlikely that the relationship between crime, race, and poverty was ignored—or that the

White House viewed the urban constituencies as politically insignificant. On the contrary, the Task Force on Poverty probably chose not to focus openly on urban unrest only because, as deputy director Adam Yarmolinsky observed, "we were all aware of the work in the Justice Department. The conclusions were so self-evident" that there was no need. We assumed that "as you deal with poverty, you deal with crime and delinquency."[76]

The evidence for this assertion is circumstantial but suggestive. Despite endless denials to the contrary, top officials at both the Delinquency Commission and the Office of Economic Opportunity understood the racial dimensions of the emerging urban crisis. By 1963 Robert Kennedy also knew that the committee's focus was on black teens—Hackett had made it explicit. And at the poverty task force, memos such as "Why the Poverty Program is Not a Negro Program" virtually begged the question. A blatantly and calculatedly even-handed appeal to conservatives in Congress, it claimed that the program "opens the way for pouring cold water on a situation of growing explosiveness, the thousands of white and Negro school dropouts who are on the streets of the cities." In the margins Shriver wrote: "This is fantastic—almost unbelievable—but very, very good." As Yarmolinsky later said: "We were busy telling people it wasn't just racial because we thought it'd be easier that way, and we thought it was less racial than it turned out to be."[77]

That description seems accurate, but it is also important to note that officials such as Yarmolinsky operated in a city where racial considerations permeated almost all discussions of social policy. According to the 1960 census, Washington was 54 percent black, with 33.8 percent of black children in single-parent homes (compared to 18.9 percent of white children). The median family income for blacks was $4,763 compared to $8,466 for whites. Between 1961 and 1962 the crime rate among juveniles in the capital rose 17.7 percent, to a rate 13 percent above the national average.[78] Not surprisingly, Hackett made clear to Robert Kennedy in June 1962 the political necessity of funding the Washington Area Youth Project.[79] The attorney general in turn informed his brother. "I thought you'd be interested in seeing this," he wrote to the president, referring to an attached *Washington Post* article. It declared that while poverty, not race, underlay the delinquency crisis, "the most volatile tinder lying around the Washington 'powder keg' is the idle Negro juvenile."[80]

The *Post* article was no exception. During the early 1960s, the media scrutinized the urban ills of the nation's capital. In a well-publicized speech, a prominent female journalist noted that 85 percent of the district's crimes were committed by African Americans and said that "fear haunts the average citizen. Women who live alone do not feel safe in their houses and dare not go even across the street at night to mail a letter."[81] In a three-part series, the *New York Times* reported that although Washington was not the nation's most crime-ridden city, the "rise of violence here has been the most widely dramatized symptom of what everyone concedes is an alarming case of urban decay."[82] In an editorial, conservative commentator Arthur Krock contended in loaded language that the city was unsafe day or night, a "jungle" for lone pedestrians, women, and "respectable" blacks terrorized by "urban Mau Maus [who] circulate in and out of our courts and jails and cause nearly all the violent crime."[83]

The Kennedy administration maintained a watchful eye on the situation in Washington, fearing the political fallout if it worsened or riots erupted. After a disturbance broke out between local police and "Black Muslims," the president of the District's Board of Commissioners requested a contingency plan for the rapid deployment of U.S. Army soldiers in case of a riot. The request received prompt approval.[84] In the White House, aides kept close tabs on the media coverage, monitoring reports and preparing responses if necessary.[85] At the Justice Department, Robert Kennedy pledged vigorous action but tried to lower expectations. In words liberal Democrats would repeat in endless variations endless times, he declared at a press conference that "no matter how long we stay here and how vigorous we might be, we are not going to end crime in the United States."[86]

Despite the attorney general's efforts, expectations and anxieties would continue to mount from 1961 to 1964. Ironically, however, public concern over juvenile delinquency would wane even as the rate of youth crime rose dramatically. The news media shifted its attention to street crime and black criminals, who were less often perceived or defined as juveniles.[87] But regardless of whether youths or adults committed the offenses, they led to a growing sense that the streets of America's cities were unsafe—and that race was an integral element of the problem. In that climate, the poverty planners naturally saw their efforts as at least a partial response. "Like the staff of the [Delinquency Commission] before them," a writer has noted, "the poverty warriors thought of themselves as an advance guard worrying about the racial issues that lay over the next hill (whose true dimensions even they severely underestimated), while most of the government was still focused on the Civil Rights Act."[88]

But even as civil rights received top priority from the Johnson administration in the aftermath of the Kennedy assassination, opposition to desegregation was growing among conservatives in general and Republicans in particular. And in 1964 one Republican would find that, amid rising crime and unrest, his most effective argument against the Civil Rights Act was not "Segregation Forever" but law and order. His name was Barry Goldwater, and in his unsuccessful bid for the presidency, he would successfully introduce the language of law and order to national politics, with fateful consequences for the Johnson administration, the Democratic Party, and liberalism itself.

2.

Law and Order Unleashed

At the Republican National Convention in July 1964, Arizona Senator Barry Goldwater gave a fiery acceptance speech. The phrase that would subsequently attract the most attention was his memorable aphorism about extremism and liberty, vice and virtue. But at the time it was his invocation of law and order that roused the delegates to a fever pitch. Demanding in loaded language that it "not become the license of the mob and of the jungle," the Republican decried the Democrats for allowing "violence in our streets" to flourish. Blending the threats to personal and national security, he declared that "security from domestic violence, no less than from foreign aggression, is the most elementary and fundamental purpose of any government."[1]

At that moment, law and order became an important part of national political discourse. In the 1950s, three major developments—the black migration, urban de-industrialization, and juvenile crime—had laid the groundwork for the issue. But now it was propelled to the forefront of presidential politics through the deliberate and calculated actions of two conservative candidates, Democrat George Wallace and Republican Barry Goldwater. In the spring of 1964, the Alabama governor had demonstrated the appeal of law and order among northern whites; in the fall, the Arizona Senator would do likewise among southern whites. But the popular perception that Goldwater and Wallace, both avowed opponents of the Civil Rights Act, were racial extremists limited the broader impact of their message, which also failed to take hold because popular fear over "crime in the streets" had not yet become widespread.

The Johnson administration, however, was alarmed by the potential effect of law and order and by the real damage caused by civil unrest in New York, which erupted within days of Goldwater's address to the Republican Convention. In an effort to control the political damage, the White House carefully staged a summit meeting on racial violence and covertly urged a cessation of civil rights protests until after the election. It also cautiously negotiated with FBI Director J. Edgar Hoover over how he would assess the urban riots. The White House nevertheless remained nervous and anxious, revealing the full extent of liberal sensitivity to the conservative bonding of civil disobedience and civil disorder.

Behind in the polls, Goldwater hoped that law and order would turn the tide in his favor. But a controversial campaign commercial, which critics lambasted as racist, discredited his efforts to package the issue in a provocative yet palatable manner. Still, the emergence of law and order had sent shock waves through the White House. Publicly, the president and his advisers paid little attention to it; privately, they were deeply troubled by it. Even as the Johnson administration cruised toward a landslide victory, it began to craft a liberal solution for the social causes and political consequences of disorder and violence. Eventually, the White House would choose to promote the War on Poverty as a War on Crime. Like many other administration initiatives, the strategy, while successful in the short term, would unleash a host of unintended and unforeseen consequences in the long term.

I

Behind Goldwater's march to the Republican presidential nomination lay many factors: his personal appeal; the clarity of his conservative message; the weakness of his moderate rivals; the organizational skill of F. Clifton White and others in the "Draft Goldwater" movement; and the enthusiasm of tens of thousands of volunteers at the grassroots level.[2] At the same time, a conservative backlash had emerged in the wake of the Birmingham protests in June 1963. "The hostility to the new Negro militancy," wrote a prominent Republican official in a confidential memo circulated among Goldwater's top advisers, "has seemingly spread like wildfire from the South to the entire country." If the Arizona Republican endorsed states' rights, he could certainly win the nomination.[3]

But to win the presidency the candidate had to eschew racial extremism and couch his strong opposition to the civil rights bill in moderate terms.

One way was to depict it as an unconstitutional violation of private property and states' rights, which he had consistently maintained it was and sincerely saw it as. Another was to attack the movement for the disorder it had supposedly produced, to allege that it was responsible for the disintegration of public safety. Goldwater first made this charge in March 1964 during the New Hampshire primary. In a reference to Johnson's effort to demonstrate fiscal frugality by dimming the lights at the White House, he demanded that the president turn on the "lights of moral leadership" as well as the "lights of law and order." Using the charged metaphor of darkness, Goldwater then declared that crime and riots ran rampant in America's streets, a development he traced to the doctrine of civil disobedience and the growth of the welfare state. In so doing, he constructed what would become the standard conservative formulation of law and order.[4]

Although an advocate of limited government and states' rights, Goldwater argued that the federal government could and should play a large role in the local fight against violence and disorder. The Supreme Court could ease restraints on police by overturning recent rulings that hampered prosecutions, and the federal courts could set a positive example by imposing harsher sentences on criminals. The president could reinforce respect for the law and promote contempt for those who violated it, regardless of motive. But because of political opportunism, Goldwater contended, Johnson had failed in his duty. In search of votes, the president had turned a blind—even approving—eye toward civil rights demonstrators when they violated what they viewed as unjust and immoral laws. As a result, declared Goldwater, "many of our citizens—citizens of all races—accept as normal the use of riots, demonstrations, boycotts, violence, pressures, civil disorder, and disobedience as an approach to serious national problems."[5]

Behind this breakdown in civic order, Goldwater continued, was the welfare state, which promoted paternalism and dependence at the expense of opportunity and responsibility. "Government seeks to be parent, teacher, leader, doctor, and even minister," he charged, exploiting the increasing association of welfare, like crime, with black Americans. "And its failures are strewn about us in the rubble of rising crime rates."[6] By targeting liberalism as the ultimate source of these problems, Goldwater implicitly downplayed the differences between urban riots, political demonstrations, street crime, and juvenile delinquency. Instead, he explicitly combined these distinct phenomena into a common threat to a society of decency, security, and harmony—in short, to a society of law and order.[7]

Of course, the conservative construction of law and order rested as well on calculated silences and symbolism. For one, it ignored how southern officials often violated the law, leaving demonstrators with little choice but civil disobedience. For another, it permitted Goldwater to sidestep the more extreme belief that the civil rights movement was the product of a communist conspiracy.[8] Finally, it represented a reversal of traditional positions on federalism, with conservatives arguing that crime control was a federal matter and liberals emphasizing that it was, in practical and constitutional terms, a local matter. Likewise, Goldwater's attacks on the Warren Court, which had expanded individual protections against police coercion in *Mallory* and *Escobedo*, reflected a significant qualification in his defense of individual rights.[9]

But the message resonated with many whites—and none more so than the man who personified unyielding opposition to civil rights. On the eve of the Democratic primaries, Alabama Governor George Wallace made a bold prediction: "If I ran outside the South and got ten percent, it would be a victory. It would shake their eyeteeth in Washington."[10] He then entered Wisconsin to scant national notice and little local fanfare. But in April his campaign gathered momentum after a dramatic appearance at Serb Memorial Hall in Milwaukee.

As Wallace took the stage, a black civil rights activist yelled, "Get your dogs out!" The angry reference to Birmingham, Alabama, where in May 1963 Commissioner of Public Safety Eugene "Bull" Connor had unleashed water cannons and police dogs on peaceful demonstrators, brought an immediate response from rally organizer Bronko Gruber, a tavern owner and ex-marine. "I'll tell you something about your dogs, padre!" he replied hotly. "I live on Walnut Street and three weeks ago tonight a friend of mine was assaulted by three of your countrymen or whatever you want to call them." Cheers and whistles erupted from the packed crowd of 700 blue-collar workers. "They beat up old ladies 83-years-old, rape our womenfolk," continued Gruber. "They mug people. They won't work. They are on relief. How long can we tolerate this?" After a near brawl, Wallace gave his speech, interrupted by at least 30 ovations in 40 minutes.[11]

As the physical embodiment of southern segregation and "massive resistance" to civil rights, Wallace clearly appealed to the anti-integration sentiments of his northern audience. But the entire incident suggests a more complicated dynamic. It illustrates, first, how intimately fear of integration was related to fear of crime. Second, it demonstrates how Gruber and the other men in the hall saw as the victims of crime the women of their community, whom they felt compelled yet unable to protect. Compounding their frustration and adding to the threat to their manhood was the perceived racial identity of the assailants. Finally, the confrontation shows how anxiety over neighborhood safety could transmute into a wider critique of the civil rights movement and the liberal welfare state.

In retrospect, the moment signified the early rumblings of a seismic shift in the American political landscape. The next day, a worried Johnson ordered his Polish-American Postmaster General to fly immediately to Wisconsin to campaign against Wallace. The trip was in vain. On primary day, the Alabama Democrat defied all expectations, including his own, and won more than 33 percent of the votes cast in the Democratic primary. Although it is unclear to what degree Wallace's success was the result of his invocation of the crime threat, it is clear that he had tapped into a rich vein of resentment, anger, frustration, and fear.[12]

Wallace continued to seek political gold in May 1964 when he claimed during the Indiana primary that the courts made it impossible to convict criminals. "If you are knocked in the head on a street in a city today," he declared, "the man who knocked you in the head is out of jail before you get to the hospital." Then he won 30 percent of the votes, including 53 percent in several blue-collar, white-ethnic counties where he had not even made an appearance.[13] Finally, Wallace climaxed his spring run by receiving 43 percent in the Maryland primary, including more than 90 percent of the white voters on the Eastern Shore. In Baltimore, ethnic counties that in 1960 went for John Kennedy by 2–1 margins now went for Wallace.[14] The "Southernization" or "Redemption" of American politics was now underway.[15]

Wallace had shaken more than a few eyeteeth. But his abortive bid for the Democratic nomination never amounted to more than a political protest, in part because the Alabama Governor never overcame his reputation as a racist and in part because most white Americans remained untroubled by the alleged loss of public safety. Nevertheless, Wallace had demonstrated how powerful the appeal of law and order was to those for whom the threat of crime and disorder was real. He had also shown how tenuous the ties of such Democrats were to the national party's liberal agenda. In mid-July he announced that he would not run for president as a third-party candidate or independent, but claimed that he had made his voice heard. He had—and he had pointed the way for others with less racial baggage.

The question now was whether Goldwater could exploit and broaden the discontent that Wallace had revealed without assuming his liabilities.

As a past member of the NAACP, a founding member of the National Urban League chapter in Phoenix, and a strong supporter of voluntary integration, his personal beliefs dictated that he avoid overt racist appeals.[16] As a staunch conservative, his political interests dictated that he send covert racial signals to Wallace's followers. With the convention at hand, Goldwater was therefore careful to praise the Alabama Democrat for his opposition to crime and disorder even as he declined to add him to the Republican ticket.

In San Francisco, Goldwater signaled his intent to harvest the votes of ethnic whites by making "crime in the streets" one of his central campaign themes. Advice and evidence that he should do so came from several quarters.[17] In addition, former President Dwight Eisenhower's speech to the convention demonstrated beyond doubt the potency of law and order. In a last-minute departure from his prepared text, he warned against false sympathy for criminals—and the delegates erupted. As journalist Theodore White noted, he was "lifting to national discourse a matter of intimate concern to the delegates, creating there before them an issue which touched all fears, North and South. The convention howled." Nevertheless, the final decision rested with Goldwater, who personally chose to include stronger law-and-order language in the final draft of his nomination speech.[18]

After the speech, Goldwater stressed to reporters his determination to make law and order a major campaign issue. "I think ... the abuse of law and order in this country, the total disregard for it, the mounting crime rate is going to be another issue [after foreign policy]," he predicted, "at least I'm going to make it one because I think the responsibility for this has to start someplace and it should start at the federal level with the federal courts enforcing the laws." He then promised that as president he would "do all I can to see that women can go out in the streets of this country without being scared stiff."[19]

In hindsight, the acceptance speech was most notable because it signaled Goldwater's deliberate decision to make law and order his major domestic issue. It also highlighted many of the themes he would later elaborate during the campaign: the connection between political corruption in Washington and street crime in America; the gendered evocation of criminals and their victims; the equation of the loss of order with a loss of freedom; and the correlation between the communist threat to security from overseas and the criminal threat to security at home. But the speech made no direct mention of civil rights or the racial complexion of urban violence.[20] Henceforth Goldwater would concentrate on what he viewed as the race-neutral refrain of "crime in the streets."[21] The refrain would provoke considerable anxiety in the White House, as would events in Harlem, 3,000 miles from the site of the convention.

II

Hours before Goldwater accepted the Republican nomination, an off-duty New York police officer in plainclothes shot and killed a black teenager armed with a knife. Two days later, a rally in Harlem to protest the Mississippi murders of three civil rights workers turned into a march on a precinct police station, where officers and demonstrators clashed. For the next week, street rallies in Manhattan and Brooklyn escalated into violent confrontations as police battled protesters hurling bricks and bottles. Arson and looting followed, with scores of injuries. One week later, a similar riot erupted in Rochester.[22] But it was in Harlem, in the symbolic and historic heart of black America, that a new dynamic in the racial politics of the nation truly began.

The riot took the administration by surprise. Ramsey Clark, an assistant attorney general at the time, later recalled "how distant Rochester and Harlem and the other major disturbances seemed to the Department of Justice We just thought they've got big fine police departments and they can take care of it." The president was firm yet evenhanded, promising to restore order, disparaging violence in all forms, and pledging to attack "the evil social conditions that breed despair and disorder." He also carefully paired his criticism of the riots in the North with condemnation of white supremacist violence in the South. "American citizens," he said, "have a right to protection of life and limb—whether driving along a highway in Georgia, a road in Mississippi, or a street in New York City."[23] Then he directed Hoover and the FBI to investigate the causes of the riots, with special attention to the possibility of communist provocation.

While Johnson maintained a calm facade in public, in private he was extremely perturbed. "Deke, you and the FBI have got to stop these riots," he told his FBI liaison, Cartha "Deke" DeLoach. "One of my political analysts tells me that every time one occurs, it costs me 90,000 votes." The next day the president called Hoover directly. "We're getting floods of wires and telegrams," Johnson told him. "Here's one. [reads aloud:] 'I'm a working girl. . . . I'm afraid to leave my house. . . . I feel the Negro revolution will reach Queens. . . . Please send troops immediately to Harlem.'"[24] The president chose instead to send the FBI director, hoping that his investigation would contain the political fallout from the riots and shield the Great Society from conservative criticism.

But the White House remained in a state of high anxiety. In conversations with New York Mayor Robert Wagner Jr. and Texas Governor John Connally, the president speculated that right-wing extremists like Texas oil millionaire H. L. Hunt were involved. "Both sides are in on these riots," he informed Connally. "Hell, these folks have got walkie-talkies. . . . Somebody's financing them big. . . . It's Brooklyn one night and it's Harlem the next night and it'll be another section of New York tonight."[25] The president's advisers were equally nervous. Addressing the riot issue directly might benefit Goldwater, one warned, but also might "blunt the further erosion of white voter passions" by reducing racial tensions. Given the possibility of future riots, that was critical. "This one issue could destroy us in the campaign," he concluded. "Every night of rioting costs us the support of thousands. Therefore we need to move swiftly to try to hold the line before it spreads like a contagion."[26]

Yet Goldwater too feared an epidemic of racial violence, telling prominent Republicans in private that he was "scared to death" at the prospect of more riots. "I know that your big cities in the Northeast and in the Middle West—not only on the West Coast—are just tinderboxes," Goldwater said, "and I'll be darned if I will have my grandchildren accuse their grandfather of setting fire to [them]."[27] And so he approached Johnson with a sincere request for a private meeting at which the two candidates would agree not to exploit the racial situation for political gain.[28]

The proposal exposed the full extent of White House concern about a possible intersection in the public mind between urban racial violence and the civil rights movement. Some aides opposed the summit meeting because it would raise the challenger's stature, blunt his image as an extremist, and give him "a buffer against criticism that he is stirring up racism by claiming he is operating within the ground rules which you discussed." Above all, it would give Goldwater "camouflage for just the kind of campaign he intends to run." Others warned, however, that rejecting the offer could enable the Republicans to accuse Johnson of "racial exploitation … and to ascribe every CORE picket ruckus to the Democratic Party."[29]

Ultimately, Johnson reached a compromise, typical of his unending search for consensus. First, the president held a preemptive press conference, pledging that he would never "lend any aid or comfort" to a violent minority and adding that he hoped Goldwater would do the same. Next he held a brief (16 minutes) and inconclusive meeting with Goldwater. Afterward, Johnson avoided all photo opportunities with his challenger and issued a joint statement notable only for its brevity and ambiguity. And then the White House moved swiftly and firmly to defuse potential trouble: white liberals were told to withhold funds from civil rights organizations until after the election, surveillance preparations for the Democratic Convention were shifted into high gear, and civil rights leaders were persuaded to cancel or postpone demonstrations.[30]

Whether the summit foreclosed the possibility of an honest debate remains unclear.[31] Johnson would later claim that, unlike his challenger, he had no intention of ducking the growing issue of racial tension.[32] But both candidates avoided the critical subject of urban disorder because it was too explosive, leaving working-class whites to vote their fears in local races while accepting the Democratic "package" in the national campaign.[33] In any event, law and order never achieved critical mass in 1964 because the Republican nominee (like Wallace) was a flawed messenger and, more important, because social conditions had not yet reached a crisis point. But the issue also failed to gain traction because the White House managed to contain the racial unrest and control the political agenda of the campaign.

In August, the White House debated whether to hold a conference on law enforcement. Advocates contended that it would reduce racial tensions and the possibility of future riots. Moreover, failure to act would allow Goldwater to "seize the initiative on this most crucial domestic issue of all" and to make a dramatic gesture similar to Eisenhower's 1952 campaign pledge to visit Korea. But opponents contended that the conference would redound to Goldwater's credit and "might become a forum for civil rights discussions—something we do not need at the present time." The conference was quietly shelved, showing once again the administration's anxiety over the conservative equation of street crime and civil rights.[34]

In September, the administration took proactive measures as well. It had prominent black spokesmen like Carl Rowan, the African-American director of the U.S. Information Agency, denounce the disorder. "Some Negroes believe that extremism in pursuit of the black man's liberty is no vice," he declared, paraphrasing Goldwater, "but I say that stupidity is never a virtue. . . . The hour has come when bold, uncompromising efforts must be made to free the civil rights movement from the taint of street rioters, looters and punks who terrorize subways." When Press Secretary Bill Moyers suggested more "non-political speeches" by Rowan, Johnson readily agreed. "Get him in 10 important states," he demanded. "New York, Illinois, Ohio, California, et al."[35]

The White House also hastened to influence the FBI report Johnson had commissioned in the aftermath of the Harlem Riot. It stated that "there was no systematic planning or organization of any of the city riots," not by communist individuals or the Communist Party. It also refused to characterize the disorders as race riots or contend that they were the direct result of civil rights agitation. "A common characteristic of the riots was a senseless attack on all constituted authority without purpose or object," declared the report, which in addition stressed the impact of slum conditions and youth crime.[36] The report's moderate tone won it praise from liberals and scorn from conservatives. The *National Review* expressed outrage at the "politicization" of the FBI and the "endorsement" of the anti-poverty program. "We must hope that future attempts to conscript the FBI as a propaganda agent for the Administration's policies will fail," wrote the magazine, "and one bases one's hopes that it will fail on a high regard for the integrity of John Edgar Hoover."[37]

But Hoover had hopes and designs of his own. The report's ghostwriter was former presidential candidate Thomas Dewey, whom Johnson had selected with the expectation that he would restrain Hoover. Instead, the roles were reversed, with the director currying the president's favor by moderating Dewey's analysis. In the end, the arrangement benefited both parties. Johnson, as one historian has noted, had "covertly maneuvered a prominent Republican and overtly maneuvered his anticommunist FBI director into issuing a report that endorsed the War on Poverty and helped blunt the Goldwater Republican challenge." In exchange for his moderation, Hoover had gained a freer hand with surveillance operations. The tacit bargain would have significant consequences in the years to come.[38]

In the weeks to follow, the report would serve as political cover for liberal Democrats across the nation. Although top officials differed on its merits, the White House circulated it widely, emphasizing Hoover's conclusion that the Civil Rights Act had not contributed to the urban racial violence.[39] But the law and order issue would not fade because an increasingly desperate Goldwater could not and would not let it.

III

In late summer the situation for Goldwater was bleak. He lagged in the polls and was vulnerable to Democratic charges that he opposed Social Security and favored a nuclear confrontation with the Soviet Union. His only hope—and it was a long shot—was to identify the breakdown in law and order with the Johnson administration. But his attempts to persuade a broad cross-section of the American public backfired, leaving him saddled with the image of a racial extremist, which in turn blunted any success he might have had.

Goldwater's first task was to sell moderate Republicans on the legitimacy and potency of law and order. At a closed "Unity Conference" held in Hershey, Pennsylvania in mid-August, some were openly skeptical.[40] In one exchange, New York Governor Nelson Rockefeller, Goldwater's main opponent in the primaries, asked the nominee to "oppose any and all efforts that would make our party appear to be a party of lawlessness, a party of racism, or a war party." In frustration, Goldwater replied that "I don't know how I can say it any more candidly or clearly than I have said it." For his part, Eisenhower urged extreme caution in word selection, noting that his reference to switchblades at the Republican Convention had drawn criticism from blacks. He also suggested that Goldwater repudiate any backlash support. "Well, I have said that," the candidate retorted. Congressman Robert Wilson then urged him to attack the president's efforts to curtail any civil rights protests until after the election. "I think we can make some political capital with this rather cynical situation," he said with Goldwater's approval.[41]

To raise some political capital, Goldwater now moved to boost the political profile of law and order. A confidential campaign memo reveals that the deployment of the issue was largely a calculated political tactic. It noted that Johnson was very popular, with an aura of invincibility and consistently high Gallup approval ratings. What Goldwater therefore needed to do was to strip away the president's "victory psychology," stem the defection of moderate Republicans (the "frontlash" as the Democrats called it), and erase "the 'trigger happy,' 'nuclear war-mongering' image which has been fastened on the Senator." Avoid Democratic strengths like peace and prosperity, advised the memo rather wishfully, and seize the initiative from the president, who polls showed was vulnerable in only one area: law and order.[42]

Goldwater should therefore declare the country in crisis and the president incapable of action because of his lack of moral conviction and his alliance with minority organizations and political bosses. Equally critical, the memo continued, was that every aspect of the crisis—street crime, urban riots, juvenile delinquency, government corruption—"be treated as a prong of a single fork—a fork labeled 'moral crisis' [and] jabbed relentlessly from now until election day." Noting that Kennedy had turned a virtual non-issue, the alleged missile gap, into the decisive issue of the 1960 campaign by hammering away at it constantly, the memo urged Goldwater to do the same with law and order regardless of whether the strategy yielded immediate results.[43]

Others offered similar advice, which found favor with the candidate.[44] Goldwater may not have approved of every aspect of the memo, but his campaign speeches indicate that he faithfully adhered to the suggested approach and established themes. The gendered construction of crime, in which criminals were invariably men and victims were invariably women, remained a central element of his conception of law and order. The doctrine of civil disobedience, he reiterated, gave license to lawbreakers, whom the president had for political gain first encouraged and then discouraged. At the same time, law enforcement received little support as the Supreme Court expanded the rights of criminals and reduced the ability of police to arrest, prosecute, and convict them. Urging better judicial appointments, Goldwater called for a constitutional amendment to curb the Warren Court.[45]

The welfare state remained at the heart of the crisis. "Telling people again and again that the federal Government will take care of everything for them," Goldwater contended, "leads to the decline of personal and individual responsibility which is the base cause of the rise in crime and disregard for law and order."[46] But the creators of the welfare state had exacerbated this problem twofold. After all, argued Goldwater, it was the liberal who was "concerned for the criminal and careless about his victims, who frowns on the policeman and fawns on the social psychologist." And it was the liberal who, through disregard for discipline, had fostered "the deterioration of the home, the family and the community, of law and order, of good morals and good manners."[47]

Nowhere was the failure of the administration's approach to law and order more evident, declared Goldwater, than in the District of Columbia. In the nation's capital, often within sight of the White House, crimes against persons occurred at four times the national average and major crimes had risen 34 percent in first six months of 1964—double the national average. Rape, assault, burglary, and robbery had jumped 47 percent, in "the one city which should reflect most brightly the president's concern for law and order, for decent conduct. Instead, it is a city embattled, plagued by lawlessness, haunted by fears."[48] Left unsaid—but understood—was Washington's image and reputation as a heavily African-American city.

The media in particular understood—or chose to interpret—Goldwater's statements and omissions as a form of racial code.[49] Not all journalists took that position.[50] But the conventional wisdom soon depicted Goldwater as desperate to attract the "backlash" vote by laying the blame for civil disorder on the White House. "By harping on the very subject which he denies exploiting," asserted one commentator, "he is keeping it alive—or trying to do so—and the objective is so transparent that his rather pious denials begin to lack credibility." Significantly, the journalist added, Goldwater had never alluded to the other side of the equation: that the denial of civil rights had led to the protests in the first place; that comparable violence was committed by white segregationists in the South; and that the northern riots had involved only small numbers of unemployed youths.[51]

Many in the media nonetheless saw law and order as a legitimate issue raised in response to real concern. In the charged climate of the Cold War, observed ABC News commentator Edward P. Morgan, the clamor for a tougher police response to crime and disorder sprang from a constellation of rational and irrational anxieties and fears "spawned by the explosive insecurity of the nuclear age in which we live, and ... triggered by the knowledge of clear and present danger stalking city streets and parkways." He worried, however, that Republican rhetoric would enflame racial tensions and prejudice. And Morgan regretted that "the Goldwater tactic of seeming to lump civil rights demonstrations, race riots, and individual assaults in the streets together in one column has made it appear—to the delight of the white backlashers—as if the American Negro population had invented and maintained a monopoly on crime."[52]

In response to such criticism, Goldwater and his advisers consistently disavowed any racist intent. In a television interview, the candidate said race had not played a major role in the riots, claiming that whites, blacks, and Puerto Ricans—"organized gangs" and "undesirables from every branch of American society"—had participated. He was not asked for his thoughts on civil disobedience. Republican National Committee Chairman Dean Burch stated that neither he, Goldwater, nor anyone connected with the campaign was a racist. Pressed by the interviewer, Burch admitted that the campaign had aired commercials which illustrated the breakdown of law and order by showing footage of the Harlem Riot. The "Negro riots" were part of the problem, he conceded in a revealing statement, "but they're not the *only* [emphasis added] aspect of the problem."[53]

The disclaimer by Burch failed to satisfy Roy Wilkins, president of the National Association for the Advancement of Colored People (NAACP), who maintained that "every utterance touching on this issue by the Republican nominee and by his vice presidential running mate has had ill-concealed racial overtones, undertones, and just plain out-and-out tones." Predicting that the Goldwater campaign would concentrate on foreign policy and "crime in the streets"—the "Communist bogey-man" and the "Negro bogey-man"—Wilkins noted correctly that the Republican never attacked segregationist violence in states like Mississippi or drew a distinction between violent and peaceful protests. Additional ammunition for his charges would come from television commercials prepared by the Republican campaign.[54]

The most notable was a thirty-minute, racially charged film called "Choice," which in many respects was the forerunner for the notorious Willie Horton commercial that the Republicans would run in the 1988 presidential campaign.[55] Produced by a supposedly independent organization called "Mothers for a Moral America" (MFMA), the film was nonetheless conceived, funded, and backed by top officials in the Goldwater campaign.[56] The candidate himself gave initial approval, although in response to sharp criticism he also made the ultimate decision not to show the film on national television.[57] "Choice" nonetheless attracted widespread attention in the mainstream media and was shown on numerous local stations.[58]

The grainy, black-and-white film began with a selective review of American history and then presented voters with a "choice" between two nations: in Johnson's America, interracial couples gyrate wildly to rock music, scantily clad women dance on tables, cars careen down highways, the "Fast Deal" mentality flourishes, blacks constantly clash with police, and pornographic books with titles like "Call Me Nympho" and "Jazz Me Baby" are available on every street corner; in Goldwater's America, well-scrubbed white children recite the Pledge of Allegiance, middle-class whites attend church, and neighborhood committees composed of white homeowners keep order in their communities. "Choice" concluded with a personal appeal from John Wayne and a montage of convention shots, including a sound bite of Goldwater warning that "tonight, there is violence in our streets."[59]

Between the history and the hysteria, the film's racial insinuations were numerous and obvious: in graphic footage, white policemen confront unidentified blacks, perhaps rioters, looters, or demonstrators.[60] No mention is made of civil rights—but no distinction is made between violent civil disorder and nonviolent civil disobedience. The one crime victim given a face is an ethnic white male beaten by a gang, and the one policeman given a voice is a white Philadelphia cop who complains that "during the riots we were told our only weapon was to be our night sticks. How the hell do we defend ourselves?"[61] According to a draft of the script, the Pledge of Allegiance scene called for the faces of "some negroes and minorities"—though none are apparent in the film. Other instructions specifically requested Harlem Riot footage, the "best we have." The opening scene was originally supposed to feature the gang mugging of a lone woman on a dark street, but it apparently wound up on the cutting-room floor.[62]

A memo attached to the draft further revealed the calculation behind the film's creation and distribution. Goldwater could win, it asserted, by targeting women voters, seeking free media coverage, and combining "the whole complex of juvenile delinquency, crime, violence, riots, narcotics, pornography, and immorality in government." The memo further advised that MFMA be "an entity in itself, a spontaneous public movement"—but also be "carefully coordinated with and through" the official campaign organization. As for the candidate, he cannot "be directly connected with this manipulation" until the conclusion of the campaign.[63] If that was the plan, it failed badly.

The day before "Choice" was to air nationally on NBC-TV, news of its contents leaked. Outraged, Wilkins telegrammed NBC President Robert Sarnoff and threatened to boycott the network if it showed the film, which the NAACP president called "an unprincipled attempt to arouse anti-Negro feeling and to play upon the anxieties of some white people regarding alleged criminality and irresponsibility of Negro citizens."[64] The storm of criticism forced Goldwater to withdraw and then repudiate "Choice," which he termed "nothing but a racist film."[65] His actions allowed him to sidestep accusations of racial prejudice, but undercut his claim to be the candidate of traditional morality and reinforced the impression that he had little control over his own campaign.

Above all, the controversy over "Choice" discredited Goldwater's contention that law and order was not, at heart, a form of racial code. It also distracted public attention from the extent to which the issue had privately rattled the administration, particularly when the nominee framed his charges in the martial rhetoric that Johnson himself loved to employ.[66] "Now we have heard of and seen many wars in the time of the present administration," said Goldwater, referring both to the War on Poverty and the war in Vietnam. "But have we yet heard of the only needed war—the war against crime?"[67] The question would linger as the campaign moved into the final stretch and the White House agonized over how best to contain the threat posed by law and order.

IV

During the fall the White House chose not to confront the Goldwater challenge directly. Although the administration quietly began to lay the groundwork for the War on Crime, which it would launch early in 1965, the strategy was to keep the focus on Goldwater and the threat he supposedly represented to Social Security, nuclear peace, and economic prosperity. In late October, however, the president decided to portray the antipoverty program as an anti-crime measure; in so doing, he expressed the liberal faith that the War on Poverty would complement the War on Crime by ameliorating the social conditions that bred violence. It was a fateful choice, one that would have a major impact on national politics, race relations, and public policy in the years to come.

A remarkable memorandum prepared by Deputy Attorney General Norbert Schlei and others in the Department of Justice highlighted the administration's continuing anxiety about the potential impact of law and order. Entitled "Riots and Crime in the Cities" and drafted at the behest of Moyers, it outlined in thirty-two pages the approach that the president would, with few deviations, undertake in the next few years in an effort to address what was rapidly emerging as the nation's most pressing domestic problem.[68] As such, the memo provides both a candid snapshot of White House attitudes toward law and order at the time as well as a road map of where those attitudes—and the policies they prescribed—would lead.

Schlei began by identifying Goldwater's emphasis on law and order as a racial appeal coded so that "those to whom racial issues are dominant will identify 'crime in the streets' with crime by Negroes in major urban centers such as New York, Chicago and Philadelphia." Nevertheless, he insisted (unlike many non-administration liberals) that street crime represented for many a real threat, not a statistical mirage or political smokescreen. At the same time, Schlei rejected the conservative contention that the main cause was an erosion in the moral standards of Americans in general and youth in particular. On the contrary, he asserted that crime was on the rise primarily because the number of young men (who historically have tended to commit most acts of violence) was increasing at a far faster rate than the general population.[69]

To combat delinquency and crime, Schlei recommended that the White House place "principal emphasis" on initiatives already in place, such as the Juvenile Delinquency and Youth Crime Program, the Manpower Development and Training Act, and the Civil Rights Act. But, as he readily conceded, this focus on factors like poverty and unemployment was unlikely to yield "immediate and dramatic improvements" and could complicate efforts to treat street crime and urban riots as distinct phenomena. Moreover, although the federal government could assist local police, especially with gambling and narcotics operations run by organized crime, responsibility for law and order would remain with state, county, and municipal authorities.[70] In time, these notes of caution would become hallmarks of the liberal position.

Given these reservations, Schlei advised Johnson to appoint a presidential commission after the election, a step that the president would take in March 1965 when he convened the President's Commission on Law Enforcement and the Administration of Justice. In the meantime, the administration should sit tight and enact no new measures "on a crash basis or upon the basis of an unbalanced or hysterical view of the [crime] problem."[71] For the most part, the White House heeded this advice. But ultimately neither Schlei nor anyone else in the administration could control Johnson's penchant for rhetorical excess, particularly his fateful decision to identify the anti-poverty program as an anti-crime measure.

In July and August, aides gathered material on the administration's anti-delinquency efforts. The purpose was patently political—"for use in connection with Ike [Eisenhower] and Barry [Goldwater] emphasis on crime in the streets."[72] The Economic Opportunity Act, it was noted, struck at the heart of two of the main sources of crime: poverty and unemployment. Therefore the administration should promote "its proposed war on poverty as an assault on the conditions under which juvenile delinquency flourishes."[73] Adding urgency to the situation was a new Harris Poll showing that in September 61 percent of Americans (up from 53 percent in August) now worried more about their personal safety than they had a year earlier.[74]

In mid-October Johnson moved to ease the fear. At the ceremony to swear in Sargent Shriver as Office of Economic Opportunity chief, the president uttered the words that would come back to haunt his administration in the years to come: "The war on poverty ... is a war against crime and a war against disorder." Reinforcing this theme, he criticized Goldwater directly (though not by name): "There is something mighty wrong when a candidate for the highest public office bemoans violence in the streets but votes against the war on poverty, votes against the Civil Rights Act, and votes against major educational bills that have come before him as a legislator. The thing to do is not to talk about crime; the thing to do is to fight and work and vote against crime."[75]

For the remainder of the campaign, the White House was virtually silent on "crime in the streets." The only official to address the issue was Nicholas Katzenbach, who in September had become the acting attorney general when Robert Kennedy chose to run for the U.S. Senate in New York. A large man with a deliberate manner and distinctive profile, Katzenbach had served in the Air Force during World War II and was a prisoner of war in Italy. In 1945 he returned to Princeton to finish his degree. Then he went to Yale Law School and became a Rhodes Scholar. For eight years he taught law at Yale and Chicago before joining the Justice Department in 1961. Two years later, he confronted George Wallace on the steps of the University of Alabama and presented him with a court order to admit two black students.

Now Katzenbach acknowledged, in a speech before the Federal Bar Association, that urban disorder was a serious problem. But in a concise statement of liberal principles, he challenged the conservative correlation of race with crime and riots. "I do not mean to imply that Negroes do not commit crimes," he said bluntly. "Of course they do. What I do mean to show is that to draw a causal connection between membership in the Negro race and crime is wrong. The relevant link is not between riots and race, but between riots and delinquency, between lawlessness and lawless environments." Above all, there were, contrary to Republican rhetoric, no simple or easy answers. Calling partisan attacks on the Supreme Court "uninformed and irresponsible," Katzenbach stated firmly that order without law was unacceptable, that civil liberties were not mere technicalities.[76] It was a refrain that he and other liberals would repeat many times in the coming years.

Ultimately, the strategy of silence paid dividends in 1964. By avoiding issues where Goldwater was strong (like law and order) and attacking those where he was weak (like Social Security and nuclear war), Johnson protected his early lead and roared to a landslide victory. His popular vote margin was 16 million (61 to 39 in percentage terms), and his electoral college margin was 486–52. The president captured 94 percent of the black vote, 90 percent of the Jewish vote, 62 percent of the women's vote, 20 percent of the registered Republican vote (as "frontlash" proved a reality), and a majority of the white vote (a feat no Democratic presidential candidate has managed since). He also carried every state, with the exception of Arizona (Goldwater's home state) and the Deep South (Mississippi, Alabama, South Carolina, Georgia, and Louisiana).[77]

But buried within the rubble of Goldwater's political defeat lay glimmers of future electoral gold for the Republicans. For a variety of reasons—a divided party, internal staff conflict, a healthy economy, and a popular incumbent—the Goldwater campaign had never gained momentum.[78] It had introduced law and order to presidential politics, but conditions were not yet ripe for the issue to take hold. In a sense, the conservative diagnosis remained unproven and the liberal cure remained untested. That would soon change. But in 1964 Goldwater was, like Wallace, a prophet ahead of his time—and one who also bore the burden of ideological and racial extremism.[79]

At the grassroots level, however, the election had energized a new generation of conservative activists.[80] In addition, the enhanced level of racial polarization—Goldwater had attracted 6 percent of the black vote compared to the 40 percent Eisenhower had earned in 1956 and the 32 percent Nixon had received in 1960—hinted at opportunity for the Republicans, who at little political cost could now appeal directly to southern whites opposed to black demands for civil rights.[81] By contrast, the overwhelming allegiance of black voters portended problems for the Democrats, who by principle and necessity were now committed to racial equality but were also faced with the potential defection of urban whites angered by street crime, neighborhood integration, and workplace competition.[82]

But the backlash bombed in 1964. It failed to ignite in South Philadelphia, Brooklyn, and Queens, where Italian, German, and Irish voters rejected Goldwater in greater numbers than they had Nixon. It also failed to detonate in Polish precincts in Cleveland and Chicago—and even in cities under economic and social strain like Gary and Milwaukee, where Johnson captured 82 percent of the vote. On the whole, the news from the liberal perspective was good. As a confidential AFL-CIO memo put it, "Since the only substantial reward outside the South for the use of civil rights as a political issue, however indirectly or delicately phrased in terms of safety in the streets, was the massive mobilization of a large and effective Negro vote, there is reason to hope that this nation may be spared a repetition of this most cynically immoral and degrading ploy."[83]

The president also had reason to hope. By bonding the War on Poverty to a War on Crime, he had garnered political support and expressed the liberal belief that it was vital to attack the "root causes" of crime. But at the same time, Johnson had also increased the exposure of each war to a withering conservative counterfire.[84] Moreover, by failing to dispel the conservative coupling of crime and riots he had complicated any serious attempt to reform police practices or separate the real from the imagined fears of urbanites and suburbanites. Nevertheless, the White House entered 1965 confident that it could contain the issue of law and order. The optimism would prove misplaced.

3.

The War on Crime

In the fall of 1964, Lyndon Johnson blunted the threat of law and order by promising that the War on Poverty would constitute a virtual War on Crime. In the fall of 1965, he declared an actual War on Crime. "I will not be satisfied," the president announced in gendered language that echoed the Inaugural Address of John Kennedy, "until every woman and child in this Nation can walk any street, enjoy any park, drive on any highway, and live in any community at any time of the day or night without fear of being harmed." The rhetoric was ambitious and risky. By promoting the idea of victory and hailing the policeman as "the frontline soldier in our war against crime," Johnson had staked a great deal of his political credibility on a domestic struggle no less dangerous than the foreign conflict in South Vietnam.[1] "It proved to be a dreadful mistake," recalled Nicholas Katzenbach. "You are meant to win wars, and the War on Crime was in a sense an unwinnable war."[2]

A combination of confidence and anxiety motivated Johnson. On the one hand, the nation's economic abundance emboldened him to claim that he could eradicate a seemingly intractable peril. "We really had a sense that government could do things," recalled domestic adviser Joseph Califano, "that we could get the country organized in ways to deal with these problems."[3] On the other, the president understood well the latent potency of law and order, which had caused his campaign such trepidation and continued to resonate in the months after the election. In December 1964, for example, a Harris Poll showed that 73 percent of those surveyed felt that crime in their neighborhood had increased in the past year, a figure that was consistent in rural areas, small towns, suburbs, and cities.[4]

Accordingly, the president moved aggressively in the spring of 1965. To demonstrate both personal toughness and political determination, he lobbied Congress to pass the Law Enforcement Assistance Act (LEAA), which established the Office of Law Enforcement Assistance (OLEA), a small but significant expansion of the federal role in crime control. To gain time and build consensus for further action, Johnson convened a Presidential Commission on Law Enforcement and the Administration of Justice (hereafter the Crime Commission), which would lay the liberal groundwork for future legislation. In policy terms, the War on Crime was the logical extension of his earlier pledge. In political terms, it was a liberal attempt to neutralize or capture the conservative issue of law and order. Either way, however, the War on Crime was not without risk. For one, it might spotlight and validate the crime issue in the eyes of anxious Americans. For another, it might lead to rhetorical oversell by the president and excessive expectations by the public. Finally, it might spark conservative and radical opposition—as well as reveal liberal uncertainty.

The War on Crime nonetheless appeared headed for a decisive victory. But then came the Watts Riot in Los Angeles, which in the summer of 1965 stunned Johnson and most Americans. It also foreshadowed conflagrations to come and highlighted the political danger the administration faced in assuming greater responsibility for civil order. And Watts complicated the White House's efforts to separate street crime and civil disorder in the public mind. In the aftermath, official reports generated more controversy than consensus as liberals, conservatives, and radicals debated the larger meaning of the riot. Watts thus exposed and exacerbated the racial and ideological fissures that permeated the nation as it reached a fault line between the optimism of the early 1960s and the pessimism of the late 1960s. Despite the president's hopes and ambitions, demands for law and order would continue to escalate.

I

In the spring of 1965, the president found no shortage of suggestions as he prepared, in what would become an annual ritual, to deliver his Special Message to Congress on Law Enforcement. From the Department of Labor came the recommendation—courtesy of Daniel Patrick Moynihan, not yet notorious for his controversial report on black families—that the administration first devote more study to organized crime and juvenile delinquency, particularly among black youths.[5] The Department of Health, Education, and Welfare called for more social programs even as it claimed that cynical conservatives had "often distorted and exaggerated" the crime issue for political gain.[6] By contrast, the Department of Justice wanted Johnson to take a harder line, with less emphasis on juvenile delinquency and social services. "We feel the president must place a much greater emphasis on crime and law enforcement if he is to strike the right note with Congress and the public," it advised.[7]

In March, Johnson reached for that note in his Special Message. He was careful to avoid areas of contention, such as whether the greatest threat to personal security came from criminal-coddling courts (a favorite target of the right) or Constitution-shredding policemen (a favorite target of the left). Praising the War on Poverty, the president observed that "laws are less likely to command the respect of those forced to live at the margins of our society," but added that "we should remember that not all crime is committed by those who are impoverished or those denied equal opportunity." Because neighborhood violence was now a "national concern," he lauded federal initiatives such as the Crime Commission. But because street violence remained the practical and constitutional responsibility of local authorities, the president forswore—as he would repeatedly in the years to come—any intention of building a national police force.[8]

Johnson's moderate tone reassured Democratic Senator Sam Ervin of North Carolina, a strong supporter of states' rights, who invoked the federalism issue immediately upon introduction of the LEAA. "We cannot and should not establish a Federal police force," he declared. "[W]e cannot and should not attempt to write, enforce or interpret the laws of the States; and we cannot and should not dictate the methods and tools to those responsible at the state level."[9] Congress followed his lead, appropriating small sums and attaching few strings. In final form, the act authorized the attorney general to make grants-in-aid to state and local police for experimental programs, research projects, specialized training, and modern equipment. The OLEA in turn administered the grants, evaluated their success, and publicized the results to police departments around the country.[10]

At the signing ceremony for the LEAA, which won overwhelming approval in Congress, the president warned that critics would judge the Great Society a failure if it met the material needs of every American but was unable to curb the rising crime rate.[11] He was right. But most conservatives would find little fault with the OLEA. In the end, few considered the agency a federal boondoggle, the first step in the creation of a national police force, or an unconstitutional usurpation of state power—perhaps because most federal funds for law enforcement ultimately went to Republican-leaning suburbs, where voters were most plentiful, rather than to Democratic-dominated cities, where crime was most prevalent.[12]

Radicals, however, soon developed a harsh critique of the federal program. One charge was that the OLEA functioned like an embryonic Department of Defense, importing battle-tested technology like guerrilla sensor devices from Vietnam for coercive purposes at home. A second fear was that the agency would aid the construction of a police-industrial complex. A third concern was that the OLEA would promote local surveillance and harassment of citizens, particularly those critical of the government. A final contention was that efforts to enhance police professionalism reinforced the notion of police infallibility and eroded the credibility of police critics.[13]

Police professionalism was one focus of the Crime Commission, which the president convened in February 1965 with a two-year deadline and a broad mandate to explore all aspects of law enforcement. It would serve the interests of the administration by deferring the crime issue to a nonpartisan body of impartial experts, who in turn would produce a milestone in crime research and a set of policy recommendations that would become the cornerstone of the Safe Streets bill introduced in 1967. But the Crime Commission was unable to deflect the politics of crime indefinitely. The final report, a clear statement of liberal thought on crime control, ultimately attracted sharp criticism from radicals and conservatives. It also revealed the fragility of the consensus the White House had carefully sought to construct. Above all, it failed to educate the public about the complexities of law enforcement or the distinctions between crime and riots, which became more critical in the wake of Watts.

In the fall of 1964, Katzenbach suggested that Johnson appoint a high-level committee to study street crime and "rioting by Negroes" (a reference to the Harlem Riot). The attorney general feared that unless the administration acted it would promote "the impression that we are doing nothing and that the president is not giving the leadership which I think is important."[14] The White House was hesitant, however, to act during the campaign lest it seem to panic in the face of Goldwater's charges.[15] But after the election, the Crime Commission quickly began to take shape. From the start, James Vorenberg was the obvious choice for executive director. A veteran of the Air Force (where he had met Katzenbach), professor at

Harvard Law School, and director of the Office of Criminal Justice, he was appointed without delay or dispute. The position of chair proved more problematical, but eventually it went by default to Katzenbach after two Republicans declined the post.

The Crime Commission faced a number of obstacles. One was the ever-present danger of excessive expectations. A prime culprit was Johnson himself, who told members in September 1965 that "today we have taken a pledge not only to reduce crime but to banish it."[16] Such promises delighted the media but daunted Vorenberg and Katzenbach, who warned the White House that "to the extent we inadvertently appear to make promises about the rapid reduction of crime we can complicate the political problem." Yet the attorney general was confident—excessively so in retrospect—that a campaign of public education would gain public acceptance "because most of the press is sufficiently sophisticated to appreciate the hard facts."[17]

Another obstacle was the Crime Commission's commitment to consensus. On the one hand, it made sense to sidestep "red-light" issues like the *Miranda* decision, the death penalty, police surveillance, and marijuana decriminalization in order to concentrate on attainable reforms and available funds for law enforcement. As Vorenberg recalled, "It was clear to me . . . that if we got embroiled in them, the effort to understand the criminal justice system, to make the case for additional resources, would go down the drain."[18] On the other hand, the avoidance of controversy raised the possibility that the Crime Commission had squandered a rare opportunity.

The commitment to consensus also fostered the perception of liberal bias among conservative members, most notably American Bar Association President Lewis Powell Jr. Insisting that actual cases of police brutality were rare, he contended that false accusations harmed police morale, recruitment, and performance—especially when it came to protecting the poor and minorities. Asserting that *Miranda* was a flawed ruling, Powell claimed that the Supreme Court had created an imbalance of rights in favor of the accused.[19] Accordingly, he drafted a "Supplemental Statement on Constitutional Limitations." Although not a formal dissent—which would have shattered the consensus Johnson, Katzenbach, and Vorenberg sought—the statement maintained that *Miranda* had hindered the ability of the police to conduct reasonable interrogations and solicit voluntary confessions. Yet Powell also expressed understanding of the Court's difficult role, voiced regret for the unfair criticism it had received, and pledged support for its rulings until lawfully overturned or superseded. He had, noted his biographer, "established [himself] as a critic—a respectful and responsible but unmistakably conservative critic—of the Warren Court."[20] And Powell had gained the attention of the man who would eventually nominate him for the Supreme Court, Richard Nixon.

In the end, the Crime Commission unanimously approved the final report. Ironically, however, Johnson at first refused to accept it because he believed, mistakenly, that the report had recommended permitting wiretaps in cases not involving national security. He changed his mind only after Vorenberg told Califano that he "would either deliver it peaceably or . . . throw it over the back fence of the White House with some reporters around."[21] Faced with little choice, the administration in early 1967 carefully timed and staged the release of the report for maximum political exposure and mileage. And even the president would later praise it, claiming in his memoirs that when he read it "the effect was like a light cutting through the darkness."[22]

The report was a thorough, wide-ranging, and balanced effort to explain the complexity and diversity of crime. It offered more than 200 specific recommendations for the police, the courts, and corrections facilities, although they were listed in no order of priority, leaving it unclear which the Crime Commission considered the most essential. A constant refrain was that more research and resources, financial and intellectual, were needed, as well as a public commitment to steps as easy as locking one's car and as painful as paying higher taxes. The report was modest in tone and moderate in ideology. It acknowledged the reality of crime, but stressed that the crimes most Americans most feared—acts of violence committed by predatory strangers—were relatively rare. Warring on poverty and unemployment, the Crime Commission maintained, was warring on crime, whose existence often stemmed from social conditions such as inadequate schools and poor housing. Yet the report also conceded that lawlessness resulted from affluence and immorality, particularly in the suburbs. Finally, it was careful to avoid taking sides on controversial issues, such as whether marijuana was a major contributor to violent crime or wiretaps represented a significant threat to individual privacy.[23]

The Crime Commission nevertheless attracted criticism from both conservatives and radicals. Conservatives attacked the report because it defended the constructive role of Great Society programs and ducked the corrosive impact of Warren Court rulings. Columnist James J. Kilpatrick was blunt: "A feeling that will not go away is that the Commission's staff talked with too many sociologists, and not with nearly enough cops. . . . What matters to the average citizen is not so much the abstract of statistical problems or

even the sociologists' long-range solution. His concern goes to the mugger, the rapist, the dope-crazed thief, the arrogant young punks who infest his streets. What can be done about them now? One of the Commission's answers is to provide textbooks for slum schools that are written in slum English. Okay, okay. But what can be done tomorrow, next week, next month, to lock up the hoods and thieves?"[24]

Radicals engaged the report on two fronts. First, they contended that the Crime Commission had mistakenly accepted the idea that laws are predicated on absolute moral standards rather than contemporary political and economic imperatives. Thus it ignored how most laws were class-biased and protected the interests of class elites by trivializing crimes like insurance fraud and sensationalizing crimes like armed robbery. Other laws became engines of crime by producing either a widespread sense of injustice (such as segregation statutes in the South) or enlarged classes of criminals (such as prostitution and narcotics offenses). The report's call for a new wave of social programs represented not a revolution in thinking about crime and justice, radicals argued, but a recycling of tired and stale liberal ideas intended at great cost to excuse legislators and authorities for their present failure to create and administer practical and just laws.[25]

The other radical contention centered on the role of the police, the alleged agents of class, racial, sexual, and cultural oppression in the United States. Conservatives tended to welcome and celebrate that role—or at least stress the need to maintain proper authority and hierarchy. Liberals tended to sidestep or deny the issue. Contending that the police had an unfortunate but essential function given the problems that inevitably arose in a complex and diverse modern society, they saw the commission's proposed police reforms as the best possible outcome short of long-term social reforms. The radicals disagreed with both premises. "Behind both the liberal and conservative views of the police there is a basic pessimism about the possibilities for human liberation and cooperation, a pessimism that we do not share," declared a group of radical criminologists unwilling to take for granted the existence of the police. Instead, they advocated the creation of a new society, one "without grinding poverty, ill-health, mutual exploitation and fear—and, therefore, without a vast, repressive police apparatus."[26]

Despite the contemporary criticism, scholars have subsequently praised the work of the Crime Commission, citing it as a model presidential commission. "National dismay over rising crime was so acute, Katzenbach's commission was so superbly led and staffed, and the total effort was so brilliantly orchestrated by the masterful chief legislator in the White H that the Katzenbach Commission remains a prime example of the presidential commission's strategic potential," concludes one historian. "It carefully and professionally nurtured consensus between hard-line demands for crack-down and constitutional solicitude for civil liberties and due process." It also, he added, yielded a "bumper harvest" of legislation, including the Safe Streets and Gun Control Acts of 1968.[27]

The Crime Commission had not, however, educated the public or the politicians as well as it might have. To achieve consensus, it had sidestepped the question of how useful or harmful surveillance was. Congress would subsequently attach provisions to the 1968 Safe Streets Act that were at best ineffectual against crime and at worst menacing to civil liberties.[28] Moreover, because the Crime Commission had dodged the debate surrounding *Miranda*, it had neglected to provide studies that answered directly the question of whether the ruling had handcuffed the police. Research would eventually show that it had a minimal impact on the confession and conviction rate.[29] But by then conservatives were able to allege that the report had deliberately excluded the "disastrous effects" of the Warren Court.[30]

The Crime Commission also failed to demystify or depoliticize the issue of street crime. Despite the report's concrete recommendations and analysis, the public continued to gravitate toward the conservative vision of law and order. In particular, the Crime Commission never succeeded in uncoupling street crime from urban riots and antiwar protests. Perhaps no commission could have. But as a result, the liberal agenda came to appear either inadequate or irrelevant in the face of what many whites saw as critical challenges to the authority of the government and the fabric of society.

II

On a hot August evening in 1965, days after Johnson had signed the Voting Rights Act into law, the Watts section of Los Angeles exploded in violence. Before the National Guard could restore order, 34 were dead, hundreds were injured, almost 4,000 were arrested, and roughly $35 million in damage was done.[31] The optimistic vision of a Great Society built on material prosperity and racial harmony also lay in ashes. The proximate cause was the arrest of a young black motorist by a white highway patrolman. The deeper causes sparked a debate whose repercussions echoed for years. Ultimately, the official investigation conducted by the McCone Commission would come under fire from partisans of all perspectives, foreshadowing the stormy reception that the Kerner Commission would receive three years later.

Like the Harlem Riot, Watts began with an alleged act of police brutality—although in typical Los Angeles fashion, it involved a traffic violation. On Wednesday, August 11, a white officer with the California Highway Patrol (CHP) stopped two African Americans and the situation rapidly escalated out of control.[32] On Thursday the situation exploded, with the outmanned Los Angeles Police Department (LAPD) forced to retreat and surrender the streets to the rioters.[33] With Chief William Parker not capable of command at the time, newly promoted Inspector Daryl Gates was left temporarily in charge. On Friday, he decided to abandon the passive strategy of containment in favor of an active strategy of rollback, with mass arrests and more force. But the department lacked the firepower to implement the new strategy. In desperation, LAPD officers brought guns from home and bought others from gun shops—some supposedly with the price tags still affixed.[34]

On Saturday, the overwhelmingly white National Guard arrived and the rate of killing—of black civilians in particular—rose sharply. Unprepared to wage guerrilla war in an urban environment, the 10,000 "weekend warriors" joined with 6,000 LAPD, Sheriff's Department, and CHP officers to confront an estimated 35,000 adults who were "active as rioters" and another 72,000 who were "close spectators." In the end, more than 3,400 individuals were arrested, most for looting within one mile of home. The typical rioter was a juvenile male, 17, with little or no prior contact with the police. He was a native of California who had lived in Los Angeles for more than five years and came from a one-parent home with an annual income of $3,600, at or slightly above the official poverty level of $3,335.[35]

The riot generated shock waves that rattled the country. Reports of racial conflict came from large cities like Philadelphia and Chicago as well as small cities like Springfield, Massachusetts and Morristown, New Jersey. Near the epicenter in southern California, there was near panic. Movie theaters closed. Freeway traffic halted. And gun sales to whites more than doubled during the weekend after Watts. "We've been getting a conglomeration of all kinds of people here—doctors, lawyers, businessmen, motorcycle messengers—from the lowest to the highest," said one firearms dealer. "Some don't even know which shoulder to put a gun to, but they want a weapon to protect themselves."[36]

In Washington and Austin there was dismay and confusion at first. "We just simply hadn't seen the warnings," conceded deputy Attorney General

Ramsey Clark, who had also failed to anticipate the Harlem Riot in July 1964. "The president, and all of us, were baffled by it for a long time," recalled special counsel and speechwriter Harry McPherson, a 36-year-old Texan who had joined the staff that month. "Our data was almost nonexistent. It took us several days to understand that Watts was not a conventional eastern city tenement area, but that it was an area of small houses." During those critical first few days, the president was paralyzed, unable to act or react.[37] Even more shocking for a man who treated the telephone as a virtual appendage, he was incommunicado, creating a breakdown in communications with Califano that paralleled the problem Gates had with Parker. Eventually the administration moved to limit the damage, but by then the physical destruction was considerable and the political fallout was almost as serious. Caught by complete surprise, the White House hastily launched an investigation from Washington, headed this time by Clark rather than Hoover. The strategy had worked well in 1964; it would not work nearly as well in 1965.

On Friday and Saturday, Califano attempted to reach Johnson at his Texas ranch, but the president refused to take his calls. It was a tense moment for Califano, a 34-year-old Harvard Law School graduate who had recently moved from the Defense Department to the White House. Already he had received a call from Lieutenant Governor Glenn Anderson, who was in charge while Governor Pat Brown was on vacation in Greece. "If you don't provide support," Anderson warned Califano, a diminutive Brooklyn native with an agile mind and quick wit, "the violence will rest on the White House's head." Meanwhile, General Creighton Abrams, vice chief of staff of the Army, had requested permission to provide supplies and transportation to the Guard. After conferring with Secretary of Defense Robert MacNamara and Attorney General Nicholas Katzenbach, Califano wired a presidential order and proclamation to Texas. Then he gave Abrams authorization to act, telling him he had White House approval and sidestepping his query as to whether he had presidential approval as well. On Sunday Califano finally heard from Johnson, who demanded to know who had authorized the airlift and reminded him: "You work for the president. Not for McNamara. Not for Katzenbach. Not for Brown. And damn sure not for [LA Mayor Sam] Yorty."[38]

By then the president had recovered some of his characteristic decisiveness. Worried that the riots were premeditated (or might be viewed as such) and that Ronald Reagan would "make political hay out of the riots" (which the actor-turned-politician would do during his successful gubernatorial bid in 1966), Johnson told Califano to ask Brown to make Los Angeles businessman John McCone head of the state inquiry: "An ex-CIA director, conservative, if he says there's no communist conspiracy and describes the conditions in Watts, we'll be able to help those Negroes out there. Do it now. Today. Not tomorrow. Not next week." Yet Johnson also was pessimistic, even fatalistic. With an acute if misinformed sense of history, he wondered if the Second Reconstruction was now, like the First Reconstruction, doomed because of blacks "pissing in the aisles of the Senate" and making fools of themselves. "What came through to me was how much Watts had depressed him," observed Califano. "Johnson lived his presidency in a race against time. . . . He knew it was essential to arouse the oppressed, and that, once aroused, their clock ticked impatiently."[39]

Convinced that time was running out, Johnson prepared to send federal anti-poverty assistance to Los Angeles. Refusing to believe that the riot had enjoyed widespread support, he stated that "we cannot let the actions of three or four thousand rioters stay our compassion for the hundreds of thousands of people in the city of Los Angeles—of every race and color—who neither participated in nor condoned the riots."[40] He announced that Clark, a lean and laconic fellow Texan with a soft drawl and an unassuming manner, would head a federal task force to investigate the causes of the riot. But while the president in public expressed great confidence that the task force would get to the bottom of what had happened, in private he had serious reservations.[41] Clark shared them, noting that "there was great concern that what we would do might appear to reward rioters."[42] In retrospect, he was politically prescient.

The task force report provided a snapshot of liberal thought and optimism at the time. Riots were "manifestations of defects in our development as a democratic society"—but not structural defects, as evidenced by the fact that most residents of Watts were law-abiding. Although the report briefly noted the need for order and "adequate police protection," it identified the real causes of the riot as urbanization and discrimination, unemployment and poverty. Contrary to what conservatives alleged, moral decline and personal evil were not significant factors. In the long run, the report maintained, "we cannot solve the problems of our slums by police power. . . . It is no more possible to suppress rioting where its causes are fermenting than it is to hold the lid on a boiling pot." But the task force was confident that more social programs could and would lower the heat.[43]

Political pressure shaped the report's form and future. The White House wanted it made clear "that not everyone in Watts was involved in the riot."

It also wanted the report to include praise for Brown and the president, particularly "his prompt statements of concern during the riot and his continuing interest."[44] The changes were made. But the report was never released, foreshadowing the administration's hostile reaction to the Kerner Commission report. The reason, according to Clark, was that the task force had incorporated the voices of angry community members in its report, which "didn't pull any punches . . . it was not tender in its treatment of many important interests." He added that Johnson was also reluctant to overshadow the work of Brown's own commission, which was chaired by the president's personal choice, John McCone, who reportedly threatened to resign unless the federal findings were shelved.[45]

The chairman's reaction involved more than personal pique or jurisdictional jousting. It also reflected the clashing ideological perspectives of Clark, a staunch liberal, and McCone, a moderate conservative. A longtime Los Angeles resident, prominent local businessman, and former CIA director under John Kennedy, he engineered an analysis of the riot that provided a degree of political cover for Brown and disputed several of the task force's conclusions. On the one hand, McCone and Executive Director Warren Christopher (then a Brown adviser and later a deputy attorney general in the Johnson Justice Department) identified similar "underlying causes" such as the heavy black migration to Los Angeles, the resultant housing strains, and an overtaxed public education system. On the other hand, the McCone Commission placed considerable blame on "aggravating events" such as the false expectations raised by the federal poverty program and the wide publicity given to unlawful violence across the nation. Above all, the report claimed that the rioters were "riffraff" with "no legal or moral justification for the wounds they inflicted" because Watts was no slum and Los Angeles offered unequaled opportunities for black advancement. "What happened," it concluded, "was an explosion—a formless, quite senseless, all but hopeless violent protest—engaged in by a few but bringing great distress to all."[46]

The explosion occurred even though there was "no reliable evidence of outside leadership or pre-established plans for the rioting." But the commission harshly criticized black leaders who had supposedly failed to take personal responsibility for their community's lack of progress, promoted the promiscuous use of civil disobedience (a clear reference to the civil rights movement), and, in some cases, issued "brutal exhortations to violence." Although the report favored the establishment of a City Human Relations Commission, it rejected the creation of a Civilian Review Board because it "would endanger the effectiveness of law enforcement, which would be intolerable when crime is on the increase throughout the country." The commission acknowledged that blacks harbored a deep-rooted and widespread hatred and distrust of the LAPD, but the report defended Chief Parker as well as the department and denied the existence of systemic police brutality.[47]

The conservative tone of the report was in part a reflection of the personal beliefs of McCone and Christopher, who were cautious pragmatists by nature. The chairman in particular had limited the scope of his staff's inquiry because "I felt that those broad pronouncements so common in the writings of political sociologists would, if accepted by a commission such as ours, raise [unrealistic] hopes . . . resulting in more frustrations, more anger, and finally more rage." Christopher likewise felt that the task was to present recommendations that were feasible in policy terms and defensible in political terms: "We felt that our mission or our role was to draw together the facts of the riots themselves and see if anything could be learned from the circumstances, the cops-and-robbers part of it. And then to look at what we thought were perhaps not the deepest underlying causes, but the ones that were susceptible of some immediate remedial efforts, some immediate improvement."[48]

The immediate reaction to the work of the McCone Commission was mixed. White Californians gave it a favorable review, since a substantial majority (64 percent) of those surveyed attributed Watts to "outside agitators" or a "lack of respect for law and order."[49] The then-conservative *Los Angeles Times* also gave the commission's findings an initial endorsement—albeit a tepid one—but it was virtually alone among major publications. In a typical comment, *Newsweek* described the report as "a flawed accounting" and cautioned that it "could become a substitute instead of a catalyst for visible, meaningful action."[50] The later reaction was even more hostile. In a narrow sense, it revealed how charged the issues were and how critical the official effort to define the larger significance of Watts was. In a broader sense, the debate over the riot's meaning, which was contested from all ideological directions, underscored the intensity of the racial crisis.

The left viewed the work of the McCone Commission as fundamentally and fatally flawed. Radicals condemned both the chairman and the executive director as committed to the status quo and content to heed the accommodating but artificial voices of black leaders rather than the angry but authentic voices of the Watts ghetto. "'Politically and psychologically,' wrote one critic, "they were unprepared to face the reality of the social cancer destroying the heart of the city and country." Spreading the cancer were capitalism and colonialism—two factors ignored by the McCone Commission—but of more immediate relevance was how the symptom of deprivation, widely and deeply felt, had fueled the anger that the riot revealed.[51]

Underpinning this analysis was a direct refutation of the "riffraff theory." Central to the radical critique was the assertion that far more blacks than officially estimated had "participated" in the riot and that they were far more representative of their community than McCone had contended.[52] This assertion in turn had two corollaries. First, it meant that the black leadership was hardly to blame for Watts—not when the crisis of the slum was so systemic and conditions were so oppressive.[53] Second, the widespread support for the riot—and the deliberate decision to leave churches, homes, and libraries untouched—indicated that Watts was a conscious political protest, not the "formless" explosion that the report had contended. In sum, concluded one scholar, the McCone Commission "offered inadequate assumptions based on erroneous analyses derived from untenable assumptions. And in so doing it demeaned the rioters, belittled their grievances, misunderstood the ghetto, misconstrued the riots, and thereby discouraged efforts to devise imperative and more drastic reforms."[54]

At significant junctures, the analysis offered by the left and the right overlapped. Like most radicals, many conservatives tended to depict Watts as organized and orchestrated with political intent. Behind the riot undoubtedly lay the insidious actions of activists—possibly communists engaged in a conspiracy to destabilize society—and the invidious appeal of civil disobedience. This interpretation resonated among ordinary citizens and prominent journalists. "If you are looking for those ultimately responsible for the murder, arson, and looting in Los Angeles," wrote one conservative of King and his followers, "look to them: they are the guilty ones, these apostles of 'non-violence.' They have taught anarchy and chaos by word and deed—and, no doubt, with the best of intentions—they have found apt pupils everywhere, with intentions not of the best."[55]

Both conservatives and radicals also preferred to describe Watts as a rebellion or insurrection rather than a riot. As a conservative local CBS radio commentator in Los Angeles asserted: "This was not a riot. It was an insurrection against all authority. This was not a riot. If it had gone much further, it would have become a civil war."[56] The language choice reflected ideological predilection and facilitated multiple agendas. Raising the stakes and turning what might appear an isolated incident into a wider indication of society's breakdown served the interests of both camps by increasing the sense of crisis. It also enabled radicals to assign political agency to the rioters and conservatives to assign moral responsibility to them. Thus the more extreme definition of Watts served the common interest of the left and the right by highlighting the apparent failure of liberalism.

That point was critical because it buttressed the core conservative contention that the disorder was the responsibility of individuals, not society. Moral failure, not social conditions, was to blame. Most immigrants, argued conservatives, had peacefully and quietly endured far worse poverty and deprivation. Therefore the fault belonged first and foremost to the black rioters themselves and then to their unwitting accomplices, the white liberals who had inculcated a culture of dependency and entitlement. According to this interpretation, Great Society planners in remote Washington had imposed confiscatory taxes on hard-working middle-class whites, squandered the funds on undeserving minorities, raised false expectations among them, and constructed an expansive as well as intrusive bureaucracy that trampled on the prerogatives of municipalities and the values of communities. Finally, the War on Poverty had compounded the mistake by rewarding lawless individuals with millions of dollars and thousands of jobs.[57]

Conservatives thus offered a variety of arguments, with racist, materialist, and localist flavors designed to appeal to audiences hungry for a sense of order and an explanation of the chaos around them. Taken separately, each element had limited appeal. Taken collectively, they satisfied the intellectual appetites of those who felt besieged by forces both seen and unseen, immediate and indeterminate. Liberals, by contrast, were buffeted externally and fragmented internally, with little agreement beyond the need to confront what they suddenly saw as the crisis of the ghetto.

White leaders were divided as to whether more anti-poverty programs were the answer.[58] By contrast, black leaders were united—in public—in condemnation of the report's assertion that they had to shoulder a share of the blame for the riot. "It is white leadership, not Negro leadership, which has caused millions of Negroes to be born and grow up in poverty and ignorance," charged Norman Houston, president of the Los Angeles NAACP.[59] But elements of the commission's work won a qualified endorsement from other officials—in private. "The truth is the majority of Negro citizens were in their homes just as frightened as the white citizer ” claimed Leonard Carter, the NAACP regional director in Los Ang who also conceded that the organization had no branch in Watts a spokesmen who lived in the immediate area.[60]

By the end of 1965, the Johnson administration faced trouble from every direction on the issue of law and order. The left feared official repression and saw signs of it everywhere; the right feared social anarchy and saw signs of it everywhere. At every step, White House officials who were, for the most part, pragmatic and perceptive—not idealistic or inept—had to calibrate the costs of their next move, fully aware of the difficulty of attempting to steer a moderate course. But they saw little choice, on policy or political grounds. Ultimately, their failure was testament more to the complex and treacherous environment in which they operated—including the shrillness of their critics on both ends of the spectrum—than to a shortage of political acumen or a surplus of liberal naïveté.

In Watts, hope that the riot would act as a catalyst for progress soon faded, as poverty remained rampant and the LAPD adopted a militaristic approach to ghetto policing that relied on helicopters for surveillance and pursuit.[61] In Washington, the president prepared for future riots by establishing a civil disorders command center.[62] Aides meanwhile reported that the Republican Party would probably employ law and order more in the coming year since "the Democratic Party has not convinced the voting public that it is especially concerned with solving this growing problem."[63] In the White House, the dilemma of how to pursue both social order for conservatives and social justice for liberals appeared acute.

Above all, Katzenbach counseled the president, do not predict quick results or engender false expectations. "Fear and frustration about crime," he warned, "[are] already making people susceptible to unfair, yet effective, political appeals and to a tendency to find simple answers to complex problems." Like the war in Vietnam, the War on Crime promised no immediate victory. Johnson therefore had to temper his penchant for rhetorical oversell. "It makes no political sense for the president annually to engage in an all-out war on crime and annually lose," advised the attorney general.[64] The advice was sound. But Johnson would find it increasingly difficult to follow as the political climate shifted dramatically in 1966.

4.

The Conservative Tide

In December 1966 California Governor-elect Ronald Reagan took a moment to bask in the glow of victory and contemplate the challenge of governing. "It is fantastic from my present vantage point," he wrote in a thank-you note to conservative activist and author William F. Buckley, an early supporter, "to discover what really faces one when the chance comes to put order into the chaos our little liberal playmates have created."[1] His was not a unique position. Across the nation, a rising tide of public anxiety over law and order had helped sweep incumbent liberals from power and presented insurgent conservatives with new opportunities.

Conservatives took decisive control of the issue in 1966, incorporating street crime, urban riots, and student protests into a comprehensive critique of liberalism's failure to contain the crisis of authority that seemed pervasive in America. At the same time, law and order functioned as a "bridge," enabling the right to tap into existing streams of conservatism at the municipal level and divert them into national politics. The rhetoric constructed at the national level also mobilized grassroots conservatives, giving them a language of protest and a vocabulary of ideas with which to link troubling changes in their communities to broader developments in American society and culture. The symbiotic and symbolic qualities of law and order thus enhanced its political power and potency.

The conservative current flowed from coast to coast. In California, Ronald Reagan rode law and order to a decisive victory in a gubernatorial race that garnered national attention and catapulted the former actor to national prominence.[2] In New York, the issue exposed the growing gaps in the liberal coalition during the campaign over whether to retain a civilian review board for the New York Police Department (NYPD). By the end of 1966, the conservative capture of law and order was on the horizon—with ominous overtones for the White House.

I

In November 1966 Ronald Reagan astounded the political world when he easily upset two-term incumbent Democrat Pat Brown in the race to become governor of California. In the end, the contest was not even close. Reagan won 58 percent of the votes, received almost one million Democratic votes, and carried all but three counties. In Orange County, he took 72 percent of the votes, even though 50 percent of the residents were still registered Democrats and 44 percent had cast their ballots for Johnson in 1964.[3] The outcome was the result of many factors, including socioeconomic developments in places like Orange County; the rise of a powerful and well-organized grassroots conservative movement; the charm and charisma of the former actor whose communications skills compensated for his lack of political experience; and the telegenic weakness and overconfidence of Brown.[4] But equally if not more important was law and order. The amorphous quality of the issue enabled conservatives to combine fear over the Watts Riot, disgust over the demonstrations at Berkeley, and alarm at rising crime into a powerful denunciation of the inequities and inefficiencies of the liberal state.

"If there had been no Barry Goldwater," one scholar has written, "there could have been no Ronald Reagan." Although exaggerated, the statement contains an ample amount of truth. Reagan first achieved conservative prominence with "A Time for Choosing," his famous 1964 speech on behalf of Goldwater's presidential bid. Two years later, he would employ many of the themes and much of the rhetoric that Goldwater had pioneered—but with little of the stridency.[5] Goldwater's campaign also accelerated the mobilization of a broad constituency dedicated to the triumph of conservative principles and candidates.[6]

Nowhere was the growth of grassroots conservatism more apparent than in Orange County. A confluence of factors made it possible. One was the emergence of a strong and racially homogeneous middle class, with a median family income higher than either the U.S. or California average and a homeownership rate of 70 percent. Many of Orange County's new residents were young veterans with families, lured to the area by the economic boom fueled by Cold War military spending. Often migrants from the Midwest, they brought with them traditional values that they clung to amid the sense of dislocation engendered by geographic mobility and spatial privatization, an unintended consequence of the rapid and unregulated development of highways, malls, and suburbs.[7]

Churches attempted to fill the void left by the loss of community. Preeminent were Protestant denominations led by fundamentalist ministers such as "Fighting" Bob Wells and the Reverend Carl McIntire of the American Council of Christian Churches. Holding apocalyptic theological views, they saw the world as doomed by many forms of "evil" including crime, abortion, pornography, even centralized power. Accepting some aspects of progress, such as materialism, the ministers rejected others, among them secularism and rationalism. "That such thinkers held an appeal in high-tech Orange County is at first surprising," one historian has noted. "But on a closer look, it is precisely such a new, rootless and hyper-modern environment that created anxiety about the consequences of modernity." The anxiety and emptiness felt by many residents, particularly women, motivated them to seek to reassert control over their lives and the community through conservative political activism.[8]

A major beneficiary of their activism was Ronald Reagan. A former actor, president of the Screen Actors Guild, and corporate spokesman for General Electric, he had no previous political experience, little knowledge of California, and a tendency to speak without restraint. However, in characteristic fashion he quickly turned his negatives into positives. He described himself as a citizen-politician. His top aides, Stu Spencer and Bill Roberts, taught him to watch his remarks and keep his temper under control, which he successfully accomplished for most of the campaign.[9] And Reagan hired as campaign consultants two behavioral psychologists to pinpoint issues, prepare position papers, and provide research data.[10]

Reagan's opposition took him lightly, assuming that like Goldwater in 1964 he was too conservative, too far from the mainstream, to be a viable candidate.[11] That assumption proved a serious miscalculation, but the Brown record gave Democrats additional cause for confidence. He had defeated two formidable opponents, William Knowland and Richard Nixon, in his 1958 and 1962 gubernatorial contests. And he had compiled an enviable set of accomplishments. Brown had built a new water system, upgraded perhaps the nation's finest system of higher education, and signed into law a battery of liberal legislation. Finally, he had presided over an economic boom that had made California the envy of the nation and the world.

None of it would ultimately matter, however. Reagan rolled over Brown, who placed much of the blame for his defeat on the "white backlash" and his image of softness. As he recalled: "People always felt that I was too friendly with the blacks anyway. . . . They just tarred me with it and said, 'Put a guy in there that'll put these colored guys in their place.'"[12] Operatives for both campaigns highlighted the pivotal role played by white working-class Democrats, who deserted Brown in droves.[13] Spencer noted that 1966 was the first time he had directly targeted such voters. Coupled with the blue-collar whites' resentment toward the incumbent, maintained Brown campaign manager Donald Bradley, was the sense that it was time for a new face in the governor's mansion. Reagan press secretary Lyn Nofziger concurred. "My mother could have run his campaign and he'd have won," he said bluntly. He also credited above all Reagan's personality, which meshed perfectly with the spirit of the times and the people's perception of what the times demanded.[14] Three words captured that mood: law and order.

Although the vulnerabilities which beset Brown's candidacy predated the election year, they were glaringly exposed during his bitter primary fight with Sam Yorty, the conservative mayor of Los Angeles. Yorty pledged a hard line on law and order, vowing to crack down on crime, prevent a repeat of Watts, and restore order to Berkeley. He offered full support to Los Angeles Police Chief William Parker, whose explanation of the riot's origins went as follows: "One person throws a rock and then, like monkeys in a zoo, others start throwing rocks."[15] Yorty loathed Brown, personally and politically, and the feeling was mutual. But the governor knew he was in political peril when the man he viewed as a "yokel" attracted almost one million votes (to Brown's 1.3 million). Yorty's totals matched almost exactly the nearly one million, mostly white working-class Democratic votes that Reagan would later receive.[16]

In Washington, the White House monitored the situation closely. Brown had long received favored treatment from first Kennedy and then Johnson. In 1962, for example, the Kennedy administration had overcome opposition from several federal agencies and staged a White House Conference on Narcotic and Drug Abuse largely so that Brown could counter Nixon's charge that he was "soft on dope peddlers."[17] By contrast, there was no love lost between Johnson and Yorty, who chafed at what he saw as the "step-child treatment" the president extended to him during visits to Los Angeles. For his part, Vice President Hubert Humphrey viewed the mayor as an unprincipled opportunist and had a private laugh—which he shared in a confidential note to Brown—at Yorty's request in March that he not endorse the governor. But there were few smiles after the primary in June, with polls showing Reagan ahead by a 51–37 percent margin and journalist Drew Pearson reporting privately to Johnson (via an aide) that Yorty might well endorse Reagan in October and thereby doom Brown's prospects for a comeback.[18]

More importantly, the primary had demonstrated beyond doubt the visceral appeal and volatile force of a campaign based on law and order, whose three touchstones in California were the Watts riot, the Berkeley protests, and street crime. In a political world increasingly dominated by the televised sound bite, the issue had extraordinary appeal because it was simple and malleable. Politicians could tailor it to specific audiences and situations—or remain imprecise and allow listeners to assign whatever meanings they wished to it. At the same time, law and order had become a powerful symbol of the perceived failure of liberal government.

When questioned, Reagan had a ready response for why Watts had occurred and how to prevent a recurrence. The riot had erupted, he contended, because a small minority in the community (most of them recent arrivals to Los Angeles, many of them migrants from the South) viewed the police as oppressors rather than protectors. Then Brown had failed to deploy the National Guard immediately to restore order—a mistake that Reagan pledged he would not make. Using rhetoric borrowed directly from Goldwater, he promised not to tolerate individuals who broke the law under the guise of civil disobedience, which he said had no place in a democracy. During the campaign, when riots broke out near San Francisco, Reagan declared that "the leaders of the Negro community who have urged civil disobedience have forfeited their right to leadership."[19]

Reagan also insisted that under his administration riots would become less common because he would not implement new anti-poverty programs that raised false expectations among poor minorities while discouraging individual initiative, fostering personal dependency, and building a bloated bureaucracy.[20] Thus he offered anxious whites the promise of personal security, reduced spending, and a development plan that seemed to many at least as likely to curb future riots as the liberal alternative. It was a popular message reinforced by the popular appeal of the messenger. Above all, it was perfectly appropriate given what even one of Brown's own staffers conceded was not Republican-induced hysteria but an "underlying and spontaneous welling up" of racial fear and tension.[21]

Unlike Reagan, Brown had neither abundant personal charm nor a compelling political message. On vacation in Greece when Watts occurred, the governor could only promise to deal swiftly with future unrest—which he did when riots erupted in Oakland and San Francisco in 1966. But that merely raised the issue of Brown's political sincerity and begged the question of why he had allowed the disorders to develop in the first place.[22] In addition, the governor's oft-stated desire to attack the root causes of civil unrest—poverty, unemployment, poor housing, and poor education—with expensive social programs lacked credibility with both conservatives and liberals by 1966. The *National Review* questioned whether the millions Brown proposed to spend would make a difference, while the *Nation* contended that his "tiresome clichés" would not alter how invisible communities like Watts were in the eyes of most whites.[23]

Visible to most everyone was the disorder at Berkeley. Since October 1964, when the Free Speech Movement (FSM) began to confront the authority of President Clark Kerr, demonstrations had regularly rocked the campus. At first Brown remained on the sidelines. Then, in the wake of a direct challenge to the university administration in December 1964, the governor launched the largest mass arrest in California history. Less than 24 hours later, the FSM called for a campus-wide strike, thousands of sympathetic students gathered, and Kerr decided to accede to the demands of the demonstrators. The next year, the Filthy Speech Movement emerged, bringing to the fore cultural matters such as drug use, human sexuality, and personal appearance.[24] Finally, in May 1966, the California Senate Subcommittee on Un-American Activities, chaired by State Senator Hugh Burns, charged that the Berkeley campus had become a haven for communism, homosexuality, and immorality. Public disgust at what seemed like subsidized sinfulness and silliness soon reached a crescendo.

Less than one week after the release of the Burns Report, Reagan gave a dramatic address at the Cow Palace in San Francisco. Relying on a study prepared by the Alameda County district attorney's office (where future Attorney General Ed Meese was employed), the candidate first stated that he could not cite specific incidents—they were supposedly too offensive and indecent. Then Reagan proceeded to give a graphic description of a dance sponsored by a Berkeley anti-war group that had attracted a crowd of more than 3,000 juveniles.

> Three rock 'n' roll bands were in the center of the gymnasium playing simultaneously all during the dance, and all during the dance movies were shown on two screens at the opposite ends of the gymnasium. These movies were the only lights in the gym proper. They consisted of color sequences that gave the appearance of different-colored liquid spreading across the screen, followed by shots of men and women[;] on occasion, shots were of the men's and women's nude torsos, and persons twisted and gyrated in provocative and sensual fashion. The young people were seen standing against the walls or lying on the floors and steps in a dazed condition with glazed eyes consistent with the condition of being under the influence of narcotics. Sexual misconduct was blatant.

According to Reagan, the breakdown in morality dated from 1964, when the Berkeley administration had first permitted student demonstrators to defy the police, the symbol of law and order.[25] Now liberal tolerance had become permissiveness. And the question he posed to audiences was how far they would permit the epidemic of immorality to spread.[26] At the same time, Reagan and other conservatives drew analogies between the contemporary crisis, the rise of fascism, and the spread of communism. Like appeasement at Munich, they contended, tolerance at Berkeley had placed freedom and decency in jeopardy. Liberals who were soft on anti-containment communists in the 1950s were now soft on anti-war communists in the 1960s.

Berkeley quickly became, recalled Spencer, a "a sub rosa emotional issue with people. . . . We felt this underlying feeling, and we jumped on it. . . . I think Reagan escalated it as an issue and it started showing up in the polls." Borrowing a page from the Goldwater playbook, the campaign also commissioned a five-minute film on the Berkeley protests that contained actual footage from police libraries. A "brutal show" and "hairy, hairy film," it was never shown because, as Spencer remembered, "we had that issue under control. . . . We didn't have to go out and do wild things about it."[27] He was right. As a Brown staffer recalled: "Berkeley, in our polls, was the most negative word you could mention."[28]

To maintain that negative rating, the Reagan campaign monitored the situation closely. In August, it solicited advice from H. R. Haldeman, who would later join the Nixon White House as Chief of Staff. He advised that Berkeley "is clearly an issue to be thoroughly and effectively exploited—Brown is scared of it, and for good reason."[29] In October, Reagan responded quickly when he learned that "Black Power" advocate Stokely Carmichael planned to attend a rally on campus later that month. Fearing that further disorders might benefit Brown, who would have another opportunity to demonstrate his newfound toughness and resolve (he had recently won acclaim for removing demonstrators promptly from Sproul Hall), Reagan wired Carmichael and requested that he not attend the upcoming rally for the sake both of his cause and a peaceful election.[30]

In the end, Berkeley became a figurative quagmire for Brown, who could do little to defuse the issue. Although the campus protests would ironically grow in size and intensity after 1966, he could not act tougher than Reagan in part because he was on record as praising the colleges for encouraging student activism on behalf of civil rights and migrant workers. Nor could he appeal to the students as an ally, since the rift between them over the Vietnam War was by then irreparable. With no way to advance or retreat, he was frozen in place by prior rhetoric, previous commitments, and his popular image as a liberal committed to cultural tolerance and civil disobedience.[31]

For many Californians, the disorder at Berkeley was a potent symbol of the seeming collapse of moral standards and constituted authority. It also represented a potential threat to their children's future. Street crime was, however, an even more immediate menace. Following a ten-year pattern, murder rose 14.4 percent in 1966, with robbery up 9 percent and rape over 5 percent.[32] Anxiety was particularly prevalent among the elderly, reported Brown's senior citizen coordinator for northern California. A majority of the victims as well as the assailants were black—a fact of which many were aware. But campaign officials were also aware that Brown was in a poor position to reassure voters, given his general opposition to capital punishment and his sixty-day stay of execution in the Caryl Chessman case.[33]

By contrast, Reagan was in a perfect position to make street crime a top priority. "Narcotics traffic has mushroomed like a rush hour jam on the free way, and directly in its path—as its prime target—is our youth, our sons and daughters," he announced during his Kick-off Telecast. But after grimly reciting the statistics and correctly predicting that Brown would challenge their validity, he announced a series of rather anticlimactic proposals.[34] Emotions, not substance, would dictate how the campaign approached the issue, as was evident in a television commercial aired during the campaign.

Using his acting background and coded language, Reagan painted a dramatic picture. Every day, he announced, the sun goes down "and the jungle comes a little closer." Vowing to protect the treasured "way of life" in

California, he noted that the state had a crime rate well above the national average. The blame, he argued, rested with the Supreme Court, whose rulings had handcuffed the police, and with Brown, who had promised to solve the drug problem in 1958, 1962, and now again in 1966. The camera then cut to the audience composed exclusively of middle-class and middle-aged whites. "There isn't a city street that's safe for our women after dark," he declared as the camera zoomed to a shot of concerned women.[35]

Equally concerned was Brown himself, who knew how critical the crime issue was. "I think people are primarily concerned with law enforcement," he told *ABC News* in October. "I think this is the thing that has now become the overriding issue."[36] But nothing Brown tried seemed to work. To bolster his pro-police credentials, he declared that civilian review boards were an unneeded additional layer of bureaucracy. To counter Republican commercials, his campaign prepared and aired several commercials about "crime in the streets." To quiet criticism of the fact that he had not permitted the execution of anyone since 1963, he offered to let the state legislature decide the death penalty issue once and for all. And to disprove the crime statistics cited by Reagan, he quoted FBI figures showing that in 1965 California had the lowest increase in violent crime of any major state; that youth crime had actually declined the past year; and that the ratio of crime increase to population increase since Brown had taken office in 1958 was lower than in any other state.[37]

His efforts were to no avail. Brown even proposed a California version of the Law Enforcement Assistance Administration to aid local departments, a family court to address juvenile crime, and an expanded drug rehabilitation program to assist addicts.[38] But these solutions smacked of big government and exacerbated his image as an unreconstructed liberal. In the end, on street crime as well as the Watts Riot and the Berkeley protests, Brown was unable to quench the public thirst for law and order. In the meantime, Reagan promised to do so in no time, at little cost, and with plenty of moral righteousness. Not surprisingly, the audience applauded enthusiastically.

For Reagan, who turned 55 in 1966, it was the start of a remarkable second or third act to his career, an act that would culminate with his election as president. But for Brown, a victim in large part of forces beyond his control, it was a bitter defeat—one that he had seen coming months earlier. "The Republicans are attacking me more viciously than at any time in my career and there are a whole slew of them who slug me every hour on the hour," he wrote to Humphrey in a confidential letter. "The things they complain about are the Watts riots, but they had those in New York and Pennsylvania where they have Republican governors; the University of California turmoil, which was immediately stopped when they violated the law . . . and some of the crime picture that every incumbent Mayor or Governor in the land has had to face."[39] Three thousand miles away, a liberal Republican, New York Mayor John Lindsay, shared his predicament if not his pain.

II

In November 1966 the politics of law and order engulfed New York City, where street crime was rampant and race relations remained tense following the Harlem Riot of 1964.[40] At stake was a referendum to abolish the revised police review board established by the newly elected Lindsay, who sought to solidify his fragile coalition of blacks and Jews. The purpose of the new board, which had a civilian majority unlike the previous board, was to investigate allegations of police brutality, provide more effective oversight of the NYPD, and promote better police-minority relations. The image that dominated the campaign, however, came from the Patrolmen's Benevolent Association (PBA).

In opposition to the review board, the PBA distributed a powerful campaign poster. Employing racial, class, and gender code to tap into the widespread and well-founded fear of crime, it showed a young middle-class white woman exiting nervously from the subway and emerging alone onto a dark and deserted street. "The Civilian Review Board must be stopped!" read the accompanying text. "Her life . . . your life . . . may depend on it." The reason, it added, was that a "police officer must not hesitate. If he does . . . the security and safety of your family may be jeopardized."[41] The message was pointed and persuasive. A poll taken on November 4 showed that a clear majority of those surveyed felt that the CRB would hinder police performance; four days later, buoyed by a near-record turnout, the referendum passed by an almost two-to-one margin. Of the five boroughs, only Manhattan narrowly voted to retain the review board.[42]

The result, although not entirely unexpected, was a stunning blow to liberalism.[43] In the nation's largest and arguably most progressive city, which two years earlier had given Lyndon Johnson a decisive victory and Robert Kennedy a comfortable margin of victory in his race for the U.S. Senate, a measure identified by supporters as an extension of the civil rights cause and endorsed by every prominent liberal politician and organization had met disastrous defeat. But the municipal referendum had broader implications. It revealed the growing power of conservatism as well as the widening fault lines within the suddenly fragile liberal coalition. Contested under the spotlight of the nation's media capital, it also reflected and reinforced the fragmentation of the New Deal order by strengthening the perception among urban whites that any vote at any level could directly affect—or even cost them—their lives.

A sample of white ethnics in Brooklyn revealed how it had happened. Over 80 percent of Catholics had voted against the review board—a level of support higher than John Kennedy had received in 1960. Only 40 percent of Jewish voters had voted for it—evidence of class-based divisions within the Jewish community and symptomatic of the overall lack of liberal enthusiasm for the measure. And over 60 percent of those who had backed Johnson in 1964 now took their cue from Goldwater supporters and opposed what they saw as a dangerous restraint on the NYPD—a sign of growing unease with liberalism and a portent of trouble to come for the Democrats.[44] The backlash had blossomed.

At its heart was race. But it was not bigotry per se; rather it was the growing sense that personal safety was now of necessity a political priority.[45] This sense had emerged in part as a result of demographic developments. During the 1950s, black migration and Puerto Rican immigration had altered considerably the complexion of New York, making boroughs like Brooklyn significantly poorer and younger, less white and more minority.[46] At the same time, the crime rate had skyrocketed among youths of color, who numbered disproportionately among both the victims and perpetrators.[47] Many white residents of Brooklyn now had to struggle to reconcile their faith in liberalism with the increased incidence of mugging, murder, and mayhem on their blocks.[48] They also had to confront the real and material threat to their life savings and economic security, which were often tied to apartments and homes whose value plummeted when neighborhoods changed. By the end of the decade, the mainstream media no longer hesitated to report the apparent conjunction of race and crime. Yet a relative silence surrounded the issue of police brutality even as the civil rights movement and urban white flight gained momentum and publicity.[49]

A concurrence of events in 1964 decisively and permanently shattered the silence. In April, the City Council debated a proposal to form an all-civilian review board reporting directly to the mayor, not the police commissioner. The measure stood little chance of passage but produced a heated reaction from the NYPD that anticipated later PBA rhetoric.[50] Meanwhile, a series of incidents—including the infamous Kitty Genovese assault—alarmed whites and led the *National Review* to warn on July 16 that "What is happening, or is about to happen—let us face it—is race war."[51] That very day an off-duty NYPD officer in plainclothes shot and killed a black teenager.[52] Two days later, the Harlem Riot erupted.

As the first major riot of the 1960s, Harlem ensured that police brutality—with racial overtones—would have a prominent place in the public vocabulary. It also made riot prevention or causation a central theme in the debate over the civilian review board, whose necessity was now beyond doubt according to black leaders like James Farmer, who contended that the riot was at bottom "a war between the citizens of Harlem and the police."[53] White residents by contrast tended to see it as a war between the races.[54] But elsewhere white liberals were divided. On the one hand, they were uncertain whether the denial of civil liberties, economic opportunity, or racial equality was the root cause.[55] On the other, they were uncertain whether the creation of a civilian review board would hinder or encourage future disorders.[56]

Conservatives harbored no such doubts. During the 1965 mayoral campaign (which Lindsay won with a plurality), Conservative Party candidate William F. Buckley Jr. employed a Cold War analogy to equate liberals with fellow travelers. Once the latter had jeopardized national security by providing aid to communists; now the former threatened personal security by providing comfort to criminals. Buckley also contended that criminals were active agents of evil, not passive victims of society. Yet liberals endorsed the Supreme Court's expansive view of civil liberties, encouraged cries of police brutality regardless of proof, and excused "political" violence in the name of favored causes. In so doing, they exalted above all the absolute rights of individuals in general and criminals in particular over the abstract rights of the community in general and victims in particular.[57] Buckley thus provided a framework through which many conservatives could relate the apparent chaos and anarchy in their neighborhoods and communities to larger developments in the country as a whole.

During the 1966 campaign, the shadow of the Harlem Riot loomed over the referendum, making the flashpoints of race and crime, civil rights and civil unrest, impossible to avoid.[58] Opponents insisted that a civilian review board would hinder the ability of police to respond to future disorders. A PBA television commercial surveyed damage allegedly caused by a riot, with the announcer commenting that "the police were so careful to avoid accusations that they were virtually powerless."[59] The assertion proved particularly compelling to those whites whose suspicions about the communist origins of the Harlem Riot reinforced their doubts about the liberal rationale behind the board.[60] Supporters portrayed civilian review as a riot preventive because it would improve police-community relations. Lindsay himself noted proudly that the civilian review board had not kept the NYPD from keeping the peace in the summer of 1966.[61] Yet his public boast may have backfired by adding to the racial cast of the measure and reinforcing the conservative conflation of crime and riots.[62] It also helped make civilian review a cause célèbre among conservatives nationally, with the PBA receiving donations from wealthy individuals and a network of newly politicized police organizations.[63]

Backers of civilian review likewise tried to generate public support by stressing the national implications of the election. One strategy Lindsay employed was to make the confrontation a liberal litmus test, a question of whether the commitment to civil rights remained paramount.[64] Another was to highlight the danger of defeat and warn that the referendum was, in the words of Senator Jacob Javits, "the most important issue of the ultra-conservative cause in this country." Then he and fellow Senator Robert Kennedy released an Anti-Defamation League (ADL) Report, prepared at their request, purporting to show that right-wing groups like the John Birch Society were actively campaigning against the CRB and had successfully recruited policemen to their ranks.[65]

The city's core white liberal constituency nevertheless remained divided. With Irish and Italian voters conceded to the opposition by pro-review board forces, the critical target became Jewish voters, for whom class, culture, and concern collided. From the outset, lower-middle-class and working-class Jews in the outer boroughs were wary of civilian review—a fact highlighted when the Bronx chapters of the American Jewish Congress voted unanimously to disregard the parent body's endorsement of the board. But even professional Jews with college degrees and Manhattan addresses proved reluctant to back civilian review unless they combined an overriding commitment to civil rights with a strong sense of personal security. At Temple Rodeph Shalom in the heart of the Upper West Side, for example, congregants barraged Lindsay's press secretary with questions about why the mayor always seemed to side with lawless minorities against law-abiding taxpayers. Ultimately, despite liberal efforts to cast civilian review as a referendum on racism—"DON'T BE A YES MAN FOR BIGOTRY—VOTE NO" read thousands of posters—55 percent of Jews sided with their Catholic neighbors and voted against the board.[66] The scale of the Jewish defection from the liberal banner startled observers.

By contrast, the minority vote as expected was heavily in favor of civilian review, although precise figures are not available.[67] Within the PBA itself, the only significant support for civilian review came from the Correctionaires (representing 1,000 blacks in the Corrections Department) and the Guardians (representing 1,300 black police officers).[68] Nevertheless, it is not clear how seriously blacks viewed the problem of police brutality. In the wake of the Harlem Riot, only 12 percent of blacks surveyed told *The New York Times* that there was "a lot" of it. And a confidential survey conducted for the NAACP in August 1966 revealed that Harlem residents considered street crime and poor housing more important issues.[69]

Nor is it clear that civilian review enjoyed universal support within the black community. For moderates like Martin Luther King, the police tolerance of ghetto crime was the real problem. For radicals like Eldridge Cleaver, civilian review provided a rallying point for the black bourgeoisie only, disguising how the police were merely the instrument of those who waged social, economic, and political brutality against minorities in America and Vietnam. And for conservatives, the main threat was violent crime, which affected minorities the most and warranted better policing, harsher sentences, and more black officers. "There is police brutality," declared the chairman of the Harlem NAACP's anti-crime committee, "but that isn't what makes people afraid to walk the streets at night."[70]

On election night, Lindsay was asked after his concession speech what had caused the review board defeat. "Emotion and misunderstanding and fear," he replied. Then he added that "the important thing is that we did what we thought was right. It was worth fighting for, even though we lost."[71] Perhaps it was. But the election had also offered a dramatic demonstration of how law and order divided liberals and united conservatives, who now had conclusive evidence of how the issue connected municipal causes to presidential campaigns and energized grassroots activists by imbuing their local struggles with a larger significance. The review board referendum thus represented the fulcrum point at which neighborhood and national politics intersected as well as collided.

III

In October 1966 officials within the White House continued to insist that while urban violence was a serious problem, there was no crime wave, no racial causation, and no cause for "political demagoguery or scare tactics designed to make women afraid to go out in the evening."[72] But by November the impact of law and order was obvious and ominous to the administration. On the eve of the election, Johnson appealed to Americans not to cast their ballots on the basis of fear and hate. Acknowledging that those who fostered disorder were just as bigoted as those who sought to exploit it, he nonetheless declared that "the answer to their bigotry is not more bigotry in return."[73] It was a hopeful message.

It fell, however, on deaf ears. Although analysts had expected a "correction" after the sweeping victories of 1964, the election results were extremely disturbing for Democrats. Overall, the Party lost 47 House seats, 8 governorships, and 3 Senate seats. Among the celebrated casualties was Illinois Senator Paul Douglass, a liberal stalwart who was defeated by Republican newcomer Charles Percy. Pollster Richard Scammon counseled Johnson to avoid panic or retreat from the Great Society despite the loss of 11 of 12 senate and gubernatorial races in the ten largest states. But, he added, "[t]he president must grasp the nettle of violence in the streets very firmly and unequivocally. . . . This is one problem that will not go away, and which will cause even more difficult political problems in the next two years unless some dramatic and successful efforts are made."[74]

From the political trenches, a confidential survey of Democratic officials and defeated candidates confirmed Scammon's analysis and revealed the full extent of the damage. Commissioned by the White House, it detailed how no state seemed immune from the corrosive combination of race and disorder. Even in states with negligible minority populations like Iowa and Wisconsin, the reaction against civil disturbances was the decisive factor.[75] In cities like Chicago, Democratic vote totals—in both black and white wards—declined by more than 40,000 over the previous low set in 1950.[76]

Chicago was not unique. Across the nation, blue-collar white ethnics chose not to switch parties—at least not yet—but instead elected to stay home. In selected wards in Detroit, the Democratic percentage dropped by only 9 percent but turnout plummeted 40 percent while Republican totals remained stable. The comparison, moreover, was with 1962—not with 1964, when the presidential race inflated voter turnout. Similar results were reported in Cincinnati, Philadelphia, and Louisville. Non-voting, not party-switching, was the trend. And it would increase in the years to come.[77]

For labor in general and the AFL-CIO in particular, the results from 1966 were extremely discouraging because 36 incumbents with Committee on Political Education (COPE) voting records of better than 75 percent lost and less than half of all COPE incumbents from competitive districts retained their seats. In the House, the number of Congressmen considered favorable to labor dropped from 248 to 199; in the Senate, COPE lost 13 of 22 races in which it issued an endorsement. The outcome was discouraging too because, according to political director Alexander Barkan, COPE was better organized and better funded in 1966 than ever before. "If there were any weaknesses in COPE," he conceded to the AFL-CIO Executive Committee in mid-November, "it might have been in the area of political understanding of our members." But he laid primary responsibility on the unpopularity of Johnson; the failure of certain Great Society programs; the decline in key wards of the labor and black vote; factional conflict in selected states including New York and California; the bankruptcy of the Democratic National Committee; and, above all, the existence of "a tide that we did not see."[78]

That tide of reaction was swelled, at least in part, by the popular appeal of law and order among those who perceived that their personal and economic security—as well as that of their families and friends—was at risk. It was also clearly a national phenomenon that boded ill for the Democratic Party and the Johnson administration. Polls in the fall of 1966 showed that most Americans felt that the Republican Party could better handle urban riots and racial violence—and that a majority of whites believed that the War on Poverty was not curtailing the unrest.[79] The White House might have minimized the damage had it found a way to address the race and disorder issue effectively and to strike a persuasive balance on the need to provide for both social justice and social order.

But the administration was filled with shrewd political operatives and headed by one of the most astute politicians of his era. Therefore the failure of liberals to find a compelling voice on law and order suggests that the success of conservatives was due in large measure to the potency and cogency of their message as well as the heightened level of public concern. During the "Long Hot Summer" of 1967, riots in Newark and Detroit would further fan the fear—and doom the efforts of the White House to regroup in preparation for 1968.

1. In July 1964, with the presidential race in full swing, Barry Goldwater and Lyndon Johnson met briefly and privately in an effort to defuse the racial tensions surrounding the Harlem Riot and civil unrest in other cities.

2. In 1965, Lyndon Johnson declared a War on Crime, which would cause him numerous political headaches in the years to come.

3. In 1966, former actor Ronald Reagan made law and order the centerpiece of his successful campaign to become governor of California. His victory made him a national figure and highlighted the growing power of the emerging issue.

4. The "long hot summer" of 1967 began in Newark, New Jersey, where rioting and looting led to 23 deaths, 21 of whom were black residents of the city.

5. One week after the Newark Riot, President Johnson and, from left to right, Marvin Watson, FBI Director J. Edgar Hoover, Secretary of Defense Robert McNamara, General Harold Johnson, and Joe Califano had to confront the crisis in Detroit, where the worst civil disorder of the decade would require the intervention of the U.S. Army.

6. Following the riots in Newark and Detroit in 1967, Mayor John Lindsay of New York agreed to serve on the Kerner Commission. A year earlier, Lindsay had campaigned in vain to preserve a civilian review board for the New York Police Department.

7. In October 1967, opponents of the Vietnam War staged a March on the Pentagon. Antiwar demonstrations were the third leg (in combination with street crime and civil unrest) of the law-and-order triad.

8. Robert Kennedy (left foreground) and Theodore Sorenson share a pleasant moment on April 3, 1968. The next day, Martin Luther King, Jr. was assassinated and riots erupted across the nation. Two months later, Kennedy himself was assassinated in California.

9. On April 5, 1968, President Johnson met with a host of civil rights leaders to discuss how to control the urban riots that had erupted across the nation in the aftermath of the King assassination.

10. At Columbia University, there was chaos on campus when conservative and radical students clashed in front of Low Library in April 1968.

12. In August 1968, anti-war demonstrators massed on the streets of Chicago outside the Democratic Convention. Police and protestors later clashed in what became known as the "Battle of Michigan Avenue."

11. President Johnson and Joe Califano plot the progress of the Washington Riot, which came within blocks of the White House in April 1968.

13. The politics of law and order doomed the campaign of Vice President Hubert Humphrey, who could never find a compelling or convincing position on the critical issue during the 1968 campaign.

14. Alabama Governor George Wallace promised in 1968 to restore law and order by any means necessary, including shooting rioters and looters. His position ultimately proved too extreme for most voters.

15. Richard Nixon declared in 1968 that "freedom from fear" was the first civil right of all Americans. In a close election, he defeated Hubert Humphrey by pledging to restore law and order, the issue that was most important to most Americans.

5.

The Politics of Civil Unrest

On July 24, 1967, Detroit was in a state of chaos and the White House was in a state of crisis. One week earlier, the Newark Riot had "put the country near to a psychic flash-point" according to speechwriter Ben Wattenberg, who had joined the staff a year earlier. Now the latest and most serious riot of the decade was escalating out of control.[1] Within the administration, officials debated whether Johnson should address the American people in an effort to reassure them. Special Council Harry McPherson opposed the idea since the president would have to assume responsibility for a situation over which he had little or no control. Wattenberg disagreed. "To say that it's a responsibility without real power to cope with it may be true," he contended, vision fixed firmly on the 1968 presidential race, "but [it] ignores the fact that Wallace for sure, and probably Nixon and Reagan (and maybe others as well) will ultimately try to stick the blame on the president and the Democrats (as they did in 1964 and 1966)—whether or not any speech is delivered." Wattenberg was right. The politics of civil unrest was already in full force. That night U.S. Army paratroopers began to patrol the streets of Detroit.[2]

During the "Long Hot Summer" of 1967 more than 100 cities experienced riots. The aftermath revealed the depth of the divide between white and black perceptions of what had happened. A Harris Poll in August showed that although most whites and blacks tended to agree that ghetto residents were the main victims of the riots and that new federal programs would reduce the chance of further unrest, they held starkly different views on what had caused the disorders. Twice as many whites as blacks saw the riots as organized. Twice as many blacks as whites, by contrast, blamed the unrest on discrimination, poor housing, and unemployment. Blacks typically (by a 2–1 margin) cited police brutality as a major factor. Whites overwhelmingly (by an 8–1 margin) rejected it.[3]

The riots in Newark and Detroit shredded what confidence remained among most liberals. The critical distinction that they had tried to draw between race and crime was shattered, perhaps permanently. The careful emphasis on federalism—the notion that law and order was a local responsibility—lay in ruins. And the abiding faith that the Great Society would calm social unrest was replaced by the gnawing fear that it had somehow contributed to the civil disorders. By the fall of 1967, restoring law and order meant repulsing urban riots. Polls showed that the racial crisis was now the nation's chief domestic concern.[4]

In the eyes of critics on the left and the right, the riots had discredited the entire liberal enterprise and generated predictions of a society in meltdown. Even the White House was not immune from apocalyptic visions. In the wake of the civil unrest of the summer, the administration in the fall prepared a confidential report entitled "Thinking the Unthinkable," which outlined four potential policy outcomes. In the first scenario, "The Armed Fortress," whites flee to suburban enclaves when "unprecedented violence" erupts in central cities. Congress guts urban aid. Police forces soon resemble "occupation armies." Blacks become the majority in large cities and capture City Hall only to discover that no resources are available for social programs. The United Nations flees New York for Paris and "Reagan Republicans" take over the GOP, which dedicates itself to the interests of white suburbanites. The Democrats jettison their commitment to civil rights and concentrate on retaining the labor vote, causing young liberals to abandon the party. "Everyone," it concludes on a bleak note, "becomes increasingly convinced that there is no way out."[5]

Scenario II—"The Pacified Ghetto"—was only marginally less grim. Black radicals conclude that initiatives like Model Cities will work and forego violence. With more funds available due to the end of the Vietnam War, urban conditions improve. The cities retain sufficient commercial and cultural assets to wield political clout. Black moderates maintain middle-class enclaves and attain political power; adventurous whites continue to visit what has become a de facto "foreign country." Over time conditions begin to deteriorate due to segregation but remain bearable because suburban whites are willing to send their tax dollars "into the central cities as the price of Negro exclusion from their communities."[6]

Scenarios III and IV were more optimistic. In "The Mini Ghetto," strong open-housing legislation breaks down segregation, granting middle-class blacks access to suburban life and fostering urban renewal that lures young whites back to the city. In "The Vanishing Ghetto," society achieves virtually complete residential and political integration. Yet the report concluded that only Scenarios I and II depicted realistic outcomes—a clear indication of how Newark and Detroit had eroded whatever liberal optimism and confidence remained after the events of 1965 and 1966.[7] On the left, the Black Power movement had emerged, with Stokely Carmichael as its charismatic spokesman. On the right, the conservative movement had revived, with Ronald Reagan as its new hope. For the White House, under siege from every direction, no relief appeared in sight.[8]

I

Although Newark had remained quiet during the Harlem outbreak in 1964, it was as promising a place for a riot as any other in America. The poverty, unemployment, and crime rates were high. It had a police department that was, proportionately, the largest in the country—yet was, by most accounts, riddled with corruption and rife with brutality. On both the Board of Education and the City Council, seven of nine seats were filled by whites. But since 1960 more than 70,000 whites had departed, leaving the city "majority minority"—52 percent black and 10 percent Puerto Rican or Cuban. Feelings of political powerlessness exacerbated tensions over urban renewal plans to build a new state medical and dental college in the heart of the black district. Turmoil also ensued when the mayor, a liberal former Congressman, appointed as secretary to the Board of Education a white ally with a high school degree rather than the city's budget director, a popular black with a master's degree. Although Newark had relatively little taxable property and a declining tax base, it had a per capita outlay on health, welfare, police, fire, and other municipal services several times greater than that of nearby communities—in part because of the large poor population, in part because of the large commuter population. As a result, taxes were twice as high as in neighboring suburbs—a point of contention for anti-tax conservatives. Yet the schools were overcrowded and dilapidated. And with the arrival of summer, more than 20,000 teens were on the streets, unemployed and unoccupied because of budget cutbacks in the recreation program.[9]

On the evening of July 12 (a Wednesday) a black cab driver named John Smith sustained serious injuries after he was arrested by Newark Police. As rumors of police brutality spread, a confrontation between officers and bystanders erupted outside the Fourth Precinct Police Station, near the massive Hayes Housing Project. A barrage of rocks and a few Molotov cocktails smashed against the station. Scattered looting was later reported. The next day, the mayor called the Smith affair an "isolated incident" but promised an investigation by a panel of citizens and the appointment of the city's first black police captain. Meanwhile, the director of police, Dominick Spina, extended shifts from 8 to 12 hours and mobilized half of his officers. That evening, they were needed as a protest march disintegrated into widespread looting. At midnight the overwhelmed police were told to use "all necessary means—including firearms—to defend themselves." Early Friday morning, the mayor requested that Governor Richard Hughes dispatch the State Police and National Guard. "The line between the jungle and the law might as well be drawn here as any place in America," declared Hughes, who sent in more than 3,000 Guardsmen. By dawn the first contingent had arrived.[10]

Despite their arrival, the looting spread on Friday as rioters chanting "Kill white devils" rampaged through the downtown. *Newsweek* described how "self-service shoppers" selectively raided a liquor store, taking expensive Scotch first and then moving to inexpensive wine. A member of the National Urban League felt despair. "I came dangerously close to flipping my lid as I watched the wholesale looting and destruction in the Central Ward of Newark," he reported. "It was sickening to see the hundreds of kids—and I mean kids, not teenagers, but five- and six- and seven- and eight- and nine-year olds—looting and having a ball. The unkindest cut of all was to see so many adults herding the very young into stores and directing them in what to take." There was, he added, a "carnival air about the tragedy," with much drinking and laughter. He recounted a conversation between two black women outside a drug store: "One said, 'This is a colored place.' And the other said, 'Yeah, but there's a lot of stuff in there. Wait until tonight!'" People, he related, had so much loot they could not carry it all: "There was enough stuff . . . left on the sidewalks and in the streets for someone to have filled a store—records, furniture, clothing, baby things, foodstuffs."[11]

That afternoon the violence intensified. Police gunfire directed at looters instead hit a three-year-old in the left eye as well as the brother and father of the associate director of the Washington Urban League. The father eventually died. Snipers allegedly killed a white policeman and a white fireman. A National Guard unit at a roadblock opened fire and claimed the life of a ten-year-old black child whose father had swerved in panic at the sight of the soldiers. But panic also gripped the troopers and Guardsmen, ill-prepared whites in a hostile and alien environment. On Saturday Spina encountered a young white soldier who had shattered the temporary calm by firing a shot because he was under orders to keep everyone away from the windows of a nearby housing project. "Do you know what you just did?" asked the police director. "You have now created a state of hysteria. Every Guardsman up and down this street and every State Policeman and every city policeman that is present thinks that somebody just fired a shot and that it is probably a sniper." His intervention made little difference. Later that day two columns of Guardsmen and troopers directed mass fire at a reputed sniper's nest in the Hayes Project. In the hail of bullets, three women—a grandmother, a two-year-old, and her mother—died. By Monday evening the state police and National Guard forces had withdrawn. Left behind were 23 dead, 21 of whom were black residents of Newark.[12]

The deaths left even temperate observers angry. During his appearance on "Meet the Press" that Sunday, Roy Wilkins bristled at assertions that he should have done more to halt the riot. "Nobody ever asked the Chamber of Commerce to stop a white riot; nobody ever asked the Ministerial Alliance to stop the riot," he retorted. "They realize rioters are not part of the church or part of the business community, but the minute something happens in a Negro community they say, 'Why don't you Negroes get together, you law-abiding Negroes, and stop all the rest of these Negroes?'" When columnist Robert Novak asked whether he favored a "massive effort to disarm the Negroes in the ghettos," the NAACP director replied that "I would be in favor of disarming everybody, not just the Negroes." Brushing aside Novak's objection, he then added "I wouldn't disarm the Negroes and leave them helpless prey to the people who wanted to go in and shoot them up." But why, interjected Novak, should blacks in Newark have rifles? What do they have to fear? "Why does anyone have rifles?" responded Wilkins. "The NRA is carrying on a tremendous lobbying campaign for Americans to own rifles. Every American wants to own a rifle. Why shouldn't the Negroes own rifles?"[13] Even in air-conditioned studios far from the ghettos, tempers were rising.

In Washington, the president anxiously watched the situation unfold. Ready to help an old friend and fellow Democrat, Johnson on Friday had offered Hughes whatever he needed—support the governor declined. But the president remained sensitive to conservative claims that his administration rewarded rioters and that poverty workers had helped to incite the riot. He also was determined to maintain the division of responsibility mandated by federalism. When Humphrey on Saturday confirmed that the White House had offered assistance, Johnson was furious. Inform the vice president, he told Califano, that "he has no authority, spell it out, N-O-N-E, to provide any federal aid to Newark or any other city, town or country in America." Four days later, the president met with Roy Wilkins and Whitney Young. "I was struck by their despair," recalled Califano. "The nation was at a flash point with pent-up frustration and anger, and these leaders seemed bewildered by the rush of events . . . [and] numbed by their lack of influence."[14] They were not alone.[15]

At the cabinet meeting on Wednesday, Johnson urged his officials to do more for the cities, to challenge critics about what they would do, and to redouble efforts to get the administration's story told. At his press conference the day before, the president had followed his own advice. "No one condones or approves—and everyone regrets—the difficulties that have come in the Wattses, the Newarks, and the other places in the country," he said. Then, after defending OEO, Model Cities, and the entire poverty program he acknowledged the depth of the crisis in the ghetto. "We can't correct it in a day or a year or a decade," he declared. "But we are trying at this end of the line as best as we can."[16] By the end of the weekend, it was clear that was not good enough.

II

Unlike Newark, Detroit was not a textbook case of a riot waiting to happen. Led by respected liberals like Mayor Jerry Cavanagh and Commissioner Ray Girardin, it was seen by many as a "model city."[17] Black incomes were significantly above the national average—and the gap between blacks and whites had narrowed dramatically since 1960. The unemployment rate was also low in comparison to other urban areas, in part because the federal government had pumped $360 million into Detroit during the 1960s through various anti-poverty programs. More important was the good health of the auto industry. With economic growth strong, the engine at the heart of the "Motor City" continued to hum. "Detroit probably had more going for it than any other major city in the North," declared an editorial in the *New York Times* as the riot mushroomed.[18]

But the "Motor City" was not truly a "model city." Despite "white flight," blacks lacked an equitable share of political power. Although many of the unions had finally begun to accept African Americans, discrimination remained rampant, with blacks concentrated in unskilled or low-skill jobs. The city schools were overcrowded. Black housing was segregated and in poor quality, if not in national terms then in comparison to white housing. And at the grassroots, federal spending had little impact except in the case of urban renewal, which was widely unpopular.[19] Above all, the police had a local reputation for brutality that poisoned community relations, particularly among blacks in the troubled 12th Street section. Despite reforms instituted by City Hall and lauded by the Justice Department, many African Americans were outraged by the department's seemingly slow reaction to the murder of a young black Army veteran by white youths.[20] Once again, the stage was set.

Early Sunday morning, July 23, four days after Johnson spoke to the Cabinet about Newark, Detroit police raided five "blind pigs" or private social clubs. At the last club, located on a corner of 12th Street, there were more customers than expected because of a celebration for several soldiers, one of whom had just completed a tour of duty in Vietnam. Thus it took over an hour to transport the prisoners. The critical delay allowed time for a crowd to form. To complicate matters, the Tactical Mobile Unit, the department's crowd control squad, had already completed its shift, leaving fewer than 200 officers to patrol the entire city during what was typically the most quiet period of the week. By mid-morning allegations of police mistreatment had spread and the riot was underway. The police, however, were content at first to establish a cordon around its epicenter, refraining from the use of force and allowing the looters to operate for the most part unimpeded.[21]

Although the example of Watts would seem to indicate otherwise, the tactic of containment seemed appropriate based on previous success and the shortage of officers. "If we had started shooting in there . . . not one of our policemen would have come out alive," said Commissioner Ray Girardin later. "I am convinced it would have turned into a race riot in the conventional sense." To maintain an air of normalcy, the city asked businesses to remain open and permitted the Detroit Tigers game to proceed (despite the drain on scarce officers). Community leaders also attempted to calm the crowd. Their efforts were in vain.[22]

By Sunday afternoon, the crowds had grown and become more belligerent. Rumors and rocks began to fly. As the looting and burning spread,

Cavanagh first asked for the State Police and then the National Guard. It was too late. As the Kerner Commission would later report, "A spirit of carefree nihilism had taken hold." Not all agreed. Congresswoman Martha Griffiths voiced a common suspicion when she declared that the riot "was a professional, well organized looting job." But Cavanaugh and others characterized the looting as spontaneous and disorganized, a description that many participants themselves endorsed, albeit implicitly. "I heard a friend of mine say, 'Hey! They rioting up on 12th,'" recalled one black man. "I said what are they doing and he said looting. That's all it took to get me out of the house. He said the police was letting them take it; they wasn't stopping it; so I said it was time for me to get some of these diamonds and watches and rings. It wasn't that I was mad at anybody or angry or trying to get back at the white man." As another black looter recalled: "I thought it was a lot of fun. People see'n what they could get for nothing and they went out and got it. It wasn't no race riot. They was white and Negro both going into stores and helping each other pass things out. Having a good time."[23]

The Detroit Police Department, proportionately among the smallest in the nation, was not sharing in the good time. Overwhelmed, it was unable to provide cover for the Fire Department, which was also overextended and under attack. A typical radio message underlines why the firemen had to retreat from over 280 locations:

> There is no police protection here at all; there isn't a policeman in the area. . . . If you have any trouble at all, pull out! ...We're being stoned at the scene. It's going good. We need help! . . . Protect yourselves. Proceed away from the scene. . . . They are throwing bottles at us so we are getting out of the area. . . . All companies without police protection—all companies without police protection—orders are to withdraw, do not try to put out the fires. I repeat, all companies without police protection are to withdraw, do not try to put out the fires![24]

When Governor George Romney flew over central Detroit Monday evening, he said the landscape resembled the aftermath of a bombing raid. Then came the first of countless—and usually false—reports of sniper fire. The arrival of the Michigan State Police and National Guard, however, merely added oxygen to the fire. The latter in particular were poorly prepared, with little training for riot control. They were ill-equipped, with obsolete weapons, inadequate maps, and a severe shortage of radio equipment (so severe that at times they had to depend upon pay telephones). And they were overwhelmingly non-urban whites (only 42 of the 8,000 Guardsmen in Detroit were black), with little knowledge of the city or respect for African Americans. "I'm gonna shoot at anything that moves and that is black," declared one Guardsman upon arrival.[25] His sentiments were typical.

His declaration also highlighted both the racism of many Guardsmen and their lack of fire discipline. Discharging their weapons indiscriminately, they endangered citizens, policemen, firemen, street lamps, and each other. Fear and fatigue were major factors. Deployed in piecemeal fashion—"They sliced us up like baloney," complained their commander later—the troops lost unit cohesion, which contributed to the panic. Exhausted after 30 hours without sleep, they were also "scared pissless" according to Girardin. "They're always shooting their own people," he added. "I was scared stiff to bring them in. It's not their fault, and I'm forever grateful to them: they did help to save this city. But they just don't have the training for this kind of thing." Their on-the-job training cost the black residents of Detroit dearly.[26]

What little faith most blacks had in law enforcement evaporated. "Man, these peckerwoods is itching to kill," said one teen pointing to a squad of National Guardsmen. "Lookit'em. They want to kill them a nigga so bad they can taste it."[27] The mother of a young man allegedly executed by a National Guard warrant officer was equally outraged. "I want justice done so bad I can taste it," she demanded. "And I ain't never had larceny in my heart, but I got it there now. I feel something should be done about it. And if I live, I'm going to stand there and tell them about it." In a sermon entitled "The Fear is Gone," a minister preached that "America is set on a disaster course of conflict and violence. The black man cannot accept America as it is. The white man refuses to make the changes necessary for the black man to live in America with dignity and justice. These are two facts. . . . There is no solution except conflict and violence."[28]

On Monday, the riot reached a crescendo as the temperature climbed to 90 degrees. In a desperate effort to restore order, the Detroit Police, National Guard, and State Police began to shoot looters. As in Watts and Newark, "official violence" mounted as fatigue and fear and rage and resentment fueled a loss of restraint on the part of law enforcement. The situation now clearly demanded the U.S. Army. Yet throughout the day Romney and the White House shadowboxed. Legally, the governor had to issue a formal request affirming that a state of insurrection existed and that all available resources were exhausted. Politically, Romney had higher political ambitions and was loathe to admit (like New Jersey Governor Richard Hughes) that he could not handle the situation himself.[29] For his part, Johnson mistrusted the Republican Romney (unlike the Democrat Hughes) and was not eager to assume responsibility for the racial crisis.[30]

The president had little choice, however. While Romney and Clark negotiated the timing, language, and details of the deployment, Johnson agreed that the paratroopers should assemble at Selfridge Field, 30 miles outside Detroit. He also sent former Deputy Secretary of Defense Cyrus Vance to survey the situation. At first Vance reported that the unrest was under control—an assessment that received a mixed reaction from community leaders as well as state and local officials. Then night fell and the violence intensified. "The situation is continuing to deteriorate," Vance reported to the president shortly after 11 p.m. He advised that Johnson sign the Executive Order. "Well," said the president glumly, "I guess it's just a matter of minutes before federal troops start shooting women and children." Twenty minutes later, FBI Director J. Edgar Hoover informed him that "Harlem will break loose within thirty minutes. They plan to tear it to pieces." With no apparent alternative, Johnson committed the Army paratroopers and federalized the National Guard.[31]

The president's worst nightmare was not realized. Under the command of General John Throckmorton, a veteran of World War II, Korea, Vietnam, and Mississippi, the paratroopers from the 101st and 82nd Airborne, many of whom had protected black children at Central High and James Meredith at Ole Miss, soon restored relative peace with minimal force.[32] By late Tuesday most of the looting and firebombing had ended, although scattered reports of sniper fire continued. By Thursday the worst civil disorder of the century to date—until the Los Angeles Riot of 1992—was over. On Saturday the paratroopers departed, followed by the National Guard three days later. Left behind were 43 dead, 33 of whom were black, 15 of whom were looters. Despite the constant cry of sniper, rioters were responsible for three deaths at most. Insurance payments of approximately $32 million covered 65 to 75 percent of the estimated damage.[33]

The intervention of the U.S. Army had saved lives and property—and might have saved more if it had happened sooner.[34] Yet it had also significantly weakened the facade of federalism so carefully maintained by the administration. No longer could the White House assert with plausibility that law and order was exclusively a local matter. Moreover, the deliberate manner in which the president ultimately agreed to intervene—combined with the defensive way he presented his actions—contributed to the perception that the administration had played politics while Detroit burned.[35] The result was a further loss of credibility for Johnson, who could ill-afford it. Afterward, the White House faced the additional challenge of aiding the victims without appearing to reward the rioters—a delicate task that was complicated by a bitter internal debate over whether black radicals had conspired to produce the riots.[36]

At around midnight on Monday, July 24, the "spin control" began with an appearance by Johnson on national television. With Hoover, Clark, and McNamara at his side, the president demonstrated his continued sensitivity to the potential intersection between racial violence and civil rights by emphasizing that the movement was in no way connected to the events in Detroit, which the "vast majority of Negroes and whites" condemned. In legalistic language, the brief speech also managed to mention six times in seven minutes how Romney's inability to maintain order had forced Johnson's hand.[37] Califano and McPherson thought the wording politically maladroit, a clear case of shifting the blame, but the president was swayed by the advice of an old friend, Justice Abe Fortas.[38] In retrospect, Johnson should have ignored Fortas' input because the heavy-handed message backfired and instead generated sympathy for the governor.[39]

A week later, Romney fired back at a press conference, charging that the administration's hesitation had cost lives and property. "I think the president of the United States played politics in a period of tragedy and riot," he said strongly. At his press conference that same day, Johnson brushed aside the charge. But clearly it stung. First, the president had Clark respond the next day. Then he had the attorney general issue a statement immediately after Romney repeated his allegation before the Kerner Commission on September 12. In the statement, Clark went through the chronology of July 24 hour-by-hour. "Any delays in dispatch of federal troops resulted from Governor Romney's indecision," he concluded, noting that the governor had not even fully deployed the National Guard when he finally made his request. "This is excellent," commented Johnson, who had also arranged to have the Vance report on the riot released that day. "Pity it didn't get out properly and get better play."[40]

A similar level of defensiveness was evident in the administration's handling of the poverty programs, which came under fire precisely because of Detroit's reputation as a city of racial progress and harmony. Even as paratroopers patrolled the streets in Detroit, officials in the White House were tabulating telegrams to see whether the public blamed the War on Poverty.[41] On July 27, Califano's office put out the word: "No new programs for Detroit without clearance from us." In response, Shriver asked "how to get out of the dog house," noting that of the 23,000 OEO workers in riot cities, only five were booked by police and none were convicted. Two days later, the OEO director informed Califano that 40 VISTA volunteers would arrive in Detroit that day and that he was trying to find others to keep the schools open. Shriver's efforts met with scant approval. To his aide Califano was blunt: "Call OEO and make sure they don't send anything into Detroit" without prior authorization.[42]

The difference in outlook between Califano and Shriver mirrored how divided and uncertain the White House was about how to proceed, especially given the difficulty of distinguishing between extraordinary riot-induced needs and ordinary inner-city needs. "Should applications from these cities for ordinary HEW, HUD, Labor, OEO projects be given special treatment?" asked an aide. Most officials, he reported to Califano, felt the answer was no for "political (we don't want to reward rioters), economic (we should not use our limited resources inefficiently by subsidizing a poor project just because it is from Detroit), and administrative (we don't want to bother altering our routine) reasons." The debate posed a larger dilemma for the White House, which McPherson summarized succinctly: "We talk about the multitude of good programs going into the cities, and yet there are riots, which suggests that the programs are no good, or the Negroes past saving." Neither explanation held much appeal. The loss of liberal confidence was evident—and growing.[43]

The August 2 meeting of the Cabinet exposed other deep divisions within the White House. Johnson, Shriver, and Secretary of Labor Willard Wirtz sparred over the political and policy merits of the poverty program.[44] The issue which generated the most heated exchanges, however, was whether black radicals like Stokely Carmichael and Rap Brown had incited the riots. In his presentation, Clark said that relatively few blacks were involved, making it imperative that the administration seek to support responsible blacks and isolate the radicals. A candid if stubborn man who consistently placed principle ahead of politics, he contended that the best response to the riots was to pass the Safe Streets Act, impose effective gun control, and upgrade National Guard training.[45] Citing incidents of police and Guard overreaction, which could trigger "guerrilla war in the streets," the attorney general said that "a racial war can only be avoided by [the] disciplining of ourselves." Talk of a conspiracy, he added, merely drew attention away from the deeper social roots of the riots. In any event, he maintained, at present the Justice Department could not make a case against either Brown or Carmichael.[46]

The reaction was fast and furious. "It is incredible to think you can't make a case," declared Secretary of the Treasury Henry Fowler. Clark replied that there was little evidence of a conspiracy based on arrest figures. "But there are 52 cities potentially about to explode," stated Humphrey. Both HEW Secretary John Gardner and Secretary of State Dean Rusk also expressed disbelief at Clark's statement. Rusk said that Carmichael had personally threatened his life—as well as the lives of McNamara and the president. And Gardner warned that "those who organize or incite riots are generally the last to be picked up and arrested." The final word came, naturally, from the president. "I don't want to foreclose the conspiracy theory now," he said. "Keep that door open. . . . Even though some of you will not agree with me, I have a very deep feeling that there is more to that than we see at the moment."[47] Later he would express to Califano in private his deep disappointment with Clark.[48]

The debates inside the Cabinet were reflective of the debates that were taking place outside the government. More than 70 percent of whites felt that the riots were organized. Five times as many whites as blacks blamed outside agitators for the violence. "The Black Muslims are finally putting through the plan they threatened years ago," said a white college student from Rhode Island. But a black farmer from Mississippi disagreed: "The Negro has been down and mistreated all his life, and the Federal government has opened doors for him and he is determined to keep them open." The races also differed predictably in their assessment of the extent of racial progress, police brutality, and white exploitation. And more than 60 percent of whites thought the police should use deadly force against looters compared to less than 30 percent of blacks, although a substantial majority of both groups agreed that looters were criminals.[49]

Other points of consensus existed. Americans of all races agreed that the riots had hurt the civil rights cause, harmed blacks the most, and attracted only limited support. They also shared the belief that the federal government needed to bulldoze the slums and establish summer camps for inner-city youths. But behind the apparent consensus lurked racial ambiguities. African Americans saw their demands as a principled response to white discrimination. White Americans saw their concessions as a practical response to black unrest. "They need food, work, and education," said an elderly Californian, "but . . . they just use these as excuses to riot." A Michigan housewife complained, "They have everything I have and some have even more."[50]

Underlying these sentiments was more evidence that race relations remained confused and contradictory. In the aftermath of the riots, a substantial and increasing number of whites said that they had no problem with the presence of blacks in public spaces like restaurants, bathrooms, and theaters. Yet a disturbing and increasing number also continued to express prejudiced attitudes. In July 1966, 65 percent of whites thought blacks had less ambition and 50 percent thought they had "looser morals." In August 1967, the respective figures rose to 70 percent and 58 percent. Survey questions about whether blacks had "less native intelligence" or desired "to live off the handout" generated similar though lower numbers.[51]

One sentiment, however, united all Americans: fear. Both races now felt more uneasy on the streets than a year ago. The number of whites fearful for their personal safety rose from 43 to 51 percent by August 1967. "You just never know what's going to happen," declared a white mother from suburban Michigan. "I'm afraid to go downtown any more." The comparable figure among African Americans was 65 percent. "On Fridays and Saturdays I don't walk the streets," said a young black man from Philadelphia, who added that the police, not the rioters, were his main concern. But a black laborer from Dayton, Ohio refused to draw distinctions. "Rocks and bullets have no names on them," he said simply.[52]

By the end of the "Long Hot Summer," the combustible combination of race, radicalism, and riots had exploded the liberal faith that the War on Poverty would constitute a war on disorder. Outside the White House, anger and anxiety mounted. Inside the White House, dismay and disarray reigned. The administration seemed to have lost its sense of direction. With the intellectual foundations of the liberal agenda under challenge from conservatives and radicals alike, the ship of state drifted dangerously in a narrow channel bordered by a reef on one side and rocks on the other.

III

The riots in Newark and Detroit dashed the administration's flagging hopes that the Great Society would generate both social justice and social peace. From the left and the right came rhetorical assaults that echoed the interpretations offered in the wake of Watts. Conservatives charged that the riots were criminal acts incited or exploited by radical conspirators armed with revolutionary intent and aided or abetted by liberals whose social programs had first instilled a sense of entitlement among the rioters and then rewarded them for their lawlessness. Radicals charged that the riots were political rebellions triggered by acts of police repression and suppressed by white elites determined to preserve a racist and exploitative political and economic system. According to this view, the War on Poverty was a cruel hoax, an insidious effort to prop up rather than tear down a fundamentally flawed system. Thus by 1968 both conservatives and radicals were united and vocal in their condemnation of the Great Society and the "false expectations" it had supposedly bred. The criticism rang loud and clear.

By contrast, liberals were divided and hushed, unable to offer a unified or amplified defense of the anti-poverty program. Outside the administration, the belief grew that the Great Society was too modest in scope and had failed to bridge the considerable and corrosive gap in economic achievement between blacks and whites (the "relative deprivation" thesis). Inside the administration, the sense was that the War on Poverty was a victim of its own success, however limited (the "rising expectations" thesis). Neither explanation would prove persuasive in the aftermath of the riots in Newark and Detroit.

Perhaps the clearest statement of how ideological foes viewed the civil unrest came from a somewhat unlikely source: Tom Hayden, co-founder of Students for a Democratic Society and a Newark resident from 1964 to 1968. "To the conservative mind the riot is essentially revolution against civilization," he wrote. "To the liberal mind it is an expression of helpless frustration. While the conservative is hostile and the liberal generous toward those who riot, both assume that the riot is a form of lawless, mob behavior. The liberal will turn conservative if polite methods fail to stem disorder. Against these two fundamentally similar concepts, a third one must be asserted, the concept that a riot represents a people making history."[53] A radical activist, Hayden had a vested interest in depicting liberalism and conservatism as two sides of the same coin. Nevertheless, he had outlined accurately how each camp generally defined—or wished to define—what the riots represented.

For the right, the riots represented the logical culmination of liberalism's failure as well as a political opportunity to drive home the point. "Rioting has become part of the American way of life, like football, strikes, conventions and picnics," wrote one conservative. Although he and others differed on whether communists had incited or exploited the riots, they agreed that radicals like Carmichael and Brown had helped to spark the riots not only through traditional means but also through the news media, which constantly transmitted images of police brutality uncontrasted with depictions of anti-police harassment. "The big scene always features a savage cop beating a fallen victim, preferably female," complained the *National Review*, conveniently forgetting that conservatives rarely neglected to depict crime victims as innocent white women. At the same time, the "electronic global village" created by television had turned rioting, like youth fashions and rock music, into a global phenomenon.[54]

Nevertheless, the main targets of conservative outrage were domestic liberalism and the Johnson administration. Whereas liberals once accused conservatives of falsely conflating race and disorder, conservatives now accused liberals of falsely conflating poverty and disorder. "There is indeed a problem of the slums," conceded the *National Review*. "And there is the problem of rioting and civil disobedience. But the two are not the same problem, and it is distinctively Liberal fatuity to suppose that they are." If the riots had a root cause, conservatives charged, it was not poverty; the American economy was in robust health. Rather, the collapse of law and order was in part due to a lack of moral leadership from the White House, which included a vice president who had declared that if he lived in a slum he would "lead a mighty good revolt." But above all, it was the unintended but inevitable consequence of the administration's War on Poverty, which had perversely fostered a dangerous degree of dependency and irresponsibility among urban blacks, many of whom were now angry and frustrated, without the individual initiative and moral integrity to make progress on their own. Sending more aid to riot-torn cities under the guise of humanitarian assistance would only exacerbate the crisis by rewarding criminality and feeding the frustration.[55]

The head of economic research for Richard Nixon expressed and extended the argument. As an advocate of "black capitalism," Alan Greenspan (now the chairman of the Federal Reserve Board) opposed preferential treatment and economic reparations. The latter were, he suggested, "dangerously inflammatory" because they reinforced among blacks the claim of injustice and provided a sanction for violence, which explained why the worst riot had occurred in Detroit, a Great Society showcase. But in his mind more was at stake than urban unrest. Although he acknowledged that African Americans were victims of discrimination, he denied that they were victims of exploitation unless "capitalism itself is exploitative," a possibility Greenspan rejected given the low rate of return relative to risk that merchants and landlords in slum areas received on their investments. Yet if the liberal agenda of redistribution and regulation made headway, the road to socialism loomed. Thus the riots were at heart "a rallying cry for an attack upon America's system of free enterprise and individual rights."[56]

The revolutionary potential of the urban unrest constituted for radicals one of several points of intersection with the conservative construction. Like the right, the left perceived the riots as spontaneous eruptions at the moment but with the potential for coordinated action in the future. As an editorial in the *Nation* predicted, with a measure of despair and excitement, "Sooner or later, sporadic local uprisings are pretty sure to escalate into action organized on a national scale with some degree of liaison and discipline instead of extemporaneous looting. And then what?"[57] Like many conservatives, radicals also sought to assign political agency and revolutionary consciousness (at least inchoate) to the rioters, whom they asserted were by no means marginal or isolated members of their community. On the contrary, as the Kerner Commission would confirm, the participants had relatively high levels of education, were active in the civil rights movement, and enjoyed substantial support from fellow African Americans.[58] And although some rioters were motivated by a combination of greed, boredom, or rage, most were careful to channel their emotions into actions aimed deliberately at those they saw as the agents of their oppression—white businessmen and policemen.[59]

Thus in Newark the first target of the rioters was the 4th Police Precinct, a symbolic site of social control and the actual location of police brutality (it was where cabdriver John Smith was beaten while in custody). Firemen were harassed, according to a local white teacher and civil rights activist, so that "the two symbols of [ghetto] degradation—white businesses and rat-infested tenements"—would burn. But careful calculation also motivated the rioters according to another white radical. "Economic gain was the basis of mass involvement," contended Hayden, who observed that the looters were careful to avoid black establishments. "The [white] stores presented the most immediate way for people to take what they felt was theirs," he added, noting that the looting took place because organized protests against gouging merchants had previously proven futile.[60]

A third piece of common ground between radicals and conservatives was their antipathy toward the Great Society. While the right attributed great influence to the anti-poverty program—if only as a negative force—the left gave it little credit and attacked it as a political sham, a token gesture motivated by white guilt and intended to deflect black demands for structural change.[61] With dispassionate statistics, socialist Michael Harrington calculated that the United States spent relatively less on welfare than any other advanced country. In passionate prose, Eldridge Cleaver argued that the "War on Poverty, that monstrous insult to the rippling muscles in a black man's arms, is an index of how men actually sit down and plot each other's deaths, actually sit down with slide rules and calculate how to hide bread from the hungry."[62] Although an obvious exaggeration, Cleaver's vivid and gendered description exemplified the depth of animosity between liberals and the left by late 1967.

With criticism coming from all directions, liberals scrambled to mount a defense. In typical fashion, they attempted to craft a balanced and inclusive message that would satisfy reasonable critics on both sides. In a typical statement, Congressman Emanuel Celler of Brooklyn told the American Jewish Committee that white flight, white racism, and the white backlash were partly responsible for the riots because they had contributed to urban frustration and violence. But, he was quick to add, law and order was as necessary for blacks as for whites. "Riots are a form of self-indulgence and ultimately boomerang," he maintained. "That we understand the reasons for the riots is important. That we do not use the reasons for excuses is equally important."[63] The speech was moderate and reasoned. Whether it or the countless others like it had any larger impact is doubtful.

A major problem for liberals was the seeming coherence and internal logic of the arguments advanced by their opposition. But important also were divisions within their own ranks, divisions caused in part by a growing lack of confidence in the correctness of their policies. Outside the White House, many liberals contended that the War on Poverty had done too little too slowly. Despite some progress, blacks remained victims of "relative deprivation," with high unemployment rates and low income levels in comparison to whites.[64] In the words of Joseph Rauh of the Americans for Democratic Action, they were "the have-nots of a society who have waited too long for the full rights, privileges, and advantages available to other citizens in this democratic society." To secure those privileges and advantages, it was time for the federal government to commit itself to all-out war, with massive jobs programs and large-scale income redistribution policies. Where the money would come from (barring an immediate withdrawal from Vietnam) and how the administration would push these measures past a hostile Congress were questions left largely unanswered.[65]

Inside the White House, both the prescription and the remedy advanced by more extreme liberals met with little favor. Instead, the preferred explanation was that the Great Society had engendered hopes that were beyond immediate realization. Ironically and tragically, the opportunities provided had only increased the frustrations felt by many ghetto residents. At bottom, then, the riots were not a product of conspiracy but of "the revolution of rising expectations," a favorite phrase of the administration. To be sure, the progress toward economic and political equality for blacks was slow and limited, especially in the inner city. As Johnson himself conceded, "God knows how little we've really moved on this issue despite all the fanfare. As I see it, I've moved the Negro from D+ to C-. He's still nowhere. He knows it. And that's why he's out in the streets. Hell, I'd be there too." But there was some progress. By 1967 the proportion of blacks in the middle class had doubled since 1960 and the unemployment rate among blacks on the whole had dropped by over 50 percent since 1958. Even Detroit reported considerable improvement.[66]

Then the "Motor City" went up in flames. How could the White House now sell the War on Poverty as a cure for disorder? With the "Model City" in smoldering ruins, the administration was forced on the defensive, uncertain how to demonstrate that the Great Society was not in fact fueling unrest in the cities. "People say the anti-poverty program helped riots," explained an aide to Califano, "and we gather statistics to show they didn't."[67] It was a losing game and the White House knew it. The riots in Newark and Detroit had raised the rhetorical and political stakes, leaving the administration in an increasingly desperate plight. The support for the War on Poverty had faded. The effort to contain the demands for law and order within the parameters of federalism had failed. The attempt to compartmentalize civil rights and civil unrest had collapsed. The future of liberalism appeared in serious doubt.

To ordinary Americans the future appeared equally uncertain. A poll taken in August indicated that the public now perceived the riots as the nation's most serious problem—more serious even than the Vietnam War.[68] The disorders also strengthened the white backlash and reduced white support for civil rights and the Great Society.[69] A North Carolina mother of two wrote that although she had supported the movement when it began, she now felt it had gone too far. She opposed sending federal aid to Newark in the wake of the riot because she worried that it would act as "an incentive to others to loot, destroy and kill." Neither her feelings nor her fears were unique. In *How To Defend Yourself, Your Family, and Your Home: A Complete Guide to Self-Protection*, readers received tips on firearms and tear gas—as well as specific information on what to do if caught in a riot or confronted by looters. "Whether you live in a big city, a posh suburb (where crime is growing fastest) or a small town," promised an ad, "author George Hunter understands your security problems."[70]

For conservatives, the riots were an essential plank in the tripartite law-and-order platform—as important as street crime and political demonstrations. In 1964 Johnson had promised that his War on Poverty would constitute a War on Crime. Now, in the aftermath of Detroit and Newark, conservatives charged that civil unrest represented the ultimate breakdown of civil society and the ultimate bankruptcy of modern liberalism, whose social programs had apparently backfired. First, the War on Poverty had encouraged irresponsibility among the disadvantaged. Then, administered by distant bureaucrats with little regard for local traditions or values, it had rewarded lawlessness, pandered to criminals, and squandered the hard-earned tax dollars of hard-working Americans. To add injury to insult, liberals in the end had failed even to protect law-abiding citizens, black and white, from the violence that threatened to engulf them. The Great Society had reaped what it had supposedly sowed—urban destruction rather than renewal.[71] By claiming that the unrest was at least in part the product of the welfare state, conservatives thus mounted a frontal assault on contemporary liberalism even as they tapped into the racial roots of white fear.

For liberals, that fear proved impossible to dispel. It affected the white residents of urban neighborhoods, who had some cause to fear black muggers and burglars, as well as the homeowners in homogeneous suburbs and small towns, who had less cause even though many of them had only recently fled crime-ridden cities where friends and family still resided. But regardless of actual circumstance, white fear of racial violence and social chaos was real and cut across class and geographical borders. It was reinforced by conservatives who successfully blended the urban disorders with street crime and anti-war demonstrations under the rubric of law and order. Contributing to the atmosphere of anarchy perceived by many middle-class whites were the rallies and rhetoric of radicals, who claimed that the riots were not criminal acts per se but political protests.[72] Ironically, the left thus strengthened the connections the right had drawn between race and crime, civil unrest and civil disobedience, violent demonstrations and peaceful rallies.

Caught in the crossfire and trapped in no man's land were moderate liberals, who tried in vain to separate the distinct phenomena (although all were often technical violations of the law).[73] On the one hand, they denied that the riots, in contrast to the anti-war protests, were "political" in any meaningful sense, in part because that would undercut what support remained for the Great Society. On the other, they strained at considerable political cost to emphasize how important yet overlooked elements of law and order, such as suburban juvenile delinquency and white-collar crime, were not driven by race.[74] Though logical, the arguments of liberals often fell on ears deafened by thunderous rhetoric from conservatives and radicals, whose opinions served to blur distinctions, exclude complications, and heighten anxieties. Above all, the conservative construction amplified the sense that the nation was coming apart at the seams, that it faced a crisis of authority unprecedented since the 1860s.

To allay that anxiety, the president in December 1967 gave a joint interview to the major television networks. He declared that the violence was the work of a "very small minority." In an implicit concession that Vietnam had exerted an impact at home, Johnson contended that the disorders stemmed from social change and tension, as they had during World War I and World War II. "Our big problem is to get at the causes of these riots," he said, remaining consistent in his focus on underlying factors. "The answer is jobs. The answer is education. The answer is health care. Now, if we refuse to give them those answers, people are going to lose hope, and when they do, it is pretty difficult to get them to be as reasonable as we think they should be."[75] It was the mainstream liberal line, spoken with apparent conviction.

In the White House, officials maintained that the country remained fundamentally healthy despite the summer's physical devastation and psychological scars.[76] Shortly after Christmas, the president's pollster reported with satisfaction that the public seemed to have accepted the administration's Vietnam policy. Therefore it was time "to shift gears to the domestic side. The big issue here is crime, civil rights, disorders, etc. Here too the Administration should seize the middle ground between the domestic hawks and doves."[77] His confidence was misplaced, as the search for that middle ground, at home and abroad, would prove futile. But his contention was correct—the politics of law and order would prove decisive in 1968.

6.

The Liberal Quagmire

Shortly after he left the White House, Special Counsel Harry McPherson recalled with regret the administration's failure to take a firm and unequivocal stand in favor of law and order. A thoughtful and courtly Texan who combined liberal instincts with political smarts, he had first arrived in Washington in 1956, when Senate Majority Leader Lyndon Johnson hired him sight unseen to work as counsel to the Senate Democratic Policy Committee. A decade later, McPherson was the president's favorite speechwriter, but he was often dismayed by how the White House would issue a strong statement against rioters and then follow it with "an apologetic 'Of course, we understand why you rioted.'" It was, he rued, "that ambivalence of the liberal."[1] That fateful ambivalence—which in domestic political terms would prove so costly by the fall of 1968—stemmed in part from the nagging sense that the Great Society might have catalyzed rather than contained the social turbulence that now seemed endemic in America.

Nowhere was the loss of liberal certainty and unity more clearly on display than in the divided reaction to the final report of the Kerner Commission (known formally as the National Advisory Commission on Civil Disorders). The Kerner Commission was born in a moment of crisis. In a desperate and predictable search for political cover and comfort, Lyndon Johnson convened it days after Army paratroopers arrived in Detroit, hoping that it would demonstrate his commitment to law and order as the Crime Commission had in 1965.[2] In public, the president pledged that the Kerner Commission was not "expected to put the stamp of approval on what the administration believed."[3] In private, he wished to contain the political damage caused by the riots and to receive official sanction for his social programs. But the commission dashed Johnson's hopes, ultimately producing a report that the White House could not afford (in political or fiscal terms) to endorse.

Part of the reason was that the report—like the riots themselves—had rekindled a national debate about the relationship between the war in the literal jungles of South Vietnam and the "war" in the figurative "jungles" of urban America. While the administration contended publicly that the two were not related, more and more Americans—black and white, radical and conservative—came to see a host of concrete and constructed connections between law and order at home and abroad. Adding to the loss of presidential credibility was Johnson's insistence that the country could afford both wars as well as the War on Poverty. Privately, the White House knew better and secretly authorized the U.S. military to prepare for armed conflict in the nation's cities. By the end of 1967, America seemed on the verge of a second civil war.[4]

I

The White House expected the Kerner Commission to validate the antipoverty measures already taken and forge a consensus for limited action. On both counts the commission would sorely disappoint. Its call to spend billions more on the cities spotlighted major gaps in the Great Society and funding constraints imposed by the costs of Vietnam and by conservatives in Congress. The report's assertion of "white racism" as a causal factor jeopardized the increasingly shaky Democratic coalition of northern workers, white liberals, and urban minorities.[5] By the end of March 1968 the memorable phrase—"Our nation is moving toward two societies, one black, one white—separate and unequal"—had imprinted itself on the national consciousness.[6] And liberalism was in a similar state, drifting toward two camps, polarized by America's dual "wars," separate and uneasy.

In an effort to steer the commission, the White House packed it with moderate representatives from the major Democratic interest groups. Observers saw a rough split between liberals and conservatives, but the coalitions shifted often. The senior staff contained no white radicals or black militants. The executive director, Washington lawyer David Ginsburg, was a trusted confidant of the president, ensuring close cooperation with the

White House.[7] "We tried to select men and women of experience, ability and judgment whom we felt could consider all the evidence and make a judicious finding," said Johnson. But in fact he approved their selection precisely because he assumed—incorrectly—that the commissioners would not transcend political pressures and would offer him a high degree of predictability and malleability.[8]

The president's decision to convene the commission was not, however, without risk.[9] Aides warned that although it might resolve the conspiracy debate and pressure Congress to vote more funds for existing programs like Model Cities, critics might also view it as an excuse for inaction. "To me," Califano would later write, "the commission had the potential to be a political Frankenstein's monster and it was almost inevitable that Lyndon Johnson would sour on his hasty creation."[10] But at the time the president had few attractive options and chose to place his faith in the commission's careful composition. In retrospect, it was a major miscalculation.

Ironically, the final report for the most part repeated the conventional liberal wisdom, buttressed by statistics and surveys. It issued a series of predictable suggestions for containing civil unrest. It exploded popular conservative myths, such as the widespread belief in the existence of snipers. It showed that the "typical rioter" was not a recent migrant from the South or a member of the "riffraff," a theory first advanced by the McCone Commission. And it declared that there was no conspiracy, although militant organizations had created an atmosphere ripe for riots and would undoubtedly seek to exploit future unrest.[11]

The report straddled the issue of whether the civil disorders constituted political protests. On the one hand, it rejected the McCone Commission's assertion that the riots were aimless. On the other, it denied that they were revolutionary in intent. The conclusion the commission reached was that the unrest represented efforts by demonstrators and looters to engage the political system and enjoy the consumer culture. By portraying collective violence as a political act, the report overturned the pluralist consensus on collective behavior, which attributed mass phenomena like street crime and urban riots to the failure of alienated individuals to cope with social change. Now the focus had shifted to larger causes and to American society as a whole.[12]

In particular, the commission recognized how deeply and widely shared were the frustrated hopes and sense of powerlessness in the inner city. Both had contributed to a new mood among African Americans, as had the widespread access to television coverage of the disorders. Although the commission dismissed the most serious allegations of sensationalism, it concluded that the media had exerted a "cumulative effect" on the riots, in part through a false focus on the black-white angle. An additional factor outlined by the commission was the climate of violence surrounding minorities, who faced black crime in the North and white repression in the South.[13] But two sentences in the two-page introduction overshadowed the sober discussion of these issues.

"What white Americans have never fully understood—but what the Negro can never forget—is that white society is deeply implicated in the ghetto," declared the introduction. "White institutions created it, white institutions maintain it, and white society condones it."[14] The argument was forceful and the language was dramatic. Like a lightning rod it captured the attention of the media and crystallized opposition to the report. Yet it was misleading in two important ways. First, the body of the report never defined precisely what "white racism" was. The impact of "white flight" received considerable treatment, but the commission never made clear the causal relationship between urban problems and residential segregation. The report also addressed the issues of merchant exploitation and police brutality, but concluded only that perceptions of mistreatment poisoned relations between the races.[15] Nowhere did the commission attempt a systematic or structural analysis of how whites oppressed blacks.

The second element of the "white racism" theme that few noted was how it reflected a compromise choice among liberal and conservative factions on the commission. The former wanted to stress how poverty had contributed to the riots. The latter preferred to emphasize the lure of criminality since, as one commissioner put it, "a lot of whites living on less than $3000 a year didn't throw firebombs last summer." Liberals seemed to see "white racism" as an implicit admission that fundamental societal change was needed; conservatives seemed to feel it was an explicit concession that income redistribution policies were not needed. The interpretation thus proved acceptable to the commission, which wanted to reach consensus and avoid dissent.[16]

The report also chose to make expansive and ambitious spending recommendations based on optimistic revenue projections. Increased taxes and economic growth would, it claimed, provide $30 billion for the creation of one million new jobs in the public sector (double what Johnson had recommended), the construction of 600,000 low- and moderate-income housing units in the next year (part of six million new units over the next five years), the extension of welfare assistance (including steps toward a guaranteed income), and the expansion of the Model Cities program. In an aside that no doubt infuriated Johnson, the report dubbed the president's commitment of $1 billion to the latter a "minimum start." Not surprisingly, in the media firestorm that followed the report's release, only one voice was missing—Johnson's. He maintained an ominous silence.[17]

In most respects, the Kerner Commission had broken little new ground. But in laying blame for the riots on white racism and in calling for billions of dollars in additional aid to the cities, it had touched a raw nerve with the president. Angered by the commission's failure to credit his earlier efforts, acknowledge the constraints under which he operated, or recognize the threat the "white racism" theme represented both to himself and the Democratic Party, Johnson refused to give the report even an insincere embrace or polite dismissal until it was too late. As a result, the attacks from the left and the right intensified even as the rift within liberalism continued to widen.

Liberals outside the administration praised the report for its candor, courage, and commitment to racial integration, welfare capitalism, and existing institutions. "It offered a comprehensive and plausible interpretation when it could have explained them away as the product of outside agitators and irresponsible riffraff," wrote one scholar. "It also offered elaborate and reasonable recommendations for the ghettos when it could have written them off with vague phrases about private enterprise and local initiative. And had the commission abandoned its liberal perspective and submitted a more original interpretation and more radical recommendations, it would probably have been rejected outright by most Americans."[18] Given the heated reaction from the right, that was undoubtedly correct.

Conservatives aimed their contempt at the idea that the cause of the riots was "white racism" and that the remedy was more government aid to the inner cities. "When all is said, the President's Commission reaches the insupportable conclusion that everybody in the United States except the rioters are responsible for riots," wrote Senator Sam Ervin, who termed the report's recommendations "ransom legislation." A conservative columnist chastised the commission for placing "the blame everywhere but where it belongs, everywhere, that is, except upon the rioters and upon the liberals who, with their abstract ideology, prepared the way for the riots by their contempt for social order and their utopian, egalitarian enticements and incitements." Liberals, agreed presidential candidate Richard Nixon, bore substantial responsibility for "the inflated rhetoric of the War on Poverty, which added to the dangerous expectation that the evils of centuries could be overcome overnight."[19]

Radicals were equally contemptuous of the report, which one journalist described as a "$1-million charade." But the left's main criticism was that the commission had failed to recognize the structural flaws at the heart of American society. "The very acceptance—and acceptability—of the Report is a clue to its emptiness," wrote a critic. "It threatens no real, commanding interests. It demands, by implication or explication, no real shifts in the way power and wealth are apportioned among classes; it assumes that the political and social elites now in control will (and should) remain in their positions."[20]

The debate by critics outside the commission was matched by a discussion inside the administration as to whether it should enthusiastically embrace, angrily dismiss, or politely accept the report.[21] The latter was the politically smart option, but it came with an expiration date that passed before the president had acted. As a result, Johnson found himself in the end—as Califano had feared—in the worst of all possible political worlds, absorbing blame from foes for proposing the commission and from friends for not endorsing its conclusions. The fallout contributed to the siege mentality that had surrounded the White House since the Tet Offensive in January 1968 had dashed hopes for an early victory in Vietnam.

Administration officials repeatedly urged the president to receive the report.[22] As incentive, Califano offered to "start leaking [it] to diminish its overall impact, point up its enormous cost and the unrealistic nature of its recommendations." But Johnson adamantly refused even to issue a statement. Inform Ginsburg, he told Califano, that the report "was destroying the president's interest in things like this."[23] In desperation, McPherson tried to revive it. What will people think, he asked, if the White House remained silent. "I don't mean bomb-throwing liberals, *The New York Times*' editorial writers, columnists, or militant Negroes," he explained. "I mean ordinary moderate people who, though concerned about their own safety, disturbed about black violence in their cities, and much less sympathetic toward civil rights than they used to be, are also concerned about finding some way out of the tragic tailspin we are in."[24]

Later McPherson made a direct appeal to the president. Warning that the report was becoming the "Bible of the liberals," he said that continued hostility would "turn the politics of long-term riot prevention over to Bobby Kennedy as a 'responsible politician who cares,' one who is 'willing to carry out the Kerner Commission's recommendations to save our cities.'"[25] That calculated argument seemed to strike home. In response to a planted question at a press conference in late March,

Johnson termed the report thorough and comprehensive, although he pointedly noted that he had disagreements with some of the recommendations.[26]

But by then it was too late. The window of opportunity had closed. Most blacks were not assuaged. As Roger Wilkins, son of the NAACP president and director of the Justice Department's Community Relations Service observed, "There is widespread disappointment in the Negro community that the president has not embraced this report more enthusiastically. . . . Many will say that this omission approaches the magnitude of President Eisenhower's failure to state that the [Brown] decision was correct."[27] Many whites, particularly union members, were also dissatisfied. Feeling ignored by the Democratic Party when it came to law and order and blamed by the Kerner Commission for indirectly causing the riots, they distanced themselves from the liberal coalition, leaving it without the power to push for social progress. "That's what I've been trying to tell you," Johnson told McPherson later. "There aren't that many of us that we can afford to set some of us against the rest of us. That kind of talk [placing the principal blame on white racism] only hurts us when we try to pass laws for the Negro."[28]

The future of the Democratic Party was a major reason for the president's reluctance to endorse the report. But he had other reasons as well. The Kerner Commission had failed to recognize his earlier efforts or acknowledge the budget constraints he faced. "I will never understand how the commission expected me to get this same Congress to turn 180 degrees overnight and appropriate an additional $30 billion for the same programs that it was demanding I cut by $6 billion," he wrote, noting that he was already facing long odds in his fight for the tax surcharge. "This would have required a miracle." The report had also undermined his contention that the nation could afford guns and butter, that the Vietnam War was not affecting his ability to build the Great Society.[29]

The commission disbanded in April. A disgruntled Johnson refused even to sign the thank-you letters to the commissioners. "I just can't sign this group of letters," he told McPherson. "I'd be a hypocrite. . . . Just file them—or get rid of them."[30] But the president could not get rid of the divisions he had helped to foster. By bitterly resisting the report, Johnson had highlighted the split within liberalism. He had also further polarized the debate over urban unrest. The rupture between a White House moving toward the political center and a liberal orthodoxy moving away from it now appeared irreparable.

II

During the Goldwater campaign of 1964, the political film known as "Choice" had used actual footage from the Harlem Riot, including a scene where white policemen huddle nervously near a checkpoint at night, listening to the yells of the crowd gathered around them. Suddenly one confrontational and contemptuous voice from the crowd cuts through the din: "If you want to shoot, go to Vietnam."[31] It is the voice of a young African-American male, a voice that penetrates the darkness and illuminates the complicated relationship between the war at home and abroad. In an instant, it adds a racial and global dimension to the battle for law and order, transforming it into an international struggle between blacks and whites, Asians and Americans.

During the mid-1960s, observers across the political spectrum repeatedly made connections—most rhetorical, some real—between the struggle to maintain order in the United States and overseas. At the rhetorical level, there was repeated recourse to the language of deterrence and credibility, with the White House eventually developing a "gap" in both the domestic and foreign spheres. In one, the threat stemmed from rioters, demonstrators, and criminals; in the other, it came from guerrillas, soldiers, and sympathizers. An important theme, particularly for many on the right, was that the country could not contain the communist menace in South Vietnam unless it could contain crime in the streets, protests on the campuses, and riots in the cities—and vice versa.[32] Another important theme, particularly for many on the left, was that racial considerations motivated the search for containment at home and abroad, with white men promoting colonialism and repressing legitimate demands for political self-rule and economic self-control by black and yellow men.[33]

At the material level, there were tentative connections between law and order at home and abroad. The U.S. Army and local police shared tactics, weapons, personnel, and training. Poised to assist both was the National Guard—that "ambiguous hybrid from the twilight zone where the domestic army merges with the international" in the words of black radical Eldridge Cleaver.[34] The cost of the Vietnam War also bore directly on the ability of the White House to fund the War on Poverty it had launched in 1964 and to fight the War on Crime it had promised in 1965. Yet Johnson had no recourse to raise taxes because he would not admit to the seriousness of the situation in Asia or the economic instability in America.[35] Nor could he make a compelling case for the Great Society in the face of domestic disorder and the conservative opposition it had helped to fuel.

By 1968 the analogy between America's three "wars" had taken on a life of its own and posed a serious dilemma for the White House, which sought in vain to separate local and federal jurisdiction, domestic and foreign disorder. As with its attempts to draw sharp distinctions between street crime, civil unrest, and political protests, however, the administration would ultimately fail to make a compelling case. In the end, it would have to concede, albeit privately and implicitly, that the boundary between the national and the international was permeable, as critics on both flanks had maintained. McPherson demonstrated how persuasive and pervasive the analogy had become in a memo to Califano. "Arming every white man in sight" was politically unpalatable and would not halt the riots, he wrote. "If Vietnam proved one thing, it is that heavy weapons cannot easily subdue an upheaval based even in part on social unrest."[36] Therein lay an uncomfortable truth for the White House.

A bitter irony for the administration was that it had helped set in motion the development of a bilateral discourse on law and order. In public statements beginning as early as 1965, Johnson drew direct parallels between the need to prevent violence and preserve order in the U.S. and South Vietnam. In the spring of that year, the president compared white extremists to the Viet Cong. "We will not be intimidated by the terrorists of the Ku Klux Klan any more than we will be intimidated by the terrorists in North Vietnam," he declared. By late 1966 he had invoked martial rhetoric and broadened the crime metaphor. "We are today fighting a war within our own boundaries," Johnson asserted. "The enemy is not identified by uniform, but no man, woman, or child is really free from the hostilities. . . . This war is the war against crime in America." To justify that war, the president observed that while Americans bore easily the burden of a major military effort thousands of miles away, they tolerated criminal activity in their own communities that cost them ("the taxpayers" as he repeatedly and fatefully put it) far more "both in lives and dollars than the Vietnam conflict has ever cost them."[37] The references to costs and taxes would come back to haunt him by the summer of 1967.[38]

Following the riots in Newark and Detroit, Johnson extended the analogy in an appearance before a blue sea of uniformed officers. "You, and the men who you command, are America's front line in the fight against crime," he told the International Association of Chiefs of Police (IACP). "You endanger your lives every day just as the man does in the rice paddies of Vietnam to protect freedom, to protect liberty, to protect your country." The speech came after the crisis in Detroit, when the president had decided to commit U.S. troops but wanted them deployed only in situations where they would not have to use their weapons. "I'm concerned about the charge that we cannot kill enough people in Vietnam so we go out and shoot civilians in Detroit," he told aides at the time, indicating how deeply the comparison had taken hold and begun to dominate his outlook.[39]

Most of the president's top advisers shared his acceptance of the analogy—at least to some extent. From the foreign affairs perspective, Walt Rostow declared that economic and social progress—in the United States and Vietnam—depended on the restoration of law and order in both locales. Without a "base of order and progress" at home, the U.S. could not shoulder its burdens abroad. Yet that base was threatened should "U.S. withdrawal from its responsibilities result in an international environment of chaos and violence." From the domestic affairs perspective, Califano urged Johnson to make responsibility a major theme of presidential discourse. "This responsibility must begin with order—in the international sphere, as well as at home," he suggested. "International lawlessness can no more be tolerated than lawlessness on the streets of America."[40]

Similar sentiments emerged from different perspectives at the grassroots level. As a conservative, small-town doctor put it: "We should bring our boys home to protect our home country because if we cannot protect our home country, how in Kingdom come can we do good for others?" A liberal woman from New York used different logic to arrive at the same conclusion: "How can you expect to end the crime and violence in the streets with the example our government is setting by its escalation of that brutal and violent war on the poor people of Vietnam? We are tired of spending money which should be used here to educate our deprived. We are tired of the killing and spending and brutality in Vietnam."[41] Thus the administration found itself encircled and ensnared by an analogy it had helped to popularize.

Although the Vietnam War was not an immediate political reality for domestic policy planners in the White House, it clouded the psychological atmosphere and limited the fiscal possibilities of the Great Society.[42] In public, the administration consistently maintained that it could fund its "wars" against poverty, lawlessness, and communism without unbalancing the budget or imposing new taxes. At a press conference following the Detroit Riot, a reporter asked Johnson whether he was considering cuts in either military or space expenditures in order to increase expenditures on the cities. The president said firmly that he had no intention of doing so. Even if, the reporter persisted, the Kerner Commission recommends massive new spending? "I have no doubt for a moment," replied Johnson, "but that our country will be able to do whatever is necessary to do."[43] Within months the commission itself was on the table as a possible (albeit symbolic) budget cut—a course of action the president rejected only after Califano advised him that critics would read it as yet another retreat from his commitment to the Great Society.[44]

Among those critics were Robert Kennedy and Martin Luther King Jr., two of Johnson's personal antagonists. As early as 1965, in the wake of Watts, Kennedy argued that the nation could not afford to let the demands of South Vietnam take precedence over the needs of urban slums. "We should also remember," he added, with a debatable nod to history, "that the worst race riots in our history took place during World War II, in Detroit and Harlem—perhaps because Negro soldiers were asked to give so much, and their families at home were allowed so little." King was even more succinct. "Flame throwers in Vietnam fan the flames in our cities," he declared in the spring of 1968.[45]

In the wake of the riots in the summer of 1967, observers across the political spectrum disputed the president's contention that economic growth would allow the government to meet all of its commitments. Republican Senator Charles Percy of Illinois questioned the wisdom of spending "$66 million a day trying to 'save' the 16 million people of South Vietnam while leaving the plight of the 20 million urban poor in our own country unresolved." A *Nation* editorial pointedly noted that the war in Vietnam claimed $27 billion annually while the War on Poverty received only $2 billion. "What guns and what butter?" it asked. "The guns in Newark and the butter on Premier Ky's table?" A year later, the magazine predicted that without a rapid and massive redeployment of funds for social reform, which was not even on the present agenda, the nation might soon "see armed helicopters firing at snipers on rooftops."[46]

Although the White House publicly paid little heed to such dire predictions, it privately anticipated trouble and acknowledged the budget constraints imposed by the war in Vietnam and by conservatives in Congress angered by the civil disorders. "It will do little good to think up new ideas for dealing with the problems of our cities if we sit and watch programs we have already launched go down the drain," Johnson told the cabinet in August 1967, citing cuts in the Teacher Corps.[47] An aide to Califano recalled that "all domestic programs were absolutely starved" for funds, even those aimed at improving public safety. In a fit of optimism or wishfulness, the administration formed a Post-Vietnam Planning Committee whose draft report contained tables showing how postwar reductions in military spending combined with tax cuts of various sizes could lead to a possible expansion of both anti-poverty and anti-crime initiatives. Fiscal Year 1970 was the target date.[48]

Of course, the constraints theoretically cut both ways. For every soldier, weapon, troop carrier, and intelligence dollar sent to Detroit, there was potentially one less available for Saigon—a reality Califano well understood when he advised Secretary of Defense Robert McNamara to exercise caution during his Senate testimony on anti-riot legislation and to restrict his answers to specific military issues rather than broader policy matters.[49] Yet the instructions from Califano actually left McNamara with considerable latitude because of the extent to which the U.S. Army, with the acquiescence of the White House, had become a full partner in planning for future civil unrest in the wake of Detroit.

From tactics and training to intelligence and equipment, the military placed its stamp on virtually every aspect of riot control. Borrowing heavily from its experiences in Vietnam, it developed close ties to local law enforcement—ties that raised many legal and logistical questions. Among them were: What role if any should the Army play in domestic affairs? What kinds of intelligence should the military gather? In what types of preparation should it engage? How much publicity should the Pentagon's planning efforts receive? Under what conditions and whose control should the president commit troops domestically? What kinds of weapons were appropriate for riot control? Perhaps most controversial was how it should handle potential problems with black soldiers, both during and after their tours of duty.

In a real sense, the intervention of the military "nationalized" and "internationalized" the crisis of law and order. It made the conservative construction more persuasive by breaching the barriers of federalism—barriers that the administration itself had constructed—and by discrediting the claim that civil unrest was primarily a local matter. It rendered the radical critique more plausible by reinforcing the left's contention that the Pentagon's participation in riot control threatened civil liberties. And it weakened the liberal assertion that Vietnam had not hindered the struggle for social justice—a claim on which the White House had staked much credibility.

Advocates of an expanded military role in riot control offered several rationales. One was that only professional Army units had the training, discipline, and diversity to carry out urban pacification effectively. Since the Dominican crisis, reported a former Pentagon official, all soldiers had received training in situations with "similarities to those which you find in an urban conflict in a domestic situation." Army units also had considerable minority representation and fire discipline, in sharp contrast to the virtually all-white National Guard whose indiscriminate discharge of weapons had inflated casualty rates so dramatically in Newark and Detroit.[50]

A second rationale, popular with conservatives, was the sheer scope of the counter-insurgency challenge in the wake of the summer of 1967. In *Army Magazine*, retired Colonel Robert Rigg predicted that the nation's cities faced years of guerrilla warfare. "The fighters by night could be workers by day," he warned. "Rooftops, windows, rooms high up, streets low down, and back alleys nearby, could become a virtual jungle for patrolling police or military forces at night when hidden snipers could abound, as they often do against U.S. and allied forces in Vietnam in daylight."[51] Providing a counterpoint to Rigg's rather extreme analysis was the equally violent rhetoric of Stokely Carmichael, who declared that urban guerrillas were prepared to fight to the death.[52]

Critics noted that there were logistical as well as legal objections to the use of soldiers in riot-control situations. In tactical terms, the doctrine of "flexible response" (a concept ironically discredited in Vietnam) was easier to define than implement rapidly. Troops took time to mobilize in large part because their commanders often placed a priority on force and firepower. Thus the Army could not constitute a reliable front-line defense against riots. Military intervention was also costly—a constant concern for the administration.[53] And the soldiers themselves might act as a provocation. Finally, most disorders were local in origin and required only local action. "If we adopt an 'Army first' policy, we will encourage irresponsibility and unpreparedness at the local level," noted one official. "This will result in more frequent calls for federal troops by mayors and governors eager to pass on their problems, and escalation of racial tension in the long-run." Clark voiced a similar concern to the cabinet in March 1968: "The Army is ready—but don't talk about it. Since Governor Romney's action last summer, a call for federal help is the safe political thing to do. A call without maximum need imposes an impossible burden on us."[54]

In legal terms, the issues of federalism and civilian control remained paramount. Under the Constitution, the power to use the Army to control domestic disorders was carefully delineated. Only if the state was unable to maintain order and the governor requested assistance—as Romney ultimately had in Detroit—could the president send troops.[55] But at that point the problem of civilian control emerged. In general, the troops displayed a high level of discipline when it came to discharging their weapons. But the officers often demonstrated little patience with civilian personnel. "Their insensitivity to civilian consideration has been quite manifest," contended Clark, particularly when it became necessary for them to coordinate procedures with local, state, and federal officials.[56] At the same time, the principle of "flexible response" left open the possibility of a "massive response" that could leave cities in shambles and civil liberties in shreds—a possibility that seemed less remote as the war in Vietnam escalated and the unrest at home mounted.

Even moderate African Americans feared that the use of soldiers marked the first juncture toward a police state. Although not at war, maintained Roy Wilkins, "too many cities and states are permitting the far-out threats of a tiny sliver of the Negro population to convert our urban communities into battlefields, complete with troops, command posts, general headquarters, deployed weaponry, communications centers and the horrifying war implements of destruction." Hoping to build a common cause with students at Berkeley, he warned that a police state would provide order at the expense of the rights of white as well as black demonstrators. Other civil rights leaders were more alarmist. Fearing "mass genocide on the black people," the president of the New York NAACP decried the "homicidal approach" of the state National Guard, whose commander had declared in July 1967 that he was prepared, if necessary, to authorize the use of hand grenades, bazookas, and other heavy weaponry.[57]

The prospect of mass violence was on the minds of many. In the streets, the human horrors of Vietnam had numbed or desensitized many to the human costs of the riots. In the Senate, Arkansas Democrat William Fulbright charged the war with "poisoning and brutalizing our domestic life," leaving America a "sick society" rather than a "great society." In the White House, the air of crisis softened support for the principle of federalism. It also led the administration to take steps to prepare for what it viewed as the inevitable next round of civil disorders, which would probably take place during the politically critical summer months of 1968. "We had a responsibility—that was our view," said an aide. "After the Detroit Riots, our view was that next summer we might have even more riots and that we had to do something about it. We would have been negligent, in our view, if we hadn't."[58]

The first step was to acquire reliable intelligence about when and where future riots would occur. In September 1967 Clark ordered the FBI to use "the maximum available resources" to investigate whether any organization of any size had engaged in a conspiracy to "plan, promote or aggravate riot activity." The action demonstrated yet again how sensitive the White House was to the notion, promoted by the left and the right, that the riots were somehow premeditated.[59] Then in November the attorney general formed the Interdivisional Intelligence Unit (IDIU), a secret committee to coordinate, assess, and disseminate information gathered by the FBI, Army Intelligence, the Justice Department, and, possibly, the CIA.[60] Clark had acted partly on the advice of Assistant Attorney General John Doar of the Civil Rights Division, indicating once more how blurred the line between civil rights and civil unrest had become even for moderate liberals within the administration.

The IDIU faced a difficult task. In comparison to the Klan and the Communist Party, Black Nationalist groups proved tough to infiltrate because little was known about them and the FBI had few black agents.[61] The new unit also faced sharp criticism once its existence was discovered and viewed in light of the later abuses of COINTELPRO.[62] In the words of one historian: "Clark thus emerged as one of the founding fathers of community surveillance," which was "as much a Great Society legacy as the Civil Rights Act of 1964 or the Voting Rights Act of 1965."[63] Not surprisingly, administration officials for the most part disagree, citing the need to save lives, protect property, and calm fears. They also note that there were no clear guidelines as to what was legal at the time. And they contend that an important distinction existed between the legitimate reasons for which they sought the intelligence and the illegitimate purposes to which Hoover later put it.[64] The distinction has merit.[65] Yet what the formation of the IDIU fundamentally reflects is the desperate mindset of the White House, which knew that it had to find firm footing fast on the shaky ground of law and order.

Once authorized, the military began in secret to gather its own intelligence as part of its preparations for the next round of riots. In a domestic "War Room" in the Pentagon, it listed 124 cities in order of deployment priority, with detailed maps of sensitive spots (power plants, water treatment facilities, housing projects, etc.), staging areas, bivouac points, and landing sites. It drafted complete plans for each city, including the placement of equipment stockpiles and timetables by which to move them. And it designated liaisons for interagency task forces, prepared intelligence outlines in conjunction with the FBI, and compiled lists of local civic leaders. "The key thing is to get [the Departments of Defense and Justice] working together," an aide wrote to Califano, "but the Army stuff is so advanced, and so sensitive that I do not believe most of the operational stuff should be spread in the civil agencies where leaks are likely."[66]

The Army's deployment plans and intelligence assessments remained secret because the administration feared that, if leaked, they might generate self-fulfilling prophecies and encourage local officials to shirk their own responsibilities. As Califano recalled: "One, we didn't want people to say, 'God, these guys are preparing and therefore they expect riots.' ...Two, we did not want to take anything off of the back of local authorities." The White House moreover maintained a de facto "don't ask, don't tell" policy in regard to the military's domestic intelligence operation, in part because the FBI jealously resisted any encroachment on its turf. Also part of the consideration, according to an aide, was sensitivity to potential criticism for wasteful expenditures.[67]

Yet the reality was that local officials now looked to Washington for assistance when trouble erupted—and the administration expected it. And so, at the risk of further criticism and controversy, it consciously permitted the military to take other measures to increase readiness for future trouble. Conservatives watched with pleasure. Radicals watched with trepidation.[68] Liberals watched with the realization that a Pentagon partnership would bring Vietnam home in tangible ways. It would also complicate their efforts to contain the law-and-order crisis, to compartmentalize local and federal duties, domestic and foreign crises. Never directly addressed or fully answered was the question of how involved the military should become.

Into the void advanced the Pentagon, which established military-police ties across a broad front. At Fort Gordon, the Army conducted a one-week Civil Disturbance Orientation Course for all active-duty officers as well as those in the Reserve and Guard. Slots were reserved for civilian law enforcement personnel from selected cities. At Camp Pendleton, the Marines gave instruction in counter-insurgency tactics and guerrilla warfare to Daryl Gates and other officers in the LAPD.[69] The administration also discussed ways to encourage Army personnel, particularly military police, line sergeants, and petty officers, to enter police work after discharge. Moreover, through the LEAA the Pentagon distributed technological innovations field tested under combat conditions, including electronic movement sensors, armored troop carriers, and sophisticated scout helicopters like the Bell 204B, "the very type machine and operation presently being used successfully by our armed forces in Vietnam."[70]

Similarly, the Army made new and improved tear gas available at no charge to police departments around the country. Although the offer posed issues of cost effectiveness, quality control, and technical expertise, it met with widespread acceptance from the police. The reason was that tear gas promised to give law enforcement the means to deter looting without resorting to deadly force or appearing helpless before humiliating lawlessness.[71] The former approach risked an escalation of violent retribution; the latter risked an escalation of political pressure. Both were analogous to the situation in Vietnam. As a White House memo to the president observed: "The pictures of police and troops standing by while looters have a field day is very upsetting. It probably will be tolerated as long as the violence is directed against property. But it will not be when the violence is aimed at people. The tactics raise the same deeply frustrating questions as the Vietnam War. How can this great country allow itself to be pushed around and humiliated by a violent minority?"[72]

That question haunted the administration even as it remained sensitive to the political costs associated with riot control. In early 1968 it convened a series of closed conferences at Airlie House in Virginia, where hundreds of federal, state, and local officials—as well as representatives of the Army and Guard—discussed how to coordinate anti-riot procedures with police chiefs from the nation's 125 largest cities. Clark was especially eager that "competent Negroes" attend; consequently, he contacted the NAACP to see if local branches would submit the names of possible participants.[73] The desire to have minorities help police the ghetto was paralleled by anxiety over the loyalty of African-American recruits both during and after their period of enlistment.

The provocative and explosive issue hinged on two questions. The first was whether urban unrest would affect the morale of black troops in the field. Would they refuse to fight if they felt that the institution they served, the U.S. Army, was harming their families and friends back in the states? The second was what would happen if discharged African-American soldiers returned home proud of their service and sacrifice only to find themselves unemployed and their communities impoverished.[74] Would they then become converts to the radical cause, decide to put their Army skills to good use, and enlist in a new struggle at home? Back in the ghetto, noted one scholar, demobilized black soldiers could serve as the point men for future violent clashes: "Trained, battle-tested, and embittered they could be the source of the guerrilla army that a Negro leader would need for the task of disrupting an American society from which he was totally alienated."[75] The prospect was tantalizing to some, terrifying to others.

On the left, there was an air of inevitability and a tone of restrained glee. For Cleaver, 1965 was the point of no return, when a "community of interest began to emerge, dripping with blood, out of the ashes of Watts." With white soldiers now shooting both blacks at home and Vietnamese abroad, he predicted that ultimately blood would tell, that black soldiers would fight to liberate the ghetto once they realized how the U.S. government had exploited them. "They are asked to die for the System in Vietnam," he wrote. "In Watts they are killed by it." A young rioter in Los Angeles displayed a visceral understanding of Cleaver's point: "If I've got to die, I ain't dying in Vietnam, I'm going to die here." Following Newark and Detroit, another radical saw Harlem as the decisive battleground because it was the symbolic heart of black America and the geographic heart of New York. Black veterans would act as snipers, attacking commuter trains and severing road arteries.[76]

Many radicals saw confrontation as the means of demonstrating the connection between official repression in America and Vietnam. In October 1967 the General Counsel of the General Services Administration met with representatives from the National Mobilization Committee. He urged them to allow the White House to facilitate their protest at the Pentagon in exchange for the abandonment of their plans to engage in civil disobedience. But David Dellinger, Jerry Rubin, and other activists nixed the deal, contending that the administration's refusal to cooperate would lead to black riots and street disorder, which would aid the anti-war cause because it would compel the public to see the analogy between "police violence" in Saigon and "police repression" in Washington.[77]

The prospect was not a source of sleeplessness for most policymakers. But a source of concern was the nexus of military service, racial tension, and domestic disorder, which came sharply into focus in August 1968 when 43 black GIs at Fort Hood, unwilling to use force against fellow African Americans, chose military arrest rather than riot duty at the Democratic National Convention in Chicago. The administration was also careful to track the extent to which black veterans had participated in the 1967 riots and had borne a disproportionate share of combat duty in South Vietnam. The latter issue posed an acute dilemma for the White House. On the one hand, it was reluctant to trumpet excessively the contributions of African Americans for fear that it would reinforce the accurate perception that they were fighting and dying in disproportionate numbers in South Vietnam. On the other, it was eager to praise the efforts of black soldiers to counter the contention, popularized by conservatives and fostered by the riots, that black Americans were behind much of the breakdown in law and order.[78]

At a deeper level, a confidential report enthusiastically endorsed by the vice president outlined the need for a comprehensive strategy that would create opportunities for returning black veterans, provide new leadership for the War on Poverty, neutralize communist propaganda, and prevent realization of the radical vision of domestic civil war. The report, entitled "Political Stability, National Goals and the Negro Veteran," called for the recruitment of up to a thousand black officers who had served with distinction in Vietnam. These "father figures" and "symbols of authority" would then join community action programs in the nation's 35 to 50 largest cities and spur a new infusion of "civic initiative." More important, they would become natural leaders not "inclined to link the cause of civil rights in America with the Communist doctrine of 'anti-imperialist wars of national liberation.'" They would also prevent radicals from "harnessing unemployed Negro servicemen to sinister causes."[79]

The report assumed that the guerrilla war in Vietnam would continue for three to five years, "exploited on the terrain of world public opinion by official Moscow and Peking propaganda, concealed Communist agitators, uncritical pacifists and various peevish zealots on campus." Meanwhile, the "internal front"—the Communist Party's "emotional bridge" to leftists in the anti-war and civil rights movements—was unlikely to disappear given the rise of black power. Therefore America faced possible polarization and paralysis when next confronted with a Vietnam-type crisis. "If irresponsible radicals are permitted to organize the Lobby for the Poor," warned the report, "it is even possible that within a decade we will witness urban insurgency in the streets of American cities." But no public discussion of this threat was necessary or advisable. "It will be enough," concluded the report, "to present the case for Social Justice in making certain that veterans of the Vietnam War are given every opportunity to make a successful re-entry into civilian life."[80]

Whether the report was reflective of broader thinking within the administration is unclear. What is clear is that many officials were conscious of links between domestic and foreign disorder. And whether those links were real or rhetorical ultimately made little difference. Like the conservative conflation of race and crime, civil rights and civil unrest, the intersection of law and order at home and abroad—as well as on the local and federal level—complicated the efforts of liberals to draw clear distinctions that would engender popular support for policy initiatives. The Vietnam War also curtailed the administration's ability to build a Great Society based on order and opportunity—even as his denials to the contrary eroded Johnson's credibility. As 1968 approached, the future of liberalism appeared uncertain at best.

7.

The Politics of Street Crime

In July 1968 the Senate Judiciary Committee held hearings to determine whether Associate Justice Abe Fortas should replace Chief Justice Earl Warren, who had resigned. The hearings immediately became a forum for conservative assaults on the White House and the Supreme Court. The most dramatic moment came when Republican Strom Thurmond of South Carolina unleashed a blistering attack on the *Mallory* decision, which in 1957 had ruled that lengthy interrogations prior to arraignment violated due process. "Do you believe in that kind of justice?" Thurmond asked Fortas, who had joined the court in 1965 and had a legal reputation as a civil libertarian. "Does not that decision—*Mallory*—I want that word to ring in your ears . . . shackle law enforcement? Mallory, a man who raped a woman, admitted his guilt, and [was] turned loose on a technicality?" For several minutes Fortas was silent. Then he declined to answer, citing his position on the bench.[1]

The silence was symbolic. Unlike conservatives, who spoke with a clear voice on law and order, liberals never found their voice on the issue. In October, Johnson withdrew the nomination of Fortas, his long-time friend and advisor, who became a prominent victim in large part of the politics of crime.[2] But three earlier developments highlighted how conservatives had already wrested control of the political agenda from liberals. The first was the debate over the validity and reliability of crime statistics. The second was the effort to bring law and order to Washington. The third was the battle over the Safe Streets Act, the most important piece of federal anti-

crime legislation to date, which in final form demonstrated how po
conservatives had become and how powerless liberals were to stop

In response, the White House shifted political tactics and moved to make gun control—not poverty programs—the main front in the liberal war on crime and disorder. It was a significant shift. But it was also too late. By the fall of 1968, the conservative vision of law and order dominated the political sphere because it meshed with a trajectory of events that seemed to signal a fundamental erosion of stability and security in American society. The outcome was therefore not due primarily to miscalculation or miscommunication by hubristic or disengaged liberals. It was, instead, an affirmation and confirmation of the strength and solidarity of conservatives, who capitalized on a climate of crisis and turned the politics of street crime to their lasting advantage.

I

At face value, the statistics were scary. According to the Uniform Crime Reports (UCR) compiled and published by the FBI, the rate of property crime (burglary, larceny, and auto theft) rose 73 percent between 1960 and 1967. The rate of violent crime (murder, robbery, forcible rape, and aggravated assault) rose 57 percent—and doubled by 1969. Between 1965 and 1969 the overall crime rate increased by double digits every year.[3] And although crime per capita was highest in urban centers, it grew fastest in small towns and rural areas. In August 1964, *U.S. News & World Report* asked "Is Crime Running Wild?" One year later it had an answer—and a new question: "Crime Runs Wild—Will It Be Halted?"[4]

Liberals, however, maintained that the figures were inconclusive. It was unclear, argued Attorney General Nicholas Katzenbach in late 1965, "whether all women in a city should be constantly terrified by the possibility of being raped by a stranger, or whether in fact, the odds of that happening may be about the same as those of being hit by lightning—which may, indeed, be closer to the truth." False information, he added, often intimidated or misled the public.[5] In similar fashion, the president in early 1967 cautioned—in words that echoed the inaugural aphorism of Franklin Roosevelt—that the fear of crime was as serious as crime itself, whose "extent and gravity" remained in doubt.[6]

Conservatives harbored few doubts. They eagerly accepted the crime statistics, using them as proof that lawlessness was rampant.[7] By contrast, liberals carefully probed the FBI figures for statistical errors and analytical flaws, using them as proof that law and order was a phony issue. "We talk of 'crime waves' as certainly as though we were measuring snowfalls," complained Katzenbach, "and we discuss the 'crime problem' as though it were as palpable as the parking problem."[8] But not only were such objections in vain—they often backfired, leading many whites to question whether liberals truly had their best interests at heart.

The crime statistics reflected in part demographic changes. As the "Baby Boomers" reached adolescence, the number of juveniles rose 22 percent between 1960 and 1967. With more young men in their crime-prone years, the number of juveniles arrested rose 59 percent.[9] The problem, reported FBI Director J. Edgar Hoover, was now as acute in the suburbs as in the cities.[10] The main cause, conservatives concluded, was youthful disrespect for adult authority, private property, and traditional morality. Liberals, by contrast, continued to emphasize social conditions. But in the debate over the causes and nature of lawlessness, both sides found common ground on the issue of suburban delinquency. Liberals used it to discredit the notion that crime correlated with race; conservatives used it to discredit the notion that crime resulted from poverty.

The increasing availability of guns was another factor. In 1966 almost 60 percent of all homicides (6,500 in all) were committed with firearms, an increase of almost 17 percent over 1965. The number of aggravated assaults with guns rose 23.8 percent over the same period. In addition, there were 10,000 suicides and 2,600 accidental deaths attributable to guns. In 1967, Washington, with weak firearms restrictions, had a murder rate of 9.1 per 100,000 residents; New York, with tough firearms restrictions, had a murder rate of 1.7 per 100,000. Such figures and the constant carnage led even Hoover to endorse gun control. "There are licenses for automobiles and dogs," he observed. "Why not guns?"[11]

The growing popularity of drugs compounded the sense of chaos. Curious teens and affluent whites who had not used or experimented with marijuana and heroin prior to the 1960s now indulged, perhaps because real incomes had grown, perhaps because social constraints had loosened and personal liberation had become a popular quest. At the same time, a new federal law—the Drug Abuse Control Amendments—replaced medical supervision with police enforcement in 1965. By 1967 state and local narcotics arrests—especially of juveniles—had risen 165 percent over the 1960 level. The number of addicts as well as the consumption of illegal drugs had increased. But so too had the sense that they challenged American values, which added both to the appeal of the substances and the arrest of their users. "Since the use of marijuana and other narcotics is widespread among members of the New Left," Hoover informed all FBI field offices in 1968, "you should be alert to opportunities to have them arrested by local authorities on drug charges."[12] No doubt the agents were.

But liberals had their doubts—with good reason—about the accuracy of the crime data, particularly the way it was collected. The UCR, issued quarterly by the FBI, relied on voluntary reporting by the nation's police departments, many of whom may have had a vested interest in either underreporting crime (to demonstrate effectiveness) or overreporting it (to receive more funding). Crime statistics "represent little more than exercises in the use and abuse of the talents of an IBM tabulating machine," declared a sociologist. "National figures were put together by adding local figures collected by corrupt or efficient, slothful or diligent local police forces," observed a journalist. "If a fairly effective police force, like New York City's, collected its figures honestly, it made New York seem like the Death Capital of the nation. If a city like Dallas slapped its figures together haphazardly, Dallas glowed by contrast."[13] But even the New York Police Department apparently manipulated the data at times. In 1967 the chief inspector ordered his subordinates to report all crimes—and suddenly robberies and burglaries surged by 200 to 300 percent in certain precincts.[14]

The crimes often ignored were the crimes of the ghetto. For minorities, police neglect was often as much of a problem as police brutality. But for liberals it was a dangerous issue to raise. First, it might make the figures on black crime even more disturbing. By 1971, for example, African Americans constituted less than 10 percent of the total population, but accounted for more than two-thirds of all robbery arrests and almost two-thirds of all homicide arrests.[15] Second, it might reopen the wounds inflicted by the race and crime correlation, which remained extraordinarily sensitive.[16] Liberals, black and white, therefore tried to invert the correlation by asking why the selective enforcement of white-collar crime—"crime in the suites"—received so little attention. It was part of their effort to diversify the crime threat, to create alternative symbols of public menace such as the corporate criminal.

White-collar crime, liberals maintained, cost the country far more in economic terms than "blue-collar" crimes like robbery, larceny, burglary, and auto theft. Moreover, by not making it a priority, the police also indirectly reinforced the pervasive image of the black criminal. A focus on embezzlement and fraud, claimed the president of the Urban League, would reveal that middle-class whites were at least as criminal-minded as their black counterparts.[17] But white-collar crime never received equal public attention because its costs were dispersed and its threat was amorphous. Liberals, however, preferred to blame the media, which dramatized sensational crimes to the point where there was often no direct correlation between the level of crime and the level of fear.[18]

Liberals also contended that even if impartial experts collected and processed the data, shifts in the public's willingness to report certain crimes (such as rape) and the police's willingness to enforce certain laws (such as drunk driving) would render the statistics of dubious value. Economic changes further complicated matters. Because larceny involved theft in excess of $50—a fixed figure—inflation alone made increases inevitable. In addition, prosperity may have contributed to the "growth" in crime since it encouraged more Americans to purchase insurance coverage, which then gave them a material incentive to report burglaries they knew the police were unlikely to solve.[19] Finally, it was hard to know what the "increases" actually represented since the Crime Victims Survey would later reveal that many if not most crimes were never reported.

Even the crimes that were reported were often open to interpretation. For example, the murder rate—the figure best kept and least open to interpretation—rose 22 percent between 1960 and 1967.[20] But liberals noted that although the rate had risen, it was low in historical terms (4.5 per 100,000 in 1965 compared to 8.9 in 1930) and resulted primarily from family disputes, not predatory strangers. The average American, Clark told the Kerner Commission, was probably safer in 1967 than in 1937 (although not in 1957—a point Clark omitted). Of course, medical advances also meant that many victims of violent crimes now survived whereas before they would have died. "Our statistics are far from reliable," he admitted, "our ignorance greater than our knowledge."[21]

It was an honest answer, typical of the constant search for accurate information by liberals who placed their faith in social science.[22] But it was a hopeless quest. And it distracted them from a larger reality. Simply put, the fear was real.[23] Yet rather than address that fear in emotional terms, liberals offered an intellectual response that was dismissive of what many Americans had experienced in their own streets, neighborhoods, and communities. They lost sight of how crime shattered the lives not only of victims but of their friends and families, relatives and co-workers as well. Liberals also failed to see how violence affected even those it did not touch directly, particularly when it became enmeshed in a larger sphere of cultural and political anxieties. The miscalculation would have grave and long-lasting consequences.[24]

II

While most liberals denied the reality of crime, Johnson was attuned to the perception of crime, particularly in Washington, his long-time residence.[25] As the nation's capital, the District of Columbia had symbolic significance to many Americans. As the seat of the federal government and home to a disenfranchised community (prior to Home Rule), it presented a unique opportunity for the president to demonstrate the effectiveness of his urban policies—or to assume the consequences for their failure. As a city with a majority African-American population, it offered a charged environment in which to wrestle with the dilemmas and dramas of racial discrimination, urban poverty, and street crime. And as a test case for the pet policies and theories of liberals and conservatives, Washington served as a crucial political battleground under the spotlight of national media attention.

In August 1964, amid the summer heat and Goldwater's charges, the White House requested that Walter Tobriner, president of the Board of Commissioners, consult with presidential aides and the Justice Department prior to naming a new police chief.[26] The administration also solicited advice from Hoover on ways to bolster the performance of the District of Columbia Police Department (DCPD). The FBI director recommended hiring additional staff to free police officers from desk duty. During the campaign, Johnson quietly shelved Hoover's recommendation—additional evidence of his sensitivity to the issue of "crime in the streets"—but days after the election he directed Charles Horsky, his aide in charge of district affairs, to ascertain what steps Tobriner was taking to implement it.[27]

The White House's intervention in the District led to tension on both sides. Tobriner apparently responded with alacrity to the president's request for consultation privileges.[28] Johnson in turn reacted angrily when the Board of Commissioners unilaterally and unexpectedly announced the appointment of John Layton as the new police chief in mid-November. Facing the full force of the president's wrath, Tobriner hastily apologized for what he termed an error in judgment.[29] Two weeks later, Horsky explained to Tobriner that, in light of Johnson's interest in crime in the District, "I would appreciate it very much if for the time being important changes in either the organization and structure of that Department or appointments to positions of substantial responsibilities within it be discussed in advance with me." He added that of course the White House had no interest in interfering with the day-to-day operations of the District.[30]

By May 1965, the level of coordination and cooperation between the White House and the DCPD had improved considerably. In response to Johnson's insistence that the District take "emergency measures" to improve public safety over the summer, Tobriner and Layton agreed to double the number of nighttime foot patrols in high-crime areas, appropriate more money for walkie-talkies, and order the security guards of federal buildings to take perimeter walks to increase their night-time visibility. In return, the White House pledged the funds to hire more than 200 more officers, making Washington second in the nation to Boston in its police-citizen ratio.[31]

But the "emergency measures" were ineffective. In the past year, crime in the District had risen almost 20 percent—rapes 40 percent, robberies 56 percent.[32] Johnson soon grew impatient. "I want to make the crooks tremble," he told a speechwriter on the eve of the signing of the annual appropriations bill for Washington.[33] He received the rhetoric—if not the results—he wanted. "The wave of crime must be met and it must be checked," he declared in July 1965, "and our citizens must be protected, and our streets must be made safe, and our Nation's Capital City must be a safe and secure showplace for visitors." He added harshly that "we are not going to tolerate hoodlums who mug and rape and kill in this city of Washington."[34]

Despite the powerful rhetoric, the politics of crime brought the president his first legislative defeat in September, when Congress voted down Home Rule for the District in the wake of the Watts Riot. Within the administration, others now urged Johnson to discuss law and order with more restraint and moderation. "We do not favor a comprehensive crime bill which pledges to make the District a model city and leads the public to expect immediate and drastic reductions in crime," explained Katzenbach. "The probabilities are that this cannot be accomplished in a short time."[35] The administration, however, faced an acute dilemma. On the one hand, officials in the White House needed to promise dramatic results in order to win substantial funding for anti-crime initiatives. On the other hand, officials in the Justice Department worried that their credibility—and the credibility of law enforcement in general—was jeopardized by grandiose and unrealistic pledges to restore order. "The president had a way of taking any idea and treating it as a solution," recalled one. "Our biggest problem was managing the expectations that he would create."[36]

Other problems soon emerged as well. Racial politics ensnared the White House when it sought to replace Tobriner with Walter Washington, whom Johnson intended to make the nation's first big-city black mayor once Home Rule was enacted. But prominent white liberals like publisher Katherine Graham of the *Washington Post* and lawyer James Rowe felt that the District was not ready to have a black commissioner in charge, especially if his portfolio included the police department. After an elaborate series of shuffles designed to make Washington president of the Board of Commissioners without police oversight, he surprised the president by informing him that he would not accept the position without such responsibility. Stunned, Johnson withdrew the offer. Finally, Washington became president in September 1967. But the appointment came only after Johnson received a personal appeal not to change his mind once more. "Credibility will be the issue again," McPherson warned. "Call for tougher police . . . and though you may lose some Negroes, you would gain some white support. Turning off Washington is all hurt and no gain."[37]

For the administration, much hurt and little gain also resulted from the fight over a District crime bill. In November 1966, less than one week after the Democratic Party had suffered the largest losses in an off-year election since 1946, the president had to decide whether to sign a crime bill for Washington. The controversy rested on whether to permit the police to question suspects and material witnesses not charged with any crime in violation of *Mallory*; to impose mandatory-minimum sentencing guidelines (even though District judges already issued among the harshest sentences in the country); and to prevent the publication (through prior restraint injunctions) of materials deemed pornographic.[38] The decision revealed deep divisions within Johnson's staff and foreshadowed the national debate that would erupt over the Safe Streets Act.

Hoover and Katzenbach urged the president to sign the bill, although the latter wanted Johnson to emphasize that the lower courts had to interpret it in accord with existing Supreme Court decisions. But from the bench Fortas recommended a veto because he viewed the pornography provision as unconstitutional. Acting Attorney General Ramsey Clark also opposed the bill because it would not aid long-term efforts to alleviate the root causes of urban crime. Nor, he added, would it assist short-term efforts to improve law enforcement; on the contrary, it might have the opposite effect. Califano and McPherson agreed with Clark. A veto might prove harmful in the short run, they conceded, but "a statement highly praising District policemen" would limit the damage. "[I]n the long run," they added, "history would judge a veto as the correct decision." Johnson accepted their advice and pledged instead to increase the pay for officers in Washington.[39]

But controversy soon erupted anew, this time over whether Johnson should propose an anti-riot bill for Washington in the wake of the riots in Newark and Detroit (which ironically had hastened passage of Home Rule in August 1967). Clark and Califano again demurred. "It will be taken as a sign that the president is predicting riots in the District," they argued. "It deposits riots right on the White House doorstep." Far better, they argued, to let Congress take the lead, particularly with the national anti-riot bill, which Johnson could always sign if Congress passed it by a veto-proof majority.[40] Finally, in December 1967 the president signed a revised crime bill for Washington, minus the pornography provision but with the minimum sentencing and police interrogation sections intact. The bill also contained an anti-riot provision. By then, however, Johnson's legislative attention had shifted to the Safe Streets Act before Congress.[41]

Yet the president's personal attention remained fixated on the District. With an interest that bordered on the obsessive, he demanded and consumed details that ordinarily were beneath the notice of a chief executive. In July 1968 an incident occurred in which a pair of white officers were killed by black males. Johnson insisted upon constant updates late into the night, including in-depth background information on the shootings and the assailants.[42] Thus as the end of his term approached, the president remained—or so it seemed—almost as consumed by what happened on the streets of Washington as by what happened in the jungles of Vietnam.

III

By the fall of 1967, the crime bill was the centerpiece of the White House's policy aims and political strategy. But the complicated legislative history and altered final form of the Safe Streets Act demonstrate how, when forced to respond, liberals lost control of the politics of law and order. By the summer of 1968, conservatives had reshaped the measure to their own ends, to the point where it was no longer recognizable or acceptable to many liberals. The outcome also highlighted the impact of rhetoric and race—as well as the unexpected and often unintended consequences of events themselves.

As originally conceived, the administration bill would have provided federal grants to police departments for equipment, training, and pilot programs. The preferred method was through categorical grants to municipalities (with specific federal mandates on how to spend the money) rather than block grants to states (with vague federal mandates on how to allocate the funds). Califano sought to name the bill the Safe Streets Act to make it politically unassailable; Clark feared the title would raise unrealistic expectations and offered as an alternative the Crime Control Act. Ever in search of compromise, Johnson decided to combine the two and call it the Omnibus Crime Control and Safe Streets Act.[43]

In the House, floor debate on the administration bill began in August 1967. In the wake of Newark and Detroit, the credibility and popularity of the administration on law and order were at a low point. Amid strident rhetoric, the House as a whole ignored the recommendations of the Judiciary Committee and insisted that the federal government employ block rather than categorical grants. The House also voted to add $25 million to the original appropriation, mandating that the money go to riot control, not research or training. The revised measure passed by a 377 to 23 margin and a careful effort to shape the contours of national law enforcement became a series of subsidies to local law enforcement.[44]

As the new year approached, the administration attempted to regain the initiative. "I don't think you can hit law and order too hard," advised Califano.[45] Johnson tried to court public opinion. In his State of the Union speech, he strongly denounced criminal violence and praised the Safe Streets Act—the only sections of the speech to draw sustained applause.[46] But he was unable to strike the proper tone, given his unwillingness to support a national police force or adopt the conservative anti-crime agenda. Despite a cacophony of counsel, the Special Message on Crime remained excessively soft to many.[47] Fortas, for example, said it "does not come to grips with the problem of safe streets and safe homes in simple, specific terms." He even recommended a federal law making it a crime to use an unregistered weapon to injure a person engaged in interstate work or business. He conceded, however, that such a law was "necessarily drastic and constitutionally dubious."[48]

The Senate version of the crime bill merited a similar description. The Judiciary Committee followed the House's lead and substituted block grants (Title I) for categorical grants, in part because of lobbying pressure from the International Association of Chiefs of Police (IACP), whose members came largely from small towns or rural areas.[49] Then the Senate added provisions challenging the authority of the Supreme Court (Title

II), broadening the legal use of electronic surveillance (Title III), limiting the mail-order sale of handguns (Title IV), and disqualifying from federal employment any person convicted of any felony committed in a riot (Title V). In May 1968, the altered measure passed by a margin of 72 to 4.[50] Like the House version, it bore little resemblance to the administration's bill.

Conservatives had hijacked the program of the liberals. Part of the reason was that the president had become a lame duck in March when he announced that he would not seek re-election. Although the White House insisted that the crime bill remained atop the legislative agenda, others viewed matters differently. "There was none of that presidential muscle that could have made it a real race," claimed one Democratic aide. "As far as I heard, [Johnson] didn't make a single phone call over here. And when the bill came to a vote, I never saw anyone from the White House. I guess after the president withdrew from politics everybody else over there did too."[51] In reality, the administration remained deeply engaged, as numerous internal memoranda make clear. But the perception that it no longer took an active interest weakened the White House's political leverage.

Equally important was the inability of liberals to build popular support for their proposals. Like conservatives, they resorted to arguments that represented a blend of principle and politics, but they won few debates, as the outcome of the clash over how to transfer federal funds to police departments demonstrated. Liberals favored categorical grants because in theory that would allow experts in the Justice Department to evaluate local requests impartially and to earmark federal funds directly to large cities where the crime problem was most severe.[52] Of course, left unsaid was the fact that most large cities were headed by Democratic mayors and filled with Democratic voters. Conservatives favored block grants to state planning agencies because in theory that approach would promote a balance of power and responsibility between the states and the federal government.[53] Of course, left unsaid was the fact that the governors, a majority of whom were now Republican, would appoint the members of the agencies. They in turn could allocate a larger share of the money to small towns and suburbs, where the crime problem was less severe but many Republican voters happened to reside.

Although the administration was unhappy with the block-grant system (Title I), it objected most strongly to Titles II and III. The former was a direct assault by conservatives on the Warren Court's rulings in *Mallory* and *Miranda*. It declared that in federal cases a confession was admissible so long as the trial judge deemed it voluntary. Title II also stated that a delay in pressing charges, whether caused by holding the suspect incommunicado or questioning him at length, was not in itself grounds for deeming a confession involuntary. The provision further declared void the Supreme Court's authority to review federal and state criminal cases in which voluntary confessions were ruled admissible. Finally, it prohibited the federal judiciary from issuing writs of *habeas corpus* to prisoners who felt unjustly imprisoned.[54]

Title II was symbolic politics at its best or worst. It epitomized, above all, the conservative contention that the Supreme Court's rulings had handcuffed the police, making it almost impossible to arrest and convict criminals. In a letter to a colleague, Senator Ervin was blunt: "Those who are in favor of self-confessed murderers and rapists going free should vote against" Title II. Such rhetoric and the logic that lay behind it resonated with most Americans, 75 percent of whom had a negative opinion of the Supreme Court, 70 percent of whom were convinced that liberal judges at all levels had encouraged the loss of order.[55] "It is senseless for the police to track down criminals, when the Supreme Court sets them free on 'nit-picking' technicalities," read a typical letter to liberal Democrat Emanuel Celler, a senior Congressman from Brooklyn and chairman of the House Judiciary Committee. The police chief of Garland, Texas offered a typical reaction. "We might as well close up shop," he asserted.[56] In fact, the Supreme Court probably had complicated police procedure and conduct.

But *Miranda* certainly had not crippled law enforcement. Conviction rates in general remained steady after the decree, an unsurprising outcome since experienced criminals of all ages needed no reminder of the value of silence and legal representation. Moreover, studies showed that in most prosecutions confessions were rarely decisive and rarely excluded. Yet Title II would, according to more than 100 legal scholars from top law schools, inflict serious harm on the Constitution.[57] Fundamental liberties, charged Democratic Senator Ted Kennedy of Massachusetts, were in jeopardy "because some Americans have panicked about crime and want scapegoats to flay and panaceas to grasp at. They are threatened because other Americans want revenge against a Constitution and a Court which denounced prejudice and discrimination in large segments of American life. They are threatened because this is a presidential year, and it is so easy to play politics with questions of law and order."[58] That was undoubtedly true.

Less obvious is whether racism lay at the heart of the conservative position toward the Safe Streets Act in general and Title II in particular. The evidence for this liberal assertion, which pulsed within Kennedy's statement, is circumstantial but suggestive. Most of the proponents of Title II were vocal and long-time critics of the Supreme Court, whose power they had sought to curb since the Brown decision in 1954. During hearings held in the heat of the "Long Hot Summer," Thurmond relentlessly questioned an evasive Clark as to whether the act gave the Justice Department the power to withhold funds from police departments that lacked "racial balance."[59] Ultimately, the Senate explicitly exempted police departments from Title VI of the 1964 Civil Rights Act.

The administration viewed Title II as bad but tolerable, particularly after Clark chose to interpret it as applicable only to the federal courts, which tried less than five percent of all criminal cases.[60] The attorney general also directed the Justice Department to interpret Title II as unconstitutional, leaving it ignored and untested until a conservative legal challenge forced the Supreme Court to reaffirm *Miranda* more than three decades later.[61] Title III, on the other hand, was both bad and intolerable. Under the original administration proposal (The Right of Privacy Act), only the attorney general could deploy electronic surveillance—and then only with judicial authorization and in cases of "national security" (admittedly a significant loophole). Under Title III as revised by the Senate, however, any federal assistant attorney general, state district attorney, or local district attorney with the appropriate judicial approval could plant a bug or tap a phone if the crime or potential crime in question would result in a prison sentence of at least one year. The surveillance could last for 30 days, with renewable 30-day extensions. If a serious crime were imminent, law enforcement officials could even engage in wiretapping and bugging for 48 hours without a court order.

The administration reaction verged on hysteria. An aide to Califano wrote that Title III would allow "total wiretapping for any purpose at the whim of any county prosecutor or district attorney with the support of a local judge." The measure, he added, "may do more to turn the country into a police state than any law we have ever enacted." Ironically, he concluded, "the 'liberals' of the country have been so worried about protecting the Supreme Court's rules that prevent effective questioning of criminals that they have dropped the ball completely on this much more important issue."[62]

In fact, liberals criticized Title III harshly and repeatedly. They even made a last-minute effort to substitute the administration's original proposal, which narrowly failed.[63] But on the whole the liberal opposition was ineffective, in part because its libertarian arguments fell on deaf ears amid the clamor for law and order and in part because its practical arguments were not wholly accurate. To be sure, electronic surveillance would not have a major impact on street crime—as conservatives claimed—because ordinary criminals rarely discussed their plans in advance. Yet bugs and wiretaps had proved important in the war against organized crime, which liberals contended was a vital front in the larger war against crime. Moreover, Title III in effect merely codified what many states, including New York, had practiced for years, with minimal consequences for civil liberties.[64] Of course, the central irony is that the measure was promoted most strongly by limited government and states' rights advocates like Ervin, demonstrating the malleability of ideology in such matters. Once again, when it came to the politics of crime, both sides were guilty of exaggeration and hypocrisy. But once again, conservatives dominated the discourse.

Nevertheless, Johnson was not prepared to yield immediately. For a complex and not altogether clear set of reasons, he was firmly opposed to electronic eavesdropping.[65] Yet at the same time he was a man of considerable contradictions. On the one hand, he avidly consumed FBI and CIA reports loaded with information he must have known was gathered by bugs and taps. He also installed a Dictabelt recording system on his telephone and in 1967 acquiesced in the formation of a secret interagency task force dedicated to gathering and analyzing information related to the riots. On the other, he issued a memorandum to cabinet officers and agency heads in June 1965 prohibiting wiretapping except in national security cases. Then, when the Right to Privacy Act was under consideration in February 1966, he indicated to Califano that he preferred to ban all surveillance even in national security cases.[66]

By contrast, the handgun-control section (Title IV) represented a partial victory for the administration. Although it excluded rifles and shotguns, it was still the first major piece of gun-control legislation to clear Congress since 1938. It also served as the springboard for the Gun Control Act of 1968 and illustrated the unintended effects of unexpected events. In the aftermath of the murders of Martin Luther King, Jr. and Robert Kennedy, Title IV above all reflected and reinforced the liberal shift from social programs to gun control as the primary response to violent crime and urban unrest.

The liberal focus on gun control emerged gradually as the White House maneuvered for political advantage. In 1965, the National Rifle Association (NRA) had pinned down the Federal Firearms bill, which covered handguns, rifles, and shotguns, in the House Ways and Means Committee.

Ironically, the gun manufacturers then sought a compromise based on the exemption of "long guns" because they worried that armed racial conflict in Louisiana might lead to still more stringent legislation.[67] But Katzenbach, while privately in favor of a deal, counseled the administration to hold firm publicly.[68] Since the White House had other strategic options, he advised that it let Congress construct a compromise measure. Then the administration could redraft and reintroduce it, steering clear of conservative committees.[69]

The deadlock continued during the 1966 legislative session. Despite the knowledge that a bill excluding rifles and shotguns was attainable, Katzenbach remained convinced that the White House had to stand its ground. "The politics and tactics . . . are such," he wrote Califano, "that it would be inadvisable at this point for us to abandon the request for controls on rifles and shotguns."[70] But that stance angered liberal stalwarts like Ted Kennedy, who wondered whether the administration valued the crime bill more than firearms legislation.[71] It also meant that the carnage from guns, which in 1966 accounted for almost 60 percent of all homicides (a 17 percent increase since 1965), went unabated and unchecked.[72]

The "Long Hot Summer" of 1967 and pressure from police associations turned the tide.[73] In early 1968, the White House began to promote gun and riot control measures as related.[74] On April 4, Democratic Senator Thomas J. Dodd of Connecticut, who as chair of the Senate Subcommittee on Juvenile Delinquency had introduced legislation as early as 1963 to ban the mail-order sale of handguns to minors and felons, tried without success to add a provision to the crime bill that would regulate the sale, distribution, and importation of all firearms. Then word arrived that a sniper had assassinated King. The next day, a riot in Washington erupted. On April 6, the Judiciary Committee reconsidered Dodd's motion and approved it, albeit for handguns only. By late April a white public fearful of further racial violence favored regulating gun sales and registering gun purchases (a significant additional step) by a 71–23 margin, with even gun owners in favor by a 65–31 margin.[75] For a brief moment, a broad consensus existed on the urgent need for firearms control, and liberals raced to take advantage of it.

Virtually overnight, gun control became the liberal counterpoint to conservative criticism of the Supreme Court (Title II) and legal restrictions on police surveillance (Title III). Both the liberal and conservative positions enthused and energized partisans on opposite ends of the political spectrum; neither promised to exert any dramatic or lasting effect on street crime. Sales restrictions on guns were unlikely to prevent experienced criminals from acquiring firearms. Phone taps were unlikely to prevent the commission of most street crimes. Police interrogations without the Miranda warning were unlikely to lead to more convictions based on confessions. The politics of symbolism thrived as the legislative process reached a climax.

Both sides exploited the assassination of Robert Kennedy in June 1968. Liberals used the tragedy to advance the cause of gun control. Conservatives used it to accelerate passage of the crime bill. On the very day that news of Kennedy's shooting reached the floor, the House was debating a motion by Celler to convene a conference committee, where he and other liberals hoped to reconcile the virtues and remedy the flaws of both bills. The motion failed. The next day Kennedy died and the House voted 368 to 17 to accept the Senate bill (which Kennedy might well have opposed had he lived).[76] "I am voting for this measure out of deference to so many expressions from constituents in my district who regard protection in our streets as their paramount anxiety today," said one Democrat.[77]

He was not alone. Across the nation, anxious voters pressed liberal politicians to explain why the Great Society had failed to curb urban unrest and why they opposed the conservative prescription for a restoration of law and order. Even Celler, with his seniority and popularity, was vulnerable because he represented a Brooklyn district in transition and served as the administration's pointman for crime legislation. Many of his white supporters, especially middle-class Jews, had supported the civil rights movement during the integrationist phase and continued to do so, but life on the front lines of urban decline had taken its toll. Aware intellectually that not all minorities were muggers, they wrestled emotionally with the sense that all muggers seemed either Puerto Rican or African American.

The letters to Celler reveal the depth of his constituents' anguish and the extent of the dilemma he faced. "How in God's name you would obliterate the only ray of hope existing for millions of victims of crime-ridden cities defies the imagination," declared a typical letter sent in response to Celler's public stand against the revised crime bill in May 1968. "Thousands of people of the Jewish faith have stood by helplessly to see their businesses destroyed, their lives in constant peril as politicians blithely court the Negro vote and ignore those who elected them to office. Why is it your sworn duty to protect robbers, muggers, and rapists?" The congressman's standard reply was that street crime was a local responsibility and that federal intervention would inevitably lead to a national police force and a national police state, both of which he opposed.[78] It won Celler a deserved reputation as a devoted civil libertarian, but also contributed to a bitter primary fight which he barely survived.[79]

The fate of the crime bill was in Johnson's hands after the House voted to accept the Senate bill. Would he sign it? Should he sign it? McPherson recognized that the president had little choice, given the political climate in Congress and the personal fear in the nation, where crime had skyrocketed 17 percent during the first three months of 1968. "But it is the worst bill you will have signed since you took office," he informed Johnson. A veto would, however, risk even worse legislation as well as irreparable harm to the presidential aspirations of Vice President Hubert Humphrey. Clark contended that a veto would have a "good moral effect" and that the bill, although probably constitutional, could easily lead to unconstitutional practices. He acknowledged, however, that the key point was "whether the Congress at [this] emotional and turbulent time in our national history would answer a veto with a worse bill, or override a veto and make crime the central issue in the presidential campaign leading to repressive action in the future."[80] The answer seemed obvious.

Ultimately, Johnson bowed to public pressure and in mid-June signed the Safe Streets Act with considerable reluctance. "I have decided," he said simply, "that this measure contains more good than bad and that I should sign it into law." Of Title I, he praised the fiscal support for local police and said nothing about block grants. Of Title II, he declared that it applied only to federal courts, which handled a small minority of all criminal cases. He added that the FBI would continue to advise suspects of their right to silence and representation, as it had since 1940. Of Title III, he expressed his pleasure with the ban on private wiretapping and public sale of surveillance devices but warned that other provisions could erode personal privacy. Of Title IV, he noted that it had ended three decades of federal silence on gun control, but that it was only a half step in the right direction.[81]

At bottom, Johnson probably had little choice. A diligent student of the polls and an astute politician, he knew how vociferous and virulent were the cries for law and order. He also knew that the Fortas nomination hung in the balance, as did Humphrey's candidacy.[82] A veto would hardly have accomplished any practical ends at this point. And given the margins by which the Safe Streets Act had sailed through both chambers of Congress, it might well have led to an override or passage of an even worse bill, both of which would have tarnished further the final months of his presidency.

While the president deliberated over the crime bill, liberals used the

Kennedy assassination to promote stronger gun-control measures. Days after his death, Clark recommended that Johnson convene as soon as possible a White House or Justice Department conference to stress the need for new legislation (the Gun Control Act of 1968) covering rifles and shotguns as well as firearms registration.[83] The president immediately agreed. "We have a real public groundswell now and we must keep it moving," Clark briefed the cabinet in mid-June. "We need registration, we need information, we need computer data on all the guns."[84] To nurture public support, the White House recruited Hollywood celebrities, persuading actor Hugh O'Brian (who had once chaired the NRA's Safety Committee) to head a committee with Gregory Peck. The two would later appear on the *Tonight Show* with James Stewart, Kirk Douglas, and Charlton Heston, who would later serve as president of the NRA and whose politics were evidently more liberal at the time.[85]

The Gun Control Act also received endorsements from the editorial pages of some of the nation's leading newspapers, including the *Washington Post* and *New York Times*.[86] The White House meanwhile billed it as a possible antidote to the summer riots widely feared and anticipated.[87] In October the measure passed, with a ban on inexpensive imports and interstate mail-order sales of all weapons but without registration and/or licensing provisions. "The voices that blocked these safeguards were not the voices of an aroused nation," commented a disappointed Johnson. "They were the voices of a powerful gun lobby that has prevailed for the moment in an election year. But the key to effective crime control remains, in my judgment, effective gun control."[88] A new liberal orthodoxy had taken form.

But on that note, the politics of street crime in the Johnson era ended, as much in farce as in tragedy. In the spring of 1965, the White House had launched a War on Crime amid apprehension over the political dangers but optimism that it was a winnable war that would not sidetrack the Great Society. By the fall of 1968, explosion after explosion had rocked the nation, leaving liberals on the defensive and conservatives on the march. By crafting a popular message and exploiting favorable circumstances, they had seized control of the most important domestic issue in American politics. The triumph of law and order was on the horizon.

8.

Death, Disorder, and Debate

In July 1967, *Time* published a thoughtful essay on "Violence in America." In reasoned and rational tones, it cautioned against simplistic characterizations of the "whole American panorama of violence," including street crime, civil unrest, radical protests, and political assassinations of public figures like John Kennedy and Malcolm X. Violence was a pervasive and inevitable part of life, the magazine concluded, because it was a core component of human behavior, if not an innate characteristic. Americans therefore had to learn to accept "the mystery that can turn creative energy into brute force, a peaceful crowd into a mob, and an ineffectual weakling into a mass murderer."[1]

Soon the mystery had deepened as a series of tragedies left liberals at a loss, unsure how to respond or what to do. In April 1968 the nation witnessed the murder of Dr. Martin Luther King Jr. in Memphis, leading Senator Robert Kennedy to bemoan how "we glorify killing on movie and television screens and we call it entertainment."[2] The death of King was followed by simultaneous outbreaks of rioting and looting in more than 60 cities, including Washington, which reinforced the emotional as well as intellectual sense that violence in America was out of control. The liberal bid to persuade the white public that the urban unrest was not a national affair and that a clear distinction between civil disorder and civil disobedience existed was doomed.

Then in June Kennedy himself became the next victim of the violence. A period of intense national self-examination followed. In life, Kennedy had personified the liberal approach to law and order. In death, he became both a national symbol and trigger point in the debate over disorder. The question of whether America was a "sick society" generated conservative contempt and liberal confusion. But in the wake of the assassination a new liberal agenda would emerge, organized around the need to legislate gun control and limit media violence.

In August, however, events would continue to overwhelm liberal efforts to contain the chaos and fear. In Chicago, site of the Democratic National Convention, police and demonstrators clashed. As the delegates nominated Vice President Hubert Humphrey for president, the convention climaxed with what an official report termed a "police riot." At first the media sided with the students, blaming Mayor Richard Daley and the Chicago Police Department for the bloodshed. But it soon became clear that most Americans felt the police had done their job appropriately and given the protesters precisely what they wanted and deserved. The conservative capture of law and order was virtually complete.

I

It was a year of upheaval. In 1968, political assassinations, urban riots, student demonstrations, and street crime—filmed in color and televised in homes nightly—left many Americans convinced that their society was in meltdown. Overshadowing all was the Vietnam War. Following the Tet Offensive in January, it constantly occupied the hearts and minds of millions of Americans. But another issue had a physical proximity as well as an immediate reality that made it more tangible to more Americans than the conflict in Southeast Asia. That issue was law and order.

When Congress reconvened in late January, the Associated Press polled the legislators on what most troubled their constituents. "Overwhelmingly," it announced, "the members reported that anger over riots and crime overshadowed all other domestic issues and, in many cases, even the war in Vietnam." *Time* contended that "law and order looms, with the possible exception of Vietnam, as the nation's prime preoccupation in Election Year 1968."[3] And in late February the Gallup Poll reported that, for the first time in history, "crime and lawlessness" (including riots, demonstrations, and delinquency) was the most important domestic issue. Almost one-third of Americans indicated that they were afraid to walk in their own neighborhoods at night—a figure that rose to 40 percent among city residents and 44 percent among women.[4]

Even more troubling, warned the president's pollster, was that the clear line between local and national responsibility "seems to be blurring." Increasingly, Americans expected the federal government to ensure public safety in their neighborhoods—an expectation that was almost impossible to meet and promised political peril for the president. "We want to avoid putting him in the position of taking the blame for every robbery, rape, and mugging that takes place in the United States," maintained the aide.[5] Given the level of public anxiety, however, it is doubtful whether the administration could have regained control of the situation. Richard Scammon, head of the Elections Research Center, informed the White House that lower middle-class whites wanted and demanded protection—not a repeat of the "legalistic" response to the Detroit riot, which could prove "politically disastrous." It was now time, according to Scammon, to back the "thin blue line of police."[6]

On March 12, Johnson received a taste of voter anger in the New Hampshire Democratic primary as Senator Eugene McCarthy of Minnesota, an antiwar candidate recruited by activist Allard Lowenstein and assisted by thousands of college students, almost defeated the president. The unexpected outcome opened the door to an even more potent challenger, New York Senator Robert Kennedy, who entered the race on March 16.[7] Two days later, McPherson warned the president that the current administration course would probably lead to Kennedy's nomination, Nixon's election, or both. Americans were tired of the Vietnam War, troubled by economic stagnation, and, above all, traumatized by black violence and street crime. "[T]he number one 'public' problem for millions of people [is] physical fear," he asserted, a problem which the White House seemed unable to solve in large part because, "in the eyes of some whites, it was unwilling to offend the Negroes upon whom it depended for votes."[8]

Whether Johnson was culpable was irrelevant according to McPherson. The breakdown of law and order had occurred on his watch. But the president could still win re-election if he handled future riots decisively. "Make no speeches about Constitutional inhibitions," urged McPherson, a moderate whose hard-line advice thus carried extra weight. "Back up law and order in a hurry; be seen to be more concerned with securing the peace than with protracted legal discussions or political advantage."[9] The White House had clearly absorbed the lessons of Detroit. But Johnson would never put McPherson's advice to the test. On March 31, he voiced his intention not to seek or accept his party's nomination for another term. His withdrawal would silence many of his critics; it would not, however, silence the cries for law and order.

On April 4, James Earl Ray shot and killed King outside his motel room in Memphis.[10] For conservatives, the event was tragic but expected. "We are now witnessing the whirlwind sowed years ago when some preachers and teachers began telling people that each man could be his own judge in his own case," stated Senator Strom Thurmond of South Carolina.[11] For liberals, it was another chance to reflect on what Kennedy, on the campaign trail in Cleveland, eloquently called the "mindless menace of violence" in American society. "No one no matter where he lives or what he does can be certain [who] next will suffer from some senseless act of bloodshed," he said in one of his most poignant orations. "And yet it goes on and on and on in this country of ours. Why? What has violence ever accomplished? What has it ever created? No martyr's cause has ever been stilled by an assassin's bullet, no wrongs have ever been righted by riots and civil disorders."[12]

The nation, Kennedy continued, was degraded by violence at home and abroad. "Yet we seemingly tolerate a rising level of violence that ignores our common humanity and our claims to civilization alike." It was clear, he concluded, that "violence breeds violence, repression breeds retaliation, and only a cleansing of our whole society can remove this sickness from our souls. For there is another kind of violence, slower but just as deadly and destructive as the shot or the bomb in the night. This is the violence of institutions, indifference, inaction and decay. This is the violence that afflicts the poor, that poisons relations between men, because their skin is different colored." As Kennedy spoke, major riots erupted in over 60 American cities, leading to 43 deaths, more than 3,000 injuries, and 27,000 arrests.[13]

In search of an antidote, the president met on the morning of April 5 with prominent blacks. After a plea from Secretary of Defense Clark Clifford not to judge all whites by the actions of one "demented maniac," Whitney Young of the Urban League said, "We need more than patience and non-violence. We need funds for the cities." Other leaders like Bayard Rustin, Clarence Mitchell, and Leon Sullivan agreed. Johnson was noncommittal, noting that he had made repeated efforts to reach young people. "How well I have gotten through remains to be seen," he said to the assembled leaders. But, the president added, "how well have you gotten through?"[14]

The question lingered as the White House went into crisis mode, mobilizing more than 50,000 U.S. Army soldiers and National Guard troops. As violence erupted, officials debated what to do. A proposal for an additional $5 billion in social spending generated little enthusiasm. "New programs won't stop riots now," said one aide. "The question is whether we can buy some peace for the next generation." Another asked how the cities would survive. Repeatedly, the refrain was why now, why was law and order in crisis when progress was at last evident? Some officials argued that it was because the progress itself had engendered unrealistic expectations; others maintained that it was because "human misery" remained largely untouched. All agreed, however, on the need for the president to take some sort of action, to address Congress, call it into special session, or make a televised appeal to the American people, perhaps at the Lincoln Memorial, a traditional site of national reconciliation.[15]

In Washington, reconciliation was nowhere in sight on April 5. "I remember that day vividly," recalled an aide to Califano. "We got calls from the police in the afternoon saying, 'Things are going to be out of control. There is just no way we can control this city. Everything is going to go.'" The administration, however, faced a difficult choice. Requesting soldiers would dramatize the inability of the federal government to control disorder in its own backyard.[16] It would also highlight the weakness of local law enforcement. But delay could prove fatal as well. The troops might take as long as 20 hours to man their stations—time the District might not have. "We were scared to death," said another official. "The country was exploding, and it was pretty hard to figure out how the hell we were going to contain it."[17] To control violence in the District, Johnson imposed a curfew as well as a ban on the sale of liquor and guns.

Neither action could restrain the looters, who gave the riot a carnival air. "Cohen's is open," said one woman in reference to a local store. "Take everything you need, baby." Nor could the president silence Stokely Carmichael. "Go home and get your guns," he told a crowd. "When the white man comes he is coming to kill you. I don't want any black blood in the street. Go home and get you a gun."[18] At 4 p.m. Johnson ordered the U.S. Army into position after the burning and looting had come within two blocks of the White House. By 5 p.m. a company of troops with bayonets patrolled the grounds of the White House and a machine-gun post guarded the west steps of the Capitol, commanding the approach to the mall. Eventually, 14,000 soldiers would join the 2,800 officers of the Metropolitan Police Department. The sight left Johnson in a melancholy mood: "I remember the sick feeling that came over me the next day as I saw the black smoke from burning buildings fill the sky over Washington, and as I watched armed troops patrolling the streets of the nation's capital for the first time since the Civil War. I wondered, as every American must have wondered, what we were coming to."[19]

For many District officials, wonderment quickly turned into panic.

Mayor Walter Washington telephoned the White House to insist that the troops not release any looters they arrested. "That's just insanity," he said, even though the detention centers were overwhelmed and unable to process more serious offenders. "I don't give a Goddamn what the Constitution says. We just can't release them and let them go out again."[20] Senator Robert Byrd of West Virginia called to state for the record that he wanted martial law imposed and looters shot (killed if they were adults, wounded if they were juveniles).[21] But calmer voices prevailed. Three of the administration's top black officials, noting that the riots hurt poor African Americans the most, counseled "immediate but reasonable" force against the looters.[22] Both the federal troops and District police would follow that course of action as they struggled to end a riot that seemed spontaneous and unpredictable.[23]

By April 10, the situation had cooled. But an upset Johnson, transformed personally by the riot, now retreated from his expressed intention to address Congress or appear on television. In a blunt memo, Califano informed the president that although he favored a televised speech to the nation, "I do not believe you can substitute that statement for a message to a joint session of Congress. You are publicly on record in promising a message. Failure to deliver will be considered a breach of faith by the entire Negro community and a good deal of the influential white community, including many big businessmen." Militants would also, Califano warned, cite it as another broken promise. The administration could find money for the cities from space cutbacks and new taxes—a smart long-term investment. In the short term, the president could balance his compassion with a pledge to preserve public order regardless of the cost. "The situation at home is as critical as it is in Vietnam and deserves the same kind of reassessment," Califano pleaded.[24]

The president would have no part of it. On Califano's memo Johnson scrawled "NO!" next to the suggestion that he had contemplated a television speech. In the margins next to the statement that he was on record in promising a message to Congress, the president was petulant: "I promised nothing. I stated my intention only! Since changed by riots."[25] Ultimately, Johnson made little effort to exert leadership or unite Americans. The president, noted a staffer later, always looked at matters in practical and political terms. In this instance, he calculated that the riots had destroyed much of the sympathy for the cause of civil rights that King's murder had engendered. They had also crippled Johnson's chances of persuading Congress to provide more aid to the cities. And so, explained the aide, the president saw no point in lobbying Capitol Hill. His attitude was "what am I going to talk about—crime in the streets again?"[26]

Johnson's anguish and dismay were understandable. The riots across the nation had shaken his faith in the distinction between civil disorder and civil disobedience that he had tried so hard to draw since the Harlem Riot of July 1964. The riot in the District had also smashed his hopes of depicting law and order as a local responsibility. If he could not keep the peace in Washington without the assistance of the U.S. Army, how could he reasonably expect any mayor to do so? In the twilight of his presidency, Johnson had little choice but to watch as the liberal bulwarks he had labored mightily to build collapsed speedily around him.

II

While the nation was convulsed by riots, the Democratic Party was convulsed by Johnson's withdrawal from the presidential race. It set the stage for a bruising primary battle between McCarthy and Kennedy, with Humphrey on the sidelines awaiting the Democratic Convention in August. For McCarthy, law and order was a peripheral issue—indeed, he never used the phrase because he felt it was code for the repression of blacks.[27] But for Kennedy, law and order was a central theme. As the attorney general, he had tempered his ruthless image and revealed his soft side, his commitment to social action, by making juvenile delinquency a national priority. As a candidate, he would try to use law and order to reconnect with his hard side and recapture the ethnic whites who were so vital to the Democratic Party.

In early 1967, Kennedy took a broad and balanced view of the issue. "Crime is not just in the streets," he noted. "It is in the suburbs too. It is in white-collar offices and business. And it is organized."[28] Following the summer riots, however, many of Kennedy's supporters, including long-time aide Joe Dolan, advised him to take a tougher stand on law and order, that as a former attorney general it was a "natural" issue for him.[29] In early 1968, Kennedy began to shift to the right, arguing that what most afflicted America was a "poverty of values." Many people, Kennedy later told aide Jeff Greenfield, "think I'm the black people's candidate, so I have to show I care about what the white people care about in order to be their candidate."[30]

That attitude caused some generational discord within the campaign, especially between older advisers like Dolan and younger ones like Greenfield, Adam Walinsky, and Peter Edelman. It also led the press to speculate about the "new Kennedy" and his supposed conservative conversion. The speculation angered the candidate, who felt that he had not changed, the country had. What he had learned on the campaign trail was that everyone wanted him to talk about law and order, even labor officials who privately admitted that the rank and file were more worried about riots and crime than wages and hours.[31]

Where Kennedy had learned it was in Indiana. A confidential survey conducted by the campaign showed that crime was one of the two main issues. Most Indiana residents had little to fear in their homes and communities, concluded ABC correspondent Marshall Frady, but television coverage of urban violence made them "feel menaced by confrontations and figures remote from their existences, which in another time would have remained quite abstract to them." Quite real to them were taxes, the other dominant issue. Therefore Kennedy had to confront among white voters what one official termed "the triple threat of racial fears"—namely, that the candidate would coddle rioters, leading to more handouts, more taxes, and more riots. To defuse the threat, Kennedy would have to restore hope to blacks and security to whites.[32]

The candidate wasted little time in Indiana. In campaign speeches, Kennedy stressed that the loss of public safety would lead to the erosion of community cohesion.[33] In television commercials, Kennedy reiterated how intolerable crime was and how qualified he was to restore order.[34] The appeal to law and order worked—or at least that was how the press mistakenly interpreted the outcome, which gave Kennedy a solid victory over McCarthy, who made little effort in the state. Joseph Kraft contended that Kennedy had united "Black Power and Backlash." Tom Wicker of the *New York Times* wrote that Kennedy had revived the Democratic coalition by attracting the support of white southerners near the Ohio River, Eastern Europeans in the industrial areas, and African Americans in urban centers. Reporters even composed an ode to the candidate in honor of his past reputation: "He has the Poles in Gary / The Blacks will fill his hall / There are no ethnic problems on the Ruthless Cannonball."[35]

In the White House, officials correctly concluded that the media analysis was flawed, noting that in Gary 75 percent of Kennedy's votes had come from blacks and only 15 percent from whites, most of whom actually voted for McCarthy. Moreover, he had lost the suburbs decisively. "The theory that Bobby Kennedy has the magic ability to weld together a new coalition of Negroes and ethnic groups is wrong," observed an aide. "Politicians who buy it—and him as the Democratic Party standard bearer—will be faced with the difficult problem of trying to win a national election from a narrow base of Negro support." But another adviser warned the White House that it had to preempt the issue of law and order so "as not to leave a void for Kennedy."[36]

The critical primary was California, where Kennedy repeatedly cited his experience as attorney general. In a television spot aimed at women, Kennedy stated that he knew how to contain riots: "Cordon off the area in which the rioting or disturbances take place, move in rapidly with sufficient force to deal with it, and cut it off from the rest of the community." In a print ad entitled "Law Enforcement and the Cities," he listed his proposals on the left and McCarthy's—a blank space—on the right. Kennedy also took a jab at Humphrey (who still controlled a plurality of the convention delegates): "I don't think it is 'the politics of joy' if we have rioting, if we have the police and the National Guardsmen and army soldiers patrolling our streets—our city streets in the Nation's capital."[37]

But the message failed to resonate with many voters. Kennedy therefore took aim directly at the fears of white suburbanites during his last televised debate with McCarthy. The issue was how to rescue the inner city. Kennedy favored a strategy of reconstruction through job training for residents and tax incentives for businesses. McCarthy favored a strategy of redistribution, with mass-transit systems to enable the unemployed in the cities to reach jobs in the suburbs. In response, Kennedy offered a loaded rejoinder: "[Y]ou say you are going to take ten thousand black people and move them into Orange County?" That line was all many would remember later. On June 4, Kennedy narrowly won the California primary.[38] The next day he died, the victim of a gunshot from a 24-year-old Jordanian immigrant named Sirhan Sirhan.

The assassination of Kennedy led to an intense period of hand-wringing and soul-searching. "The country does not work any more," lamented *Philadelphia Inquirer* columnist Joe McGinniss. "All that money and power have produced has been a bunch of people so filled with fear and hate that when a man tries to tell them they must do more for other men, instead of listening they shoot him in the head."[39] McCarthy speculated that the killing was linked to the violence in Vietnam. Across the country, the young blamed their unyielding elders; the elders blamed the disorderly young. Black militants blamed white racism; fearful whites blamed black power. "Has violence become an American way of life?" asked one newsmagazine.[40]

In the White House, Johnson's press secretary and long-time confidant George Christian warned against any assumption of national guilt. "Unless evidence to the contrary is developed," he contended, "[the shooting] must be regarded as a formless act committed by a psychopath who found as his victim the most prominent man in sight." Don't speculate, he advised the president. Get the facts and disseminate them immediately to "check the wave of emotional speculation" and "maudlin hysteria" which could breed further acts of violent desperation. "This nation cannot afford to wallow in another orgy of self-flagellation," he concluded. The shooting of Kennedy had nothing to do with "sickness in our society but with sickness in [an] individual."[41]

In his address to the nation, the president followed most of Christian's suggestions but predictably reached for the middle ground. "It would be wrong, it would be self-deceptive, to ignore the connection between that lawlessness and hatred and this act of violence," he said. "It would be just as wrong, and just as self-deceptive, to conclude from this attack that our country itself is sick, that it has lost its balance, that it has lost its sense of direction, even its common decency." A lone and troubled assassin had killed Kennedy, not 200 million Americans. "But those awful events give us ample warning that in a climate of extremism, of disrespect for law, of contempt for the rights of others, violence may bring down the very best among us." He then called for strict gun control legislation, extended Secret Service protection to all the remaining candidates, and announced the formation of a National Commission on the Causes and Prevention of Violence, headed by Milton Eisenhower.[42]

In the days that followed, more sober thoughts began to prevail and the search for a deeper explanation started. In an essay on "Politics and Assassination," *Time* identified the root cause of the violence as industrialization, which had heightened expectations of, and demands for, affluence and equality. Impatience combined with generational and racial conflict had fostered "a charged emotional climate that inflames inherently violent minds." Adding to the heat was the incendiary language of American political discourse, particularly on issues like race, crime, and the war. Lowering the temperature was difficult—it would mean that institutions would have to become more responsive to social needs—but essential, for otherwise "verbal assassination becomes physical assassination." On a practical level, given how the "politics of personality" made it inevitable that candidates would take risks in pursuit of votes, the federal government would have to provide them with better protection and enable them to make more effective use of television, perhaps at public expense. On a moral level, what the nation needed above all was a "national restoration of reason rather than emotion."[43]

Other commentators took a critical look at the glib connections drawn between recent events and past trends. When it came to individual violence, the nation had a homicide rate greater than any other industrialized country. But the murder rate was lower than in the 1930s (though not in the 1940s or 1950s). Moreover, when it came to collective violence none of the urban riots of the 1960s were more deadly than the draft riots of the 1860s or the labor conflicts of the late nineteenth century. And nothing in the contemporary American experience compared to the recent massacres in Indonesia or the Congo. On the basis of data from the past year, hardly a random sample, the nation had a troubling pattern of political assassination and a disturbing level of youth violence. But no clear connection existed between such disparate phenomena as crime, riots, assassination, and protests.[44]

In essence, a new liberal consensus had formed. After the murder of King, Kennedy had proclaimed that "only a cleansing of our whole society can remove this sickness from our souls." But now liberals urged calm and suggested that society was not fatally flawed. Only marginal changes were necessary. Gun control was a vital start.[45] So too was a more careful examination of the impact of television, which brought home nightly the horrors of Vietnam and enabled the average American child between the ages of 5 and 14 to see 13,000 violent deaths. In Hollywood and New York, television executives promised to remove gratuitous violence from their productions. The movie industry, indicated Motion Picture Association President Jack Valenti (formerly of the White House), was eager to cooperate with the Eisenhower Commission and, as a sign of good faith, had prepared a voluntary rating system.[46] A new liberal agenda centered on media violence and gun control was in place.[47] Henceforth liberals would routinely decry the casual violence depicted in popular culture—a position conservatives would eagerly and ironically embrace as their own in the 1990s when school shootings in California and Colorado led to renewed calls for gun control.[48]

But in the meantime, a conservative backlash had crested. One target was the emotional hysteria generated by the press. The *National Review* decried the "orgiastic frenzies" whipped up by "liberal ideologues" and added that "it is these same wailers of Guilt who have promoted the permissive, responsibility-destroying, criminal-coddling, police-hounding, law-eroding ideology that has been a primary stimulus to law-breaking and violence." Conservatives also condemned the idea that America was sick. If public order had declined, it was due to the widespread acceptance of civil disobedience, which was the root cause of the epidemic of murders, riots, protests, and assassinations. Compounding the crisis were individual permissiveness and governmental passivity. "In a civilized nation it is not expected that public figures should be considered proper targets for casual gunmen," charged William F. Buckley. "But in civilized nations of the past it has not been customary for parents to allow their children to do what they feel like; for students to seize their schools and smash their equipment; for police to be ordered to stand by while looters empty stores and arsonists burn down buildings."[49]

In the face of such rhetoric, Humphrey, the presumptive nominee, chose his words with care. "I reject casual or cynical talk about a 'sick society,'" he told the National Press Club on June 20. But the death of Kennedy marked, he later contended, the death of his own candidacy: "I said it and I meant it that the bullet that shot and killed Bobby Kennedy fatally wounded me." Ahead in the polls in late May, his lead over everyone—Kennedy and McCarthy, Nixon and Rockefeller—evaporated. His momentum dissipated. "I think that the people really then turned against us," Humphrey recalled. "I think they thought that all this violence and everything else was a kind of byproduct of the way that the country had been operated, the way it had been managed, the way it had been governed. And I was caught up in that." Had Kennedy lived, he remarked with certainty, a Democrat would have occupied the White House in November.[50]

Humphrey's optimism was predictable but premature. Within two months the whole world would watch as the Chicago police beat, kicked, clubbed, and punched antiwar demonstrators outside the Hilton Hotel while inside the delegates at the Democratic Convention nominated him for president. From Moscow to Tokyo, newspaper reporters and television commentators expressed outrage at the police violence and depicted America as a police state.[51] At first the U.S. media took a similar line. But it soon reversed course, dealing a devastating blow to the Democratic nominee, who appeared helpless and complicit in the face of the latest round of domestic disorder.

III

Anti-war demonstrators comprised the third leg of the law-and-order triad. By the summer of 1968, spokesmen for the right had chosen to portray protesters in the same light as criminals and rioters, as products of the same excessive permissiveness and false tolerance. Conservatives also used the student activists as proof that law and order was not a racist ruse since most of the latter were middle-class whites. Liberals were left to contend, rather weakly, that the antiwar movement likewise showed how public disorder was not solely a racial phenomenon.[52]

At the same time, events in Chicago highlighted other elements at work in the clash between police and protesters. The first was the extent to which a sense of localism and a distrust of distant authority permeated law and order. The second was the extent to which both sides held different definitions and conceptions of public space.[53] Finally, the demonstrators in Chicago, through their dress and behavior, challenged middle-class social norms and moral traditions, adding another dimension to the police reaction. In a sense, then, Chicago was Berkeley writ large—it had the same impact on the presidential campaign as the Free Speech movement had on the gubernatorial campaign in California in 1966.

The Democratic Party chose to hold its convention in Chicago for a number of reasons. The city was in a central location and had submitted the best bid. The party owed Mayor Daley for past services rendered, especially for the Cook County machine's vital role in carrying Illinois for John Kennedy in 1960. And of course Illinois remained a critical state in the electoral calculations for 1968.[54] But of equal if not greater importance was the belief that Daley could and would keep order if the convention were held in his city. "The Convention may be one of our easier problems logistically during the 1968 campaign," Clark reassured Johnson in private in December 1967.[55] In public, Clark was equally sanguine as late as August 1968. "I am confident that the convention in Chicago can and will be held without any significant civil disorders," he told a press briefing.[56] In retrospect, his forecast would prove as misguided—though not as famous—as General William Westmoreland's confident prediction of imminent victory on the eve of Tet.

Clark's optimism would prove misplaced because the antiwar movement was no longer confined to small teach-ins on college campuses. Since 1965 it had grown into massive protests in the streets. In October 1967, demonstrations at the Pentagon and the Lincoln Memorial attracted tens of thousands of participants.[57] In April 1968, the National Mobilization Committee (MOBE) rallied hundreds of thousands of protesters around the country. Little over a week later, an "action faction" at Columbia University led by Students for a Democratic Society (SDS) seized Low Library (an administration building) and held it until the police violently removed them. In response, Tom Hayden called for "two, three, many Columbias."[58]

The student demonstrations coincided with the urban riots that followed King's assassination on April 4. In Chicago, the toll was 11 dead, 90 policemen injured, 162 buildings gutted by fire, 268 businesses and homes looted, 3,120 arrested, and $14 million in property damage. "Why did they do this to me?" asked Daley during a tour of the scarred West Side, demonstrating how he personalized any threat to what he saw as his city. Two days after the riot, in an editorial entitled "Law and Order First," the reactionary *Chicago Tribune* made it clear where it stood: "We hope Mayor Daley will not fall into the same category as the spineless and indecisive mayors who muffed early riot control in . . . Los Angeles and Newark."[59]

Daley would not disappoint. In sadness and frustration, he declared that officers "should have had instructions to shoot arsonists and looters—arsonists to kill and looters to maim and detain." Reaction was swift and furious. The Reverend Jesse Jackson, head of Operation Breadbasket, called it a fascist idea. Clark said the indiscriminate use of deadly force risked a further escalation in urban violence. Chastened, Daley backtracked, claiming he was misquoted. But in the same breath he asserted, seemingly correctly, that on the whole the white public was supportive of his position.[60] Certainly the Chicago police were.

As preparations began for a state of siege, the officers were confident. "If the fight starts, don't expect it to last long," said one, as the 12,000-man force switched to special 12-hour shifts. "We'll win in the first round and there won't be a rematch." The city denied the demonstrators permits to camp in Lincoln Park or to hold protests anywhere near the convention hall. The federal government stationed 7,000 Army troops at nearby bases and airfields. And the state government mobilized more than 5,600 National Guardsmen, with another 5,000 placed on alert.[61] Arrayed against them were at most 10,000 demonstrators—probably no more than 5,000 at any one time—from MOBE, SDS, and the Youth International Party (YIP), which was "led" by Abbie Hoffman and Jerry Rubin.[62]

A major fear among officials was that white radicals would form an alliance with black militants, who would take advantage of the focus on the demonstrators to stage a riot aimed at distracting the police or, worse, devastating the city. Consequently, no expense was spared when it came to surveillance and penetration operations.[63] Between FBI plants, Army Intelligence, and police informants, an estimated one of six demonstrators was an undercover agent. The possibility of police provocation was immense—and rhetorical escalation on both sides increased the likelihood of violence.[64] "We are coming to Chicago," said Hayden, "to vomit on the politics of joy, to expose the secret decisions, upset the nightclub orgies, and face the Democratic Party with its illegitimacy and criminality." Daley would have no part of it. "As long as I am mayor, there will be law and order in Chicago," he stated with conviction. "Nobody is going to take over this city."[65] But Daley's reaction was more complicated than it would first appear.

On one level, the mayor's outlook reflected his profound sense of place. Rooted in the bungalows of Bridgeport, Daley embodied the idea that in Chicago "the neighborhood proclaims the man." The threat posed by the demonstrators was personal and political—it challenged his control of the city—but the two were synonymous in his mind. "No thousands will come to our city and take over our streets, our city and our Convention," was how he put it in January. In August he denied protesters the right to sleep in Lincoln Park with a similar explanation: "[W]hy should we let anyone from outside the city sleep in the park?" Like many conservatives, Daley (at heart a moderate liberal of 1950s vintage) saw himself as the defender of his community and the personification of its values. Both were under siege from "outsiders," from riot agitators, federal judges, government bureaucrats, street criminals, political demonstrators, and arrogant reporters. Thus a common thread in the right's opposition to the antiwar protesters, poverty programs, and Supreme Court verdicts (and later to forced busing) was distrust of elite power and disembodied authority. In reasserting a variant of American populism, conservatives decried the undue and undemocratic power of institutions that were physically distant from the communities of "real" America. They also decried the disproportionate influence of individuals who were philosophically distant from the values of "real" Americans.[66] When from the convention podium Senator Abraham Ribicoff of Connecticut would denounce the Chicago Police's "gestapo tactics," Daley would offer a simple and symbolic retort: "Go home."[67]

On another level, and of equal importance, was the mayor's conception of public space as a concrete and defined piece of public property. For Daley, it was a literal place where local citizens—taxpayers or at least residents with a stake in the community—could interact so long as they followed his rules. In practice, that meant they could sleep in Lincoln Park if they had official approval and kept a low profile. For the demonstrators, public space was a figurative place where individual rights took precedence. In theory, that meant that neither official approval nor a low profile was necessary to use the park. In Chicago, these visions collided. In the heat of the moment, the media saw the clash as, in CBS commentator Eric Sevareid's words, "the litmus test for politicians on the issue of free expression vs. law and order." But for Daley, as one historian has noted, "the state of his streets and his parks and his neighborhoods was far more important than abstract ideas about free speech, free assembly, or even national stability and calm."[68] And so it was.

Beginning on Sunday, August 25, nightly clashes took place in Lincoln Park, where the protesters intended to camp and the police intended to enforce the curfew. On Wednesday afternoon demonstrators in Grant Park threw garbage, rocks, and bottles. They chanted "Dump the Hump," "Fuck the pigs," "Fuck you LBJ," "Hell no, we won't go," and "Ho Ho Ho Chi Minh." As police arrested a young man who had lowered an American flag from a flagpole, they were bombarded by eggs, pieces of concrete, and balloons filled with paint and urine. Enraged, officers waded into the crowd with fists and nightsticks. "The city and the military machinery it has aimed at us won't permit us to protest in an organized fashion," Hayden told the protesters. "Therefore, we must move out of this park in groups throughout the city, and turn this overheated military machine against itself. Let us make sure that if blood flows, it flows all over the city. If they use gas against us, let us make sure they use gas against their own citizens." Hayden would have his wish.[69]

That evening, after constant harassment, the marchers collided in front of the Hilton with two separate groups of angry officers.[70] What happened next was a "police riot" on Michigan Avenue that lasted for 20 minutes under the glare of television cameras. Exhausted after three days of extended duty and faced with mounting verbal and physical provocation, the officers responded with unrestrained and indiscriminate violence, shouting "Kill 'em! Kill 'em!" as they attacked demonstrators and onlookers alike. "The police attacked with tear gas, with Mace, and with clubs, they attacked like a chain saw cutting into wood, the teeth of the saw the edge of their clubs, they attacked like a scythe through grass, lines of 20 and 30 policemen striking out in an arc, their clubs beating, demonstrators fleeing," wrote author Norman Mailer from his hotel room. "Seen from overhead, from the 19th floor, it was like a wind blowing dust or the edge of waves riding foam on the shore."[71]

The police violence had numerous layers of meaning. One was a class resentment of affluent college students who seemed to express contempt for authority and consider themselves above the law. A departmental spokesman expressed surprise that the protesters thought they had a right to run from police or resist arrest. Any kid from the streets knows you don't do that, he said, but "a group of intellectuals from the suburbs of the 1950s and 1960s didn't understand that." Another was vented anger (and possibly repressed envy) at the sexual freedom or ambiguity that long-haired male demonstrators seemed to represent. "You'd better get your fucking ass off that grass or I'll put a beautiful goddam crease in your fucking queer head," a policeman screamed at one point. Later a group of officers shouted at male hippies, "How would you like to fuck a man?" Conflict between the generations was a third layer. The actions of the demonstrators seemed, to many officers, like a rebellion against the authority of both the state and the family. These students had subverted the hierarchy of the patriarchal family structure. Now they would receive a reminder of who was in charge both in the streets and at home. "If they'd gotten beaten like this when they were kids," said one policeman, "they wouldn't be out here starting riots."[72]

The police performance generated mixed reviews from the actors themselves, some of whom saw nothing discreditable in their work. "The force used was the force that was necessary," said Superintendent James Conlisk, noting that no one was killed. A patrolman saw it as a simple matter of following orders. "We were ordered to sweep the street, clear the street, and that's what we did," he declared.[73] But others were more self-critical. "What happened didn't have anything to do with police work," said one officer. An expert witness also voiced criticism. "I don't have any doubt but that it's the worst instance of police misconduct that I have ever witnessed," said Deputy Attorney General Warren Christopher, who was in Chicago to observe events and act as a liaison. "It was perfectly plain to me that from the law enforcement standpoint the Chicago police there in front of the Conrad Hilton Hotel were utterly and completely out of the control of their superior officers."[74]

Critics with ideological perspectives also gave the production mixed reviews. "In the name of law and order," wrote the radical editor of a student newspaper, "the police attacked peaceful demonstrators, putting down their right to assembly and halting their freedom of speech and by brutal attacks on scores of newsmen they attempted to muzzle the press." Conservatives claimed that version of the incident was a "myth." The reality was that the protests were planned, the police were provoked, and the demonstrators were not denied their rights. The entire event was distorted by the press, which manipulated coverage and tried to "gangbang the cops." Not surprisingly, both the left and the right had contempt for the liberal media.[75]

The early reviews offered by liberal commentators were uniformly negative. The police "went on a sustained rampage unprecedented outside the most unreconstructed boondocks of Dixie," wrote *Newsweek*. The demonstrators had provoked the police, *Time* acknowledged. "Yet the Chicago police department responded in a way that could only be characterized as sanctioned mayhem. With billy clubs, tear gas, and Mace, the blue-shirted, blue-helmeted cops violated the civil rights of countless innocent citizens and contravened every accepted code of professional police discipline." Most of the marchers were "idealistic, demonstrably brave, concerned about their country and their fellow men," wrote columnist Tom Wicker of *The New York Times*. "The truth is that these were our children in the streets and the Chicago police beat them up."[76]

But a hasty reevaluation soon followed. The most prominent example was Walter Cronkite of CBS News. Earlier in the convention Cronkite had called the security forces "thugs." Angered, Daley demanded equal time, which the network granted. During a live interview with Cronkite, the mayor defended the police, saying "You don't know the abuse they take. How would you like to stand around all night and be called names not even used in a brothel house?" The most influential figure in broadcast journalism offered little resistance. "The mayor overwhelmed the newsman as if Cronkite were a Republican alderman," commented *Newsweek* accurately.[77]

The reason for the change of heart was simple—the audience had weighed in with its own reviews, which stunned newsrooms across the country. CBS alone received 9,000 letters, 90 percent of which were critical of its coverage. The Gallup Poll reported that by a 56 to 31 percent margin Americans approved of Daley's actions. A Harris Poll showed that 66 percent of those surveyed sided with Daley and the police; only 14 percent felt the demonstrators were denied their lawful rights. Even among those opposed to the war, 50 percent had a negative reaction to the protests and 23 percent reported feelings of "extreme hostility." Unlike Wicker, most Americans apparently felt that it was not *their* children in the streets of Chicago.[78]

The Nixon campaign moved quickly to exploit the situation. In a commercial known as "Failure," the announcer asked, "How can a party that can't unite itself unite the nation?" As frozen images of the chaos in Chicago appeared on the screen, he repeated the message: "How can a party that can't keep order in its own backyard hope to keep order in our 50 states?" One week before the election, an even more controversial ad appeared during the top-rated program *Rowan and Martin's Laugh In*. Called "Convention," it juxtaposed scenes of street protests and wounded soldiers with photos of a smiling Humphrey in Chicago. As the images shook, musical excerpts from "Hot Town" alternated with discordant tones. The

Democrats complained vociferously—shades of "Choice" in 1964—and the Republicans pulled the commercial immediately. But the damage was done.[79]

If Chicago had produced any winners, it was at the extremes. The Yippies rightly viewed Chicago as a success. "We wanted exactly what happened," claimed Rubin. "We wanted to create a situation in which the Chicago police and the Daley administration and the federal government and the United States would self-destruct. We wanted to show that America wasn't a democracy, that the convention wasn't politics."[80] But for the police it was—their rout of the demonstrators had given them clout with the electorate. They have "emerged as an important political force," *The New Republic* warned. "No candidate in America can run from now on without coming to terms with the police."[81]

As the liberal candidate mired in the middle, Humphrey had to come to terms both with what had happened and what it meant to his candidacy. "Look, I'm going to work my tail off for you," Larry O'Brien told him, "but as your [campaign] manager I have to say to you—right now, you're dead." The candidate concurred. "Chicago was a catastrophe," he admitted. "My wife and I went home heartbroken, battered, and beaten." He also left badly behind in the polls and with a campaign that was becalmed, without momentum or money. More importantly, his "silence" on the police behavior threatened to alienate him from the liberal activists, the most enthusiastic elements of the Democratic Party.[82] Yet even as his advisers told him he needed to demonstrate decisiveness, he waffled, perhaps because he was genuinely torn, perhaps because the polls showed that his own followers were split.[83]

In his acceptance speech, Humphrey adopted a moderate and balanced tone. "We do not want a police state," he declared, "but we need a state of law and order, and neither mob violence nor police brutality have any place in America." Then, however, he lashed out at the protesters in a CBS interview:

> I think we ought to quit pretending that Mayor Daley did anything wrong. He didn't. . . . I know what caused these demonstrations. They were planned, premeditated by certain people in this country that feel all they have to do is riot and they'll get their way. They don't want to work through the peaceful process. I have no time for them. The obscenity, the profanity, the filth that was uttered night after night in front of the hotels was an insult to every woman, every

mother, every daughter, indeed every human being, the kind of language that no one would tolerate at all. You'd put anybody in jail for that kind of talk. And yet it went on for day after day. Is it any wonder that the police had to take action?[84]

Later Humphrey would reverse course a third time, suggesting that the police had overreacted, which made his situation worse.[85] "Certainly if we do not make some serious attempt to clear the analytical air, no one is going to believe our tired 'plague on both your houses' rhetoric," protested one aide. "Those who oppose repression will not believe us because of our seeming support of Mayor Daley. . . . And the 'law and order' crowd is not going to vote for us anyhow. . . . At present we are taking the position best calculated to alienate everyone."[86] As the presidential campaign shifted into high gear, the political dilemma for Humphrey would grow more acute as the political climate grew more hostile.

9.

Law and Order Triumphant

"Law and order," reported *Time* in August on the eve of the Democratic Convention, "now looms as the No. 1 issue of 1968, even overshadowing a war that keeps more than 500,000 American servicemen in combat in Southeast Asia." By October the newsmagazine maintained that law and order had "virtually anesthetized the controversy over Vietnam."[1] Many subsequent accounts of the election have, however, emphasized the role of the war. "Nothing is clearer," states one popular history, "than the imperative that an account of the politics of 1968 must start with Vietnam, the progress of which dominated the struggle for the Presidency from first to last."[2] But a close look at media opinion and anecdotal impressions—as well as archival evidence and confidential analyses from political experts in all camps and at all levels—indicates that law and order was the decisive issue of the fall campaign.[3]

The impact of Vietnam was ambiguous for two reasons. First, although voters generally ranked the war as the most critical issue facing the nation, they also indicated—with the exception of liberals and the young—that Vietnam was a distant, impersonal concern. By contrast, private polls commissioned by the Democratic Party indicated that law and order was an immediate, personal priority with virtually all Americans.[4] Second, most voters could not distinguish between the candidates, both of whom pledged to bring the war to an end. Even in late October, survey data led the President's pollster to conclude that Vietnam was "cutting for neither Humphrey or Nixon."[5] Nor was inflation—an important political issue and economic problem by 1968—providing a significant edge to either party. By contrast, when it came to law and order most Americans had a clear idea where the two men stood—and by a considerable margin preferred the conservative Republican to the liberal Democrat.[6]

But in the aftermath of the Democratic Convention, the candidate who most effectively articulated the visceral demand for law and order was George Wallace. He would help ensure that the issue would dominate the election.[7] He would also leave an indelible impression on American politics for years to come. Like most third-party candidates, however, his challenge would eventually fade, suggesting that he was a flawed messenger and that there were limits to how far most Americans would go in the name of law and order. Wallace's decline, however, was small consolation to his Democratic opponent.

Behind in the polls and hindered by an image of softness, Humphrey staged a desperate comeback, pledging to attack the root causes of crime and provide Americans with "order and justice." Nixon countered with a promise to restore order without violence—and ridiculed the Democratic agenda. The terms of debate had changed little since 1964. But the unrest of the past three years had transformed the political and cultural landscape, enhancing the appeal of the conservative platform and eroding the credibility of the liberal program. In the end, Humphrey was—like Johnson before him—unable to articulate a popular position or close the critical gap on law and order. It is doubtful, however, that any candidate could have. The result was a narrow victory for Nixon but a crushing defeat for liberalism.

I

The candidacy of George Wallace was a vehicle for the hopes and fears of whites on the lower margins of the middle class. His core comprised Goldwater voters in the South and union members in the North. The southern bloc consisted of rural white Protestants. The northern bloc consisted of urban ethnic Catholics. Almost three-quarters of Wallace supporters wanted to halt racial progress, but almost 70 percent also expressed anxiety about urban riots and street crime—a reflection of their close physical proximity to the threat, particularly in the North.[8] To them Wallace offered a more brutal form of law and order than Nixon—rollback versus containment in the words of one historian—as he vowed to restore personal security by any means necessary.[9]

Wallace deliberately courted the police.[10] Days after the chaos in Chicago, he gave the keynote address at the annual gathering of the Fraternal Order of Police. Greeted by campaign banners and buttons, he was in his element, giving the officers an outlet for all of the rage and frustration and anxiety that had spilled from the fists and clubs and nightsticks at the Chicago Convention. "People cannot walk the streets at night without fear of bodily harm," he said. The cause of this crisis, he argued, was international communism, organized in the Soviet Union, aided by the Supreme Court, and abetted by "bearded beatnik bureaucrats" in Washington.[11] Standing ovation followed standing ovation.

In speeches Wallace conveyed a clear sense of malice and menace—a southern style of political rhetoric that had rarely surfaced in national politics before then. With little or no hesitation, he countenanced the deliberate use of massive retaliation against rioters and protesters. "We don't have riots in Alabama," he said at one rally. "They start a riot down there, first one of 'em to pick up a brick gets a bullet in the brain, that's all. And then you walk over to the next one and say, 'All right, pick up a brick. We just want to see you pick up one of them bricks, now!'" If a riot began, he vowed to halt it by shooting arsonists and looters first, and asking questions later. One of his most popular lines was his promise that a demonstrator who laid down in front of his car would never do it again.[12]

The extreme rhetoric fostered a gender gap as many women found Wallace—and his running mate, Air Force General Curtis LeMay—too threatening for their tastes.[13] But it had considerable appeal to alienated men in organized labor. In mid-summer, straw polls showed the Alabama Democrat decisively in the lead among auto workers in New Jersey, textile workers in the Carolinas, and steel workers in Indiana. One reason was that many whites saw blacks as a threat to their employment security and union seniority. But law and order was another reason. "The problem in the streets is more important" than workplace issues, said one unionist. "Wallace seems to be the man who can straighten the country out."[14]

To counter that image, the AFL-CIO leadership struck back hard, pouring money, manpower, and mailings into the campaign.[15] Convinced that Nixon was a greater threat than Wallace, it warned members that a vote for the latter would only aid the former. Union officials also put out the word that Alabama was not hospitable to the interests of workers, even though the governor had vetoed right-to-work legislation. "We are making a particular effort to go after Wallace," reported the director of the Committee on Political Education (COPE). "We are staying away from the civil rights area all together." It was an implicit concession that on law and order the unions could do little for the vice president.[16]

But Wallace was less of a threat to the Democrats—and more of a threat to the Republicans—than he first appeared. Most disaffected Democrats, Humphrey aides soon realized, would vote for Nixon rather than Humphrey if Wallace were not in the race.[17] For their part, Nixon aides quickly understood that Wallace threatened to siphon far more potential voters from the Republicans in the South than from the Democrats in the North. Even more critically, Wallace might force Nixon to the right, damaging his efforts to appeal to moderates in the border states and the industrial North. Or he might throw the election into the House of Representatives, which the Democrats controlled. Ultimately, Nixon adopted a two-pronged strategy. One was to appeal to Wallace sympathizers in the South—especially the Upper South and the border states—not to waste their vote (a traditional pitch to backers of third-party candidates). The other was to give them a reason to join Nixon by moving to co-opt the issue of law and order.[18]

A Nixon interview in Dallas illustrates how the candidate made his pitch. First he defended Wallace supporters against charges of racism. Next Nixon emphasized how he shared their anxieties. "I feel just as strongly about what has happened to law and order in this country as does George Wallace," he said. Then he sidestepped the question of whether Wallace employed racist rhetoric. "I would have to ask his listeners whether or not they think so," replied Nixon, careful not to alienate anyone. "I am not going to get into this business of charging that George Wallace or Hubert Humphrey is basically racist or something else."[19]

That Wallace harbored racist sentiments, however, seems beyond dispute. In a section of Los Angeles known as "Little Dixie," he criticized liberal "pseudo-intellectuals" who rationalized criminal behavior by claiming that "the killer didn't get any watermelon to eat when he was 10 years old."[20] On another occasion, he asked a reporter, "Did you see those women in there? They were hysterical about their children. Folks are mad about law and order and about schools. . . . Race mixing doesn't work. Show me a place where it's worked."[21]

It also seems beyond dispute that some of his followers were racists. "George Wallace sure told them niggers a thing or two," recalled an elderly Italian man who had attended a sold-out campaign rally at Madison Square Garden. A cabdriver in Baltimore offered a similar view: "I like his stand on 'law and order.' You know—the niggers."[22] But racial animosity was not the main motivation for many of his supporters. "[Wallace] stands for what this country is built on," one white male told an NBC reporter. "Law and order."[23] Former Press Secretary Bill Moyers, now a political commentator with ABC News, attended a Texas rally and found that the crowd was not racist or even conservative. "They were just plain folks, who have voted Democratic ever since Franklin Roosevelt saved their farms and their homes and put them to work during the Depression," he reported.[24]

For those Democrats and others, the appeal of Wallace was due to more than race.[25] Beset by falling real income as well as rising street crime and civil unrest, they were attracted to his populist positions. As governor, Wallace had signed progressive housing legislation. As candidate, he had crafted a platform that accommodated the New Deal, calling for the expansion of social security and health care. His opposition to welfare and busing, moreover, usually centered on the self-evident need for local control and the self-interested role of distant elites, the "pointy-headed intellectuals" who designed or administered social programs to the detriment of blue-collar workers, civil-service employees, and small-business owners. Finally, his campaign subsisted on small donations and relied on enthusiastic volunteers to collect signatures to qualify for the ballot in all 50 states.[26]

Wallace would also claim consistently—and correctly to a point—that most blacks wanted law and order (by which they meant better protection and more respect from the police) as much as whites.[27] "It is a sad day in our country when you cannot speak out against the destruction of cities, burning, arson, looting, and murder, and I'm not talking about race because the overwhelming majority of people of all races in this country are against this breakdown of law and order," Wallace told Cronkite. Later, when asked on "Face the Nation" whether he had blacks in mind when he spoke of "crime in the streets" and "violence in the cities," Wallace had a ready reply: "Oh, no, I am not talking about Negroes. I am talking about law violators . . . anarchists . . . criminals . . . Communists . . . activists in the country."[28]

Between the spring and fall, Wallace's support doubled, reaching a peak of 21 percent in early October. But then it started to erode in the face of Democratic attacks and Republican overtures. Wallace's intemperate remarks were also a factor. By late October, the percentage who thought he was a racial extremist had soared from 51 to 69 percent. More importantly, the percentage who thought he would handle law and order well had fallen dramatically from 53 to 21 percent. On Election Day, Wallace received only 13.5 percent of the vote.[29]

It was, however, still an impressive total for a third-party candidate—the best showing since Robert La Follette in 1924 (and until Ross Perot in

1992). Wallace carried the Deep South (Alabama, Georgia, Louisiana, and Mississippi) in addition to Arkansas. He was second in the Carolinas and Tennessee. Of his nine million votes, eight percent came from outside the South (compared to less than one percent of Strom Thurmond's "Dixiecrat" vote in 1948).[30] In the end, 1968 was a close call. If Wallace had carried North Carolina or Tennessee (he lost both to Nixon by tiny margins), a shift of less than one percent from Nixon to Humphrey in Ohio or New Jersey would have put the election in the House. But it is probably incorrect to state that the Alabama Democrat denied the Minnesota Democrat victory. To be sure, with Wallace out of the race, Humphrey probably would have won Ohio, Illinois, New Jersey, Missouri, Wisconsin, and Kentucky. However, Texas would have gone to Nixon, who could have claimed the election without any of the other states.[31]

In any event, Wallace had made a lasting impact despite his fading finish. He had guaranteed that law and order would dominate the fall campaign. He had demonstrated that a sizable bloc of voters no longer felt that either party truly addressed their fears. And he had shown that too extreme a message—or messenger—mattered. Like Goldwater, Wallace was easy to discredit when it came to law and order. Unlike in 1964, however, the issue would not subside in 1968. Most white Americans wanted to halt the violent disorder, but remained unconvinced that brutal repression was the answer.[32] It was for those voters that Nixon and Humphrey would vie.

II

In mid-September, the top officials of the Humphrey campaign gathered for a confidential strategy session. "I don't think there's any realization in this country of where Humphrey stands on law and order—that we're intensely interested in preserving law and order," said Larry O'Brien, chair of the Democratic National Committee (DNC), who added that "we haven't gotten to the gut." Liberal lawyer and lobbyist James Rowe offered a note of caution: "We can't compete with Nixon and Wallace on law and order, but we're going too far on the 'justice' emphasis. Let's emphasize 'order and justice.'" However, a third official cautioned that any talk of "order" alienated liberals. "If the election depends on law and order," he said bluntly, "we won't win."[33]

But law and order was, in the words of Evron Kirkpatrick, Humphrey's chief opinion analyst, "the major issue, no doubt." Citing private surveys that canvassed more voters than public polls, he reported in late September that "Humphrey is soft in the area of law and order, and this softness is hurting him more than anything else. Crime prevention is at the top of what people—as many as 89 percent—want." In early October, Kirkpatrick restated his position. "There is no doubt that this perceived 'soft' position on law and order is hurting Humphrey far more than any position he does or does not take on bombing pauses," he emphasized. "Strong, immediate, repeated measures should be taken to communicate Humphrey's understanding of the importance of order and his determination to maintain and extend it; and his detestation of crime and criminals, agitators, radicals, and disrupters of the social order. This should have the highest priority, because we now know that he is not getting through on this terribly important issue."[34]

Internal reports from Democratic insiders confirmed Kirkpatrick's assessment. From Tennessee came word that law and order—not Vietnam—was the main issue. From Florida, Mississippi, Maryland, and Texas came similar sentiments. "It is vitally important that the vice president come through strongly for law and order, [for] crime prevention," said an Illinois official. "He must make it crystal clear that he will not tolerate people, no matter who they are, resorting to violence and rioting." Even in progressive and homogeneous states, law and order was the cry. "Humphrey must be absolutely firm in his insistence on an end to rioting and violence," a Wisconsin survey found. "The people here are clear. Stop it. Period."[35]

But Humphrey could never find a firm and consistent voice on law and order. Although he agonized in private, trying to reconcile what his head and his heart told him, in public he could not express a clear conviction. In a sense, Humphrey's failure marked the culmination of Johnson's failure the past four years. Once again, liberals were unable to draw meaningful distinctions between race and crime, crime and riots, civil disobedience and civil disorder, lawful and unlawful protest. Once again, they were unable to sell social programs as a remedy for social unrest. The failure was not, however, entirely their own. With public anxiety over street crime, urban riots, and political demonstrations at a fever pitch, the liberal defeat was virtually inevitable, especially given the broad appeal of the conservative vision of law and order.

Humphrey tried to show voters that he understood their fears, but he could rarely find the right words or tone. "I believe the number one issue that troubles the American people today is how you can have both civil order and civil justice," he told Frank Reynolds of ABC News in July. "I think what the American people want is a law-abiding country." Reynolds then asked whether Humphrey believed that law and order was the most important issue. "There are two kinds of politics," replied the vice president. "There is the politics of fear and despair, which I do not indulge in, and then there is the politics of hope and inspiration. That is more my kind."[36] His kind would encounter serious setbacks in the coming months.

The nature of the Democratic coalition limited Humphrey's options.[37] A substantial majority of white voters rejected the idea that reducing poverty would restore law and order. They also wanted to see looters shot. But Humphrey could not co-opt either position (even if he had felt so inclined) because Jews and blacks, two core constituencies, were so adamant on both. For example, African Americans (22 percent of the Democratic base) opposed the use of deadly force against looters by a decisive margin. The vice president was trapped. Move to the left and he would antagonize the majority. Move to the right and he would alienate his base. Stay where he was and he would get caught in the crossfire.[38]

But Humphrey compounded the danger by repeatedly blurring the distinction between crime, riots, and demonstrations. Following the assassination of Robert Kennedy, he said that "violence, crime, looting, burning cannot be condoned and must be stopped." He added that the "escalation of protest" had at times degenerated into "an escalation of violence." His casual conflation of disparate phenomena earned him rebukes from supporters.[39] Aides also wondered why Humphrey gave aid and comfort to the conservatives with his rhetoric. Arresting civil rights activists was sometimes unavoidable, noted a speechwriter, "but that should not lead us to confuse civil rights militancy with 'violence in the streets.'" Another official noted that such rhetoric "confuses the issue and plays into the hands of the 'law and order' claque." David Ginsburg, executive director of the Kerner Commission and a close advisor, informed Humphrey that "to confuse urban riots—stemming from problems of poverty and race (Newark and Detroit)—with dissent from our policies in Vietnam (Chicago) is grotesque and evil."[40]

The quagmire of race and crime also posed a challenge for Humphrey, who knew he had to decouple the conservative connection. Whenever possible, he would substitute the word "poor" for "black." In front of white audiences, he would stress that the problem was "American crime, not black crime, not white crime." In front of black audiences, he would emphasize that the "poor" wanted security as much or more than the affluent.[41] "Law and order is something desperately needed in the ghetto by the poor man," Humphrey told a television interviewer, noting that blacks were five times as likely as whites to be murdered, four times as likely to be robbed. Moreover, although minorities committed a disproportionate number of crimes, few were interracial.[42] With the liberal image of black as victim, Humphrey thus sought to counter or balance the conservative image of black as criminal.

In Humphrey's view, social order and social justice were complementary. Conceding that there was not always a "direct relationship between poverty and lawlessness," he nonetheless contended that there was a "causal relationship between poverty, deprivation . . . and crime." For every prison Nixon vowed to build, Humphrey pledged to build new schools, "a new city and a new neighborhood." He also promised to enforce the law and implement the recommendations of the Kerner Commission.[43] At the same time, he maintained that law and order was necessary to protect the quality of life for all and promote an assault on the roots of crime. "Americans have a right to personal safety," he declared, as well as a right to "a new freedom from fear and the constant threat of violence."[44] The phrase "freedom from fear" was one of Nixon's personal favorites, an indication of Humphrey's growing desperation.

The vice president himself recognized one source of the desperation. "The blue-collar worker, the lower-middle income white feels that the government has no interest in him," he wrote to campaign manager Orville Freeman. "[He feels] that the Great Society programs are only oriented to the black man and to the poorest of the poor." White workers were frustrated at how the federal government seemed to squander their tax dollars on lawless minorities. "This is the key," the vice president added. "There isn't any doubt that this matter will win or lose the election." Aware of the wide rift between white workers (another important Democratic constituency) and the Humphrey campaign, Freeman recalled how "we wrote speech after speech and planned program after program, trying to hit a balance where we could bridge that gap and we never succeeded."[45]

In an effort to bridge the gap, Humphrey relentlessly advocated federal assistance to local departments to improve the pay, training, and equipment of the police. It was time, he declared, to replace talk with money. On the whole, however, his crime-control package won him limited support among law enforcement and the general public.[46] Part of the problem was that Humphrey had a hard time countering Nixon's assaults. When the Republican nominee criticized *Escobedo* and *Miranda*, the vice president asked how a candidate who "denounces the Supreme Court, which is the center of justice in this country," could claim to advocate law and order. The response was ineffective, which Humphrey privately acknowledged in a letter to Attorney General Ramsey Clark.[47] By contrast, when Nixon blamed the rise in crime on Clark, Humphrey noted that of the 15 states with crime rates above the national average, 13 were governed by Republicans. "Crime is committed by criminals," he stated correctly in a clever twist on a conservative argument, "not by governors, Republican or Democrat, or by attorney generals, Republican or Democrat."[48] But by then Clark's image as soft on crime was already firmly fixed in the minds of most Americans.[49]

The climax of Humphrey's efforts to wrest law and order from the conservative stranglehold came in a televised address in mid-October. Careful preparation went into the speech. In response to a personal request from O'Brien, Califano ignored the President's explicit instructions and slipped into DNC headquarters to offer comments on a draft. He and his staff recommended, among others, the deletion of black from "black riots"; the addition of "black and white" to the section which described how afraid Americans were; the substitution of the phrase "The Constitution forbids a national police force" with "Americans don't want a national police force"; and the insertion of a sentence reading "the few students who have tried to tear down some of the nation's great universities are not black and not poor."[50] The revised speech met with immediate and general acceptance because, as a Humphrey staffer noted, it avoided "offending any important political group which we now count as supporters—particularly the Negroes. The political fallout resulting from the reference to the phrase 'Black riots' . . . would be severely damaging politically."[51]

The political impact of the broadcast was nevertheless small, in part because it contained little that was exciting or innovative. Most of the "new" programs Humphrey endorsed, including improved street lighting, drug rehabilitation centers, gun control, corrections reform, and a ten-fold increase in funding for the Safe Streets Act, were old ideas repackaged. Some—like the creation of local "Councils of Civil Peace" to curtail riots—seemed inadequate at face value.[52] Another problem of equal or greater importance was that Humphrey had neither the resources nor the personality to mount an effective media campaign.[53]

In the final weeks, the campaign aired as many commercials as it could afford. But the style and substance of the ads diluted their impact. In a typical spot, Humphrey simply faced the camera and, speaking rapidly, promised a "Marshall Plan" for America's cities. With florid rhetoric, he became almost a liberal caricature. "We can find the path to American change, not to the left or to the right or even to the center, but up," he said. "By reaching for the stars, we will at least get out of the slums." The script left him sounding more like a disk jockey than a presidential candidate.[54] Even surveys conducted by the Humphrey campaign revealed that, in comparison to his Republican rival, the vice president seemed less likable, less sincere, less believable, less experienced, and less statesmanlike.[55]

The Humphrey camp remained optimistic, however. "Nixon has all the Republican votes he is going to get," wrote one official, who outlined what the campaign had to do to retain wavering supporters and attract undecided voters. The strategy was to avoid law and order altogether since a "hard" position would alienate the former and a "soft" position would antagonize the latter. In that category were millions of middle-aged, middle-income, blue-collar, white women. Although they tended to find Wallace too extreme, they also tended to see Humphrey as too weak—an alternative and unexpected manifestation of the gender gap. The candidate should therefore trumpet the historic accomplishments of the Democratic Party and warn of the economic consequences of a Republican victory. Above all, Humphrey should "not talk about anti-poverty programs, racial integration, civil rights, welfare handouts, or social justice." He should also "stay out of the ghettos and away from minorities."[56]

As the campaign moved into the stretch drive, Humphrey adhered to the strategy in his prepared remarks.[57] In the final week, during rallies before mostly blue-collar crowds in the Midwest, he made little reference to the War on Poverty or law and order. Instead, he spoke about trust, the economy, and what the Democratic Party stood for in comparison to the Republican Party. When questioned, he hewed to established themes, although he acknowledged for the first time that he would replace Clark as attorney general (Nixon had already promised that he would). Humphrey also was noncommittal when asked if he would replace Hoover after the election (Nixon had already declared that he would not).[58]

On November 3, in suburban Levittown, New York, Humphrey returned briefly to law and order for the last time. "Campaign oratory never caught a criminal," he said, rehashing his police program. "Bumper stickers won't help your local police. I know how to do it. I've done it. And I will take action when I am your President."[59] He would never get the chance. Two days later, despite defections by Jewish and labor voters, he lost to Nixon by less than one-half of one percentage point.[60] The Republican nominee had avenged 1960 and reversed 1964 in large part because a significant majority of white Americans believed that, unlike his Democratic opponent, he could and would restore authority, stability, and security, that under his leadership the nation would at last have law and order.

III

In mid-September, Nixon's position was almost the inverse of Humphrey's. Ahead in the polls and with his base secure, the Republican had no need for desperate measures. Powered by a well-oiled and well-funded campaign machine, he could afford to remain above the fray, making selected appearances and using television commercials to broadcast his message of law and order. Positioning himself between the perceived punitiveness of Wallace and permissiveness of Humphrey, Nixon reassured voters that his was the voice of reason and restraint.[61] Making no effort to distinguish between street crime, political protests, and urban riots, Nixon charged that liberals had promised a Great Society but had delivered great disorder. In the heated environment of fall 1968, it was a persuasive message.

Nixon tailored his argument to appeal to middle-class white voters, to the "Forgotten Americans, those who did not indulge in violence, those who did not break the law, people who pay their taxes and go to work, people who send their children to school, who go to their churches, people who are not haters, people who love this country, and because they love this country are angry about what has happened to America."[62] For the most part, those citizens lived in the suburbs. As aide Leonard Garment noted, "The people living in communities ringing the big cities are anxious to contain the spread of violence out of the urban core." The candidate eagerly added to the anxiety. "If we allow [the crime wave] to happen, then the city jungle will cease to be a metaphor," he said. "It will become a barbaric reality and the brutal society that now flourishes in the core cities . . . will annex the affluent suburbs."[63]

Two tactical goals took priority. The first was to neutralize Wallace. Speechwriter Ray Price recommended a direct assault. A young aide named Kevin Phillips, who would soon make a name for himself with his influential book, *The Emerging Republican Majority*, disagreed. He argued that Wallace would soon fade and advocated an indirect approach, which Nixon ultimately chose. When reporters asked if he and Wallace held similar views on law and order, Nixon demurred except to say that he had a "specific" and "responsible" program for "stopping the rising crime rate and for reestablishing freedom from fear."[64]

The second goal was to broaden Nixon's support. The candidate, wrote John Sears, the national director for political research, "must continue to occupy all available ground on law and order." Humphrey would first seek to consolidate his base and then try to "label us as warmongers, fanatical on law and order and Cold War perpetuators." The objective was to deflect attention from the White House record. "Above all," Sears warned, recalling what had happened to Dewey in 1948, "we must not get so sensitive about 'highroading' it that we fall into the trap of providing issues for the Democrats to campaign against us on unless we are absolutely sure that we are on the popular side of them."[65]

To capture the "popular side" on law and order, Nixon gave a major address on CBS and NBC radio in late September entitled "Order and Justice Under Law." The speech reinforced and highlighted themes that Nixon had already raised and would continue to emphasize throughout the campaign. In forceful and plain language, it outlined the extent of the crime crisis; denounced violent demonstrators; attacked the idea that America was a "sick society"; rejected poverty as the major or sole cause of civil unrest; accused the administration and Clark of laxity; denied that law and order was a racial slogan; criticized the Supreme Court for favoring the rights of defendants; offered a series of common-sense crime-control proposals; and stressed that, fundamentally, America needed a revival of traditional morality to restore respect for law and decency. In sum, it was the standard conservative version of law and order, new and improved (or at least updated) for 1968.[66]

In the broadcast, Nixon reacted to the idea that America was a "sick society" with these words: "We're sick, all right, but not in the way they mean. We are sick of what has been allowed to go on in this nation for too long." In particular, it was time to end violent protests like those at Columbia University and the Democratic Convention, which had no place in a popular democracy. Nixon also expressed his contempt for the liberal idea that poverty caused crime—and, by extension, the Johnson administration's apparent faith that social programs could restore social order. Although he conceded that poverty was a "contributing factor," he asserted that the nation was richer than ever before, with a more equitable distribution of wealth than any other country. Yet "we have more crime and violence than ever before," with delinquents in the suburbs and rioters in the cities. "If poverty were eliminated tomorrow," he concluded, "the violent and the criminal and the depraved would not disappear."[67] Later he claimed that Humphrey's promise to implement the Kerner Commission recommendations would cost $15 billion and his "Marshall Plan" for the cities would cost $30 billion—figures Humphrey disputed but which carried increasing weight with middle-class white voters upset by increased taxes and decreased security.[68]

Nixon's favorite political target was Clark, who had no direct responsibility for crime control but served as a useful symbol of supposed administration permissiveness and softness. When the attorney general suggested that the "crime wave" was more rhetorical than real, Nixon replied that the problem was real and the result of Democratic disrespect for the law. In particular, he savaged Clark's opposition to capital punishment and government surveillance (except in cases of national security). Nixon claimed that the death penalty would have a substantial deterrent effect and that wiretapping was a crucial weapon in the fight against organized crime, which he contended had a significant impact on street crime.[69] Nixon also promised to dismiss Clark, who could do little but claim that his views were misunderstood and that calls for law and order rested on racism.[70]

The Nixon campaign consistently rejected that assertion. "Nothing could be less true," stated Nixon, whom speechwriter Patrick Buchanan advised to go on the offensive. "It is a kind of reverse racism," he counseled the candidate, "to suggest that talk about law and order is anti-Negro because it implies that Negroes are opposed to law and order—this is an outrageous calumny and indeed two recent polls [in *The New York Times* and the *Daily News*] indicate clearly that crime is the major concern of Negroes in our largest cities." Repeatedly, Nixon would follow the advice. "Law and order is not racism," he declared. "Law and order with justice is what Negroes want, what they need, and they have an even greater stake in it than do whites, because they are the main victims of disorder and of illegal activities."[71] Ironically, Nixon thus defended himself by using the liberal argument against the conservative insinuation that race and crime were related.

Nixon was less restrained when it came to the Supreme Court, although he was careful to attack the court's decisions (such as *Miranda*) rather than the court itself. "It is the court's duty to protect legitimate rights," he declared in late September, "but not to raise unreasonable obstacles to enforcement of the law." But he became more critical and less judicious as the race tightened in late October. During an appearance in Ohio, Nixon related how the Supreme Court had set free on a "technicality" a confessed criminal who had robbed and murdered a Philadelphia cabdriver. "Some of our courts have gone too far in their decisions weakening the peace forces as against the criminal forces in the United States of America," he said, pledging to appoint justices "who will respect the Constitution."[72] Of course, the justices whose views of the Constitution most offended him were appointees of President Eisenhower, whom Nixon had loyally served for eight years as vice president.

Equally ironic was that most of Nixon's crime-control proposals were either pale imitations or minor refinements of Johnson administration initiatives. Like Clark and Humphrey, he was a strong supporter of police professionalism, including a National Academy of Law Enforcement. He also called for a National Coordinating Center for anti-crime organizations and a series of local town hall conferences on crime prevention. And he advocated modest prison reform, with a greater emphasis on rehabilitation, as well as moderate gun control, with states free to set their own provisions according to federal guidelines. Nixon acknowledged the limited nature of his proposals. "They are the tools of order," he said. "They are not the sources of civic order." What was essential was moral leadership from Washington and moral regeneration at the grassroots. "The law on the books cannot replace the law in the heart," he concluded. "The sources of moral and civic order are in the family, the church, the school, and the community."[73]

On the whole, Nixon's version of law and order was similar to what Goldwater had presented in 1964. But in 1968 the political climate was far more receptive to the conservative message. Other, less significant, differences also existed. First, Nixon maintained a relative silence on urban riots, perhaps because by then they were imprinted on everyone's minds, perhaps because the anticipated summer unrest never materialized, and perhaps because his advisers were split on how to handle them.[74] Second, in 1968 the Republicans made skillful and lavish use of media. The campaign spent almost $12 million on radio and television, including last-minute buys in key states like California, Texas, Illinois, Michigan, Ohio, and Pennsylvania.[75] In the end, the televised images conveyed far more powerfully than spoken words both the "New Nixon" and his stand on law and order.

The "New Nixon" seemed calm, cool, and collected—a relaxed and statesmanlike figure in comparison to the frenetic Humphrey of 1968 and the frantic Nixon of 1960. Whether the image was real or artificial remains a source of debate.[76] In any event, Nixon himself saw the need for a change in focus if not personality. "I spent too much time in the last campaign on substance and too little time on appearance," he admitted. "I paid too much attention to what I was going to say, and too little to how I would look."[77] He would not make the same mistake again. With the assistance of advertising executives and political advisers, he devised a political strategy that bore little resemblance to the "New Politics" of Robert Kennedy and Eugene McCarthy.

In a seminal memo, aide H. R. Haldeman wrote to Nixon that "The time has come for political campaigning—its techniques and strategies—to move out of the dark ages and into the brave new world of the omnipresent eye." The old-style approach of six speeches a day sandwiched between and around hours of hand-shaking at the factory gate no longer made sense. The new-style strategy would feature one choreographed message a day, released in varied and calculated ways through "offhand" remarks, "confidential" interviews, and colorful activities that should appear "unscheduled and spontaneous." The candidate should also have a standard speech so the campaign could control the "lead" as reported by the press. Haldeman would later seek to downplay the influence of his brief, but it became Nixon's bible and the blueprint for future campaigns.[78]

The media campaign Haldeman devised served two functions. First, it enabled Nixon to convey the impression that he was in control and in touch through tightly scripted and carefully edited panel discussions with "ordinary citizens."[79] Second, it permitted the Republicans to portray law and order in graphic terms that belied the restrained rhetoric that dominated the candidate's public utterances. Substantively, the commercials broke little new ground as they restated familiar themes. In a spot entitled "Wrong Road," for example, viewers saw photos of poor blacks and whites, in rural and urban settings. At the same time, they heard Nixon denounce a litany of liberal measures. "We have reaped from these programs an ugly harvest of frustration, violence, and failure," he intoned. Now it was time to "quit pouring billions of dollars into programs that have failed."[80] The logic was dubious, since the Great Society might have kept the crime rate from rising even faster. But to a large number of white Americans the conservative argument was extremely persuasive.

The ads also repeated slogans Nixon had made familiar since his acceptance speech at the Republican Convention. "Freedom from fear is a basic right of every American," he said in one commercial. "We must restore it." In another, he stated that "I pledge to you that the wave of crime is not going to be the wave of the future in America." In a third, Nixon declared that dissent was necessary. "But in a system of government that provides for peaceful change there is no cause that justifies a resort to violence." Then he turned liberalism's moral claim and greatest achievement on its head: "Let us recognize that the first civil right of every American is to be free from domestic violence." The tag line on every ad left little doubt about what was at stake: "THIS TIME VOTE LIKE YOUR WHOLE WORLD DEPENDED ON IT."[81]

Stylistically, however, the commercials broke new ground by creating a series of visual images that tapped directly into the fear and anxiety felt by many Americans. One depicted in stark terms the gendered symbol of woman as victim. As an announcer recited crime statistics, a middle-aged, middle-class, white woman walked nervously down a deserted city street as darkness fell.[82] Others offered collages of chaos by juxtaposing still photos with atonal music. The collages depicted scenes (often interwoven) of street crime, urban riots, and student protests, using dramatic pictures of a rifle, a switchblade, a hypodermic needle inserted into an arm, a policeman silhouetted against a wall, bloody demonstrators in handcuffs, national guardsmen firing tear gas, and firemen crouched before a blazing fire. The impact was powerful and unsettling. As a journalist noted, the combined effect of the images, words, and sounds was "the whole being greater than the sum of its parts."[83] The same was true of law and order itself.

On the whole, the Nixon campaign ran smoothly and powerfully. But in the last weeks of October Humphrey rallied the faithful and recruited independents by invoking the New Deal heritage and scoring Nixon's lofty refusal to debate him. In the final days, as his lead dwindled, the "cool" Nixon disappeared and the combative Nixon reappeared. On a last-minute trip to Texas, for example, he made a veiled appeal to Mexican Americans. "They have not been rioting," he said, in implicit contrast to African Americans. "They have not been breaking the laws." How unfair it was, he added, that "the wheel that squeaks gets the grease."[84] Suddenly, the ghosts of 1960 loomed.

In the end, however, Nixon won the election by a narrow margin. Although his electoral college margin was substantial (302 votes to 181 for Humphrey and 45 for Wallace), his popular plurality was less than 250,000 votes out of 68 million cast. Not since Woodrow Wilson in 1912 had a president received as small a share of the popular vote (43 percent) as Nixon had.[85] The defeat for liberalism was nonetheless of epic proportions. In 1964, Johnson had received 43.1 million votes, 61 percent of the total. In 1968, Humphrey received 31.2 million votes, 43 percent of the total. Almost 12 million voters, including 5 million from urban areas, had either abstained or defected to Wallace or Nixon, who together claimed almost 57 percent of the popular vote.[86] The victory for conservatism was convincing. The triumph of law and order was complete.

Epilogue

The rise of law and order signaled an end to the brief era of liberal ascendancy. By 1968, amid a charged climate of danger and disorder, the conservative movement had capitalized on the pervasive sense that America was coming apart. The reign of law and order was, however, short-lived. In the two subsequent decades, the issue receded from presidential politics even as violent crime rose and the Republican Party assumed a virtual "lock" on the White House. In 1988, law and order resurfaced when supporters of Republican candidate George Bush used the brutal crimes of a black inmate in a furlough program to discredit the Democratic nominee, Massachusetts Governor Michael Dukakis. And in 1992, Arkansas Governor Bill Clinton raised the issue during the primaries to bolster his credentials as a "New Democrat" and distract attention from his extramarital affairs. But throughout the 1970s and 1980s, most conservatives on the national stage shifted their focus away from personal security in response to economic decline, political scandal, and international conflict in Afghanistan and Iran.

The decline of law and order in presidential races after 1968 was due to two main factors. First, the social landscape had changed. With new issues like Watergate and "stagflation" emerging, and old threats like the protests and riots receding, law and order lost some of the visceral appeal it had once had, although it remained a potent force in local and state elections. Second, the political context had shifted. In the national arena, liberals downplayed their faith in root-cause solutions. As a result, conservatives found that they could not exploit law and order as effectively as they once had. Moreover, once in office they discovered that controlling crime was more difficult than they had led the American people to believe. In a sense, then, the issue faded because it had served its purpose and because its advocates were reluctant to take responsibility for it.

The emergence of law and order was nevertheless of long-term significance. It helped to usher in a new age of American politics, in which nightmares of criminal chaos replaced dreams of a Great Society. The issue also deepened the divisions within the Democratic coalition of liberal activists, white southerners, African Americans, and union members, which had dominated presidential elections since 1932. Above all, law and order both reflected and exacerbated the unease and frustration felt by many urban whites. In a special report on "The Troubled American," *Newsweek* cited in 1969 what it described as a "deep crisis" in the national mood. "People are scared and they've changed," declared a Boston cabbie. "Ten years ago if you were getting beaten up you could expect some help. Now people just walk by—they're afraid for their lives."[1]

Richard Nixon was determined to address that fear. In January 1969, the new president arrived in Washington to find a city in crisis. During the campaign, Nixon had promised to restore order in the country and the capital. "D.C. should not stand for disorder and crime," he had vowed.[2] Now he had to make good on his pledge—the credibility of his administration was on the line. Accordingly, the president announced with great fanfare that he would appoint new prosecutors, reorganize the District's courts, and provide the funds to hire a thousand additional officers, which would increase the size of the force by 25 percent. The White House also drafted and submitted to Congress a controversial crime bill for Washington which would, among other provisions, allow the "preventive detention" of dangerous suspects and the use of "no-knock" search warrants in certain situations.[3] According to the administration, the measure would remove unreasonable restraints on police officers, although civil libertarians and liberal Democrats objected.

One year later, the situation in Washington remained bleak. The crime rate had risen by double digits. The crime bill remained stalled in Congress. And polls showed that fewer than one in four Americans approved of the president's actions. With mid-term elections on the horizon, the administration's strategy was to assume a defensive posture on the economy, which was in decline, and take an offensive stance on crime, which Nixon felt "can be a very effective issue if we can grab hold of it and use it."[4] In October 1970, he took to the road and campaigned for 36 candidates in 21 states.

As in 1968, he promoted law and order tirelessly and blamed the Democrats repeatedly for the "violence, lawlessness, and permissiveness" that he claimed were rampant in America. This time, however, the issue failed to resonate. Two-thirds of the candidates Nixon campaigned for lost. As the party in opposition, the Democrats retained their majority in the Senate and widened it in the House.[5] The results, although typical for a mid-term election, seemed to signal the death knell for law and order.

But in the White House, the immediate post-election analysis was that the issue remained viable nationally even though its impact varied regionally. According to internal data, law and order continued to have an effect in the urban Northeast, where crime was routine, but not in the rural Midwest or Far West, where crime was rare. The administration had also, concluded aide Charles Colson, failed to convince "the public that . . . liberal permissiveness was the cause of violence and crime."[6] Nixon concurred. It was, he believed, the execution that had failed, not the strategy. "On the issue side," he asserted, "we still haven't gotten through the strong position on law and order despite our leadership in this field, all of the public relations devices we use to get it across, and my hitting it hard in the campaign."[7]

Ultimately, however, the president chose not to make law and order the centerpiece of his reelection bid. Precisely why is not clear. Nevertheless, several explanations seem persuasive. First, the political lesson of 1968 and 1970 was that the issue worked best for the candidate in opposition, not the incumbent. Second, the political climate of 1972 was not conducive to law and order. On the one hand, the administration's record on crime, even in Washington, remained ambiguous at best.[8] On the other, South Dakota Senator George McGovern, the Democratic nominee, was not about to steal the issue, given his liberal reputation and his supposed support for "acid, amnesty, and abortion" (as the Republicans put it). By contrast, peace and prosperity were the issues that in 1972 mattered most to an anxious electorate weary of the Vietnam War and wary of the American economy. And so Nixon rode those issues to a landslide victory comparable to what Johnson had achieved in 1964.

After 1972 presidential candidates rarely invoked law and order, which Nixon himself had discredited when he resigned in disgrace in 1974 as a result of the Watergate Crisis. In 1976, Democrat Jimmy Carter narrowly defeated Republican Gerald Ford, who had pardoned Nixon and failed to stem the economic downturn. Carter in turn saw his hopes for reelection dashed when the "misery index" (a combination of unemployment and inflation) rose to double digits, the Soviets invaded Afghanistan, and Iranian fundamentalists led by the Ayatollah Khomeini held 55 Americans hostage in Tehran for more than a year. Suddenly, economic and national security were again at the forefront of public concern. "Are you better off now than you were four years ago?" asked Republican Ronald Reagan, who in 1980 easily defeated Carter by promising to restore American prosperity and greatness.[9] Four years later, with the country basking in the glow of patriotic fervor and a revived economy, Reagan handily won re-election by proclaiming that the nation's best days once more lay ahead, that it was "Morning Again in America."[10]

But candidates at the state and local level continued to employ law and order frequently and successfully. In 1970, for example, moderate Republican Nelson Rockefeller was re-elected governor of New York on a tough anti-drug platform, while in liberal Minneapolis a police detective was elected mayor by a decisive margin despite the combined opposition of the Democrats and Republicans.[11] In California, fear of crime derailed Los Angeles Mayor Tom Bradley's bid in 1981 to become the first black governor of the state, and led to repeated recall efforts against Rose Bird, the first female member of the California Supreme Court, who vacated 61 consecutive death sentences until ousted in 1986.[12] The resilience of law and order in the 1970s and 1980s illustrated how many middle-class Americans were moving to the right on issues of crime and drugs even as they were moving to the left on matters of racial equality and sexual preference. What most Americans increasingly seemed to want was both more freedom over issues of individual choice and more control over threats to home and family.[13]

In 1987, however, the ultimate nightmare for many whites became a grim reality for a young couple in a serene subdivision outside Washington. An armed black man invaded their home, which he had chosen at random. The intruder then bound and slashed the man, who had to listen helplessly while his fiancée was raped. The criminal was Willie Horton, who was serving a life sentence for murder in Massachusetts but was free on a weekend furlough program. Back in 1976 the state legislature had passed a bill that would have denied leaves to violent offenders like Horton, but the bill was vetoed by Massachusetts Governor Michael Dukakis, who contended with some justification that it would hinder efforts to rehabilitate prisoners. The veto attracted relatively little attention at the time. By the spring of 1988, however, Dukakis was the Democratic frontrunner for president and had a lead in the polls of at least 16 points over the Republican candidate, Vice President George Bush.[14]

With a degree of desperation and calculation, the Bush campaign realized that it had to depict Dukakis as an extreme liberal who was far outside the political mainstream. The Republicans had already attacked him for his opposition to a mandatory Pledge of Allegiance and his membership in the American Civil Liberties Union. Now the seemingly perfect example of his pro-criminal tendencies had appeared. As James Pinkerton, the director of opposition research, told campaign manager Lee Atwater, "The more people who know who Willie Horton is, the better off we'll be." Soon Horton was notorious. Although the Bush campaign consciously chose, on the advice of media consultant Roger Ailes, not to air commercials that included Horton's mug shot, conservative political action committees, supposedly acting on their own (as had, allegedly, the group which in 1964 produced the pro-Goldwater film "Choice"), showed no restraint in making Horton the symbol of black criminality and liberal permissiveness. The paid advertisements on cable television, which were repeatedly reshown on network news, had a devastating impact on the Dukakis campaign. It never recovered as Bush roared ahead in the polls in August and cruised to victory in November.[15]

The Dukakis debacle and the return of law and order to national politics convinced many Democrats that they would have to find a candidate with the record and rhetoric to challenge the Republicans on the issue. In 1992 he appeared and his name was Bill Clinton. During the New Hampshire primary, the Arkansas governor, who was under heavy criticism for his affair with Gennifer Flowers, flew home to Little Rock to oversee the execution of Ricky Ray Rector, a prisoner of questionable mental competence (he set aside part of his final meal so that he could eat it later).[16] On the campaign trail against President Bush, Clinton made it clear that he was a "New Democrat" who would not coddle criminals. "Those who commit crimes must be caught, those who are caught must be convicted, those who are convicted must be punished," he declared. The main issue in 1992 was not law and order—it was "the economy, stupid," as the famous sign in the Clinton campaign headquarters noted. But the tough talk decisively distanced Clinton from Democratic orthodoxy and, at the very least, insulated him from the charge that he, like Dukakis, was soft on crime.[17]

Clinton spent most of his first year in office pursuing his ill-fated health care plan. But in late 1993, with mid-term elections fast approaching, he proposed the crime bill that, along with welfare reform, would cement his reputation as a "New Democrat." In original form, the bill requested $3.4 billion, primarily to hire 50,000 more police officers. Both liberals and conservatives were dissatisfied; the former wanted more spent on prevention, the latter wanted more spent on prisons. In final form, the Violent

Crime Control and Law Enforcement Act of 1994 authorized the expenditure of $30.2 billion, including $13.5 billion for law enforcement (to hire 100,000 more officers), $9.9 billion for prison construction, and $6.9 billion for crime prevention. The measure also included a ten-year ban on semi-automatic assault weapons (although those already in possession of such weapons could keep them, a provision which failed to mollify the National Rifle Association); made 60 federal crimes eligible for the death penalty; and mandated life sentences for "three strikes" violent felons. Despite the delicate balancing act, the legislation almost failed to gain passage and came too late to help the Democrats, who lost control of the House and the Senate in the 1994 elections.[18]

Clinton had, nevertheless, transformed public perceptions of the crime issue. In 1991, the Republicans had a 37–16 percent advantage on law and order according to a Time/CNN poll; by 1994, the Democrats had a 42–34 percent edge according to a CNN/USA Today Poll. "The Republicans lost Communism and now they're losing crime," boasted a White House aide.[19] The claim was premature. Most Republicans had no intention of ceding what they saw as the most critical issue facing the country. As New York Mayor Rudolph Guiliani told a group of police cadets in 1994, echoing what Nixon had said in 1968, "It's a struggle for the most basic civil right that we possess. That is the right to public safety, the ability to use our public spaces, our public buildings, our educational institutions, our hospitals, our schools, without the fear of being the victim of a serious crime."[20]

The fear continued to have racial repercussions. As The Reverend Jesse Jackson admitted in that same year, "There is nothing more painful for me at this stage in my life than to walk down the street and hear footsteps and start to think about robbery and then look around and see it's somebody white and feel relieved." But ironically, the crime wave of the late 1980s and early 1990s had already begun to recede by the time Clinton and Congress acted in 1994. By the end of the decade, the homicide rate had fallen eight consecutive years, from 9.8 per 100,000 in 1991 to 5.8 in 1999 (a level not seen since the mid-1960s, when the murder rate first began to skyrocket). The rate of violent crime dropped by almost 33 percent between 1993 and 1999.[21]

The dramatic decline caught police officials and policy experts by surprise. It also led to a lively debate over which factor—police tactics, prison expansion, gun control, demographic change, political legislation, or economic opportunity—should receive the credit, with most scholars arguing in favor of a combination of causes. And although the media continued to sensationalize crime—"if it bleeds, it leads" remained the mantra of local television news directors—it appeared that the reduction in crime, combined with economic prosperity and the collapse of communism, might signal an end to the politics of fear and insecurity. Even public support for the death penalty, which had risen in conjunction with the crime rate, now began to fall in response to revelations of racial bias and wrongful convictions.[22]

But then came 9/11. The attacks on the World Trade Center and the Pentagon, twin symbols of America's economic and military might, instantly shattered the sense of security most Americans felt. Suddenly the war on terrorism replaced the war on crime, and the face to fear became that of a Middle-Eastern, rather than African-American, male. Now the nation faced a long, twilight struggle similar to the Cold War. Only this time the threat seemed both more immediate and more amorphous. Under those changed circumstances, the return of law and order in traditional guise appeared unlikely. As a former official in the Clinton administration put it, "national security is now personal security."[23]

Whether Americans will have to live under the shadow of fear for another generation or longer is uncertain. What does seem evident, in hindsight, is that since the New Deal the politics of security, albeit in different forms, has dominated presidential campaigns. During the 1930s, in the depths of the Great Depression, economic security was the main concern. In the 1940s and 1950s, national security became the order of the day as the United States faced first the threat of fascism and then communism. In the 1960s, personal security as defined by law and order moved to the forefront. In the 1970s and 1980s, economic and national security returned to center stage. Only in the 1990s, briefly, were Americans able to indulge in the idea that they could transcend history and live in a world without danger.

In retrospect, then, the seismic shocks generated by the rise of law and order may seem more like recurrent tremors, similar to the anti-communism charges which the Republicans used after World War II to broaden the appeal of their free-market philosophy and question the patriotism of their Democratic opponents. But in fact law and order shook the foundations of liberal credibility during the Kennedy-Johnson years by popularizing the conservative cause, equating civil rights with racial turmoil, undermining public faith in activist government, and anticipating the anti-tax revolts of latter decades. As street crime and civil unrest swept the country from 1964 to 1968, hopes for progress gave way to fears of violence. The crisis of liberalism was at hand.

Notes

INTRODUCTION

1. Curt Furr to Sam J. Ervin, Jr., June 18, 1968, Folder 669, Box 204, Legislative Files, Ervin Papers, Southern Historical Collection, University of North Carolina, Chapel Hill.

2. In 1963, civil rights activist Bayard Rustin had anticipated this development when he discussed the "dilemma of dissent" at an American Socialist Party meeting in Washington. Most middle-class white Americans believed in justice and freedom, he contended, but they believed even more in "law and order." The task of the movement, therefore, was to awaken the first set of beliefs without arousing the second because in a competition law and order would always trump justice and freedom. Lewis Chester, Godfrey Hodgson, and Bruce Page, *An American Melodrama: The Presidential Campaign of 1968* (New York: The Viking Press, 1969), p. 592.

3. They had "a reflexive, almost pathological, inability to get their hands around this issue." Ben Wattenberg, interview with author, December 19, 1997.

4. *Crime in the United States*, Uniform Crime Report (Washington: The Federal Bureau of Investigation, 1970).

5. Special Message to the Congress on Crime and Law Enforcement, February 7, 1968, *Public Papers of the Presidents of the United States: Lyndon B. Johnson, 1968–69* (Washington: U.S. Government Printing Office, 1969), 1: 185.

6. Lyndon Baines Johnson, *The Vantage Point: Perspectives of the Presidency, 1963–1969* (New York: Holt, Rinehart and Winston, 1971), p. 549.

7. By ethnic I mean primarily those of Irish, Italian, Jewish, and East European ancestry.

8. Although police departments expanded at twice the rate of population growth during the 1960s, both clearance and conviction rates fell—the direct result of court rulings according to conservatives. Lucas A. Powe, Jr., *The Warren Court and American Politics* (Cambridge: Harvard University Press, 2000), pp. 399–400, 408.

9. Even many liberals now concede that it was a mistake to extol untrammeled civil liberties at the expense of secure public spaces. See Harold Myerson, "Why Liberalism Fled the City . . . And How It Might Come Back," *American Prospect* 37 (March–April 1998): 51–52.

10. James Sundquist, *Dynamics of the Party System: Alignment and Realignment of Political Parties in the United States* (Washington: Brookings Institution, 1983), p. 383. "There was a conflation of all of these issues," recalls one administration official. "It wasn't genius—it was what the man on the street was doing." Ben Wattenberg, interview with author, December 19, 1997.

11. In an effort to broaden the definition of politics, I use "political culture" to represent the intersection of ideology, language, and symbols with issues and elections at the local and national levels. See among others Daniel Elazar and Joseph Zikmund, *The Ecology of American Political Culture* (New York: Crowell, 1975); and Lucian W. Pye and Sidney Verba, eds., *Political Culture and Political Development* (Princeton: Princeton University Press, 1965).

12. According to two political scientists, elite actors provide policy cues, which the mass electorate then chooses to respond to or ignore. Edward G. Carmines and James A. Stimson, *Issue Evolution: Race and the Transformation of American Politics* (Princeton: Princeton University Press, 1989), pp. 161–162.

13. William Hamilton Harris, *The Harder We Run: Black Workers Since the Civil War* (New York: Oxford University Press, 1982), chapters 6 and 7..

14. During the 1960s, the annual robbery arrest rate for black juveniles between the ages of ten and seventeen was typically around 20 times as high as for white juveniles. *Crime in the United States*, Uniform Crime Report (Washington: The Federal Bureau of Investigation, 1973).

15. "The Troubled American: A Special Report on the White Majority," *Newsweek*, October 6, 1969, pp. 29–48.

16. For centuries, southern whites in particular had conflated fears of racial violence, sexual relations, and social control. See among others: Martha Hodes, *White Women, Black Men: Illicit Sex in the Nineteenth-Century South* (New Haven: Yale University Press, 1997); Edward L. Ayers, *Vengeance and Justice: Crime and Punishment in the 19th-Century South* (New York: Oxford University Press, 1984); Bertram Wyatt-Brown, *Southern Honor: Ethics and Behavior in the Old South* (New York: Oxford University Press, 1982); Dan T. Carter, *Scotsboro: A Tragedy of the American South* (New York: Oxford University Press, 1971); W. Fitzhugh Brundage, *Lynching in the New South: Georgia and Virginia, 1880–1930* (Urbana: University of Illinois, 1993); Wilbur J. Cash, *The Mind of the South* (New York: Knopf, 1957); and Fox Butterfield, *All God's Children: The Bosket Family and the American Tradition of Violence* (New York: Knopf, 1995).

17. Address to the International Union of Electrical, Radio, and Machine Workers, Box 41, A. Philip Randolph Papers, Library of Congress (LOC).

18. John Kenneth White, *Still Seeing Red: How the Cold War Shapes the New American Politics* (Boulder, Colorado: Westview Press, 1997).

19. According to one historian, "the new rhetoric of 'law and order' and not the archaic rhetoric of the domestic cold war structured the nation's response to the riots. The riots led to a search for communists in the ghetto, but that search was secondary to a national and increasingly partisan debate that placed liberalism and not communism at the center of controversy." Kenneth O'Reilly, *"Racial Matters": The FBI's Secret File on Black America, 1960–1972* (New York: The Free Press, 1989), p. 229.

20. See, for example, the "Remarks of Emanuel Celler," October 7, 1968, *Congressional Record*, 90th Congress, Second Session. For a recent view, see Roger Cohen, "A Haider in Their Future," *New York Times Magazine*, April 30, 2000, pp. 54–59.

21. Gary Gerstle, "The Protean Character of American Liberalism," *American Historical Review* 99 (October 1994): 1043–1073.

22. Robert M. Collins, "Growth Liberalism in the Sixties," in David Farber, ed., *The Sixties: From Memory to History* (Chapel Hill: University of North Carolina Press, 1994), pp. 11–44.

23. In 1966, seven of ten white families were barely able to assure a "modest but adequate" standard of living according to the Bureau of Labor Statistics. See John Howard, "Public Policy and the White Working Class," in Irving L. Horowitz, ed., *The Use and Abuse of Social Science* (New Brunswick, New Jersey: Transaction Books, 1971), p. 207. See also "The Troubled American," *Newsweek*, October 6, 1969, p. 30; and Robert M. Collins, "The Economic Crisis of 1968 and the Waning of the 'American Century,'" *American Historical Review* 107 (April 1996): 401, 407.

24. In Detroit, for example, the number of African Americans in the auto workforce increased dramatically during the postwar decades. By the late 1960s, the assembly lines were rife with racial tension—and racial violence was not uncommon. Heather Thompson, "Another War at Home: Reexamining Working Class Politics in the 1960s," *Mid-America* 81 (Fall 1999): 299–314.

25. The political director of the Amalgamated Meatcutters would maintain after the 1966 elections that liberal Democrats now had to reassure "the owners of little homes who are afraid to lose their total life savings invested in their property." Alan Draper, *A Rope of Sand: The AFL-CIO Committee on Political Education, 1955–1967* (New York: Praeger, 1989), pp. 123–124.

26. Winifred Breines, "Whose New Left?" *Journal of American History* 75 (1988): 528–545.

27. Todd Gitlin, *The Sixties: Years of Hope, Days of Rage* (New York: Bantam Books, 1987); Sara Evans, *Personal Politics: The Roots of Women's Liberation in the Civil Rights Movement and the New Left* (New York: Knopf, 1979); and Clayborne Carson, *In Struggle: SNCC and the Black Awakening of the 1960s* (Cambridge: Harvard University Press, 1981).

28. Alan Brinkley, "The Problem of American Conservatism," *American Historical Review* 99 (April 1994): 409–429. See also Leo Ribuffo, "Why Is There So Much Conservatism in the United States and Why Do So Few Historians Know Anything About It?" *American Historical Review* 99 (April 1994): 441. The literature on conservative leaders, organizations, and issues has grown significantly in recent years. See among others Jonathan M. Schoenwald, *A Time for Choosing: The Rise of Modern American Conservatism* (New York: Oxford University Press, 2001); Matthew Dallek, *The Right Moment: Ronald Reagan's First Victory and the Decisive Turning Point in American Politics* (New York: The Free Press, 2000); John A. Andrew III, *The Other Side of the Sixties: Young Americans for Freedom and the Rise of Conservative Politics* (New Brunswick: Rutgers University Press, 1997); Patrick Allitt, *Catholic Intellectuals and Conservative Politics in America, 1950–1985* (Ithaca: Cornell University Press, 1993); Kenneth J. Heineman, *Campus Wars: The Peace Movement at American State Universities in the Vietnam Era* (New York: New York University Press, 1992); and Mary C. Brennan, *Turning Right in the Sixties: The Conservative Capture of the GOP* (Chapel Hill: University of North Carolina Press, 1995).

29. Thomas Byrne Edsall and Mary D. Edsall, *Chain Reaction: The Impact of Race, Rights, and Taxes on American Politics* (New York: Norton, 1991), p. 9. For a similar national perspective, see Allen J. Matusow, *The Unraveling of America: A History of Liberalism in the 1960s* (New York: Harper, 1984). For a similar local perspective, see Jonathan Rieder, *Canarsie: The Jews and Italians of Brooklyn against Liberalism* (Cambridge: Harvard University Press, 1985).

30. He also argues that miscegenation was the main fear of whites in the 1950s. I would contend that by the 1960s street crime represented the main fear. Thomas J. Sugrue, "Crabgrass-Roots Politics: Race, Rights, and the Reaction against Liberalism in the Urban North, 1940–1964," *Journal of American History* 82 (September 1995): 578. See also Thomas J. Sugrue, *The Origins of the Urban Crisis: Race and Inequality in Postwar Detroit* (Princeton: Princeton University Press, 1996).

31. Thus a Charlestown, Massachusetts housewife, Alice McGoff, could support the 1964 Civil Rights Act but later oppose forced busing. See J. Anthony Lukas, *Common Ground: A Turbulent Decade in the Lives of Three American Families* (New York: Knopf, 1985), p. 26.

32. "As issues became more salient and politics intruded on more individuals, there was a heightened awareness of discrepancies between what the parties stood for as opposed to what they were believed to stand for." Norman H. Vie, Sidney Verba, and John R. Petrocik, *The Changing American Voter* (New York: Cambridge University Press, 1979), p. 269.

33. Wattenberg to LBJ, November 21, 1967, Ex PL/Kennedy, Robert F., Box 26, White House Subject Files (WHSF), Lyndon Baines Johnson Presidential Library, Austin, Texas (LBJ Library).

34. This analogy was popular in the 1960s. See James Q. Wilson, "Crime in the Streets," *The Public Interest* 5 (Fall 1966): 26–35; reprinted in Marvin R. Sum-

mers and Thomas E. Barth, eds., *Law and Order in a Democratic Society* (Columbus, Ohio: Charles E. Merrill, 1970).

CHAPTER 1. DELINQUENCY AND OPPORTUNITY

1. Wilkins to Mary Wennergren, March 4, 1958, Box 90, Administrative File (III), NAACP Papers, Library of Congress, Washington, D.C. (LOC).

2. No doubt many delinquents were arrested for "status crimes" such as underage drinking, driving without a license, and underage sex. No doubt too that as police departments formed units to combat juvenile delinquency, more arrests were made. Nevertheless, perhaps the best authority on the subject concludes that there was a "probable increase" in youth crime that coincided with a "probable shift" in law enforcement. James Gilbert, *A Cycle of Outrage: America's Reaction to the Juvenile Delinquent in the 1950s* (New York: Oxford University Press, 1986), p. 71.

3. Jack Lait and Lee Mortimer, *U.S.A. Confidential* (New York: Crown, 1952), p. 37.

4. Alice O'Connor, "Community Action, Urban Reform, and the Fight Against Poverty," *Journal of Urban History* 22 (July 1996): 586–625.

5. John Edgar Hoover, "A 'Third Front'—Against Juvenile Delinquency," *New York Times Magazine*, February 27, 1944, pp. 8, 32.

6. "War and Delinquency," *Newsweek*, June 28, 1943, p. 100.

7. William M. Tuttle, Jr., *"Daddy's Gone to War": The Second World War in the Lives of America's Children* (New York: Oxford University Press, 1993), p. 70; Gilbert, *A Cycle of Outrage*, pp. 33–34, 38–39, 73–74.

8. In the 1950s almost 500,000 whites left Brooklyn. By the late 1960s the Jewish population in Brownsville had shrunk from more than 175,000 in the 1940s to less than 5,000 mostly elderly residents. The last synagogue closed in 1972. Gerald Sorin, *The Nurturing Neighborhood: The Brownsville Boys Club and Jewish Community in Urban America, 1940–1990* (New York: New York University Press, 1990), pp. 91, 159–163, 168. For another description of the flight of the Jews from Brownsville, see Jonathan Rieder, *Canarsie: The Italians and Jews of Brooklyn Against Liberalism* (Cambridge: Harvard University Press, 1985).

9. According to the police, arrests of juveniles rose 60 percent between 1952 and 1957, with blacks and Latinos heavily overrepresented. "Strong Arm of the Law," *Time*, July 7, 1958, p. 15.

10. Gerald Sorin, *The Nurturing Neighborhood*, pp. 91, 109, 155.

11. Philadelphia in 1953 claimed a 70 percent increase in crime over 1951—because it had installed a new reporting system. New York in 1950 likewise claimed a 200 percent rise in assaults, a 400 percent rise in robberies, and a 1,300 percent rise in robberies over 1948 levels—again because it too had installed a new reporting system. Moreover, local departments always had an incentive either to over-

report crime (to receive funding increases) or under-report it (to demonstrate effectiveness). Daniel Bell, *The End of Ideology: On the Exhaustion of Political Ideas in the Fifties* (Glencoe, Illinois: The Free Press, 1960), pp. 138–139, 141–142. See also Jackson Toby, "A Way Out of the Blackboard Jungle," *Nation*, March 8, 1958, pp. 205–207.

12. "Why Law Fails to Stop Teen-Age Crime," *U.S. News & World Report*, January 14, 1953, p. 74; "All Our Children," *Newsweek*, November 9, 1953, p. 35.

13. A black minister in Brownsville requested that the NYPD assign as many black officers as possible because most of the robbery, vandalism, and street fighting involved black gangs. Sorin, *The Nurturing Neighborhood*, p. 108. See also Daniel Patrick Moynihan, *Maximum Feasible Misunderstanding: Community Action in the War on Poverty* (New York: The Free Press, 1969), p. 14.

14. Bell, *The End of Ideology*, pp. 116, 155, 157.

15. "Despite a relatively easy time for the United States, there was more than a hint of doom in the victory," Gilbert noted. "The war rendered the extremes of human depravity commonplace. Propaganda, mass society, atomic warfare, communism, fascism, became words infused with immediate and urgent content." Gilbert, *A Cycle of Outrage*, p. 41.

16. By 1959 fear of the youth culture had begun to give way to a sense of awe about the economic potential of the youth market, which one magazine predicted might reach $20 billion by 1970. "A Young $10 Billion Power: The US Teen-age Consumer Has Become a Major Factor in the Nation's Economy," *Life*, August 31, 1959, pp. 78–84.

17. Kenneth T. Jackson, *Crabgrass Frontier: The Suburbanization of the United States* (New York: Oxford University Press, 1985), p. 283.

18. The mechanization of cotton farming after 1940 led to the exodus of five million blacks from the South. In 1940, 77 percent of African Americans still lived in the South, 49 percent in rural areas. By 1970 the corresponding figures were roughly 50 percent and 25 percent, turning "urban" into a euphemism for "black." Nicholas Lemann, *The Promised Land: The Great Black Migration and How It Changed America* (New York: Knopf, 1991), pp. 6, 70.

19. "You can take most of those poor kids, fix them up with a ball game, give them a little equipment, and they are happy as larks," claimed New Orleans Police Captain William A. Walker Sr. "Most of the defiance, the insolence, and downright viciousness is exhibited by kids from well-to-do families, or those in moderate circumstances." See "All Our Children," *Newsweek*, November 9, 1953, pp. 28–35; and "Kids Grow Worse," *Newsweek*, December 6, 1954, pp. 26–27.

20. At times his desire for balance became rather strained. In his discussion of crime comics, for example, he rejected the notion that they caused delinquency because "the need to be bad is already formed." Yet he later called for a ban on them because "repetitive dunning into the child's mind of ways to commit crime . . . can well create an attitude within the child that makes him more susceptible to

delinquency than he might otherwise be." Fine, *1,000,000 Delinquents* (New York: World, 1955), pp. 113, 344.

21. Ibid., pp. 107, 128, 139.

22. Ironically, the American Legion appears to have missed the symbolism of the climactic scene, in which a sympathetic student named Santini (played by Jameel Farah, later known as Jamie Farr) uses an American flag to knock a knife out of the hands of another student. *Blackboard Jungle* (1955). Given the level of Cold War concern, it is also noteworthy that Director Richard Brooks was able to resist the studio's insistence that the film include a scene of a similar student riot in a Moscow High School. For its part, New York City denied Brooks permission to film in its schools. Meanwhile, the Motion Picture Association of America (MPAA) had a very different concern during the filming of *Rebel Without a Cause*. "It is of course vital that there be no inference of a questionable or homosexual relationship between Plato [Sal Mineo] and Jim [James Dean]," wrote an official to Jack Warner. Gilbert, *A Cycle of Outrage*, pp. 184–185, 189.

23. Although the casting of *Blackboard Jungle* appears to follow the pattern of World War II films, in which one of every ethnic stereotype is present in the unit, the film's diversity had a basis in reality, both for New York and the nation as a whole. Changes in the American high school after 1945 increased the interaction between the middle class and the working class, as well as blacks and whites. In 1930, 50 percent of working-class students attended high school; by the early 1960s, the figure was over 90 percent. In 1940, 73 percent of children between 14 and 17 were in high school; by 1960, the figure was 87 percent. The percentage of blacks who completed high school doubled between the early 1940s and late 1950s; by the early 1960s the percentages of whites and blacks who attended high school were almost equal. Gilbert, *A Cycle of Outrage*, pp. 18–19.

24. *Blackboard Jungle* (1955).

25. *Blackboard Jungle* (1955).

26. Of course, Poitier would become a liberal icon and would eventually find himself on the other side of the desk in the role of a British teacher confronted by an assortment of white delinquents in *To Sir With Love* (1967).

27. Gilbert, *A Cycle of Outrage*, pp. 157, 178.

28 "Killers were Boys," *Newsweek*, August 12, 1957, p. 27; "Biggest City's Nightmare—Its Crime-Ridden Schools," *U.S. News*, February 7, 1958, pp. 46–50.

29. "Brutal Young," *Newsweek* March 25, 1957, p. 36.

30. In postwar Detroit, there were more than 200 incidents by whites against blacks trying to integrate neighborhoods. Thomas J. Sugrue, "The Origins of the Urban Crisis: Race, Industrial Decline, and Housing in Detroit, 1940–1960" (Ph. D., Harvard University, 1992), pp. 13, 264–265. For similar incidents in Chicago, see Lemann, *The Promised Land*, pp. 71–73.

31. Of course, some whites had trumpeted this issue for years. According to two tabloid journalists, the black migration represented a "tidal wave" of "dark-

ies" recruited by the CIO, the NAACP, the ADA, and Fiorello LaGuardia, Mayor of New York, who promised them welfare in exchange for votes. The goal of the "Democratic Raw Dealers" was to ameliorate "the racial problem in the South while bringing a different kind to the North." The authors contended that blacks were responsible for half of all urban crime despite a lack of police enforcement in the ghetto. "By common consent all Northern police departments overlook all Negro crime unless a white man is involved," they wrote, adding that black-on-black murders were typically attributed to traffic accidents. Lait and Mortimer, *U.S.A. Confidential*, pp. 5, 60–63.

32. "The Negro Crime Rate: A Failure in Integration," *Time*, April 21, 1958, p. 16. The NAACP insisted that crime stories include the race of the assailant only under such circumstances. After citing arrest and crime records from Philadelphia, another article observed that blacks were now the largest single voting bloc in the city, controlling 14 of 58 wards and enabling the Democrats to end 67 years of Republican supremacy. "The Big Story in the Big Cities," *U.S. News*, December 19, 1958, pp. 46–54.

33. "The Negro Crime Rate: A Failure in Integration," *Time*, April 21, 1958, p. 16. In an interview with *U.S. News*, the Philadelphia district attorney claimed that police were often intimidated by civil rights charges. "The Big Story in the Big Cities," *U.S. News*, December 19, 1958, pp. 46–54.

34. Michael Harrington, *The Other America: Poverty in the United States* (New York: Macmillan, 1962), p. 177. A scholar has made a similar argument in regard to the Birmingham protests in 1963. He contends that crime against other blacks declines when there is an organized direct-action campaign because race pride develops. See Robin D.G. Kelley, "The Black Poor and the Politics of Opposition in a New South City, 1929–1970," in Michael B. Katz, ed., *The 'Underclass' Debate* (Princeton: Princeton University Press, 1993), pp. 320–321, esp. n.59. For a similar if earlier view, see Robert Coles, "Race and Crime Control," in Charles E. Reasons and Jack L. Kuykendall, eds., *Race, Crime, and Justice* (Pacific Palisades: Goodyear Publishing Co., Inc., 1972), pp. 132–138.

35. Relying on the FBI Uniform Crime Reports of 1954, it stated that blacks comprised 70 percent of gambling arrests; 63 percent of murder; 63 percent of drugs; 63 percent of aggravated assaults; 55 percent of possession of deadly weapons; 53 percent of robbery; 40 percent of rape; 33 percent of burglaries; 28 percent for offenses against children and family; 22 percent for all other sex offenses. It added that out of 7,337 babies born out of wedlock in the state that year, 7,070 were black. Pamphlet attached to "NAACP Branches and the Crime Problem," April 1958, Box 90, Administrative File (III), NAACP Papers, LOC.

36. In February 1958, Obadiah Williams of Cincinnati wrote to Roy Wilkins: "Since most of the trouble in the New York Schools has come from members of our race (Negro) I feel that your group should take a positive stand against such action." Williams recommended a mass meeting or a concerted effort by commu-

nity leaders, although he was aware that blacks were not entirely to blame, despite much bad publicity. John A. Morsell to Obadiah Williams, March 7, 1958, Box 90, Administrative File (III), NAACP Papers, LOC.

37. Press Release, October 1, 1959, Box 91, Administrative File (III), NAACP Papers, LOC.

38. Wilkins to Mary Wennergren, March 4, 1958, Box 90, Administrative File (III), NAACP Papers, LOC.

39. "NAACP Branches and the Crime Problem," April 1958, Box 90, Administrative File (III), NAACP Papers, LOC.

40. John A. Morsell to Harold Williams, May 21, 1958, Box 90, Administrative File (III), NAACP Papers, LOC.

41. For an overview of Eisenhower's political philosophy, see Robert Griffith, "Dwight D. Eisenhower and the Corporate Commonwealth," *American Historical Review* 87 (February 1982): 87–122.

42. Malcolm M. Feeley and Austin D. Sarat, *The Policy Dilemma: Federal Crime Policy and the Law Enforcement Assistance Administration, 1968–1978* (Minneapolis: University of Minnesota Press, 1980), p. 39.

43. Although the play included a song ("Officer Krupke") which mocked the efforts of liberals to understand and treat delinquency, it had a wide impact. When asked by Professor Frances Fox Piven at a 1973 conference why the Kennedy administration had placed such importance on youth crime, Adam Yarmolinsky replied with a revealing quip: "West Side Story." Transcript, Poverty and Urban Policy Conference, Brandeis University, June 16–17, 1973 (Brandeis Conference), p. 49, John F. Kennedy Presidential Library, Boston, Massachusetts (JFK Library).

44. James L. Sundquist, *Politics and Policy: The Eisenhower, Kennedy, and Johnson Years* (Washington: The Brookings Institution, 1968), pp. 73–75.

45. Ibid., p. 464; James D. Calder, "Presidents and Crime Control: Some Limitations on Executive Policy Making," (Ph.D. diss., Claremont, 1978), p. 168; *Public Papers of the Presidents of the United States: John F. Kennedy, 1961* (Washington, D.C.: U.S. Government Printing Office, 1962), p. 22.

46. Hackett was a popular student and star athlete who had befriended Robert Kennedy when he arrived at Milton Academy in his junior year. Arthur Schlesinger, *Robert Kennedy and His Times* (New York: Ballantine Books, 1978), pp. 48–49; Lemann, *The Promised Land*, pp. 123–124.

47. John E. Moore, "Controlling Delinquency: Executive, Congressional, and Juvenile, 1961–1964," in Frederic N. Cleaveland, ed., *Congress and Urban Problems* (Washington: The Brookings Institution, 1969), pp. 123–138.

48. Delinquency Commission report, n.d., Box 13, Dean Markham MSS, JFK Library.

49. Ibid.

50. MFY served an area that was 27 percent Jewish, 26 percent Puerto Rican, 11 percent Italian, and 25 percent black. Over 35 percent of the housing was sub-standard

and only 14.9 percent of the adults had finished high school. Marjorie Hunter, "U.S. And City Open 12.6 Million War on Delinquency," *New York Times*, June 1, 1962, pp. 1, 4.

51. MFY received 15 percent of its funding from the Ford Foundation, 30 percent from the city and state government, and 55 percent from Washington. Moynihan, *Maximum Feasible Misunderstanding*, pp. 51, 58, 59.

52. Richard A. Cloward and Lloyd E. Ohlin, *Delinquency and Opportunity: A Theory of Delinquent Gangs* (Glencoe, Illinois: The Free Press, 1960), pp. 161–211; Michael B. Katz, *The Undeserving Poor: From the War on Poverty to the War on Welfare* (New York: Pantheon Books, 1989), pp. 96–97.

53. Delinquency Commission report, n.d., Box 13, Dean Markham MSS, JFK Library; Interview with Sanford Kravitz, December 11, 1967, Box 51, Daniel Knapp MSS, JFK Library.

54. Nicholas Lemann, *The Promised Land*, p. 129.

55. Hackett learned of the delinquency debate at his first meeting on March 16, 1961. He then resolved it by hiring Ohlin, recalling that "I quickly learned from the March meeting that you can't get consensus among professionals, so I had to pick one of the best and rely on his judgment." Moore, "Controlling Delinquency: Executive, Congressional, and Juvenile, 1961–1964," p. 127.

56. Moynihan, *Maximum Feasible Misunderstanding*, p. 170. Moley, however, completely ignored the fact that the Gluecks were careful to state that environmental and cultural factors remained important. "Teen-Age Criminals," Raymond Moley, *Newsweek* May 12, 1958, p. 108.

57. Moynihan, *Maximum Feasible Misunderstanding*, p. 118; "The Week," *National Review*, December 1, 1964, p. 1046; Victor S. Navasky, *Kennedy Justice* (New York: Atheneum, 1971), p. 444.

58. "Failure to mount an effective defense of the $10m-a-year delinquency program," wrote one scholar, "would have weakened the administration's case for its proposed $1 billion-a-year poverty program." In 1965, the Delinquency Act gained a two-year extension, with a modest increase in funding. Moore, "Controlling Delinquency: Executive, Congressional, and Juvenile, 1961–1964," pp. 169–171.

59. Navasky, *Kennedy Justice*, pp. 441–442; Statement of Robert Kennedy to the Committee on Labor and Public Welfare, 26 June 1964, Box 33, Adam Walinsky MSS, Box 33, JFK Library.

60. David Hackett OH, interview by John W. Douglas, August 21, 1970, JFK Library.

61. Lemann, *The Promised Land*, pp. 124–125.

62. Although John Kennedy understood opportunity theory, he placed more emphasis on the need to create jobs for juveniles in general and minorities in particular. Special Message to the Congress on Civil Rights and Job Opportunities, June 19, 1963, *Public Papers of the Presidents of the United States: John F. Kennedy, 1963* (Washington, D.C.: U.S. Government Printing Office, 1964), p. 488. Later

he called for a tax cut in part because "we cannot effectively attack the problem of teenage crime and delinquency as long as so many of our young people are out of work." Radio and TV Address to the Nation on the Test Ban Treaty and the Tax Reduction Bill, September 18, 1963, *Public Papers of the Presidents of the United States: John F. Kennedy, 1963*, p. 688.

63. Lemann, *The Promised Land*, p. 128. Navasky by contrast downplays the idea that his time in the Justice Department hastened Robert Kennedy's transition from ruthless Cold Warrior to champion of the oppressed. Navasky, *Kennedy Justice*, pp. 441–442.

64. Statement by Robert Kennedy, July 12, 1961, Box 55, Ramsey Clark MSS, Lyndon Baines Johnson Presidential Library (LBJ Library).

65. Address by Robert Kennedy, May 6, 1961, Box 55, Ramsey Clark MSS, LBJ Library.

66. Statement of Robert Kennedy, April 7, 1964, Box 87, Adam Yarmolinsky MSS, JFK Library. On his way to Capitol Hill, Ohlin briefed Robert Kennedy, who finally grasped opportunity theory in personal terms: "Oh, I see—if I had grown up in these circumstances, this could have happened to me." Lemann, *The Promised Land*, p. 129.

67. As Hackett recalled, "We made no distinction between the two." Schlesinger, *Robert Kennedy: His Life and Times*, p. 443.

68. "Community action appealed to me immediately," remembered Heller, who knew he needed a new selling-point given the continued pressure, from the Department of Labor and elsewhere, for a more traditional federal jobs program. "The moment I heard about it, it became part of my thinking." Lemann, *The Promised Land*, p. 133.

69. Sundquist, *Politics and Policy*, p. 138.

70. These include the relative importance of social scientists and economists, and whether the emergence of poverty as an issue reflected the cyclical nature of reform or the importance of presidential initiative and contingency. For a good discussion of these and other issues, see Carl M. Brauer, "Kennedy, Johnson, and the War on Poverty," *Journal of American History* 69 (June 1982): 98–119.

71. "A way had to be found to prod the local Democratic party machinery to cultivate the allegiance of urban black voters by extending a greater share of municipal services to them, and to do this without alienating urban white voters," they write. "It was this political imperative that eventually led the Kennedy and Johnson Administrations to intervene in the cities." They cite the fact that anti-delinquency funds flowed into the nation's ten largest cities at three times the national per capita average. Richard A. Cloward and Frances Fox Piven, *Regulating the Poor: The Functions of Public Welfare* (New York: Random House, 1971), pp. 231, 256, 259.

72. Hackett stated that to his knowledge only three grants were made on a political basis—to Harlem, Houston, and Providence. He contended that a "political animal" like Robert Kennedy would surely have pressured the Delinquency Com-

mission to give funds directly to the mayors if political patronage was his intent. Adam Yarmolinsky, deputy director of the Task Force, firmly maintained that with both the civil rights and poverty agenda "there was no concern whatsoever about holding on to the black vote, about an upsurge of revolt of the masses." Yet another former official demurred, recalling that the 1964 re-election campaign, the black vote, and the March on Washington, were present in the minds of the planners. Brandeis Conference, pp. 84, 133–134, 168, 193, 201, 203, 205.

73. Lawrence Friedman notes that the poor made no real demands, either organized or unorganized, for assistance. The War on Poverty was, he asserts, largely a top-down initiative by Washington experts. Carl Brauer states that the administration took black votes largely for granted and was much more worried about a backlash from southern whites angered by support for the civil rights movement. If poverty was a political issue, he adds, it was primarily as a way for Kennedy to protect and mollify liberal Democrats upset that his tax cut had not aided the disadvantaged, and to upbraid conservative Republicans for their insensitivity toward the poor. Still, Michael Katz observes that the debate reflects the differing perspectives of "insiders" and "outsiders." And although he values the evidence of "insiders" like Hackett and Yarmolinsky, he favors the analysis of "outsiders" like Piven and Cloward. See Lawrence M. Friedman, "The Social and Political Context of the War on Poverty: An Overview," in Robert H. Haveman, ed., *A Decade of Federal Anti-poverty Programs: Achievements, Failures, and Lessons* (New York: Academic Press, 1977), p. 26; Brauer, "Kennedy, Johnson, and the War on Poverty"; Katz, *The Undeserving Poor*, pp. 84–87.

74. At one point during the Brandeis conference, Piven declared that no evidence would change her mind, since individuals in positions of power often conceal their real motivation. Transcript, Poverty and Urban Policy Conference, Brandeis Conference. Yarmolinsky today acknowledges that he and others made decisions based on a variety of concerns. "Everybody acted from different motives," remembers Yarmolinsky, who calls Piven a "cliché thinker." Adam Yarmolinsky, interview with author, July 19, 1995.

75. A Kennedy biographer and administration participant makes this point. Schlesinger, *Robert Kennedy: His Life and Times*, pp. 446–448.

76. Adam Yarmolinsky, interview with author, July 19, 1995.

77. Hackett to Kennedy, August 5, 1963, Daniel Knapp MSS, JFK Library; Lemann, *The Promised Land*, p. 156; Nicholas Katzenbach, interview with author, March 6, 1998; "Why the Poverty Program is Not a Negro Program," n.d., Box 87, Adam Yarmolinsky MSS, JFK Library. This memo can be interpreted in two ways, as either a statement of the administration's outlook or an indication of how much they knew the contrary to be true—and feared a public outcry if discovered.

78. Fact Sheet—JD Planning Board, July 1, 1963, Box 8, Charles Horsky MSS, JFK Library.

79. "The very welcome and much needed decision to give administration leadership to the solution of the critical social problems of Washington has some definite political implications," wrote Hackett, requesting $150,000 for a study of youth problems. "Neither the administration nor the country can afford to fail." Hackett to Kennedy, June 7, 1962, Box 7, Richardson White Jr. MSS, JFK Library.

80. The article was entitled "Jobs Erase Hostility of Idle Negro Youths." Robert Kennedy to John Kennedy, August 15, 1963, Box 80, POF, JFK Library.

81. Speech by Agnes E. Meyer, April 15, 1963, Box 3, Charles Horsky MSS, JFK Library.

82. Russell Baker, "Behind Washington's Postcard Facade: Change, Trouble and Danger Afflict Capital," *New York Times*, June 10, 1963, p. 25.

83. Krock borrowed the reference to "urban Mau Maus" from an article in the *Washington Daily News*. See Arthur Krock, "Legalized Protection of Crime in the Capital," *New York Times*, March 18, 1963, p. 6.

84. Walter Tobriner to Charles Horsky, March 4, 1963, Box 3, Charles Horsky MSS, JFK Library.

85. Charles Horsky to John Kennedy, June 6, 1963, Box 3, Charles Horsky MSS, JFK Library.

86. Press Conference, April 6, 1961, Box 117, Ramsey Clark MSS, LBJ Library.

87. *U.S. Historical Statistics* Volume I (Washington, D.C.: Government Printing Office, 1988), p. 419. *Newsweek*, for example, ran only two related articles in two years. In the 1960s, the public focus on juvenile delinquency diminished, perhaps because the rise in urban violence rendered increasingly unpopular the idea that youths—especially black teens—were more deserving of a second chance and less responsible for their actions than adults. Another possible explanation is that as African-American males became the face of crime, there was less willingness on the part of whites to see a distinction between youths and adults.

88. Lemann, *The Promised Land*, p.156.

CHAPTER 2. LAW AND ORDER UNLEASHED

1. Republican National Convention, July 16, 1964, Box 10, 1964 Presidential Campaign Files (PCF), Barry M. Goldwater Papers (Goldwater MSS), Arizona Historical Foundation, University of Arizona, Tempe, Arizona (AHF). Whether words like "mob" and "jungle" represented implicit racial references or code words is debatable. Certainly Johnson used the term "jungle" as well: "We will not permit any part of America to become a jungle, where the weak are the prey of the strong and the many." American Bar Association Convention, August 12, 1964, Box 16, PCF, Goldwater MSS, AHF.

2. Goldwater's successful campaign for the nomination is described in detail in Rick Perlstein, *Before the Storm: Barry Goldwater and the Unmaking of the American*

Consensus (New York: Hill and Wang, 2001); Theodore H. White, *The Making of the President 1964* (New York: Atheneum, 1965); Robert Alan Goldberg, *Barry Goldwater* (New Haven: Yale University Press, 1995); John A. Andrew III, *The Other Side of the Sixties: Young Americans for Freedom and the Rise of Conservative Politics* (New Brunswick: Rutgers University Press, 1997); Robert D. Novak, *The Agony of the GOP 1964* (New York: Macmillan, 1965); Mary C. Brennan, *Turning Right in the Sixties: The Conservative Capture of the GOP* (Chapel Hill: University of North Carolina Press, 1995); and John H. Kessel, *The Goldwater Coalition: Republican Strategies in 1964* (New York: Bobbs-Merrill, 1968). For participant accounts, see F. Clifton White, *Suite 3505: The Story of the Draft Goldwater Movement* (New Rochelle: Arlington House, 1967); Lee Edwards, *Goldwater: The Man Who Made a Revolution* (Washington: Regnery, 1995); Stephen Shadegg, *What Happened to Goldwater?* (New York: Holt, Rinehart and Winston, 1965); and Karl Hess, *In a Cause that Will Triumph: The Goldwater Campaign and the Future of Conservatism* (Garden City, New York: Doubleday, 1967).

3. Peter H. Clayton, June 25, 1963, Box 4, Denison Kitchel MSS, AHF.

4. University of New Hampshire, March 3, 1964, Reel 9, Microform Reels (MR), Goldwater MSS; Keene, New Hampshire, March 4, 1964, Reel 9, MR, Goldwater MSS, AHF.

5. Keene, New Hampshire, March 4, 1964, Reel 9, MR, Goldwater MSS, AHF; White, *The Making of the President 1964*, p. 125.

6. Keene, New Hampshire, March 4, 1964, Reel 9, MR, Goldwater MSS, AHF.

7. American Society of Newspaper Editors, April 18, 1964, Box 1, Series W (unprocessed) Files, Goldwater MSS, AHF.

8. The John Birch Society (JBS) and other far-right groups consistently advocated the belief that the communists were manipulating black activists to foster a climate of chaos and terror that would lead to the imposition of martial law. Goldwater would eventually repudiate the official support of the JBS, though not the unofficial backing of its members. See "Revolution U.S.A., 1964," May 8, 1964, Box 247, Administrative File (III), NAACP Papers, Library of Congress, Washington, D.C. (LOC).

9. The result was "rhetorical confusion" and "intellectual chaos" according to one journalist. "A credo passionate with exhortations on constitutional rights here laments their legal enforcement," he wrote. "A candidate who decries unlimited public power here demands unencumbered police power." Emmet John Hughes, "Crime and Politics," *Newsweek*, October 19, 1964, p. 25.

10. Stephan Lesher, *George Wallace: American Populist* (Reading, Massachusetts: Addison-Wesley, 1994), pp. 272–273.

11. "Shouts Back Wallace at Rally on South Side," *The Milwaukee Journal*, April 2, 1964, pp. 1–2; Lesher, *George Wallace: American Populist*, pp. 283–285; and Dan T. Carter, *The Politics of Rage: George Wallace, The Origins of the New Conservatism,*

and the Transformation of American Politics (New York: Simon and Schuster, 1995), pp. 206–207.

12. "Wallace Bid Brings Visit by Gronouski," *The Milwaukee Journal*, April 3, 1964, pp. 1–2. Undoubtedly, the option of crossover voting, the lack of a contest in the Republican primary, and the unpopularity of Johnson's stand-in, Governor John Reynolds (who had proposed the controversial open-housing bill) contributed significantly to Wallace's success. See Charles W. Windler, "The 1964 Wisconsin Presidential Primary" (Ph.D. Thesis, Florida State University, 1983); and Michael Rogin, "Wallace and the Middle Class: The White Backlash in Wisconsin," *Public Opinion Quarterly* 30 (Spring 1966): 98–109.

13. Lesher, *George Wallace: American Populist*, pp. 292, 294; Carter, *The Politics of Rage*, pp. 209–211.

14. Carter, *The Politics of Rage*, p. 215; Lesher, *George Wallace: American Populist*, p. 301.

15. For a journalistic description of these developments, see Michael Lind, "The Southern Coup," *The New Republic*, June 19, 1995, pp. 20–29. For a scholarly analysis, see Philip Klinkner, *The Losing Parties* (New Haven: Yale University Press, 1994).

16. He also was a founder of the Arizona Air National Guard, which became the first integrated Air National Guard unit. Michael Lind, "The Myth of Barry Goldwater," *New York Review of Books*, November 30, 1995, p. 23.

17. Liva Baker, *Miranda: Crime, Law, and Politics* (New York: Atheneum, 1983), pp. 40–41; Shadegg, *What Happened to Goldwater?*, p. 166.

18. White, *The Making of the President 1964*, p. 200; Copy of Final Notes, Box 20, PCF, Goldwater MSS, AHF.

19. Remarks at the Mark Hopkins Hotel, July 16, 1964, Box 10, PCF, Goldwater MSS, AHF.

20. Goldberg, *Barry Goldwater*, pp. 215–216.

21. Goldwater would later contend that he had sought to assure Johnson that "at no time would I in any way connect civil rights with crime in the streets." Of course, prior to July 1964 he already had. "Barry Goldwater Speaks Out," *National Review*, January 16, 1968, pp. 27–28.

22. Overall, one person was killed, 141 (including 48 policemen) were seriously injured, and 519 were arrested. See "Harlem: Hatred in the Streets," *Newsweek*, August 3, 1964, p. 19; *Report of the National Advisory Commission on Civil Disorders* (New York: Bantam Books, 1968), p. 36.

23. Ramsey Clark Oral History (OH), interview by Harri Baker, February 11, 1969, Lyndon Baines Johnson Presidential Library (LBJ Library). See also Investigation by the FBI of Recent Civil Disturbances in New York City, July 21, 1964, Box 16, PCF, Goldwater MSS, AHF.

24. Cartha "Deke" DeLoach, *Hoover's FBI: The Inside Story by Hoover's Trusted Lieutenant* (Washington: Regnery, 1995), p. 279; Michael R. Beschloss, *Taking*

Charge: The Johnson White House Tapes, 1963–1964 (New York: Simon and Schuster, 1997), pp. 459, 462, 466–467.

25. Ibid., pp. 459, 462, 466–467.

26. Adam Yarmolinsky, interview with author, July 19, 1995. See also an unsigned memo, probably by Adam Walinsky to LBJ, July 27, 1964, Box 25, Ex JL 3, White House Subject Files (WHSF), LBJ Library.

27. "The big decision on my part," recalled Goldwater later, "was to attempt to keep race out of the campaign." Goldwater to the author, July 12, 1994. See also Hess, *In a Cause that Will Triumph*, pp. 205–206.

28. His most recent biographer contends that Goldwater acted out of sincerity. No evidence suggests otherwise. On the contrary, Johnson phoned Secretary of Defense Robert McNamara immediately after the meeting and told him that Goldwater had said, "I want to do the best I can to keep down any riot. It just would hurt me terribly if somebody got killed because of something I said." The president also claimed that Goldwater had told him that as "a half Jew" he was reluctant "to do anything that would contribute to any riots or disorders or bring about any violence." Goldberg, *Barry Goldwater*, 215–216; Beschloss, *Taking Charge*, 473–474; Barry M. Goldwater, *With No Apologies: The Personal and Political Memoirs of United States Senator Barry M. Goldwater* (New York: Morrow, 1979), pp. 192–193.

29. Bill Moyers, Richard Goodwin, and Jack Valenti to LBJ, July 21, 1964, Box 7, Diary Backup, LBJ Library; Horace Busby to LBJ, July 21, 1964, Box 7, Diary Backup, LBJ Library.

30. Press Conference, July 24, 1964, Box 16, PCF, Goldwater MSS. See also Press Statement, July 24, 1964, Box 10, PCF, Goldwater MSS, AHF; Lee Edwards, *Goldwater*, pp. 309–311; White, *The Making of the President 1964*, p. 236.

31. One historian has called the summit a mistake. But Goldwater's biographer has contended that it had little effect. He also maintains that it was the post-convention summit that caused Goldwater to shift his attack from the civil rights movement itself to what he saw as its connection to the growing crisis of crime and disorder. Yet his silence on civil rights in his convention address would seem to suggest that the shift was already underway. Vaughan Davis Bornet, *The Presidency of Lyndon B. Johnson* (Lawrence: University Press of Kansas, 1983), pp. 109–110; Goldberg, *Barry Goldwater*, pp. 215–216.

32. Lyndon Baines Johnson, *The Vantage Point: Perspectives of the Presidency, 1963–1969* (New York: Holt, Rinehart and Winston, 1971), p. 109.

33. White, *The Making of the President 1964*, p. 305.

34. Memo to Jack Valenti, August 26, 1964, Box 39, Ex JL 6, WHSF, LBJ Library; Myer Feldman to LBJ, August 23, 1964, Box 39, Ex JL 6, WHSF, LBJ Library.

35. Bill Moyers to LBJ, September 7, 1964, Box 4, Handwriting File, LBJ Library.

36. The report also criticized civilian review boards for handcuffing the ability of police departments to respond—a finding that would reverberate two years later during the controversy in New York over the establishment of a civilian review board. FBI Report, September 18, 1964, Box 20, White House Office Files (WHOF) of Richard Goodwin, LBJ Library. Hoover's position in the fall of 1964 is rather interesting. "Endeavor to remove the basic economic factors underlying Negro unrest in our large cities which result in sub standard living for Negroes," he wrote in a memo. "The Anti Poverty Program and the program to keep teen-agers in school to avoid drop-outs are steps in this direction." Suggestions for Handling Riots and Disorders, Hoover to Walter Jenkins, September 9, 1964, Box 5, WHOF of Lee White, LBJ Library.

37. "Bulletin," *National Review*, October 13, 1964, p. 1.

38. In particular, it would lead to expanded surveillance of black radicals during the Johnson administration—and to COINTELPRO operations during the Nixon administration. See Kenneth O'Reilly, "The FBI and the Politics of the Riots, 1964–1968," *Journal of American History* 75 (June 1988): 94–98. See also Kenneth O'Reilly, *"Racial Matters": The FBI's Secret File on Black America, 1960–1972* (New York: The Free Press, 1989), pp. 233–236.

39. Moyers thought it might provoke a "sharp backlash" among black voters but Katzenbach thought it on the whole "factual and realistic." Moyers to LBJ, September 23, 1964, Box 4, WHOF of Bill Moyers, LBJ Library; Katzenbach to LBJ, September 24, 1964, Box 39, WHOF of Bill Moyers, LBJ Library; Civil Rights Points for Democratic Speakers, attached to memo, Lee White to LBJ, September 28, 1964, Box 5, WHOF of Lee White, LBJ Library.

40. Although the meeting was private, a partial transcript soon found its way into Democratic hands and circulated widely at the White House. A complete transcript was eventually published in Hess, *In a Cause that Will Triumph*.

41. NAACP President Roy Wilkins had said the mention of switchblade knives constituted a coded reference to blacks. "This is news to me because I didn't associate switchblade knives with Negroes," said Eisenhower. "What I am saying here is merely this: language has to be followed or watched very, very carefully all the way through in every statement. . . . [A]s a matter of fact, I thought switchblade knives were always—and I hope there are no Italians here—identified with Italians. That will have to be watched because people are always talking about every mistake people make." Hess, *In a Cause that Will Triumph*, pp. 191, 212, 215, 221–222, 230.

42. Strategy analysis of campaign survey, n.d., Box 4, Series W Files, Goldwater MSS. The memo was probably written by Rus Walton for the national campaign staff. For indirect confirmation, see Shadegg, *What Happened to Goldwater*, pp. 222–228.

43. Strategy analysis of campaign survey, n.d., Box 4, Series W Files, Goldwater MSS, AHF.

44. Kessel, *The Goldwater Coalition*, p. 204; Edwards, *Goldwater: The Man Who Made a Revolution*, p. 330.

45. Consult the following speeches: Illinois State Fair, August 19, 1964; Prescott, Arizona, September 3, 1964; Minneapolis, September 10, 1964; St. Petersburg, September 15, 1964; Boston, September 24, 1964; Marietta, Ohio, September 29, 1964. All are located in Box 10, PCF, Goldwater MSS, AHF.

46. Illinois State Fair, August 19, 1964, Box 10, PCF, Goldwater MSS, AHF.

47. National Television Address, *ABC -TV*, October 9, 1964, Box 10, PCF, Goldwater MSS, AHF. See also "The Candidates Spell Out the Issues," *The New York Times Magazine*, November 1, 1964, Box 10, PCF, Goldwater MSS, AHF.

48. See the following speeches: Minneapolis, September 10, 1964; Columbia, October 31, 1964; and Philadelphia, October 21, 1964. All are located in Box 10, PCF, Goldwater MSS, AHF.

49. Edward P. Morgan, *ABC News*, September 3, 1964, Box 17, PCF, Goldwater MSS, AHF; Robert Pierpoint, *CBS News*, September 10, 1964, Box 17, PCF, Goldwater MSS, AHF; Roger Mudd, *CBS News*, Box 17, PCF, Goldwater MSS, AHF.

50. R.K. Scott, *Mutual Broadcasting System*, September 27, 1964, Box 17, PCF, Goldwater MSS; Bob White, October 19, 1964, Box 18, PCF, Goldwater MSS, AHF.

51. George Hamilton Combs, *Mutual Broadcasting System*, September 10, 1964, Box 17, PCF, Goldwater MSS, AHF.

52. Edward P. Morgan, *ABC News*, October 20, 1964, Box 18, PCF, Goldwater MSS, AHF.

53. Today Show, *NBC-TV*, September 10, 1964, Box 10, PCF, Goldwater MSS, AHF; Burch interview with *ABC News*, September 14, 1964, Box 17, PCF, Goldwater MSS, AHF.

54. Annual Meeting of the American Political Science Association, September 10, 1964, "Speakers—Roy Wilkins, 1963–1965," Box 304, Administrative File (III), NAACP Papers, LOC; campaign commercials, 1964, Anthology of Political Commercials, The Museum of Television and Radio, New York; Kathleen Hall Jamieson, *Packaging the Presidency: A History and Criticism of Presidential Campaign Advertising* (New York: Oxford University Press, 1984), p. 209.

55. Like the "Choice" film, the Willie Horton spot featured a racial image, was created by an independent organization not directly affiliated with the Bush campaign, and derived most of its impact from the attention devoted to it by the mainstream news media. For an in-depth analysis of the Willie Horton episode, see David C. Anderson, *Crime and The Politics of Hysteria: How the Willie Horton Story Changed American Justice* (New York: Random House, 1995). For a description of the "Choice" controversy, see Jamieson, *Packaging the Presidency*, pp. 212–216.

56. Although MFMA indicated in a press release that it had "conceived" and "financed" the film's production, the Goldwater campaign in fact contributed the production and airtime costs. Members of MFMA included Charles Keating, Nancy

Reagan, and the mother of William F. Buckley. George Hamilton Combs, *Mutual Broadcasting System*, October 22, 1964, Box 18, PCF, Goldwater MSS, AHF. See also *Washington Post*, October 26, 1964, p. A8 and Samuel G. Freedman, "The First Days of the Loaded Political Image," *New York Times*, September 1, 1996, p. 30H.

57. In Goldwater's defense, however, it appears that he gave his approval only to a general description of the project—and without seeing either a script or the completed film beforehand. Transcript of telephone conversation between Stephen Shadegg and Clifton White, December 1, 1964, Box 3J9, Barry Goldwater Collection (BGC), Eugene C. Barker Center for American History, University of Texas at Austin (Barker Center).

58. A campaign poster in the possession of Stephen Shadegg, a high-ranking Goldwater staffer, listed 41 states where "Choice" would air, including air times and specific stations. In all, more than 100 copies of the film were sold to local groups, which could then purchase airtime on their local stations. Advertisement for "Choice," Box 3H514, BGC, Barker Center.

59. "Choice," copy in the author's possession and the Audio-Visual Department of the John F. Kennedy Presidential Library (JFK Library).

60. Even top Goldwater officials were appalled. Burch and Kitchel opposed showing the film. Speechwriter Karl Hess later wrote, "From start to finish the film was racist provocation. It showed riot after riot, and black hand after black hand raised in violence. It showed Negroes in every bad light it could." Hess, *In a Cause that Will Triumph*, p. 140; Jamieson, *Packaging the Presidency*, p. 215.

61. "Choice," copy in the author's possession and the Audio-Visual Department of the JFK Library.

62. "Choice" transcript, September 29, 1964, Box 3H514, BGC, Barker Center.

63. Memo, attached to transcript, September 29, 1964, Box 3H514, BGC, Barker Center. Although unsigned, the memo was probably written by Rus Walton, public relations director of the Goldwater campaign, since it also made reference to Kennedy and the 1960 missile gap.

64. Presidential Campaign of 1964 (General), Box 247, Administrative Files (III), NAACP Papers, LOC.

65. Edwards, *Goldwater: The Man Who Made a Revolution*, p. 330.

66. For a good account of how Johnson used martial rhetoric—and the costs it imposed—see David Zarefsky, *President Johnson's War on Poverty: Rhetoric and History* (Tuscaloosa: University of Alabama Press, 1986).

67. St. Petersburg, September 15, 1964, Box 10, PCF, Goldwater MSS, AHF.

68. Schlei did not see crime and disorder as vital matters until "I was asked to focus on it by the White House." The linkage of crime and riots was because "[t]he focus of the memo was on responding to Goldwater's charges and concerns." Norbert Schlei, interview with author, July 6, 1995.

69. Riots and Crime in the Cities, n.d., attached to memo from Norbert Schlei to Lee White, September 24, 1964, Box 5, WHOF of Lee White, LBJ Library.

70. Ibid., pp. 2, 3, 26, and 27.

71. Ibid., pp. 4, 30–32. The president had already received the idea for a crime commission from Lee White. See White to LBJ, September 8, 1964, Box 5, WHOF of Lee White.

72. Paul Southwick to Bill Moyers, July 27, 1964, Box 177, Name Files (Goldwater, Barry), LBJ Library.

73. Paul Southwick to Jack Valenti, August 31, 1964, Box 481, WHOF of Fred Panzer, LBJ Library.

74. Hazel Erskine, "The Polls: Demonstrations and Riots," *Public Opinion Quarterly* 31 (Winter 1967–68): 670.

75. Dayton, Ohio, October 16, 1964, Box 16, PCF, Goldwater MSS, AHF.

76. Katzenbach to the Federal Bar Association, September 18, 1964, Box 33, Katzenbach MSS, JFK Library.

77. Of the 507 southern counties that Goldwater won, 233 had never voted Republican before. Goldberg, *Barry Goldwater*, pp. 232–235.

78. "Some day I may write a book about the campaign and if I do, I will call attention to a basic fact, that my defeat was insured on July the 15th by the stiletto job Rockefeller and Scranton and others had done on me." Goldwater to Stephen Shadegg, June 23, 1965, Box 2, Denison Kitchel MSS, AHF. For a description of some of the personal rivalries and resentments that ran through the Goldwater campaign, see Shadegg, *What Happened to Goldwater?*, pp. 75, 87, 89–91, 173; Hess, *In a Cause that Will Triumph*, pp. 135–137; White, *Politics as a Noble Calling*, pp. 155, 157; and Richard Kleindienst, *Justice: The Memoirs of an Attorney General* (Ottawa, Illinois: Jameson Books, 1985), pp. 30, 33, 47.

79. How Goldwater's language resonated with ordinary voters is unclear. But a sampling of his post-election correspondence reveals that, regardless of Goldwater's intent, his followers often read race into his pronouncements on law and order and based their support for him accordingly. See Thomas Haines to Goldwater, May 24, 1965; Donald Ledoux to Goldwater, n.d.; and Donald E. Fiscor to Goldwater, June 23, 1965. All are found in Goldwater post-election correspondence, October 22, 1964 to November 29, 1965, microform collection, Cornell University.

80. Between 1960 and 1964 the Young Americans for Freedom expanded significantly, the Conservative Party was founded in New York, and circulation of the *National Review* tripled. See Goldberg, *Barry Goldwater*, pp. 157–160; and Andrew, *The Other Side of the Sixties*, pp. 210–211.

81. Lind, "The Myth of Barry Goldwater," p. 27.

82. Novak, *The Agony of the GOP 1964*, p. 194.

83. Committee on Political Education (COPE) research memo, November 1964, Box 3J9, BGC, Barker Center.

84. By September 1966—over a year before the riots in Newark and Detroit—a majority of whites felt that the anti-poverty program would not reduce racial un-

rest. Hazel Erskine, "The Polls: Demonstrations and Riots," *Public Opinion Quarterly* 31 (Winter 1967–68): 673.

CHAPTER 3. THE WAR ON CRIME

1. Statement Following the Signing of the Law Enforcement Assistance Act, September 22, 1965, *Public Papers of the Presidents of the United States: Lyndon B. Johnson, 1965*, Book II (Washington: U.S. Government Printing Office, 1965), pp. 1013 (*Johnson Papers*).

2. Nicholas Katzenbach, interview with author, March 6, 1998.

3. Joseph Califano, interview with author, August 8, 1995.

4. Louis Harris, "Crime Rise Laid to Social Problems, Not Breakdown in Law Enforcement," *Washington Post*, December 7, 1964, p. A1.

5. Daniel Patrick Moynihan to Richard Goodwin, November 20, 1964, Box 25, Ex JL 3, White House Subject Files (WHSF), Lyndon Baines Johnson Presidential Library (LBJ Library).

6. Staff memo, December 1, 1964, Box 28, White House Office Files (WHOF) of Horace Busby, LBJ Library; Special Message on Crime and Juvenile Delinquency, December 2, 1964, Box 70, SP-2 3/1965/JL, WHSF, LBJ Library.

7. Memo, Norbert Schlei, December 2, 1964, Box 70, SP-2 3/1965/JL, WHSF, LBJ Library.

8. Special Message to Congress, March 8, 1965, *Johnson Papers* 1965 1: 263–271.

9. Statement by Ervin, July 22, 1965, Box 140, Senator Sam J. Ervin, Jr. Papers (Ervin MSS), Southern Historical Collection, University of North Carolina, Chapel Hill, North Carolina (SHC).

10. The most thorough analysis of the act claims that, although small in scope, it "legitimized" the federal role in law enforcement. Malcolm M. Feeley and Austin D. Sarat, *The Policy Dilemma: Federal Crime Policy and the Law Enforcement Assistance Administration, 1968–1978* (Minneapolis: University of Minnesota Press, 1980), pp. 36–37.

11. Statement Following the Signing of the Law Enforcement Assistance Act, September 22, 1965, *Johnson Papers 1965*, 2: 1011–1013.

12. Patrick V. Murphy and Thomas Plate, *Commissioner: A View from the Top of American Law Enforcement* (New York: Simon and Schuster, 1977), p. 68; Stuart A. Scheingold, *The Politics of Street Crime: Criminal Process and Cultural Obsession* (Philadelphia: Temple University Press, 1991), pp. 105–115.

13. See Joseph C. Goulden, "The Cops Hit the Jackpot," pp. 31–33, 40; Lee Webb, "Repression—A New 'Growth Industry,'" pp. 77–79; and Vince Pinto, "Weapons for the Homefront," pp. 89–90 in Anthony Platt and Lynn Cooper, eds., *Policing America* (Englewood Cliffs, New Jersey: Prentice Hall, 1974).

14. Katzenbach to Lee White, September 8, 1964, Box 5, WHOF of Lee White, LBJ Library. "Get rid of this problem," he advised Johnson. "Get a commission to study it." Nicholas Katzenbach, interview with author, March 6, 1998.

15. Lee White to LBJ, September 8, 1964, Box 5, WHOF of Lee White, LBJ Library.

16. Remarks to the Members of Commission on Law Enforcement and the Administration of Justice, September 8, 1965, *Johnson Papers 1965*, 2: 982 983.

17. "Target: Establishment of National Crime Commission," *Newsweek*, September 20, 1965, p. 26; Katzenbach to Califano, December 16, 1965, Box 170, Statements File (SF), LBJ Library. "There was always tugging and hauling between the people, particularly in the White House staff, who wanted to make as big a splash as possible, and the people who would have more responsibility for the program and were more realistic about what it could accomplish," Vorenberg recalled. James Vorenberg, interview with author.

18. The chairman concurred, contending that a commission without unanimity "won't solve anything." Nicholas Katzenbach, interview with author. James Vorenberg, interview with author; Notes on Meeting on Crime-Justice, August 18, 1966, Box 1, Legislative Background (LB), Safe Streets and Crime Control Act 1968, LBJ Library.

19. Powell to Vorenberg, July 6, 1966, Box 11, Katzenbach MSS, John F. Kennedy Presidential Library (JFK Library).

20. President's Commission on Law Enforcement and the Administration of Justice, *The Challenge of Crime in a Free Society* (Washington, D.C.: U.S. Government Printing Office, 1967). See also John C. Jefferies, Jr., *Justice Lewis F. Powell, Jr.* (New York: Scribner's, 1994), pp. 213–214; and James Vorenberg, interview with author.

21. James Vorenberg, interview with author.

22. *Life*, *CBS*, and *The New York Times* received advance copies in return for more detailed coverage. Only one volume appeared each week, so the media could digest its findings carefully. Katzenbach to Califano, January 3, 1967, Box 351, WHOF of James Gaither, LBJ Library. Lyndon Baines Johnson, *The Vantage Point: Perspectives of the Presidency, 1963–1969* (New York: Holt, Rinehart and Winston, 1971), p. 335.

23. *The Challenge of Crime in a Free Society*, passim.

24. M. Stanton Evans, "At Home," *National Review Bulletin*, May 14, 1967, p. 6; *Washington Evening Star*, February 21, 1967, p. 23.

25. Jack D. Douglas, ed., *Crime and Justice in American Society* (New York: Bobbs-Merrill, 1971). For the administration reaction, see Fred Panzer to Califano, April 18, 1967, Box 26, Ex JL 3, WHSF, LBJ Library.

26. Center for Research on Criminal Justice, *The Iron Fist and the Velvet Glove: An Analysis of the U.S. Police* (San Francisco: Garrett Press, 1975), p. 9.

27. Hugh Davis Graham, "The Ambiguous Legacy of American Presidential Commissions," *The Public Historian* 7 (Spring 1985): 20–21.

28. The commitment to consensus and secrecy, noted *The New Republic*, meant that "it will be late in the day when it becomes clear which questions were asked and which were not." "The Compromise Report on Crime," *The New Republic*, February 4, 1967, p. 16.

29. Liva Baker, *Miranda: Crime, Law, and Politics* (New York: Atheneum, 1983), p. 202; Arthur Niederhoffer, *Behind the Shield: The Police in Urban Society* (New York: Doubleday, 1967), pp. 161–4; David Simon, *Homicide: A Year on the Killing Streets* (New York: Ballantine, 1991; 1992 paperback edition), pp. 199–200.

30. M. Stanton Evans, "At Home," *National Review Bulletin*, May 14, 1967, p. 6.

31. *Report of the National Advisory Commission on Civil Disorders* (New York: Bantam Books, 1968), p. 38.

32. That the officer was white was not surprising, since only three of the more than 3,000 CHP officers were black. Gerald Horne, *Fire This Time: The Watts Uprising and the 1960s* (Charlottesville: University of Virginia Press, 1995), pp. 54–55, 57, 354.

33. The LAPD had to patrol 463 square miles to patrol with 5,120 officers. By contrast, the NYPD had 30,000 police for 365 square miles. "We're the most undermanned police force in the country," said one veteran captain. See "Troubled LA—Race Is Only One of its Problems," *U.S. News and World Report*, August 30, 1965, p. 61. This fact—in conjunction with Parker's well-publicized lack of respect for minorities—may have contributed to the LAPD's historical willingness to resort to force at the least provocation.

34. Daryl F. Gates with Diane K. Shah, *Chief: My Life in the LAPD* (New York: Bantam Books, 1992), pp. 98, 100–101; Horne, *The Fire Within*, p. 77.

35. He was also a churchgoer, usually charged with looting within one mile of home in the company of friends. See Gates, *Chief: My Life in the LAPD*, pp. 103–104; Horne, *Fire This Time* pp. 3, 205. *Report of the National Advisory Commission on Civil Disorders*, p. 258.

36. "Terror in Los Angeles: What Life Is Like When Race War Hits a City," *U.S. News & World Report*, August 30, 1965, p. 24.

37. Ramsey Clark OH, interview by T.H. Baker, April 16, 1969, LBJ Library; Harry McPherson OH, interview by T.H. Baker, April 9, 1969, LBJ Library; Joseph Califano, interview with author, August 8, 1995.

38. Joseph A. Califano, Jr., *The Triumph and the Tragedy of Lyndon Johnson: The White House Years* (New York: Simon and Schuster, 1991), pp. 59–62. The politics of blame quickly engulfed Los Angeles, with Yorty, Parker, and Brown firing accusations at each other and at targets like Sargent Shriver. See "A Dispute over Blame for the Los Angeles Riots," *U.S. News & World Report*, August 30, 1965, p. 16; and "After the Blood Bath," *Newsweek*, August 30, 1965, pp. 13–20.

39. Califano, *The Triumph and the Tragedy of Lyndon Johnson*, pp. 62–63.

40. Statement Upon Announcing a Program of Assistance to LA, August 26, 1965, *Johnson Papers, 1965*, 2: 993–994.

41. Harry McPherson OH, interview by T.H. Baker, April 9, 1969, LBJ Library.

42. Ramsey Clark OH, interview by TH. Baker, March 21, 1969, LBJ Library.

43. Report on the President's Task Force on the Los Angeles Riots, August 11–15, 1965, Box 47, WHOF of Joseph Califano, LBJ Library.

44. Not included in the report, despite White House urging, was praise for Yorty or the conduct of the California National Guard. Barefoot Sanders to Ernest Friesen and Hugh Nugent, September 16, 1965, Box 71, Clark MSS, LBJ Library.

45. Ramsey Clark OH, interview by Harri Baker, March 21, 1969, LBJ Library. See also Paul Jacobs, "The McCone Commission," in Anthony M. Platt, ed., *The Politics of Riot Commissions, 1917–1970* (New York: Macmillan, 1971), p. 294. According to one account, Johnson was prepared to publish but yielded in the face of McCone's threat to resign. See Roger Wilkins, *A Man's Life: An Autobiography* (New York: Simon and Schuster, 1982), p. 173.

46. The McCone Commission contended that only two percent of the black population had participated in the rioting and looting. It also noted that the Urban League had rated Los Angeles first among 68 cities in quality of life for African Americans. Governor's Commission on the Los Angeles Riots, "Violence in the City—An End or a Beginning?" in Platt, ed., *The Politics of Riot Commissions, 1917–1970*, pp. 264–268; Gates, *Chief: My Life in the LAPD*, p. 94.

47. Governor's Commission on the Los Angeles Riots, "Violence in the City," pp. 269–283.

48. At the same time, structural factors influenced the report. The commission had a tight three-month deadline, few funds beyond what the Ford Foundation provided, and a staff of investigators and consultants that ultimately included no professional social scientists. Warren Christopher Oral History, interview by T.H. Baker, October 31, 1968, LBJ Library; Paul Jacobs, "The McCone Commission," in Platt, ed., *The Politics of Riot Commissions, 1917–1970*, pp. 293–294.

49. Hazel Erskine, "The Polls: Demonstrations and Riots," *Public Opinion Quarterly* 31 (Winter 1967–68): 665.

50. "McWhat report: reactions to McCone report," *Newsweek*, December 20, 1965, pp. 28–29.

51. Jacobs, "The McCone Commission," p. 289; Michael T. Klare, "Bringing It Back: Planning for the City," in Anthony Platt and Lynn Cooper, eds., *Policing America*, pp. 99–103; Horne, *The Fire This Time*, p. 38.

52. If only 10,000 individuals had actively joined the riot, then the LAPD had managed to arrest 40 percent of them—a questionable assumption to many. A UCLA study also directly contradicted the assertion that those arrested were marginal members of community in terms of education and employment history. At the same time, the commission spent little time assessing how common "passive participation" was. Robert M. Fogelson, "White on Black: A Critique of the McCone Commission Report on the Los Angeles Riots," *Political Science Quarterly* 82

(September 1967): 345–346. Later studies would show that the typical rioter was not a recent arrival, with little education or political awareness. *Report of the National Advisory Commission on Civil Disorders*, pp. 127–134.

53. In a recent twist on this argument, one scholar has contended that the failure of leadership in Watts was due primarily to Cold War hysteria and "Red Squad" harassment in the 1950s. "The repression of the left," he writes, "created an ideological vacuum that would later be filled by black nationalism and this nationalism exploded in Watts in August 1965." See Horne, *The Fire This Time*, p. 3.

54. Paul Jacobs, *Prelude to Riot: A View of Urban America from the Bottom* (New York: Random House, 1966), pp. 237–262; and Robert M. Fogelson, *Violence as Protest* (New York: Doubleday, 1971), pp. 192–216. For the quotation, see Fogelson, "White on Black: A Critique of the McCone Commission Report," p. 367.

55. The author was also casual and contemptuous in his use of racial metaphor. "How could it have happened?" he asked. "After all, Los Angeles is not the Congo—or is it?" See Will Herberg, "Who Are the Guilty Ones?" *National Review*, September 7, 1965, pp. 769–770. For a less sophisticated but similar view, see Aubrey Chrisman to Ervin, August 17, 1965, Box 138, Ervin MSS, SHC.

56. Horne, *The Fire This Time*, p. 36.

57. "Interview with a Policeman assigned to the Watts Area," *National Review*, September 7, 1965, 17, p. 773. See also Ronald Reagan on "Issues and Answers," *ABC-TV*, 29 May 1966, Box 25, Ronald Reagan Papers (Reagan MSS), Hoover Institution Archives, Stanford University, Palo Alto, California (Hoover Institution); "Watts and the Welfare Riot," *National Review*, December 14, 1965, p. 1146; and Sam Yorty OH, interview by Joe B. Frantz, February 7, 1970, LBJ Library. The localist impulse received clear expression from Yorty: "I am hopeful you will give strong consideration to our argument that the War on Poverty can be most effectively waged at a local level and that consensus programs developed thousands of miles away and implemented because they appear popular and politically safe are a threat to our anti-poverty efforts." Yorty to LBJ, May 26, 1967, Box 58, WHOF of Joseph Califano, LBJ Library.

58. Carey McWilliams, "Watts: The Forgotten Slum," *Nation*, August 30, 1965, pp. 89–90.

59. Norman B. Houston to various California news agencies, March 17, 1966, Box 64, Administrative File (IV), NAACP Papers, Library of Congress (LOC).

60. Leonard Carter to Roy Wilkins, September 10, 1965, Box 333, Administrative File (III), NAACP Papers, LOC. Carter later seemed to support the "agitator theory" advanced by some on the right, writing that since Watts "Communist, Black Nationalist, Black Muslems [sic] and John Birch Society followers have been at work fanning the seeds of unrest and hatred." Carter to Gloster B. Current, March 18, 1966, Box 64, Administrative Files (IV), NAACP Papers, LOC.

61. Mike Davis, *City of Quartz: Excavating the Future in Los Angeles* (New York: Vintage Books, 1992).

62. The command center generally included Califano, Hoover, Clark, and McNamara, with other aides often present, including McPherson and Fortas. In 1967 it helped Johnson to avoid the paralysis he had experienced during the first days of Watts in 1965. Donald Scruggs, "LBJ and the National Commission on Civil Disorders (The Kerner Commission): A Study of the Johnson Domestic Policy Making System," (unpub. Ph.D., University of Oklahoma, 1980), p.196.

63. Jim Jones to W. Marvin Watson, November 11, 1965, Box 25, Ex JL 3, WHSF, LBJ Library.

64. Katzenbach to LBJ, December 8, 1965, attached to Califano to LBJ, December 9, 1965, Box 25, Ex JL 3, WHSF, LBJ Library; Katzenbach to Califano, February 25, 1966, Box 77, SP-2–3/1966/JL, WHSF, LBJ Library.

CHAPTER 4. THE CONSERVATIVE TIDE

1. Reagan to William Buckley, December 7, 1966, Box 37, Ronald Reagan Papers (Reagan MSS), Hoover Institution Archives, Stanford University, Palo Alto, California (Hoover Institution).

2. The best account of this race is Matthew Dallek, *The Right Moment: Ronald Reagan's First Victory and the Decisive Turning Point in American Politics* (New York: The Free Press, 2000).

3. Lisa McGirr, "Suburban Warriors: Grass-Roots Conservatism in the 1960s" (Ph.D. diss., Columbia University, 1995), p. 250. See also Lisa McGirr, *Suburban Warriors: The Origins of the New American Right* (Princeton: Princeton University Press, 2001).

4. Of Reagan one Brown campaign official noted: "He is an attractive, plausible, persuasive 'good guy' whose synthetic packaging is not apparent. . . . [H]e is a 'natural' not only in the TV era but for the emerging cultural, psychological wavelengths to which much of the country is attuned. The Governor, in contrast, belongs to an earlier political era in terms of personal projection." Frederick Dutton to Bill Moyers, June 10, 1966, 6/10/66, Box 1057, Vice-Presidential Papers (VPP), Hubert H. Humphrey Papers (Humphrey MSS), Minnesota Historical Society, St. Paul, Minnesota (MHS).

5. Stuart Spencer, interview by Sarah Sharp, February 23, 1979, in *Issues and Innovations in the 1966 Republican Gubernatorial Campaign*, The Bancroft Library, University of California, Berkeley (Bancroft Library).

6. Mary C. Brennan, *Turning Right in the Sixties: The Conservative Capture of the GOP* (Chapel Hill: University of North Carolina Press, 1995), p. 141. Gaylord Parkinson, interview by Sarah Sharp, November 21, 1978, in *Issues and Innovations in the 1966 Republican Gubernatorial Campaign*, Bancroft Library.

7. In Orange County, more than 50 percent of adult males were veterans (the national average was 37 percent). Between 1950 and 1960 California received al-

most twice as much in federal military expenditures as any other state, most of which went to southern California. McGirr, "Suburban Warriors," pp. 29, 37, 61, 65, 110–111, 113.

8. Ibid., pp. 115, 126, 290–291.

9. Roger Kent, interview by Amelia R. Fry, February 23, 1977, in *Building the Democratic Party in California, 1954–1966*, Bancroft Library; Matthew Dallek, "Liberalism Overthrown," *American Heritage* 47 (October 1996): 50.

10. Stanley Plog, interview by Steven Stern, June 5, 1981, in *More Than Just An Actor: The Early Campaigns of Ronald Reagan*, Bancroft Library.

11. In 1970 Brown wrote of Reagan: "Ronald Reagan for governor of California? We thought the notion was absurd and rubbed our hands in gleeful anticipation of beating this politically inexperienced, right-wing extremist and aging actor in 1966." Dallek, "Liberalism Overthrown," p. 44.

12. Brown also admitted, rather backhandedly, that Reagan was "a very, very adroit politician. There's no question about it at all. In my opinion, [he] is a liar too. I mean, he doesn't tell the truth." Edmund "Pat" Brown OH, interview by Joe B. Frantz, August 19, 1970, Tape #2, Lyndon Baines Johnson Presidential Library (LBJ Library).

13. In union households, Brown's support dropped from 74 percent in 1958 to 57 percent by 1966. Kurt Schuparra, *Triumph of the Right: The Rise of the California Conservative Movement, 1945–1966* (New York: M. E. Sharpe, 1998), p. 138.

14. Stuart Spencer, interview by Sarah Sharp, February 23, 1979, in *Issues and Innovations in the 1966 Republican Gubernatorial Campaign*, Bancroft Library; Donald Bradley, interview by Amelia R. Fry, January 16, 1979, in *Managing Democratic Campaigns, 1943–1966*, Bancroft Library; Lyn Nofziger, interview by Sarah Sharp, October 10, 1978, in *Issues and Innovations in the 1966 Republican Gubernatorial Campaign*, Bancroft Library.

15. Sam Yorty to LBJ, July 28, 1965, Box 40, FG 763, White House Subject Files (WHSF), LBJ Library.

16. Edmund G. Brown, Sr., interview by Amelia R. Fry, November 15, 1978, in *Years of Growth, 1939–1966: Law Enforcement, Politics, and the Governor's Office*, Bancroft Library. For an analysis of Yorty's showing, see Totton J. Anderson and Eugene C. Lee, "The 1966 Election in California," *Western Political Quarterly* 20 (June 1967): 535–536, 549.

17. Jake Jacobsen to LBJ, October 4, 1966, Box 33, Ex PL/ST5, WHSF, LBJ Library; Lee White to John Seigenthaler, December 28, 1961, Box 13, Dean Markham MSS, John F. Kennedy Presidential Library (JFK Library). For an analysis of the larger significance of this conference, see Michael Woodiwiss, *Crime, Crusades, and Corruption: Prohibitions in the U.S., 1900–1987* (Totowa, New Jersey: Barnes and Noble Books, 1988), p. 166.

18. Yorty to LBJ, June 8, 1964, Box 3, Handwriting File, LBJ Library; Humphrey to Brown, April 4, 1966, Humphrey to Jack Conway, June 23, 1965, and Humphrey

to Bill Connell, June 23, 1965, Box 1057, VPP, Humphrey MSS, MHS; Robert Kintner to LBJ, June 25, 1966, Box 76, PL/Name Political Affairs, WHSF, LBJ Library.

19. Appearance at Boalt Hall, Berkeley, n.d., Box 25, Reagan MSS, Hoover Institution.

20. Press Conference, January 4, 1966, Box 25, Reagan MSS, Hoover Institution; Transcript, "Issues and Answers," *ABC-TV*, May 29, 1966, Box 25, Reagan MSS, Hoover Institution.

21. Frederick Dutton to Bill Moyers, June 10, 1966, Box 1057, VPP, Humphrey MSS, MHS.

22. There was, conceded a Brown campaign official, "a general impression, in a period of increasing conservatism, of Pat overshifting to the liberal side and at the same time vacillating at times and seeming to be too much a politician." Frederick G. Dutton, interview by Amelia R. Fry, August 15, 1978, in *Democratic Campaigns and Controversies, 1954–1966*, Bancroft Library.

23. "The Week," *National Review*, April 5, 1966, p. 301; Carey McWilliams, "Watts: The Forgotten Slum," *Nation*, August 30, 1965, pp. 89–90.

24. In California, narcotics arrests of juveniles rose almost 35 percent in 1966. See *U.S. News and World Report*, November 21, 1966, p. 53.

25. Dallek, "Liberalism Overthrown," p. 50.

26. The Reagan campaign moved to make pornography part of the "culture wars," noting how California had become the nation's leading producer of smut and lending support to Proposition 16, an anti-obscenity initiative. See for example the TV commercial "Crime," 1966, RNC Series—Film, Audio-Visual Department, JFK Library.

27. Stuart Spencer, interview by Sarah Sharp, February 23, 1979, in *Issues and Innovations in the 1966 Republican Gubernatorial Campaign*, Bancroft Library.

28. Frederick G. Dutton, interview by Amelia R. Fry, August 15, 1978, in *Democratic Campaigns and Controversies, 1954–1966*, Bancroft Library.

29. Reagan would later appoint Haldeman to the Board of Regents. Haldeman to Henry Salvatori, August 23, 1966, Box 9, Series II, Richard M. Nixon Presidential Library (RMN Library).

30. BASICO Staff to RR, October 12, 1966, Box 36, Reagan MSS, Hoover Institution.

31. "Ammunition!" from the Research Center, March 1966, Box 35, Reagan MSS; Edmund G. Brown, *Reagan and Reality: The Two Californias* (New York: Praeger, 1970), p. 143.

32. "Reagan Interview," *U.S. News and World Report*, November 21, 1966, p. 55.

33. Emerson Midyett to James Cuff O'Brien, November 11, 1966, Box 1057, VPP, Humphrey MSS; Frederick G. Dutton, interview by Amelia R. Fry, August 15, 1978, in *Democratic Campaigns and Controversies, 1954–1966*, Bancroft Library.

34. Reagan proposed the establishment of a foundation for the widows and children of police and firemen killed in the line of duty; the installation of a three-

digit statewide phone number to report crimes; and the construction of a central crime laboratory and a police training academy (modeled on the FBI's facilities). See "Men from Clean," *Newsweek*, September 5, 1966, pp. 23–24; Reagan Kick-Off Telecast, September 9, 1966, Box 25, Reagan MSS, Hoover Institution; and Reagan to Hoover, August 19, 1966, Box 37, Reagan MSS, Hoover Institution.

35. "Crime," 1966, RNC Series—Film, Audio-Visual Department, JFK Library. Reagan would reinforce the gender theme constantly. In October he asked the Highway Patrol Commissioner whether "he's willing to let his wife walk the streets of his hometown at night, alone." News Release, October 5, 1966, Box 34, Reagan MSS, Hoover Institution.

36. Transcript, "Issues and Answers," *ABC-TV*, October 2, 1966, Box 25, Reagan MSS, Hoover Institution.

37. "Meet the Press," *NBC News*, September 11, 1966, Box 34, Reagan MSS, Hoover Institution; Roger Kent, interview by Amelia R. Fry, February 23, 1977, in *Building the Democratic Party in California, 1954–1966*, Bancroft Library; Research Department to Reagan, May 4, 1966, Box 37, Reagan MSS, Hoover Institution; Brown News Release, September 5, 1966, Box 37, Reagan MSS, Hoover Institution.

38. Brown News Release, September 5, 1966, Box 37, Reagan MSS, Hoover Institution.

39. Brown to Humphrey, January 19, 1966, Box 1057, VPP, Humphrey MSS, MHS.

40. In New York the crime rate set a record in 1962 and climbed steadily in 1963. See "Crimes Set Mark, Rising 3% in 1961," *New York Times*, July 13, 1962, p. 50 and "Crime Here Rises 9.1%; Murders Increase by 9.3%," *New York Times*, October 15, 1963, p. 78.

41. Ruth Cowan, "The New York City Civilian Review Board Referendum of November 1966: A Study in Mass Politics" (Unpub. Ph.D. diss., NYU, 1970), pp. 6, 393. Other PBA commercials were even more graphic, featuring brass knuckles, switchblades, and a voice-over that emphasized how only "the policeman stands between you and the threat of mounting violence." James Priest Gifford, "The Political Relations of the PBA in the City of New York, 1946–1969," (Unpub. Ph.D. diss., Columbia University, 1970), p. 386.

42. The turnout was 2.08 million votes—more than were cast in the 1964 presidential race. The final margin was 1,313,161 (63 percent) in favor of the referendum and 765,468 (32 percent) opposed. In Manhattan, the vote in favor of civilian review (and against the referendum) was 234,485 to 168,391. In the Bronx, the vote against civilian review was 235,310 to 128,084; in Brooklyn, 414,133 to 201,836; in Queens, 426,821 to 191,787; and in Richmond, 63,083 to 12,800. See Thomas R. Brooks, "'No!' Says the PBA," *New York Times Magazine*, October 16, 1966; David W. Abbott, Louis H. Gold, and Edward T. Rogowsky, *Police, Politics, and Race: The New York City Referendum on Civilian Review* (Cambridge: American Jewish

Committee and the Joint Center for Urban Studies of Massachusetts Institute of Technology and Harvard, 1969), pp. 7–8; and "Tally of Votes for Governor, Statewide Offices, Police Review Board, and Judgeships," *New York Times*, November 10, 1966, p. 10.

43. Both Lindsay and Aryeh Neier of the New York Civil Liberties Union (NYCLU) had deep doubts about the outcome. Woody Klein, *Lindsay's Promise: The Dream that Failed* (London: Macmillan, 1970), pp. 245, 250; Cowan, "The New York City Civilian Review Board Referendum of November 1966," p. 354.

44. On the whole, 68 percent of Brooklyn voters opposed the review board in comparison to 65 percent of the sample. Over 93 percent of Goldwater supporters opposed the review board. Among Jews, 55 percent who supported the civil rights movement *and* felt safe backed the review board; only 38 percent of those who supported the civil rights movement *but* felt unsafe did so. Abbott, Gold, and Rogowsky, *Police, Politics, and Race*, pp. 8, 17–18.

45. In the survey of Brooklyn whites, 85 percent said blacks learned as well as whites; 75 percent said they "would not mind if a Negro with the same income and education" moved into their neighborhoods; and 62 percent rejected the idea that some groups were better than others. Thus it appears that the results reflected less racial animus and more fear of what whites felt blacks represented—violence, poverty, welfare, property deterioration, and family disintegration. They "voted to support the police—the symbol of order and the defender of life and property—against the threat to their way of life, which they believed the Negroes posed." What was critical wasn't racism but a shift in the liberal perception of blacks, "from victims and objects of violence and prejudice, to perpetrators of violence and social disorganization." Abbott, Gold, and Rogowsky, *Police, Politics, and Race*, pp. 38, 42–44.

46. Gerald Sorin, *The Nurturing Neighborhood: The Brownsville Boys Club and Jewish Community in Urban America, 1940–1990* (New York: New York University Press, 1990), pp. 91, 159–163, 168.

47. Ibid., pp. 108, 109. See also "Strong Arm of the Law," *Time*, July 7, 1958, p. 15.

48. "The situation in New York City is getting out of hand," wrote one resident. "Violence, horror, looting, rioting, stabbing, raping, purse-snatching are all around. . . . It is not safe walking in the streets and parks and riding in the elevators." Charles Shamoon to Nelson Rockefeller, July 24, 1964, Reel 17, RG 15 (Subject Files), Nelson A. Rockefeller Papers (Rockefeller MSS), Rockefeller Archive Center, Tarrytown, NY (RAC). A survey of correspondence to Democratic Congressman Emanuel Celler of Brooklyn reveals similar sentiments. See Box 298, Emanuel Celler Papers (Celler MSS), LOC.

49. In 1952, a flurry of complaints about alleged NYPD misconduct led to the creation of a police review board composed of three deputy commissioners. But the issue of police brutality received little attention for the remainder of the decade.

50. The proposal, which originated with the NYCLU and Reform Democrats like future Mayor Ed Koch, vested the board with the power to pursue cases independently regardless of any ongoing criminal investigations. During the hearings, NYPD Commissioner Michael Murphy said the charges of police brutality were "maliciously inspired" and were a "calculated mass libel of the police." Cowan, "The New York City Civilian Review Board Referendum of November 1966," pp. 116–117, 126.

51. In March, Kitty Genovese bled to death from multiple stab wounds while 38 people listened to her screams and failed to act. In April, a gang of 50 black teenagers attacked a group of Hasidic children. And in May, the NYPD confirmed the existence of the "Blood Brothers," an anti-white gang in Harlem believed responsible for the murder of four whites. In Brooklyn, Hasidic Jews formed a civilian patrol named the Maccabees to protect their community after repeated beatings, muggings, and the attempted rape of a rabbi's wife by a black man. Finally, over Memorial Day weekend 20 black teens vandalized and terrorized a subway train, beating and robbing passengers. "Maccabees and the Mau Mau," *National Review*, July 16, 1964, pp. 479–480.

52. The shooting fit a tragic if familiar pattern. For a balanced description, see James Lardner, *Crusader: The Hell-Raising Police Career of Detective David Durk* (New York: Random House, 1996), p. 75. A grand jury would later find Gilligan not criminally liable for the shooting. But witnesses interviewed by the NAACP contended that Powell was shot while moving away from Gilligan, that he was shot without warning or identification by the officer, and that the student was unarmed. See Statement and Recommendations of New York Branch NAACP, Box 103, Branch Files (III), NAACP Papers, LOC.

53. "The black man is mad," agreed Adam Clayton Powell Jr., "mad with the continued police brutality of white policemen." Woody Klein, "Harlem: The Ghetto Ignites," *Nation*, August 10, 1964, pp. 50–51. Klein later became Lindsay's press secretary. See also Statement and Recommendations of New York Branch NAACP, Box 103, Branch Files (III), NAACP Papers, LOC.

54. See the correspondence to Governor Nelson Rockefeller, Reel 17, RG 15 (Subject Files), Rockefeller MSS, RAC.

55. Theodore H. White, *The Making of the President 1964* (New York: Atheneum, 1965), p. 231.

56. Official reports suggested the latter. The FBI report on the Harlem Riot and the McCone Report on the Watts Riot suggested that civilian review boards hindered a prompt response. Katzenbach to LBJ, September 24, 1964, Box 39, WHOF of Bill Moyers, LBJ Library; Governor's Commission on the Los Angeles Riots, "Violence in the City—An End or a Beginning?" in Anthony M. Platt, ed., *The Politics of Riot Commissions, 1917–1970* (New York: Macmillan, 1971), p. 276.

57. William F. Buckley, Jr., "Remarks to the NYPD Holy Name Society," *National Review* April 20, 1965, p. 326; William F. Buckley Jr., "Statement by Wm. F.

Buckley Jr. Announcing His Candidacy for Mayor of New York, June 24, 1965," *National Review* August 13, 1965, p. 587.

58. The campaign did feature other issues, such as the so-called "sleeper clause," which proponents of civilian review contended at the last moment would insulate the NYPD from all graft and corruption investigations. In fact, however, the clause would not prohibit investigations by the district attorney, grand juries, or Internal Affairs. In any event, the issue proved to have less "bite" than many liberals, including Robert Kennedy, had hoped. See Bernard Weinraub, "Kennedy Sees Peril to Civilian Control of Police," *The New York Times*, November 4, 1966, p. 29; and Sidney E. Zion, "'Sleeper Issue' on Police Referendum Wakes Up," *The New York Times*, October 30, 1966.

59. Bernard Weinraub, "Kennedy Sees Peril to Civilian Control of Police," *The New York Times*, November 4, 1966, p. 29.

60. New York Citizens Committee to Support Your Local Police, Box 19, Legal Department (III), NAACP Papers, LOC.

61. The civilian review board, he contended, had boosted confidence in the police and would also protect officers from malicious or groundless accusations. Press Releases, May 2, 1966 and September 22, 1966, Box 68, Departmental Correspondence, Lindsay MSS.

62. On July 12 Lindsay met in private with Cassese and Frank and told them that he would hold them responsible if the PBA inflamed racial tensions. Klein, *Lindsay's Promise*, p. 202.

63. H. L. Hunt of Dallas contributed a reported $10,000. More than 50 police unions sent donations to the PBA and the International Association of Police Chiefs passed a resolution in July 1966 affirming its opposition to civilian review boards. See William W. Turner, *The Police Establishment* (New York: Putnam's Sons, 1968), p. 225; Cowans, "The New York City Civilian Review Board Referendum of November 1966," p. 369; and Press Release, September 22, 1966, Box 68, Departmental Correspondence, Lindsay MSS, New York Municipal Reference Library (NYMRL).

64. "This is an historic moment," said Lindsay on October 26 at the Overseas Press Club. "Perhaps the most important fight I have ever seen. I am appalled to discover, after passage of many civil rights bills, that many of the wonderful liberals are slightly doctrinaire, it appears. This fight is the guts of it. This separates the men from the boys." Klein, *Lindsay's Promise*, p. 232; Press Release, September 22, 1966, Box 68, Departmental Correspondence, Lindsay MSS, NYMRL.

65. The JBS launched a "Support Your Local Police" campaign because it saw local law enforcement as a bulwark of freedom against the communist conspiracy and the federal government. The JBS also used the campaign to recruit members and to raise needed funds through the sale of bumper stickers, buttons, etc. When the JBS sponsored a Town Hall rally against civilian review, a crowd of almost 500 gathered, most of them off-duty officers with PBA badges. See "Let's Go," John

Birch Society Newsletter, February 1965, Goldwater post-election correspondence, Microform Reel # 2 (October 22, 1964–November 29, 1965), Cornell University; and Arnold Foster, "John Birch in Uniform," The ADL Bulletin, November 1965, Box 19, Legal Department (III), NAACP Papers, LOC.

66. David Garth, campaign manager for the Federated Association for Impartial Review (FAIR), later termed the pursuit of Irish and Italian votes "a waste of time." Cowan, "The New York City Civilian Review Board Referendum of November 1966," pp. 317, 331; Klein, *Lindsay's Promise*, p. 255; and Abbott, Gold, and Rogowsky, *Police, Politics, and Race*, p. 15.

67. No exit polls of blacks and Puerto Ricans appear to exist. The vote totals for certain districts support the statement, however. In South Harlem, the margin was 10,507 to 3,332 in favor of the review board; in Central Harlem, it was 11,044 to 2,658; in Harlem, it was 15,206 to 3,255. In Bedford-Stuyvesant, it was 9,002 to 3,312 and in Fort Williamsburg it was 9,148 to 2,581. "Tally of Votes for Governor, Statewide Offices, Police Review Board, and Judgeships," *New York Times* November 10, 1966, p. 10.

68. After the referendum the president and chairman of the Guardians filed a suit against the PBA alleging illegal use of their funds. Press Release, March 15, 1966, Box 68, Departmental Correspondence, Lindsay MSS, NYMRL; Press Release, December 14, 1966, Box 2, Printed Matter (IV), NAACP Papers, LOC.

69. Joseph P. Viteritti, *Police, Politics, and Pluralism in New York City: A Comparative Case Study* (Beverly Hills: Sage Publications, 1973), p. 12; Cowan, "The New York City Civilian Review Board Referendum of November 1966," pp. 153, 162; Attitudes of Harlem Residents toward Housing, Rehabilitation, and Urban Renewal, August 1966, Box 32, Administrative Files (IV), NAACP Papers, LOC.

70. Martin Luther King Jr., "Beyond the Los Angeles Riots: Next Stop, the North," *Saturday Review*, November 13, 1965, p. 34; Eldridge Cleaver, *Soul On Ice* (New York: Dell, 1968), pp. 132–133; *Associated Press*, December 13, 1968, Box 109, Clark MSS, LBJ Library. See also Lionel H. Mitchell (a black conservative), "When Law and Order Fail," *National Review*, July 30, 1968, pp. 741–742.

71. Klein, *Lindsay's Promise*, pp. 255–276. For a thorough analysis of what the defeat meant for the mayor, see Vincent Cannato, *The Ungovernable City: John Lindsay and His Struggle to Save New York* (New York: Basic Books, 2001). For a critical assessment of whether the battle was worth it, see Aaron Wildavsky, "The Empty-Head Blues: Black Rebellion and White Reaction," *The Public Interest* 11 (Spring 1968): 3–16; reprinted in Marvin R. Summers and Thomas E. Barth, eds., *Law and Order in a Democratic Society* (Columbus, Ohio: Charles E. Merrill, 1970).

72. Wattenberg to Moyers, October 4, 1966, Box 18, WHOF of Ben Wattenberg, LBJ Library.

73. Statement by the President, November 6, 1966, Box 6, WHOF of Ceil Bellinger, LBJ Library.

74. James Rowe (actually written by Richard Scammon) to LBJ, January 6,

1967, attached to memo, Marvin Watson to LBJ, January 12, 1967, Box 77, PL 2, WHSF, LBJ Library.

75. Civil Rights and Backlash, Box 1057, VPP, Humphrey MSS, MHS.

76. According to AFL-CIO political analysts, the white backlash and black activism were to blame, particularly in white, blue-collar wards like Cicero. "Illinois," n.d., Committee on Political Education Research Division Files (COPE Papers), George Meany Memorial Archives, Silver Spring, Maryland (GMMA).

77. Alan Draper, *A Rope of Sand: The AFL-CIO Committee on Political Education, 1955–1967* (New York: Praeger, 1989), pp. 123–124; Wattenberg to LBJ, November 21, 1967, Box 26, Ex PL/Kennedy, WHSF, LBJ Library.

78. Draper, *A Rope of Sand*, pp. 121–123; Minutes of AFL-CIO Executive Council Meeting, November 15, 1966, GMMA.

79. A Harris Poll in early September showed that, by a healthy margin (49–31 percent), whites felt that the anti-poverty program was a failure (blacks supported it by a 67–12 percent margin). A Harris Poll in late October showed that 56 percent of those surveyed felt that the Republican Party "would be better at cutting down riots and racial violence." Only 44 percent chose the Democratic Party. Hazel Erskine, "The Polls: Demonstrations and Riots," *Public Opinion Quarterly* 31 (Winter 1967–68): 673–674.

CHAPTER 5. THE POLITICS OF CIVIL UNREST

1. The terminology or language of urban unrest was constantly contested. The most common term was riot, which had a precise legal meaning as well as a symbolic significance. The Kerner Commission popularized the term "civil disorder," which troubled some liberals because of its connotations to civil disobedience. Ironically, both the left and the right often preferred uprising, revolution, or rebellion because they presumed political intent and even premeditation. Likewise the term insurrection, which was also favored by insurance companies because, when invoked, it often voided coverage (although in late 1967 they agreed to honor all of that summer's claims regardless of the specific terminology used by local officials). In this study, riot, unrest, and disorder are used interchangeably because they seem more neutral than the alternatives. Today, the terminology remains contested, as a recent article on the aftermath of the 1992 LA Riots reported. While scholars and officials preferred the term "civil unrest," some blacks favored "rebellion" or "uprising," while Hispanics often used *los quemazones* ("the great burnings") and Koreans generally followed their national tradition of using the date—sa-i-ku (literally 4–2–9). Todd S. Purdum, "Legacy of Los Angeles Riots: Divisions Amid the Renewal," *New York Times*, April 27, 1997, A1 and A24.

2. Wattenberg to LBJ, July 24, 1967, Box 243, Statements File (SF), Lyndon Baines Johnson Presidential Library (LBJ Library).

3. Panzer to LBJ, August 11, 1967, Box 398, WHOF of Fred Panzer, LBJ Library. The figures on police brutality were consistent. *Report of the National Advisory Commission on Civil Disorders* (New York: Bantam Books, 1968), p. 302 (hereafter *Kerner Commission Report*). By the end of the summer of 1967, only six percent of whites believed that police brutality existed in their communities, a drop of 50 percent from 1965. Panzer to LBJ, August 29, 1967, Box 39, Ex JL 6, White House Subject Files (WHSF), LBJ Library.

4. Panzer to Marvin Watson, August 3, 1967, Box 20, FG 11-8-1 / Panzer, Fred, WHSF, LBJ Library.

5. Thinking the Unthinkable: A Scenario in Four Parts, October 18, 1967, Box 77, White House Office Files (WHOF) of Joseph Califano, LBJ Library.

6. Ibid.

7. Ibid.

8. The president felt under fire from both wings of his own party. Senator Richard Russell of Georgia "thinks that we are going to hell every year. . . . [H]e thinks that we got a warfare in our own party and that we are kind of backing the Stokely Carmichaels and the Martin Luther Kings and the only way he can defend himself is to take the Republicans and whip the hell out of us and that's what he's going to do." At the same time, continued Johnson, the liberal Democratic senators are "hitting us everyday from the inside so that our party is split wide open. I do not know what in the world they think we can do." Telephone conversation, LBJ with Katzenbach, January 25, 1967, 7:45 p.m., Tape K67.02, PNO 3, LBJ Library.

9. *Kerner Commission Report*, pp. 56–60. An application for Model Cities aid in 1967 noted that Newark had the nation's highest percentage of poor housing; the most crime per 100,000 residents; the heaviest per capita tax burden; and the highest rates of venereal disease, maternal mortality, and new cases of TB. The city was also second in infant mortality, second in birth rate, and seventh in absolute number of drug addicts despite its relatively small size. Tom Hayden, *Rebellion in Newark: Official Violence and Ghetto Response* (New York: Random House, 1967), pp. 3, 5–6; and "The Real Tragedy of Newark," *U.S. News & World Report*, July 31, 1967, p. 30. Conditions have hardly improved in Newark since. See Ronald Smothers, "In Riots' Shadow, a City Stumbles On," *New York Times*, July 14, 1997, pp. B1, B4.

10. The main characters in the drama were complicated figures. Smith was a former Army corporal, a chess-playing trumpet player with a revoked license and a poor driver with eight or nine accidents to his record. The mayor was a liberal former Congressman who had wrested control of City Hall from the Irish by forging an Italian-Black coalition. Spina was a police progressive who had implemented a series of reforms, including police-precinct councils, mandatory human relations training, and a Citizens' Observer program. Ironically, in 1966 the Justice Department had funded the nation's largest police–community relations program in Newark. See *Kerner Commission Report*, pp. 60–64; and Hayden, *Rebellion in Newark*, pp. 9, 14–16, 34, 38.

11. "Newark Race Riot: 'Open Rebellion—Just Like Wartime,'" *U.S. News & World Report*, July 24, 1967, p. 6; "Newark Boils Over," *Newsweek*, July 24, 1967, p. 22; Art Sears Jr., July 18, 1967, Box 471, Part III, National Urban League Papers (NUL Papers), Library of Congress (LOC).

12. Only 1.2 percent of the New Jersey National Guard was black and less than 1 percent of the New Jersey state troopers were black. *Kerner Commission Report*, pp. 64–69; Hayden, *Rebellion in Newark*, p. 45.

13. *Meet the Press*, July 16, 1967, Box 78, Administrative File (IV), NAACP Papers, LOC.

14. Johnson diplomatically rejected their suggestion that communists had supplied the snipers with rifles by stating that Hoover was checking into it. Joseph A. Califano, Jr., *The Triumph and the Tragedy of Lyndon Johnson: The White House Years* (New York: Simon and Schuster, 1991), pp. 210–211.

15. Newark officials were "in a state of shock" on Sunday according to Warren Christopher, who had joined the Justice Department that weekend. Warren Christopher OH, interview by T. H. Baker, November 18, 1969, LBJ Library.

16. President's News Conference, July 18, 1967, *Public Papers of the Presidents of the United States: Lyndon B. Johnson, 1967*, Book II (Washington, D.C.: U.S. Government Printing Office, 1968), pp. 701–702 (*Johnson Papers*).

17. "Detroit's Mayor," *U.S. News & World Report*, August 7, 1967, p. 16.

18. *Kerner Commission Report*, 85–86, 89–91; Sidney Fine, *Violence in the Model City: The Cavanagh Administration, Race Relations, and the Detroit Riot of 1967* (Ann Arbor: The University of Michigan Press, 1989), pp. 1–93. See also "The Fire This Time," *Time*, August 4, 1967, pp. 13–14.

19. During the 1950s, Detroit lost almost one-quarter of its white population. From 1960 to 1967, the black population rose from under 30 to almost 40 percent of the population. The unemployment rate for Detroit in the year before the riot was 3.9 percent. In July, however, it was 6.2 percent (around 8 percent for blacks in general and 11 percent for blacks in the riot area). By 1965 the median non-white family income was $6,405 compared to the national average of $3,886 and the white average in Detroit of $6,846. Fine emphasizes that blacks in Detroit compared their condition unfavorably to whites rather than favorably to blacks in other cities. *Kerner Commission Report*, 85–86, 89–91; Fine, *Violence in the Model City*, pp. 1–93.

20. Yet in the spring of 1967 the Office of law Enforcement Assistance hailed the Detroit Police Department as "the model for community relations." Fine, *Violence in the Model City*, pp. 95–125. See also Jerome Cavanaugh OH, interview by Joe B. Frantz, March 22, 1971, LBJ Library.

21. Police Commissioner Ray Girardin later explained that police feared it was a diversion. Garry Wills, *The Second Civil War* (New York: New American Library, 1968), p. 84. Another factor was that the police had put down a riot in 1966 using similar tactics—in addition to a show of overwhelming force, a point forgotten

in 1967. Jerome Cavanaugh OH, interview by Joe B. Frantz, March 22, 1971, LBJ Library.

22. Congressman John Conyers was booed and stoned when he visited his district. "You try to talk to these people and they'll knock you into the middle of next year," he said. Robert "Buddy" Battles III, UAW shop leader and president of the Trade Union Leadership Council, had a similar experience: "You couldn't speak to those kids. This was not hate the man, just looting." B. J. Widick, "Motown Blues," *Nation*, August 14, 1967, p. 103. See also the *Kerner Commission Report*, pp. 84–89.

23. Barefoot Sanders to Califano, July 28, 1967, Box 58, WHOF of Joseph Califano, LBJ Library; Jerome Cavanaugh OH, interview by Joe B. Frantz, March 22, 1971, LBJ Library; Tom Parmenter, "Breakdown of Law and Order," *Trans-Action* 4 (Sept. 1967): 13–22, reprinted in Marvin R. Summers and Thomas E. Barth, eds. *Law and Order in a Democratic Society* (Columbus, Ohio: Charles E. Merrill, 1970), pp. 105–106. For an anecdotal account of casual looting in Detroit, see John Dotson, "I Don't Care If I Die," *Newsweek*, August 4, 1967, pp. 26–27.

24. *Kerner Commission Report*, pp. 92–93.

25. Many of the soldiers held racist beliefs and few had any personal familiarity with Detroit. A reporter described an encounter with the crew of an armored personnel carrier. "We're lost!" said the officer. "Can you tell us where we are? We're from Grand Rapids." Fine, *Violence in the Model City*, pp. 196–199.

26. Wills, *The Second Civil War*, pp. 50–51, 53. Fine, *Violence in the Model City*, p. 201. For descriptions of the havoc wreaked by the Guard, which was responsible for at least seven deaths, see the *Kerner Commission Report*, pp. 97–103.

27. Dotson, "I Don't Care If I Die," *Newsweek*, August 4, 1967, p. 27.

28. John Hersey, *The Algiers Motel Incident* (Baltimore: The Johns Hopkins University Press, 1968; revised edition, 1998), pp. 333, 351–352.

29. The mayor, safety director, and governor would exchange accusations in the aftermath. The governor couldn't make up his mind, charged Girardin, a Cavanagh loyalist, claiming that he and the mayor had always wanted federal troops. Wills, *The Second Civil War*, p. 51. In Romney's defense, he was concerned that use of the term "insurrection" might void insurance coverage. Fine, *Violence in the Model City*, pp. 193–196, 199–203.

30. Johnson lacked trust or confidence in Romney. Joseph Califano, interview with author, August 8, 1995. "I knew what I had to do," recalled Johnson in his memoirs, "but I could not erase from my mind the awful prospect of American soldiers possibly having to shoot American citizens. The thought of blood being spilled in the streets of Detroit was like a nightmare. I could imagine the inflammatory photographs appearing within hours on television and on the front pages of newspapers around the world." Lyndon Baines Johnson, *The Vantage Point: Perspectives of the Presidency, 1963–1969* (New York: Holt, Rinehart and Winston, 1971), p. 170.

31. Tom Johnson's Notes of the President's Activities During the Detroit Crisis (TJN), July 24, 1967, Box 1, LBJ Library.

32. The 2,700 paratroopers fired only 201 rounds, most of them in the first few hours. They were permitted to load their weapons only if an officer gave the order. Throckmorton attempted to have the National Guard unload their weapons as well, but had less success. *Kerner Commission Report*, p. 100. See also "An American Tragedy, 1967," *Newsweek*, August 7, 1967, p. 20.

33. The death toll in Detroit and other cities may have been higher than reported. As one guardsman recalled: "We were supposed to fill out all those goddam reports after every exchange of fire. You can't fight a battle and be filling out forms. We just shot and forgot. When we killed a sniper or looter, he either died in a burning building or we threw him into one." Wills, *The Second Civil War*, p. 56. For the official figures, see *Kerner Commission Report*, pp. 106–108. For a recent analysis of the lingering impact that the riot has had, see Robyn Meredith, "5 Days in 1967 Still Shake Detroit," *New York Times*, July 23, 1997, p. A10.

34. One of the "haunting questions," according to Johnson, was what if he had deployed the paratroopers sooner. Johnson, *The Vantage Point*, p. 173.

35. "The Romney-LBJ Feud: Who Played Politics in the Rioting?" *U.S. News & World Report*, August 14, 1967, p. 14.

36. We knew, recalled Califano, "that we had to find a way to get them aid without appearing to bow to the rioters." Joseph Califano, interview with author. "In this picture," concurred Christopher, "we were always walking a difficult line of wanting to assist the cities in their relief and rehabilitation, but at the same time not wishing to have the occasion of a riot made the reason for a city to get preferential treatment on its normal programs." Warren Christopher OH, interview by T. H. Baker, November 18, 1969, LBJ Library. McPherson felt that the issue of rewarding rioters was "hollow" because the administration had a moral obligation to assist all in need and lacked the funds "to 'reward' anybody, if 'reward' means the massive rebuilding of slum areas. We didn't have it before and we don't now." McPherson, *A Political Education: A Washington Memoir* (Austin: University of Texas Press, 1972; 1995 edition), pp. 360–361.

37. Remarks to the Nation After Authorizing the Use of Federal Troops in Detroit, July 24, 1967, *Johnson Papers (1967)*, 2: 716.

38. Johnson later claimed that the language was for constitutional purposes only. "But my doubts were as deep as those of the reporters I tried to persuade," recalled a dubious McPherson. When Califano, who likewise felt the wording was too partisan and legalistic, questioned Johnson, he replied that "I had the best damn constitutional lawyer in the country write that statement." McPherson, *A Political Education*, p. 360; Califano, *The Triumph and the Tragedy of Lyndon Johnson*, p. 218.

39. Even Cavanagh, a Romney foe, believed that the Johnson's speech had engendered sympathy for the governor. Jerome Cavanaugh OH, interview by Joe B. Frantz, March 22, 1971, LBJ Library.

40. President's News Conference, July 31, 1967, *Johnson Papers* (1967), 2: 727; Ramsey Clark statement, September 12, 1967, Box 15, Warren Christopher Papers (Christopher MSS), LBJ Library. See also Califano to LBJ, September 12, 1967, Box 24, Handwriting File, LBJ Library. In a request that Hoover saw as "fraught with political dynamite," the White House also asked the FBI director to get a tape of Romney's TV and radio statement on July 24 in which he vacillated on the need for federal troops. See Fine, *Violence in the Model City*, p. 216.

41. Califano to LBJ, July 26, 1967, Box 22, WHOF of John Robson and Stanford Ross, LBJ Library.

42. Gaither to Califano, July 27, 1967, Box 43, WHOF of James Gaither, LBJ Library; Muriel Hartley to Jim Gaither, August 1, 1967, Box 43, WHOF of James Gaither, LBJ Library; Notes of the President's Meeting with the Cabinet, August 2, 1967, Box 9, Cabinet Papers, LBJ Library.

43. Nimetz to Califano, August 9, 1967, Box 58, WHOF of Joseph Califano, LBJ Library.

44. Notes of the President's Meeting with the Cabinet, August 2, 1967, Box 9, Cabinet Papers, LBJ Library. See also Minutes of the Meeting, August 2, 1967, Box 9, Cabinet Papers, LBJ Library.

45. "Ramsey ultimately did, in every instance that I saw, just what Ramsey thought the right result was," recalled an aide. Bruce Allen Murphy, *Fortas: The Rise and Ruin of a Justice* (New York: William Morrow, 1988), pp. 295–296.

46. Notes of the President's Meeting with the Cabinet, August 2, 1967, Box 9, Cabinet Papers, LBJ Library. See also Minutes of the Meeting, August 2, 1967, Box 9, Cabinet Papers, LBJ Library.

47. Ibid. Whether Johnson seriously entertained the idea that the riots were the product of a conspiracy is unclear, although he was willing to ponder the possibility at times. According to one scholar, the president became convinced a conspiracy existed, perhaps fostered by communists, an idea Hoover encouraged. "The FBI always knew when and where the next riot was going to take place and it had always taken place when and where they predicted," Johnson told Katherine Graham. Nicholas Lemann, *The Promised Land: The Great Black Migration and How It Changed America* (New York: Knopf, 1991), p. 190. For his part, Califano contends otherwise: "I don't think he thought for five minutes that there was a conspiracy. The only thing we ever worried about was whether Chinese communist money was going to the Black Panther groups." Joseph Califano, interview with author.

48. Of Clark, Johnson said: "If I had ever known that he didn't measure up to his daddy [former Attorney General and Justice Tom Clark], I'd never have made him Attorney General." Yet Johnson remained loyal to Clark and apparently never sought to replace him. Califano, *The Triumph and the Tragedy of Lyndon Johnson*, pp. 221–222.

49. "After the Riots: A Survey," *Newsweek*, August 21, 1967, pp. 18–19; Hazel Erskine, *Public Opinion Quarterly* 31 (Winter 1967–68): 655–677.

50. Ibid.

51. Ibid.

52. Ibid.

53. Tom Hayden, *Rebellion in Newark*, p. 69.

54. Phillip A. McCombs, "Who is Behind the Race Riots?" *National Review*, September 20, 1966, pp. 334–335; James Burnham, "Care and Feeding of Riots," *National Review*, September 24, 1968, p. 951. James Burnham, "The Collective Organizer," *National Review*, August 22, 1967, p. 895.

55. "Bulletin," *National Review*, August 2, 1966, p. 1; "Watts to Detroit," *National Review*, August 22, 1967, pp. 885–7; "The Permanent Insurrection," *National Review*, August 8, 1967, pp. 835–838. See also Ervin to Mrs. John Burchard, March 16, 1968, Box 200, Senator Sam J. Ervin, Jr. Papers (Ervin MSS), Southern Historical Collection (SHC).

56. Alan Greenspan to Nixon, September 26, 1967, Box 3, Series I, 1968 Presidential Campaign Papers (PCP), Richard M. Nixon Presidential Library (RMN Library). Other Nixon advisers like Ray Price held more moderate views. See Price to Nixon, 7/27/67, PPS 500.10–5, Research Files, PCP, RMN Library.

57. Editorial, "The Three Revolutions," *Nation*, August 14, 1967, pp. 98–99.

58. Surveys in Detroit and Newark confirmed that a significant number of the residents in selected neighborhoods had participated to some degree in the riots and that participants on average had more education than nonparticipants, although less than those who had actively opposed the riots. The surveys also showed, however, that a significant majority of blacks were either passive bystanders or active counter-rioters (that is, they attempted to stop the riots). *Kerner Commission Report*, pp. 7, 132–133. See also Richard A. Cloward and Frances Fox Piven, *Regulating the Poor: The Functions of Public Welfare* (New York: Random House, 1971), pp. 228–229, 233, 238–239. Newark, according to Hayden, was one of those moments when the "people take leadership in their own hands." Hayden, *Rebellion in Newark*, p. 14.

59. Almost all of the major riots of the 1960s were precipitated by a police action. Police harassment and brutality remained major causes of black resentment. Robert M. Fogelson, "From Resentment to Confrontation: The Police, the Negroes, and the Outbreak of the Nineteen-Sixties Riots," *Political Science Quarterly* 83 (June 1968): 217–247.

60. Lewis M. Moroze, "Lethal Indifference," *Nation*, August 14, 1967, pp. 105–107; Hayden, *Rebellion in Newark*, pp. 30, 32.

61. In 1965, Saul Alinsky called the War on Poverty "history's greatest relief program for the benefit of the welfare industry." Social workers were, he added, "pimps of the poor." The anti-poverty program was, he concluded, "a macabre masquerade and the mask is growing to fit the face, and the face is one of political pornography." Saul Alinsky, "The War on Poverty—Political Pornography," *Journal of Social Issues* 21 (January 1965): 41–47. In March 1968, the black caucus at the Lake Villa Confer-

ence called for an end to the War on Poverty because it was a paternalistic reform. David Farber, *Chicago '68* (Chicago: University of Chicago Press, 1988), p. 87.

62. *Kerner Commission Report*, p. 143. Harrington's statement was cited in "Crime and Insurrection," *Nation*, July 31, 1967, pp. 68–69. See also Cleaver, *Soul on Ice*, p. 136.

63. Celler to the American Jewish Committee Appeal for Human Relations, November 2, 1967, Box 540, Celler MSS, LOC.

64. Almost four times as many non-whites as whites still lived in poverty (defined by the Social Security Administration as an annual household income of less than $3,335 for a family of four). The median black family income was less than 60 percent that of whites. Only 28 percent of black families were in the middle class compared to 55 percent of white families. And although the overall unemployment rate for blacks had fallen to 8.2 percent by 1967 (3.2 percent for married black men), it remained twice as high as for whites. In the central cities it was between 16 and 20 percent. *Kerner Commission Report*, pp. 14, 251–253.

65. Joseph Rauh to Congress, July 12, 1967, Box 11, Joseph L. Rauh Papers (Rauh MSS), LOC; A. Philip Randolph to LBJ, July 19, 1967, Box 64, Administrative Files (IV), NAACP Papers, LOC.

66. James Gaither OH, interview by Michael L. Gillette, May 12, 1980, LBJ Library; Douglass Cater, interview with author, July 13, 1995; Doris Kearns, *Lyndon Johnson and the American Dream* (New York: Harper and Row, 1976), p. 305; Ben Wattenberg OH, interview by T.H. Baker, November 23, 1968, LBJ Library; *Kerner Commission Report*, pp. 14, 251–253. The White House deliberately tabulated the unemployment figures in the most favorable light, but they accurately reflected the administration's outlook. For an alternative assessment, see William Hamilton Harris, *The Harder We Run: Black Workers Since the Civil War* (New York: Oxford University Press, 1982), p. 153.

67. Douglass Cater, interview with author; James Gaither, interview with author, September 25, 1995; James Gaither OH, interview by Michael L. Gillette, May 12, 1980, LBJ Library; Matthew Nimetz OH, interview by Steve Goodell, January 7, 1969, tape #1, LBJ Library.

68. In September 1966, 24 percent viewed racial unrest as the nation's most important problem. By August 1967 that figure had jumped to 79 percent—higher even than the 76 percent who believed the war in Vietnam to be the nation's most pressing overseas concern. Fred Panzer to Marvin Watson, August 3, 1967, Box 20, FG 11-8-1 / Panzer, Fred, WHSF, LBJ Library.

69. In Cleveland 80 percent of whites voted Republican and in Boston it was 50 percent. In Gary, the figure was 90 percent. A Croatian precinct that was 68 percent Democratic in 1964 was now 93 percent Republican. Wattenberg to LBJ, November 21, 1967, Box 26, Ex PL/Kennedy, Robert F., WHSF, LBJ Library.

70. Mrs. Charles W. Ratchford to Ervin, July 18, 1967, Box 180, Ervin MSS, SHC. The book maintained that the loss of personal security resulted from liberal

programs which had transformed America "into a happy hunting ground for the thief, the rapist, the drug addict, the pervert, the arsonist, the murderer-for-kicks, the looter." It also promised "guidance that you, your wife—yes, and your children—must have as the crime rate continues to soar in the Great Society jungle." *National Review*, January 16, 1968, p. 4.

71. For a concise and typical statement, see "Senator Sam Ervin Says," August 3, 1967, Box 451, Ervin MSS, SHC.

72. This view found considerable favor in the scholarly world. See Cloward and Piven, *Regulating the Poor*, pp. 228–229, 233, 238–239.

73. In a typical response, the Attorney General declared that "I think we would have to be very careful in considering demonstrations and lawlessness and rioting as the same thing." See Law Day USA Special, April 30, 1967, Box 20, Ramsey Clark MSS, LBJ Library.

74. Daniel Patrick Moynihan, "The Politics of Stability," September 23, 1967, Box 57, WHOF of Harry McPherson, LBJ Library.

75. A Conversation with the President, December 19, 1967, Johnson Papers (1967), 2: 1164-1165.

76. Wattenberg to McPherson and Cater, December 22, 1967, Box 260, Statements File, LBJ Library.

77. Fred Panzer to Jim Jones, December 28, 1967, Box 20, FG 11–8-1 / Panzer, Fred, WHSF, LBJ Library.

CHAPTER 6. THE LIBERAL QUAGMIRE

1. Harry McPherson Oral History, interview by T.H. Baker, March 24, 1969, tape #6, Lyndon Baines Johnson Presidential Library (LBJ Library).

2. Johnson convened almost twice as many commissions annually as had his postwar predecessors. Overall, Johnson appointed 28 presidential commissions and more than 130 secret task forces in what one historian has called a "tour de force of presidential advisement." Hugh Davis Graham, "The Ambiguous Legacy of American Presidential Commissions," *The Public Historian* 7 (Spring 1985): 20. See also Donald Scruggs, "LBJ and the National Commission on Civil Disorders (The Kerner Commission): A Study of the Johnson Domestic Policy Making System" (unpub. Ph.D. diss., University of Oklahoma, 1980), p. 4; and Thomas R. Wolanin, *Presidential Advisory Commissions: Truman to Nixon* (Madison: University of Wisconsin Press, 1975), pp. 21, 23.

3. *Report of the National Advisory Commission on Civil Disorders* (New York: Bantam, 1968), p. 537 (*Kerner Commission Report*).

4. Garry Wills, *The Second Civil War: Arming for Armageddon* (New York: The New American Library, 1968).

5. For a solid contemporary account of the Kerner fiasco (from the administra-

tion's perspective), see Elizabeth Drew, "On Giving Oneself a Hotfoot: Government by Commission," *Atlantic* 221 (May 1968): 45–49.

6. *Kerner Commssion Report*, p. 1.

7. On several occasions Ginsburg conferred with Califano and assured him that he would try to steer the commission away from controversy. Califano to LBJ, August 7, 1967, Box 11, White House Office Files (WHOF) of Joseph Califano, LBJ Library; Joseph Califano, interview with author, August 8, 1995.

8. Wolanin, *Presidential Advisory Commissions*, p. 76. See also Press Conference, July 29, 1967, Box 2, WHOF of Irvine Sprague, LBJ Library; Otto Kerner OH, interview by Paige E. Mulhollan, June 12, 1969, LBJ Library; Press Conference, July 31, 1967, Box 58, WHOF of Joseph Califano, LBJ Library.

9. In general, the White House cannot dictate to commissioners because of their high visibility and prestige. At the same time, an administration often is unclear in what it wants, needs a commission with credibility and integrity, and usually lacks the resources as well as the will to try to "fix" a commission. Scruggs, "LBJ and the National Commission on Civil Disorders (The Kerner Commission)," pp. 92–94; Wolanin, *Presidential Advisory Commissions*, pp. 23, 145, 193–195.

10. Hugh Davis Graham, "On Riots and Riot Commissions: Civil Disorders in the 1960s," *The Public Historian* 2 (Summer 1980): 13; Joseph A. Califano, Jr., *The Triumph and the Tragedy of Lyndon Johnson: The White House Years* (New York: Simon and Schuster, 1991), pp. 219–220.

11. The commission was explicit: "The urban disorders of the summer of 1967 were not caused by, nor were they the consequence of, any organized plan or 'conspiracy.'" *Kerner Commission Report*, pp. 9, 202, 278–282, 323, 328–331, 336, 505. Whether Johnson was persuaded is unclear. According to Ginsburg, at their first meeting the president was certain that the riots were the product of a conspiracy. Thomas J. Bray, "Reading America the Riot Act: The Kerner Report and Its Culture of Violence," *Policy Review* 43 (Winter 1988): 33. Kerner himself had pioneered riot training as commander of the Illinois National Guard.

12. *Kerner Commission Report*, pp. 115–116; Graham, "On Riots and Riot Commissions," pp. 116–117. See also Hugh Davis Graham, "The Paradox of American Violence," in Graham and Ted Robert Gurr, rev. ed., *Violence in America: Historical and Comparative Perspectives* (Beverly Hills: Sage Publications, 1979), pp. 475–490.

13. By January 1967 over 88 percent of all black families owned a television. The figure was probably even higher in urban areas. A 1961 study in New York, for example, showed that 95 percent of black families had a television. *Kerner Commission Report*, pp. 10–11, 267–268, 274, 362–386.

14. Ibid., p. 2.

15. For data on "white flight" and the black migration, see *Kerner Commission Report*, pp. 136, 241, 245–246. For merchant exploitation, see pp. 274–277; for police brutality, see pp. 302–304.

16. Andrew Kopkind, "White on Black: The Riot Commission and the Rhetoric of Reform," in Anthony M. Platt, ed., *The Politics of Riot Commissions, 1917–1970* (New York: Macmillan, 1971), pp. 388–389; Scruggs, "LBJ and the National Commission on Civil Disorders (The Kerner Commission)," p. 453.

17. *Kerner Commission Report*, pp. i, vii, 411, 420, 457, 475, 479, 481.

18. Robert M. Fogelson, "Review Symposium," *American Political Science Review* 63 (December 1969): 1269–1275.

19. Ervin to Mrs. John Burchard, March 16, 1968, Box 200, Ervin MSS, SHC; Frank S. Meyer, "Liberalism Run Riot," *National Review*, March 26, 1968, p. 283; Radio Address, March 7, 1968, PPS 208 (1968).11.2, Speech Files, Richard M. Nixon Presidential Library (RMN Library).

20. Sherwood Ross, "LBJ's Riot Commission: The Fact-Finding Charade," *Nation*, March 4, 1968, pp. 306–308; Kopkind, "White on Black," p. 380. For a similar analysis, see Michael Lipsky and David J. Olson, *Commission Politics: The Processing of Racial Crisis in America* (New Brunswick, New Jersey: Transaction Books, 1977).

21. Only Wattenberg had serious reservations about the report. "The Kerner Commission, for my money, bought every silly cliché about Negroes in the book—every one of them without exception. . . . And I think it would have been a very bad thing for the president of the United States to say, 'I agree. We're a white racist nation,' because that would have been a disaster." But, he added, Johnson reacted poorly to the report. "He was very foolish, I think, in letting that pique show publicly." Ben Wattenberg OH, interview by T.H. Baker, November 23, 1968, LBJ Library.

22. Clark to LBJ, March 2, 1968, Box 77, Ramsey Clark, LBJ Library; Califano to LBJ, March 2, 1968, Box 16, WHOF of Joseph Califano, LBJ Library; Louis Martin to Califano, March 5, 1968, Box 9, WHOF of Joseph Califano, LBJ Library.

23. Califano to LBJ, February 27, 1968, Box 188, WHOF of James Gaither, LBJ Library; Califano to LBJ, February 28, 1967, Ex FG 690, White House Subject Files (WHSF), LBJ Library.

24. McPherson to Joe Califano, March 1, 1968, Box 32, WHOF of Harry McPherson, LBJ Library.

25. McPherson to LBJ, March 18, 1968, Box 53, WHOF of Harry McPherson, LBJ Library.

26. Califano, *The Triumph and the Tragedy*, p. 262.

27. Roger Wilkins to Harry McPherson, April 4, 1968, Box 32, WHOF of Harry McPherson, LBJ Library; Roger W. Wilkins before the Illinois Mayor's Seminar on Urban Race Relations, March 28, 1968, Box 77, Ramsey Clark MSS, LBJ Library.

28. Harry McPherson OH, interview by T.H. Baker, March 24, 1969, tape #6, LBJ Library. For the Johnson quote, see Harry McPherson, *A Political Education: A Washington Memoir* (Austin: University of Texas Press, 1972; 1995 edition), p. 376.

29. Lyndon B. Johnson, *The Vantage Point: Perspectives of the Presidency, 1963–1969* (New York: Holt, Rinehart and Winston, 1971), p. 173; McPherson, *A Political Education*, p. 376; Scruggs, "LBJ and the National Commission on Civil Disorders (The

Kerner Commission)," pp. 472, 479–480; Califano, *The Triumph and the Tragedy*, pp. 261–262.

30. Califano to LBJ, April 10, 1968, Box 17, WHOF of Joseph Califano, LBJ Library; Lemann, *The Promised Land: The Great Black Migration and How It Changed America* (New York: Knopf, 1991), p. 191.

31. "Choice," in the author's possession and the audio-visual department of the John F. Kennedy Presidential Library (JFK Library).

32. Richard Nixon, February 15, 1968, PPS 208 (1968).6, Speech Files, RMN Library.

33. See Michael T. Klare, "Policing the Empire" and "Bringing It Back: Planning for the City" in Anthony Platt and Lynn Cooper, eds., *Policing America* (Englewood Cliffs, New Jersey: Prentice Hall, 1974); Eldridge Cleaver, *Soul On Ice* (New York: Dell, 1968), p. 132; and Lewis M. Killian, *The Impossible Revolution?* (New York: Random House, 1968), p. 162. A more recent scholarly analysis contends that the form and shape of the 1960s riots was due to patterns of internal colonialism. See Ira Katznelson, *City Trenches: Urban Politics and the Patterning of Class in the United States* (New York: Pantheon Books, 1981), p. 120.

34. Cleaver, *Soul On Ice*, pp.129–130.

35. Robert M. Collins, "The Economic Crisis of 1968 and the Waning of the 'American Century,'" *American Historical Review* 101 (April 1996): 396–422.

36. McPherson to Califano, March 1, 1968, Box 32, WHOF of Harry McPherson, LBJ Library.

37. Televised Remarks Announcing the Arrest of Members of the KKK, March 26, 1965, *Public Papers of the Presidents of the United States: Lyndon B. Johnson, 1965*, Book I (Washington: U.S. Government Printing Office, 1965), p. 333 (*Johnson Papers*). The exact cost of crime was—and is—hard to quantify. Hoover estimated it at $28 billion a year while the GOP Coordinating Committee calculated it at $30 billion a year. In either case, crime cost more than the Vietnam War and was growing at twice the rate of the American economy since 1960—figures that conservatives were eager to exploit. Buchanan to Nixon, October 23, 1967, PPS 500.18–11, Research Files (1968), RMN Library.

38. By then the projected deficit (in January) had almost tripled and Johnson had to increase his proposed tax surcharge, which Congress gave him but only in return for billions in spending cuts, primarily in domestic social programs. Collins, "The Economic Crisis of 1968 and the Waning of the 'American Century,'" p. 403.

39. LBJ to the IACP, September 14, 1967, Box 7, WHOF of Matthew Nimetz, LBJ Library; Califano, *The Triumph and the Tragedy*, p. 217.

40. Walt Rostow to LBJ, July 28, 1967, Box 32, WHOF of Harry McPherson, LBJ Library; Califano to LBJ, December 16, 1967, Box 8, WHOF of Joseph Califano, LBJ Library.

41. Clifton West to Ervin, July 21, 1967, Box 180, Ervin MSS; Alma Palton to Celler, January 19, 1968, Box 299, Celler MSS, Library of Congress (LOC).

42. Matthew Nimetz OH, interview by Steve Goodell, January 7, 1969, tape #1, LBJ Library.

43. President's News Conference, July 31, 1967, *Johnson Papers* (1967), 2: 732. See also Irving Bernstein, *Guns or Butter: The Presidency of Lyndon Johnson* (New York: Oxford University Press, 1996).

44. Although it would save almost $3 million, Califano advised against it because of the political flak. "Among other things, I think it would be read as a further abandonment of domestic problems because of the Vietnam War, could easily be related to more stories about further escalation." Califano to LBJ, December 4, 1967, Box 8, WHOF of Joseph Califano, LBJ Library.

45. In fact, the Draft Riots of 1863, which in essence were race riots, were far more deadly than Watts—or even Newark and Detroit in 1967. Robert Kennedy speech, December 16, 1965, Box 24, Legal Department (III), NAACP Papers, LOC. See also "Which War?" *Nation*, March 18, 1968, pp. 362–3.

46. "An American Tragedy, 1967," *Newsweek*, August 7, 1967, p. 26; editorial, "The Three Revolutions," *Nation*, August 14, 1967, pp. 98–99; Robert G. Sherrill, "90th Congress: Slapping at Symbols," *Nation*, August 28, 1967, pp. 142–145; editorial, "The Undiscussed Issue," *Nation*, August 19, 1968, p. 100.

47. Statement by the President for the Cabinet Meeting of August 2, 1967, Box 9, Cabinet Papers, LBJ Library.

48. James Gaither, interview with author, September 25, 1995; "Crime Control and Reduction," June 15, 1967, Box 14, WHOF of Matthew Nimetz, LBJ Library.

49. Califano to LBJ, August 1, 1967, Box 185, Ex FG 135, WHSF, LBJ Library; Joseph Califano, interview with author.

50. Interview of McGiffert by Staff of Permanent Subcommittee on Investigations, April 22, 1968, Box 6, Warren Christopher MSS, LBJ Library; Califano to LBJ, February 27, 1968, Box 188, WHOF of James Gaither, LBJ Library; *Kerner Commission Report*, pp. 67,100; Hayden, *Rebellion in Newark: Official Violence and Ghetto Response* (New York: Random House, 1967), p. 42; Clark to LBJ, July 21, 1967, Box 117, Ramsey Clark MSS, LBJ Library.

51. Cyrus Vance OH, interview by Paige E. Mulhollan, November 3, 1969; Matthew Nimetz, interview with author; "Kurtz in Storyville," *Nation*, February 12, 1968, pp. 196–197. However, conservatives objected to the transfer of certain tactics: "The technique of 'gradual escalation' in riot control is manifestly inadequate to protect the public safety. It is as inadequate in Washington or any of the other riot-torn cities as it is in Vietnam." Strom Thurmond Newsletter, April 15, 1968, Box 3, Research Files (1968), RMN Library.

52. "Racial Disturbances 1967," Vol. I, Box 11, Warren Christopher MSS, LBJ Library.

53. Panzer to LBJ, February 17, 1968, Box 397, WHOF of Fred Panzer, LBJ Library; Ramsey Clark OH, interview by Harri Baker, April 16, 1969, LBJ Library. For example, the Pentagon Center for Civil Disturbances alone received more funds

than the Department of Justice received for its civil rights, community relations, and civil disturbance programs combined.

54. Nimetz to Larry Levinson, March 18, 1968, Box 43, WHOF of James Gaither, LBJ Library. Notes of Cabinet Meeting, March 13, 1968, Box 13, Cabinet Papers, LBJ Library.

55. Interview of McGiffert by Staff of Permanent Subcommittee on Investigations, April 22, 1968, Box 6, Warren Christopher MSS, LBJ Library.

56. Ramsey Clark OH, interview by Harri Baker, April 16, 1969, LBJ Library. In his book, Clark also claimed that budget cutbacks made riot-control responsibility even more attractive to the Army. Ramsey Clark, *Crime in America* (New York: Simon and Schuster, 1970), p. 277. After the Chicago Convention, the administration became concerned about police restraint as well. A former War on Poverty planner observed that "the problem of civilian control of the police is going to be as important as the problem of civilian control of the military has been in the past few years." Yarmolinsky to Paul Jacobs, October 8, 1968, Box 26, Adam Yarmolinsky MSS, JFK Library.

57. Roy Wilkins to the Federation of Protestant Welfare Agencies of New York City, April 4, 1968, Box 74, Administrative Files (IV), NAACP Papers, LOC; Roy Wilkins to Charter Day Observance at the University of California-Berkeley, March 23, 1968, Box 74, Administrative Files (IV), NAACP Papers, LOC; Donald Lee to Governor Nelson Rockefeller, July 31, 1967, attached to memo, Henry Lee Moon to Roy Wilkins, July 31, 1967, Box 64, Administrative Files (IV), NAACP Papers, LOC.

58 Tom Parmenter, "Breakdown of Law and Order," *Trans-Action* 4 (Sept. 1967): 13–22; reprinted in Marvin R. Summers and Thomas E. Barth, eds. *Law and Order in a Democratic Society* (Columbus, Ohio: Charles E. Merrill, 1970), p. 113; Kenneth Crawford, "Fulbright on Riots," *Newsweek*, September 4, 1967, p. 28; Joseph Califano, interview with author; Matthew Nimetz, interview with author; James Gaither, interview with author.

59. See Kenneth O'Reilly, *"Racial Matters": The FBI's Secret File on Black America, 1960–1972* (New York: The Free Press, 1989), pp. 245–246; and Richard Gid Powers, *Secrecy and Power: The Life of J. Edgar Hoover* (New York: The Free Press, 1987), p. 424.

60. Whether the CIA was directly involved is unclear. Indirectly, however, it provided the FBI with "racial matters intelligence" through "Project Hunter," the agency's mail-opening operation, which unsealed at least 130,000 letters addressed to Americans ranging from Richard Nixon to Coretta King. O'Reilly, *"Racial Matters,"* pp. 264–265, 270. See also Richard Kleindienst, *Justice: The Memoirs of an Attorney General* (Ottawa, Illinois: Jameson Books, 1985), p. 70.

61. Califano to LBJ, January 18, 1968, Box 185, Ex FG 135, WHSF, LBJ Library. See also handwritten notes on the back of Agenda, "Summer Riot Preparation," n.d., Box 43, WHOF of James Gaither, LBJ Library.

62. The liaison between Hoover and Johnson defends his FBI superior by contending that COINTELPRO's excesses were largely the fault of an overly ambitious William Sullivan, who saw his chance when Hoover became frustrated by the riots. Cartha "Deke" DeLoach, *Hoover's FBI: The Inside Story by Hoover's Trusted Lieutenant* (Washington: Regnery, 1995), pp. 280, 284, 291.

63. O'Reilly, "*Racial Matters*", pp. 262–265.

64. Joseph Califano, interview with author; Matthew Nimetz, interview with author; James Gaither, interview with author.

65. With Hoover's active assistance, Clark clearly set in motion a chain of events that would culminate in the abuses of COINTELPRO. But it is important to note, first, that there was in the fall of 1967 a "clear and present danger" of future disorders, which provides some justification for the formation of the IDIU. Second, there was, I would argue, a qualitative change in surveillance operations after the change in administrations in 1968. As a careful scholar of the FBI has noted: "Until 1968, Hoover's surveillance of the antiwar movement was to provide the government with advance warning of demonstrations. This in itself was intrusive and chilling, but after 1968 Hoover went on the offensive as an active participant in an effort to disrupt and discredit opposition to the war." See Powers, *Secrecy and Power*, p. 430. Third, there is little evidence that Clark was aware that Hoover and the FBI had exceeded their mandate to provide only advance warning of potential problems.

66. Nimetz to Califano, March 6, 1968, Box 43, WHOF of James Gaither, LBJ Library; Matthew Nimetz OH, interview by Steve Goodell, January 7, 1969, tape #1, LBJ Library.

67. "With a sideways wink we probably told them to go ahead," he recalled. "You'd better not bring that information here, but you'd better get it. They probably would have anyway, incidentally, whether we told them to or not." He added that "there was this enormous sensitivity . . . to the line between the Army and the Bureau, between what's domestic intelligence and who should be collecting it." Joseph Califano, interview with author; Matthew Nimetz, interview with author.

68. "Watts to Detroit," *National Review*, August 22, 1967, pp. 887; Vince Pinto, "Weapons for the Homefront," in Platt and Cooper, eds., *Policing America*, pp. 80–81.

69. Memo to Clark, January 22, 1968, Box 109, Ramsey Clark MSS, LBJ Library; Keith L. Warn, "System Engineering Approach to Law Enforcement," in S.A. Yefsky, ed., *Law Enforcement Science and Technology: Proceedings of the 1st National Symposium on LE Science and Technology* (Chicago: Thompson Book Company, 1967), p. 651; Daryl F. Gates with Diane K. Shah, *Chief: My Life in the LAPD* (New York: Bantam Books, 1992), pp. 109–110.

70. Merton Peck to Califano, October 9, 1968, Box 28, Ex JL 3, WHSF, LBJ Library Joseph C. Goulden, "The Cops Hit the Jackpot," in Anthony Platt and Lynn Cooper, eds., *Policing America*, p. 32; Gerald Horne, *Fire This Time: The Watts*

Uprising and the 1960s (Charlottesville: University of Virginia Press, 1995), p. 107; Wills, *The Second Civil War*, p. 17.

71. Nimetz to Califano, April 24, 1968, Box 43, WHOF of James Gaither, LBJ Library. The distribution came after the IACP had surveyed the needs of more than 100 major cities. On the basis of the survey, the Army calculated how many grenades per officer were needed and then sent a letter to the department, offering the grenades for free if it had appropriate gas masks and a plan on how to use the gas. Wes Pomeroy to Warren Christopher, June 18, 1968, Box 12, Warren Christopher MSS, LBJ Library; Wills, *The Second Civil War*, pp. 40–41.

72. Fred Panzer to LBJ, April 6, 1968, Box 44, WHOF of Harry McPherson, LBJ Library.

73. Not one chief rejected a "confidential invitation" from Clark. Patrick V. Murphy and Thomas Plate, *Commissioner: A View from the Top of American Law Enforcement* (New York: Simon and Schuster, 1977), pp. 101–103; Clark memo, January 22, 1968, Box 109, Ramsey Clark MSS, LBJ Library; Clark to Clarence Mitchell, January 26, 1968, Box 109, Ramsey Clark MSS, LBJ Library.

74. In 1968 the Rockefeller campaign produced a controversial commercial. Narrated by the candidate, it noted that 3,000 black soldiers had already died in Vietnam and that another 100,000 would eventually return home. "What will they make of America, these men who risk their lives for the American Dream, and come home to find the American Slumber?" he asked, adding that black veterans deserved housing, jobs, and an education. "To those who cry, 'We can't afford it,' I say, We can't afford not to do it. To those who cry, 'Law and order,' I say, To keep law and order there must be justice and opportunity." As he recited the last three words, a black man emerged from the darkness and walked toward the camera. Lewis Chester, Godfrey Hodgson, and Bruce Page, *An American Melodrama: The Presidential Campaign of 1968* (New York: The Viking Press, 1969), p. 389.

75. Killian, *The Impossible Revolution?* p. 163.

76. Cleaver, *Soul on Ice*, pp. 132, 137; Horne, *Fire This Time*, p. 59; Paul Good, "Nothing Worth Saving," *Nation*, August 14, 1967, pp. 101–102. The Vietnam metaphor remained potent into the 1970s and 1980s. "I knew if I got into South Central," said a member of the "Bloods," a Los Angeles gang, "the police's chances of apprehending me would be slim, sort of like Marines hunting for Viet Cong in their native habitat." Sanyika Shakur, a.k.a. Monster Kody Scott, *Monster: The Autobiography of an L.A. Gang Member* (New York: The Atlantic Monthly Press, 1993), pp. 165, 169.

77. Harry R. Van Cleve confidential memo, October 6, 1967, Box 8, Warren Christopher MSS, LBJ Library.

78. David Farber, *Chicago '68* (Chicago: University of Chicago Press, 1988), p. 160; Todd Gitlin, *The Sixties: Years of Hope, Days of Rage* (New York: Bantam Books, 1987), p. 326; Willard Wirtz to LBJ, August 8, 1967, Box 58, WHOF of

Joseph Califano, LBJ Library; Wattenberg to Moyers, October 4, 1966, Box 18, WHOF of Ben Wattenberg, LBJ Library.

79. Humphrey to Johnson, May 26, 1967, Box 12, Ex PE 2 [Personal], WHSF, LBJ Library. The report was generated by the National Strategy Information Center and forwarded to Califano by Morris Liebman, a Chicago lawyer who was director of the center as well as the chairman of the National Advisory Council on Economic Opportunity. See "Political Stability, National Goals and the Negro Veteran," attached to memo, Liebman to Califano, June 20, 1967, Box 98, White House Confidential Files (WHCF), LBJ Library.

80. "Political Stability, National Goals and the Negro Veteran."

CHAPTER 7. THE POLITICS OF STREET CRIME

1. Laura Kalman, *Abe Fortas: A Biography* (New Haven: Yale University Press, 1990), p. 340. See also Bruce Allen Murphy, *Fortas: The Rise and Ruin of a Justice* (New York: William Morrow, 1988), p. 426; and Ed Cray, *Chief Justice: A Biography of Earl Warren* (New York: Simon and Schuster, 1997), pp. 498–501. For a concise description of the *Mallory* case, see Lucas A. Powe, Jr., *The Warren Court and American Politics* (Cambridge: Harvard University Press, 2000), pp. 108–109.

2. The outcome was a complicated affair. One scholar contends that political, institutional, and generational tensions in Congress ultimately doomed the Fortas nomination. See Murphy, *Fortas*, pp. 220, 228, 531–532, 595. Another scholar argues that his close association with Johnson—particularly his dubious, behind-the-scenes role as legal and political advisor—was central to his defeat. See Kalman, *Abe Fortas*, p. 348.

3. *Crime in the United States*, Uniform Crime Reports, issued by J. Edgar Hoover and the FBI, 1961–1969, and Arthur L. Stinchcombe et al., *Crime and Punishment—Changing Attitudes in America* (San Francisco: Jossey-Bass Publishers, 1980), p. 20.

4. Rural crime was, moreover, often underreported because of the lower population density, a reluctance to report the exploitation of migrant labor, and a lack of manpower, skill, or technology among small departments when it came to discovering and solving crime. See Patrick V. Murphy and Thomas Plate, *Commissioner: A View from the Top of American Law Enforcement* (New York: Simon and Schuster, 1977), pp. 74–75. "Is Crime Running Wild?" *U.S. News & World Report*, August 3, 1964, pp. 19–21; "Crime Runs Wild—Will It Be Halted?" *U.S. News & World Report*, August 9, 1965, pp. 64–69.

5. Katzenbach to the American Jewish Committee, November 11, 1965, Box 10, Katzenbach MSS, John F. Kennedy Presidential Library (JFK Library).

6. Special Message to Congress on Crime in America, February 6, 1967, *Public Papers of the Presidents of the United States: Lyndon B. Johnson, 1967*, Book I (Washington: U.S. Government Printing Office, 1968), pp. 134–145 (*Johnson Papers*).

7. For an especially strong defense of the Uniform Crime Reports, see M. Stanton Evans, "At Home," *National Review Bulletin*, August 2, 1966, p. 6.

8. Katzenbach at the 25th Annual Heywood Broun Award Presentation, February 14, 1966, Box 30, Katzenbach MSS, JFK Library.

9. At 13 percent of the population, they accounted for 50 percent of the most common property crimes. Clark to the Seventh Constitutional Convention of the AFL-CIO, December 8, 1967, Box 34, Ramsey Clark MSS, Lyndon Baines Johnson Presidential Library (LBJ Library).

10. Hoover to Norbert Schlei, November 13, 1964, Box 136, Statements File, LBJ Library.

11. "Firearms Misuse—1966," Box 92, Ramsey Clark MSS, LBJ Library; Special Message to Congress: The Nation's Capital, February 27, 1967, *Johnson Papers* (1967), 1: 226–239; "Crime Runs Wild—Will It Be Halted?" *U.S. News & World Report*, August 9, 1965, p. 67.

12. *Crime in the United States*, Uniform Crime Reports, 1967; Lawrence M. Friedman, *Crime and Punishment in American History* (New York: Basic Books, 1993), pp. 267–268; James Q. Wilson, *Thinking About Crime*, rev. ed. (New York: Vintage, 1985), p. 198; and Michael Woodiwiss, *Crime, Crusades, and Corruption: Prohibitions in the U.S., 1900–1987* (Totowa, NJ: Barnes and Noble Books, 1988), p. 167.

13. Gilbert Geis, "Statistics Concerning Race and Crime," *Crime and Delinquency* (April 1965), reprinted in Charles E. Reasons and Jack L. Kuykendall, eds., *Race, Crime, and Justice* (Pacific Palisades: Goodyear Publishing Co., Inc., 1972), p. 64; Theodore H. White, *The Making of the President 1972* (New York: Bantam Books, 1973), p. 178.

14. James Lardner, *Crusader: The Hell-Raising Police Career of Detective David Durk* (New York: Random House, 1996), p. 33; David Burnham, *Above the Law* (New York: Scribner's, 1996), pp. 113–114.

15. Stinchcombe et al., *Crime and Punishment*, p. 49.

16. The president of the NAACP was eager to circulate the news that less than 10 percent of the murders committed in New York in 1966 were black on white "because we are so frequently confronted with damaging propaganda charges about Negro criminal attacks on white persons." Wilkins to NAACP branch presidents, April 28, 1967, Box 79, Administrative File (IV), NAACP Papers, Library of Congress (LOC).

17. In 1965, embezzlement, fraud, tax fraud, and forgery resulted in a \$1.73 billion loss to the nation whereas robbery, burglary, auto theft, and larceny involved only \$690 million. Moreover, 90 percent of convicted bank robbers served jail time (52 months on average), while only 20 percent of those convicted of tax fraud went to prison (for an average of 9 months). Center for Research on Criminal Justice, *The Iron Fist and the Velvet Glove: An Analysis of the U.S. Police* (San Francisco: Garrett Press, 1975), pp. 10–11. "Crime Among the Rich," May 12, 1965, Box 48, Part II, NUL Papers, LOC.

18. "Ironically," the attorney general later contended, "news coverage of violent crime tends to increase rather than deter violence, while reporting of white-collar crime is a strong deterrent to its commission." Ramsey Clark, *Crime in America* (New York: Simon and Schuster, 1970), p. 48.

19. James Q. Wilson, "Crime in the Streets," *The Public Interest* 5 (Fall 1966): 26–35; reprinted in Marvin R. Summers and Thomas E. Barth, eds. *Law and Order in a Democratic Society* (Columbus, Ohio: Charles E. Merrill, 1970), pp. 6–9.

20. *Crime in the United States*, Uniform Crime Reports, issued by J. Edgar Hoover and the FBI, 1961–1969.

21. George Shadoan, "Behind the Crime Scare," *Nation*, May 10, 1965, pp. 495–497; Remarks to the National Commission on the Causes and Prevention of Violence, September 18, 1968, Box 79, Ramsey Clark MSS, LBJ Library.

22. One memo said that the administration had to have accurate data to put the crime rate in proper perspective. Why, it asked, are there no age-specific crime rates in FBI data? How much is due to better police work? Is there more willingness to report crimes like rape? What do international and historical comparisons show? Moyers (prepared by Wattenberg) to Katzenbach, September 6, 1966, Box 60, JL 3, White House Subject Files (WHSF), LBJ Library.

23. "Violence, U.S.A.: Riots and Crime," June 16, 1968, Box 307, WHOF of Fred Panzer, LBJ Library.

24. One scholar has suggested that there was an abiding irony to the entire debate. "Even the social scientists who write articles demonstrating that the alleged 'crime wave' is a statistical illusion are likely to tell their wives (or even themselves) that, if they live near such big-city universities as Chicago, Columbia, or Pennsylvania, they should not walk the streets alone after dark." Wilson, "Crime in the Streets," p. 7.

25. "[Johnson] was really a Washingtonian with a weekend ranch in Austin," recalled Califano. Joseph Califano, interview with author, August 8, 1995.

26. Horsky to LBJ, November 19, 1964, Box 93, WHOF of Charles Horsky, LBJ Library.

27. Horsky to Walter Tobriner, November 10, 1964, Box 68, WHOF of Charles Horsky, LBJ Library.

28. Horsky to LBJ, November 19, 1964, Box 93, WHOF of Charles Horsky, LBJ Library.

29. Ibid. See also Walter Tobriner to LBJ, November 23, 1964, Box 93, WHOF of Charles Horsky, LBJ Library.

30. Horsky to Walter Tobriner, December 2, 1964, Box 93, WHOF of Charles Horsky, LBJ Library.

31. Vorenberg to Katzenbach, May 10, 1965, Box 12, Katzenbach MSS, JFK Library.

32. Horsky to LBJ, August 19, 1965, Box 184, Ex FG 135, WHSF, LBJ Library; Current Status and Effectiveness Report: Special Anti-Crime Programs, August 19, 1965, Box 38, WHOF of Harry McPherson, LBJ Library.

33. Moyers to Horace Busby, July 16, 1965, Box 153, Statements File, LBJ Library.

34. Remarks on Crime Control at the Signing of the DC Appropriations Bill, July 16, 1965, *Johnson Papers* (1965), 2: 759–762.

35. Katzenbach to Califano, December 11, 1965, Box 14, Katzenbach MSS, JFK Library. A year later, Vorenberg would offer similar advice. See Vorenberg to Califano, December 2, 1966, Box 326, WHOF of James Gaither, LBJ Library.

36. James Vorenberg, interview with author, July 18, 1995; James Gaither, interview with author, September 25, 1995.

37. Joseph A. Califano, Jr., *The Triumph and the Tragedy of Lyndon Johnson: The White House Years* (New York: Simon and Schuster, 1991), pp. 230–234; McPherson to LBJ, August 24, 1967, Box 20, WHOF of Harry McPherson, LBJ Library.

38. Ironically, in the 1970s mandatory minimums would gain the support of many liberals convinced that a racist legal system would never give minorities and the poor fair sentences. Then in the late 1980s and 1990s liberals reversed themselves once more, contending that guidelines (particularly in drug cases) unfairly condemned the poor and minorities to excessive prison terms.

39. Clark to LBJ, November 7, 1966, Box 104, Ramsey Clark MSS, LBJ Library; McPherson and Califano to LBJ, November 9, 1966, Box 25, Ex JL 3, WHSF, LBJ Library; Disapproval of D.C. Crime Bill, November 13, 1966, *Johnson Papers* (1966), 2: 1381–1383.

40. Califano to LBJ, August 5, 1967, Box 23, Handwriting File, LBJ Library.

41. Statement Upon Signing the D.C. Crime Bill, December 27, 1967, *Johnson Papers* (1967) 2: 1192–1193.

42. Califano to LBJ, July 2, 1968, Box 28, Ex JL 3, WHSF, LBJ Library.

43. James Gaither OH, interview by Dorothy Pierce, November 19, 1968, LBJ Library. Califano remains sensitive to the charge that he oversold the Safe Streets Act: "I don't mean to put [Vorenberg] down but . . . he was a professor and I was trying to get the goddamned law passed, to shape the debate and drive our legislation through." Joseph Califano, interview with author.

44. Scholars insist that while the block-grant provision marked "a first tentative step toward New Federalism and revenue sharing," it also largely defeated the bill's intent to promote planning, reform, and innovation. Malcolm M. Feeley and Austin D. Sarat, *The Policy Dilemma: Federal Crime Policy and the Law Enforcement Assistance Administration, 1968–1978* (Minneapolis: University of Minnesota Press, 1980), pp. 45–46, 89–90.

45. Califano to LBJ, December 16, 1967, Box 8, WHOF of Joseph Califano, LBJ Library.

46. Annual Message to Congress on the State of the Union, January 17, 1968, *Johnson Papers* (1968), 1: 25–33; "The Cities: The Crucible," *Time*, January 26, 1968, p. 11.

47. Califano to Christian, February 1, 1968, Box 5, Legislative Background (LB),

LBJ Library; Larry Temple to Califano, February 5, 1968, Box 123, SP-2–3/1968/JL, WHSF, LBJ Library.

48. Fortas to Califano, February 6, 1968, Box 6, LB (Safe Streets Act), LBJ Library.

49. Barry Mahoney, "The Politics of the Safe Streets Act, 1965–1973," (unpub. Ph.D. dissertation, Columbia University, 1976), pp. 208–209.

50. The best account of the legislative history of the Safe Streets Act, albeit a rather impressionistic and partisan one, is Richard Harris, *The Fear of Crime* (New York: Praeger, 1968).

51. Harris, *The Fear of Crime*, p. 85. Clark's unpopularity was also a factor. "Ramsey's ability to deal with Congress was close to zero," recalls Katzenbach. Nicholas Katzenbach, interview with author, March 6, 1998.

52. Feeley and Sarat, *The Policy Dilemma*, pp. 40–41.

53. Everett Dirksen, Roman Hruska, Hiram Fong, Hugh Scott, and Strom Thurmond to Ervin, November 21, 1967, Box 395, Ervin MSS, Southern Historical Collection (SHC).

54. Title IV also contained a provision, introduced by Ervin, to overturn *U.S. v. Wade*, which argued that when police placed a suspect in a lineup, the state had moved from the investigatory to the accusatory stage and therefore had to provide the suspect with the opportunity to have counsel present.

55. Ervin to Senator Joseph D. Tydings, April 29, 1968, Box 203, Ervin MSS, SHC; Harris, *The Fear of Crime*, p. 110.

56. Gisela Enright to Celler, June 7, 1968, Box 298, Celler MSS, LOC; Cray, *Chief Justice*, p. 461.

57. *Issues and Answers*, May 12, 1968, Box 117, Ramsey Clark MSS, LBJ Library; Senator Joseph D. Tydings to Ervin, May 3, 1968, Box 203, Ervin MSS, SHC.

58. Harris, *The Fear of Crime*, pp. 86–87.

59. Testimony by Clark before the Senate Subcommittee on Criminal Laws and Procedures, April 18, 1967, Box 84, Ramsey Clark MSS, LBJ Library.

60. Ramsey Clark to LBJ, June 14, 1968, Box 107, Ramsey Clark MSS, LBJ Library.

61. The Supreme Court ruled by a 7–2 margin that *Miranda* was a constitutional rather than a procedural finding. Congress therefore had no right to amend or overturn it by statute. Linda Greenhouse, "Justices Reaffirm Miranda Rule, 7–2; A Part of 'Culture,'" *New York Times*, June 27, 2000, pp. A1, A18. See also Roger Parloff, "Miranda on the Hot Seat," *New York Times Magazine*, September 26, 1999, pp. 84–87.

62. Nimetz to Califano, June 8, 1968, Box 5, WHOF of James Gaither, LBJ Library.

63. Harris, *The Fear of Crime*, p. 91; Mike Manatos to LBJ, December 7, 1967, Box 27, Ex JL 3, WHSF, LBJ Library.

64. Wiretapping and bugging became legal in New York in 1938 and 1958 respec-

tively. Yet since then police had installed an average of only 66 wiretaps and 19 bugs a year, all with judicial safeguards. Harris, *The Fear of Crime*, p. 52.

65. "He was wild on that subject," recalled Califano. Why? "I just don't know . . . I mean, people have all kinds of theories but they're just theories. He lived on the phone. Also, I think he always suspected that Robert Kennedy was bugging him when he was vice president. I honestly don't know. But it was like religion with him." Joseph Califano, interview with author. "Whether he felt that in his bones or whether he felt that [opposition to wiretapping] was a necessity for a liberal politician, a progressive politician, I don't know," remembered McPherson. "I think it's probably a combination of both." Harry McPherson OH, interview by T.H. Baker, April 9, 1969, tape #7, LBJ Library. Another official recalled that Johnson's position was as follows: "Wiretapping ain't right. Don't do it. Just make goddamned sure I get a transcript of every one of them." Lee White, interview with author, March 16, 1998. For a contemporary overview of several theories, see Robert M. Cipes, "The Wiretap War: Kennedy, Johnson, and the FBI," *The New Republic*, December 24, 1966, pp. 16–22. Of course, it is also possible to conclude that Johnson was a hypocrite, paranoid, or some combination of the two. And he may simply have concluded that as president he had no choice and was above the law—a not uncommon attitude for occupants of the White House. In any event, he secretly taped more than 10,000 conversations between 1963 and 1968. Robert Dallek, *Flawed Giant: Lyndon Johnson and His Times, 1961–1973* (New York: Oxford University Press, 1998), p. 407.

66. Katzenbach suggested that the alternatives to a bill to limit or control wiretapping were unlimited official wiretapping or a complete ban on it even in national security cases. In the margins next to the complete ban option LBJ wrote: "I like this best." Califano and White to LBJ, February 9, 1966, Box 79, Ex LE/JL, WHSF, LBJ Library.

67. In the town of Bogalusa, a group of black demonstrators who were denied police protection when attacked by a group of whites formed a self-defense group called the "Deacons for Defense and Justice." See Lance Hill, *Deacons for Defense: Armed Resistance and the Civil Rights Movement* (Chapel Hill: University of North Carolina Press, 2004).

68. Joseph Barr to Larry O'Brien, July 14, 1965, attached to Henry Fowler to LBJ, July 14, 1965, Box 2, LB (Gun Control—1968), LBJ Library.

69. Katzenbach to Califano, December 11, 1965, Box 14, Katzenbach MSS, JFK Library.

70. Noting that handguns were used in 70 percent of criminal actions, Barr said that "I have no comments on the political situation and the possible charge of a sell-out or on Nick Katzenbach's position that we should hold steady for the original bill. I merely feel that I should inform you that in my opinion you can strike at the major link of crime with guns if you want to in this session of Congress." Joseph Barr to Califano, August 19, 1966, Box 2, LB (Gun Control—1968), LBJ Library.

See also Katzenbach to Califano, August 25, 1966, Box 2, LB (Gun Control—1968), LBJ Library.

71. "When I talked to Ted he was a veritable buzz-saw, saying he was 'damn mad about that situation,' and that if the Administration didn't get behind the gun bill he'd have to 'blast' us." Manatos assured Kennedy that "there isn't any legislation before Congress in which we are more interested than the gun bill, as evidenced by your recent statements." In return, Kennedy promised to help get the other bills reported. Manatos to LBJ, August 16, 1966, Box 79, Ex LE/JL 3, WHSF, LBJ Library.

72. Firearms were also used in 18.8 percent of aggravated assaults (an increase of 23.8 percent over 1965) and 66.7 percent of armed robberies. They were also implicated in 10,000 suicides, 2,600 accidental deaths, and 95 percent of the murders of law enforcement officials since 1960. See "Firearms Misuse—1966," Box 92, Ramsey Clark MSS, LBJ Library.

73. The IACP and the National Sheriffs' Association were firm proponents of legislation that would prohibit the interstate sale of all firearms. They also strongly opposed the NRA-backed "affidavit procedure," which would leave the police with only seven days and inadequate resources to check the sworn statements of would-be purchasers and possible felons. Quinn Tamm to Celler, October 3, 1967, Box 433, Celler MSS, LOC.

74. Christopher to Califano, January 15, 1968, Box 106, Ramsey Clark MSS, LBJ Library. See also "The Today Show," February 12, 1968, Box 117, Ramsey Clark MSS, LBJ Library.

75. Louis Harris, "Tight Gun Rules Favored 71–23," *Washington Post*, April 22, 1968, p. A4.

76. The outcome was not a surprise to Johnson. Sanders to Johnson, June 5, 1968, Box 6, LB (Safe Streets Act), LBJ Library.

77. Peter Edelman, Kennedy's legislative assistant, lashed out in a CBS interview at those who portrayed the crime bill as a memorial to the late senator, noting that he had strongly opposed both Titles II and III. See Harris, *The Fear of Crime*, pp. 106–109.

78. George Kamenow to Celler, May 23, 1968, Box 298, Celler MSS, LOC; interview with Celler, *WNBC*'s "Man in Office," December 7, 1969, Box 540, Celler MSS, LOC.

79. Roche to LBJ, March 7, 1968, Box 3, WHOF of John Roche, LBJ Library; Finley to Clark, June 6, 1968, Box 107, Ramsey Clark MSS, LBJ Library.

80. McPherson to LBJ, June 14, 1968, Box 32, WHOF of Harry McPherson, LBJ Library; Harris, *The Fear of Crime*, p. 110; Clark to LBJ, June 14, 1968, Box 107, Ramsey Clark MSS, LBJ Library.

81. Statement Upon Signing the Omnibus Crime Control and Safe Streets Act of 1968, June 19, 1968, *Johnson Papers* (1968), 1: 725–729.

82. Califano to LBJ, June 24, 1968, Box 22, WHOF of Joseph Califano, LBJ Library. See also Califano, *The Triumph and the Tragedy of Lyndon Johnson*, pp. 305–306.

83. Clark to LBJ, June 7, 1968, Box 80, Ex LE/JL 3, WHSF, LBJ Library.

84. Notes of Cabinet Meeting, June 12, 1968, Box 14, Cabinet Papers, LBJ Library.

85. See Larry Levinson to Charlton Heston, June 12, 1968, Box 7, LB (Safe Streets Act), LBJ Library; Levinson to LBJ, June 18, 1968, Box 27, Ex JL 3, WHSF, LBJ Library; Califano to Clark H. Wales, July 1, 1968, Box 80, Ex LE/JL 3, WHSF, LBJ Library; Califano to LBJ, June 20, 1968, Box 18, Califano MSS, LBJ Library; Liz Carpenter to LBJ, June 11, 1968, Box 20, WHOF of Joseph Califano, LBJ Library.

86. Califano to LBJ, October 23, 1968, Box 43, WHOF of Joseph Califano, LBJ Library.

87. Christopher told the National Association of Attorneys General that the extensive ownership of weapons in the ghetto might mean that future riots would lead to casualty rates far in excess of what the nation had already experienced, particularly if there was an escalation in the level of violence. Press Release, June 10, 1968, Box 105, Ramsey Clark MSS, LBJ Library.

88. Remarks Upon Signing the Gun Control Act of 1968, October 22, 1968, *Johnson Papers* (1968), 2: 1059–1060.

CHAPTER 8. DEATH, DISORDER, AND DEBATE

1. "Violence in America," *Time*, July 28, 1967, pp. 18–19.

2. Robert F. Kennedy (RFK) Address to City Club of Cleveland, April 5, 1968, Box 3, 1968 Presidential Campaign Papers (PCP), RFK MSS, John F. Kennedy Presidential Library (JFK Library).

3. "The Cities: The Crucible," *Time*, January 26, 1968, p. 11; Richard Harris, *The Fear of Crime* (New York: Praeger, 1968), p. 67.

4. George Gallup, *The Gallup Poll: Public Opinion, 1935–1971* (New York: Random House, 1972), pp. 2107–2108.

5. Panzer to LBJ, February 27, 1968, Box 397, White House Office Files (WHOF) of Fred Panzer, Lyndon Baines Johnson Presidential Library (LBJ Library); Panzer to Larry Levinson, February 28, 1968, Box 342, WHOF of Fred Panzer, LBJ Library.

6. Wattenberg to LBJ, February 29, 1968, Box 20, FG 11-8-1 / Cater, Douglass, White House Subject Files (WHSF), LBJ Library; Charles Roche to LBJ, March 21, 1968, Box 3, WHOF of John Roche, LBJ Library.

7. Lewis Chester, Godfrey Hodgson, and Bruce Page, *An American Melodrama: The Presidential Campaign of 1968* (New York: Viking, 1969), p. 79; Stephan Lesher, *George Wallace: American Populist* (Reading, Massachusetts: Addison-Wesley, 1994), p. 404. See also William H. Chafe, *Never Stop Running: Allard Lowenstein and the Struggle to Save American Liberalism* (New York: Basic Books, 1993), pp. 262–315; Jules Witcover, *1968: The Year the Dream Died* (New York: Warner Books, 1997),

pp. 88–144; and Theodore H. White, *The Making of the President 1968* (New York: Atheneum, 1969).

8. McPherson to LBJ, March 18, 1968, Box 53, WHOF of Harry McPherson, LBJ Library.

9. Ibid.

10. Although Ray's attorney and the King family now contend that he was either a patsy or a member of a conspiracy, the evidence remains sketchy at best. Kevin Sack, "Tests of Gun in King Killing Are Inconclusive," *New York Times*, July 12, 1997, p. 6. In 2000, the Justice Department found no evidence to support claims of a conspiracy to assassinate King. David Johnston, "Investigation Finds No Plot in Killing of Dr. King," *New York Times*, June 10, 2000, p. A8.

11. Strom Thurmond Newsletter, April 15, 1968, Box 3, Research Files, Richard M. Nixon Library (RMN Library).

12. RFK Address to City Club of Cleveland, April 5, 1968, Box 3, PCP, JFK Library.

13. Ibid.; James T. Patterson, *Grand Expectations: The U.S., 1945-1974* (New York: Oxford University Press, 1996), p. 686.

14. Notes of the President's Meeting with Negro Leaders, April 5, 1968, Box 3, Tom Johnson's Notes of Meetings (TJN), LBJ Library.

15. Harry McPherson, *A Political Education: A Washington Memoir* (Austin: University of Texas Press, 1972; 1995 edition), pp. 367–368.

16. Notes of Cabinet Meeting, March 13, 1968, Box 13, Cabinet Papers, LBJ Library.

17. Matthew Nimetz, interview with author, July 17, 1995; James Gaither, interview with author, September 25, 1995. Wattenberg's eventual father-in-law had his liquor store on 14th Street burned out—"the great traumatic event of his life." Interview with author, December 19, 1997.

18. "Take Everything You Need, Baby," *Newsweek*, April 15, 1968, pp. 31–32.

19. Lyndon B. Johnson, *The Vantage Point: Perspectives of the Presidency, 1963–1969* (New York: Holt, Rinehart and Winston, 1971), p. 538. According to Califano, however, the president retained his sense of humor. At reports that Carmichael planned to march on Georgetown, he exclaimed: "Goddamn! I've waited thirty-five years for this day!" Joseph A. Califano, Jr., *The Triumph and the Tragedy of Lyndon Johnson: The White House Years* (New York: Simon and Schuster, 1991), p. 279.

20. Califano, *The Triumph and the Tragedy*, p. 279.

21. Califano to LBJ, April 6, 1968, Box 39, Ex JL 6, WHSF, LBJ Library.

22. Clifford Alexander to LBJ, April 6, 1968, Box 44, WHOF of Harry McPherson, LBJ Library.

23. Patrick Murphy Oral History (OH), interview by T.H. Baker, March 13, 1969, LBJ Library.

24. Califano to LBJ, April 10, 1968, Box 16, WHOF of Joseph Califano, LBJ Library.

25. Califano to LBJ, April 10, 1968, Box 20, FG 11–8-1 / Califano, Joseph, WHSF, LBJ Library.

26. Matthew Nimetz OH, interview by Steve Goodell, January 7, 1969, tape #2, LBJ Library.

27. Chester, Hodgson, and Page, *An American Melodrama*, p. 364; "McCarthy on the Record—Civil Rights," Box 2, Candidate Files, 1968 Campaign Files, Humphrey MSS, Minnesota Historical Society (MHS).

28. Address by RFK at the Columbia Law School Forum, January 19, 1967, Box 4, Adam Walinsky MSS, JFK Library.

29. Joe Dolan to RFK, November 21, 1967, Box 2, Walinsky MSS, JFK Library.

30. *United Press International* clips, January 16, 1968, Box 120, Democratic National Committee (DNC) File, LBJ Library; RFK Proposes Comprehensive Cities Program, May 31, 1968, Box 121, DNC File, LBJ Library; Jeff Greenfield OH, interview by Roberta Greene, February 24, 1970, JFK Library.

31. Jeff Greenfield OH, interview by Roberta Greene, February 24, 1970, JFK Library; Arthur M. Schlesinger Jr., *Robert Kennedy and His Times* (New York: Ballantine Books, 1967; paperback edition), pp. 730, 946–947; Milton Gwirtzman OH, interview by Roberta W. Greene, March 16, 1972, JFK Library; White, *The Making of the President 1968*, pp. 199, 206.

32. Survey of Hoosier Voters' Attitudes Toward Issues and Personalities, n.d., Box 6, PCP, RFK MSS, JFK Library; Dan T. Carter, *The Politics of Rage: George Wallace, The Origins of the New Conservatism, and the Transformation of American Politics* (New York: Simon and Schuster, 1995), p. 377; Albert Shepard to Edward Kennedy, n.d., Box 5, PCP, RFK MSS, JFK Library; Pitchell memo, April 11, 1968, Box 6, PCP, RFK MSS, JFK Library.

33. RFK address at South Bend, Indiana, April 15, 1968, Box 3A, PCP, RFK MSS, JFK Library; RFK remarks in Indianapolis, April 25, 1968, Box 120, DNC, LBJ Library.

34. "Law and Order (Indiana)," Robert Kennedy Campaign, 1968, Political Commercial Archive of the University of Oklahoma, Norman, Oklahoma (PCA); "Senator Kennedy—April 15, 1968," Box 3, PCP, RFK MSS, JFK Library.

35. Chester, Hodgson, and Page, *An American Melodrama*, p. 176; Tom Wicker, "In the Nation: Kennedy's 'Jigsaw Victory,'" *New York Times*, May 9, 1968; William L. O'Neill, *Coming Apart: An Informal History of America in the 1960s* (New York: Random House, 1971), p. 365.

36. Panzer to LBJ, May 10, 1968, Box 397, WHOF of Fred Panzer, LBJ Library; unsigned memo (presumably Wattenberg), May 9, 1968, Box 26, Ex PL/Kennedy, Robert F., WHSF, LBJ Library. See also Garry Wills, "Waiting for Bobby," *New York Review of Books*, February 10, 2000, p. 18.

37. Peter Fishbein to RFK, April 6, 1968, Box 2, Walinsky MSS, JFK Library; "Issues and Answers" transcript, June 1, 1968, Box 2, Candidate Files, 1968 Campaign Papers, Humphrey MSS, MHS; "Housewives/Lawlessness," Box 3, PCP, RFK

MSS; Kathleen Hall Jamieson, *Packaging the Presidency: A History and Criticism of Presidential Campaign Advertising* (New York: Oxford University Press, 1984), pp. 224–225; "California," Box 3A, PCP, RFK MSS, JFK Library.

38. Schlesinger, *Robert Kennedy and His Times*, pp. 978–979; Todd Gitlin, *The Sixties: Years of Hope, Days of Rage* (New York: Bantam Books, 1987), p. 310; Chester, Hodgson, and Page, *An American Melodrama*, pp. 344–345. For a critical analysis of the Kennedy mystique, see Ronald Steel, *In Love with Night: The American Romance with Robert Kennedy* (New York: Simon and Schuster, 2000).

39. "Comment: Second Thoughts on Bobby," *Time* June 21, 1968, p. 48.

40. "Between Remorse and Renewal," *Newsweek*, June 24, 1968, pp. 25–26; "Once Again," *Newsweek* June 17, 1968, pp. 20–21; "Understanding Violence," *Newsweek*, June 17, 1968, p. 43; "Comment: Second Thoughts on Bobby," *Time* June 21, 1968, p. 48.

41. George Christian to LBJ, June 5, 1968, Box 27, Ex JL 3, WHSF, LBJ Library.

42. Address to the Nation Following the Attack on Kennedy, June 5, 1968, *Public Papers of the Presidents of the United States: Lyndon B. Johnson, 1968*, I: 691–693.

43. "Politics and Assassination," *Time*, June 14, 1968, p. 21.

44. "Understanding Violence," *Newsweek*, June 17, 1968, pp. 43–46; Chester, Hodgson, and Page, *An American Melodrama*, p. 363.

45. "Guns: Like Buying Cigarettes," *Newsweek*, June 17, 1968, p. 46; "The Gun Under Fire," *Time*, June 21, 1968, pp. 13–18.

46. "Understanding Violence," *Newsweek*, June 17, 1968, pp. 45–46; "Entertainment Without Violence?" *Newsweek*, June 24, 1968, pp. 26–27.

47. Of course, public anxiety about media violence was hardly new. A Gallup Poll in 1954 showed that 70 percent of Americans agreed that comic books—as well as crime programs on television and radio—had contributed to the delinquency problem. George Gallup, *The Gallup Poll: Public Opinion, 1935–1971* (New York: Random House, 1972), p. 1284.

48. By the late 1990s, particularly in the wake of the school shootings at Columbine High School in Colorado, conservatives had appropriated the issue of sex and violence in popular culture, while liberals continued to demand gun control. See Lawrie Mifflin, "TV Ratings Accord Comes Under Fire from Both Flanks," *New York Times*, July 11, 1997, pp. A1, 19.

49. "Anything Goes," *National Review*, June 18, 1968, p. 593.

50. Speech to National Press Club, June 20, 1968, Box 29, STF, 1968 Campaign Papers, Humphrey MSS, MHS; Humphrey OH, interview by Larry J. Hackman, March 30, 1970, JFK Library.

51. "Survival at the Stockyards," *Time*, September 6, 1968, p. 24.

52. M. Stanton Evans, "At Home," *National Review Bulletin*, October 1, 1968, p. B158; Califano to John Stewart, October 9, 1968, Box 43, WHOF of Joseph Califano, LBJ Library.

53. The most thorough account of the events in Chicago is David Farber, *Chicago ' 68* (Chicago: University of Chicago Press, 1988).

54. White, *The Making of the President 1968*, pp. 304–305.

55. Clark to LBJ, December 16, 1967, Box 117, Ramsey Clark MSS, LBJ Library.

56. *Meet the Press*, February 18, 1968, Box 35, Ramsey Clark MSS, LBJ Library; Press Conference of Ramsey Clark, August 14, 1968, Box 117, Ramsey Clark MSS, LBJ Library.

57. Johnson again expressed the fear that "communist elements" would seek to "make sure that there will be big trouble in the Negro ghetto." Robert Dallek, *Flawed Giant: Lyndon Johnson and His Times, 1961–1973* (New York: Oxford University Press, 1998), p. 488.

58. Gitlin, *The Sixties*, pp. 306–309; Allen J. Matusow, *The Unraveling of America: A History of Liberalism in the 1960s* (New York: Harper & Row, 1984), pp. 331–335.

59. Roger Biles, *Richard J. Daley: Politics, Race, and the Governing of Chicago* (DeKalb: Northern Illinois University Press, 1995), pp. 144–145; "Should Looters Be Shot?" *Time*, April 26, 1968, p. 18; Farber, *Chicago' 68*, p. 143.

60. "Should Looters Be Shot?" *Time*, April 26, 1968, p. 18. See also Biles, *Richard J. Daley*, pp. 146–147; Califano and Levinson to LBJ, April 24, 1968, Box 17, WHOF of Joseph Califano, LBJ Library; Fred Panzer to LBJ, May 28, 1968, Box 27, Ex JL 3, WHSF, LBJ Library.

61. Farber, *Chicago '68*, pp. 124–125, 163. See also "Daley City Under Siege," *Time*, August 30, 1968, pp. 18–19; Biles, *Richard J. Daley*, pp. 148, 152–153; Daniel Walker, *Rights in Conflict: "The Chicago Police Riot"* (New York: The New American Library, 1968), pp. xx–xxi.

62. Farber, *Chicago '68*, p. 52; "Daley City Under Siege," *Time*, August 30, 1968, pp. 18–19; "Who Were the Protesters?" *Time*, September 6, 1968, p. 24; Walker, *Rights in Conflict*, p. xxii.

63. Clark to LBJ, December 16, 1967, Box 117, Ramsey Clark MSS, LBJ Library; "Daley City Under Siege," *Time*, August 30, 1968, p. 19. Richard E. Rubenstein and Stephen Kaplan, "Planning Ahead for the Summer in Chicago Part One: Black and Blue," *New Republic,* April 6, 1968.

64. James Ridgeway, "The Cops and the Kids," *The New Republic*, September 7, 1968, p. 11. Jerry Rubin's own bodyguard, "Big Bob" Lavin, was actually Robert Pierson, an undercover Chicago officer. The *Chicago Tribune* later claimed that he had lowered the flag in Grant Park on Wednesday, sparking the clash, but he denied the charge. "Who Were the Protesters?" *Time*, September 6, 1968, pp. 24–25; Walker, *Rights in Conflict*, p. 197; O'Neill, *Coming Apart*, p. 383.

65. "Daley City Under Siege," *Time*, August 30, 1968, p. 19; Matusow, *The Unraveling of America*, pp. 415–416.

66. "Boss Daley's Fatherly Fist," *Newsweek*, September 9, 1968, p. 40; Farber, *Chicago '68*, pp. 123, 255. Daley would proudly cite police records that showed that almost half of those arrested were not from Illinois. "Who Were the Protesters?"

Time, September 6, 1968, p. 24. For the larger point about populism, see Michael Kazin, *The Populist Persuasion: An American History* (New York: Basic Books, 1995), and Alan Brinkley, *Voices of Protest: Huey Long, Father Coughlin and the Great Depression* (New York: Vintage Books, 1982).

67. Seconds earlier, Daley had denounced Ribicoff as "a Jew son of a bitch." Biles, *Richard J. Daley*, p. 159.

68. "Commentary," *CBS Evening News*, September 2, 1968, Television News Archive, Vanderbilt University, Knoxville, Tennessee (TNA); Farber, *Chicago '68*, pp. 248, 256.

69. Farber, *Chicago '68*, pp. 188, 196–197, 199, 203. Gitlin, *The Sixties*, p. 332; "Chicago 1968," TV Documentary, *American Experience*, 1995; Walker, *Rights in Conflict*, pp. 190–202; Matusow, *The Unraveling of America*, p. 419.

70. Walker, *Rights in Conflict*, pp. 203–226.

71. Ibid., pp. 226–249; Norman Mailer, *Miami and the Siege of Chicago: An Informal History of the Republican and Democratic Conventions of 1968* (New York: Bantam Books, 1969), p. 169; Chester, Hodgson, and Page, *An American Melodrama*, pp. 581–582.

72. Walker, *Rights in Conflict*, p. 210; "Chicago 1968," *American Experience*, 1995 television documentary; "Lots of Law, Little Order," *Newsweek*, September 9, 1968, p. 39; Gilbert Geis, "Crime and Politics," *Nation*, August 14, 1967, p. 116.

73. "Dementia in the Second City," *Time*, September 6, 1968, p. 21; "Chicago 1968," TV Documentary, *American Experience*, 1995.

74. "Lots of Law, Little Order," *Newsweek*, September 9, 1968, p. 41. See also Walker, *Rights in Conflict*, pp. xix, 210; Warren Christopher OH, interview by T.H Baker, December 2, 1968, LBJ Library.

75. Thomas W. Pew Jr., "The Hilton Hotel Incident," *Nation*, September 16, 1968, p. 229; "If a Tree Falls and There Is No One to Hear, Is There a Sound?" *National Review*, September 24, 1968, pp. 945–947; "Democrats: The Ghost of Chicago," *Newsweek*, September 16, 1968, p. 24.

76. "The Battle of Chicago," *Newsweek*, September 9, 1968, p. 21; "Lots of Law, Little Order," *Newsweek*, September 9, 1968, pp. 38, 41; "Dementia in the Second City," *Time*, September 6, 1968, p. 21; "Is the Press Biased?" *Newsweek*, September 16, 1968, p. 66.

77. "Commentary," *CBS News*, September 2, 1968, TNA; "Lots of Law, Little Order," *Newsweek*, September 9, 1968, p. 41; Farber, *Chicago '68*, p. 203; "Is the Press Biased?" *Newsweek*, September 16, 1968, p. 67.

78. Ibid., p. 66; Panzer to LBJ, September 17, 1968, Box 39, Ex JL 6, WHSF, LBJ Library; Panzer to LBJ, September 20, 1968, Box 39, Ex JL 6, WHSF, LBJ Library; Richard M. Scammon and Ben J. Wattenberg, *The Real Majority* (New York: Coward, McCann, and Geoghegan, 1970), pp. 62, 162; Farber, *Chicago '68*, pp. 205–206; Biles, *Richard J. Daley*, p. 163.

79. "Failure," Nixon Campaign, 1968, PCA; "Convention," Nixon Campaign, 1968, PCA; Jamieson, *Packaging the Presidency*, p. 247.

80. Matusow, *The Unraveling of Liberalism*, p. 422.

81. Biles, *Richard J. Daley*, p. 164; James Ridgeway, "The Cops and the Kids," *The New Republic*, September 7, 1968, p. 11.

82. Matusow, *The Unraveling of Liberalism*, p. 429; White, *The Making of the President 1968*, p. 303; Yarmolinsky to John Stewart, September 5, 1968, Box 56, Yarmolinsky MSS, JFK Library. Prior to the convention, internal polls had Humphrey in the lead with 36 percent, followed by Nixon with 34 percent and Wallace with 18 percent. Afterward, he fell behind by 12 to 16 points. Voter Opinion on Campaign Issues, Box 9, Research Files, 1968 Campaign Papers, Humphrey MSS, MHS; "Survival at the Stockyards," *Time*, September 6, 1968, p. 21.

83. By a margin of 44 to 41 percent, his supporters approved of the actions of Daley and the police. By comparison, Nixon's supporters voiced their support by 63 to 25 percent and Wallace's supporters by 71 to 20 percent. Panzer to LBJ, September 17, 1968, Box 39, Ex JL 6, WHSF, LBJ Library.

84. Carl Solberg, *Hubert Humphrey: A Biography* (New York: Norton, 1984), pp. 366, 370. The vice president had apparently long harbored conspiracy fears. Because he thought he kept seeing the same faces at protests, he had a close aide ask Clark "whether a report could be authentically prepared that would show that there was common planning throughout the United States of public demonstrations, riots in colleges, and similar types of activities." The confidential memo added that Humphrey was "particularly interested not only whether it is centrally planned, but whether or not the same people appear in various demonstrations." Kintner to the Attorney General, May 19, 1967, Box 28, FG 135, WHSF, LBJ Library.

85. "Democrats: The Ghost of Chicago," *Newsweek*, September 16, 1968, p. 24.

86. Earl Dudley to Bill Welch, John Stewart, Tom Hughes, Doug Bennet, September 7, 1968, Box 2, Research Files, 1968 Campaign Papers, Humphrey MSS, MHS.

CHAPTER 9. LAW AND ORDER TRIUMPHANT

1. "The Overshadowing Issue," *Time*, August 2, 1968, p. 11; "The Fear Campaign," *Time*, October 4, 1968, p. 21.

2. Lewis Chester, Godfrey Hodgson, and Bruce Page, *An American Melodrama: The Presidential Campaign of 1968* (New York: Viking, 1969), p. 21. For an important exception, see Richard M. Scammon and Ben J. Wattenberg, *The Real Majority* (New York: Coward, McCann, 1970), pp. 39, 93. They contend that "Americans were not voting primarily on a pro-Vietnam or anti-Vietnam basis despite its 'importance.'" Although the war was probably the nation's most serious challenge, "it was not the essential issue on which votes swung yea or nay. Vietnam was not the Voting Issue of 1968."

3. House Speaker John McCormack, a Massachusetts Democrat, and House Minority Leader Gerald Ford, a Michigan Republican, both identified law and order as the main issue of the campaign. "How They Explain What Happened," *U.S. News & World Report*, November 18, 1968, pp. 82, 84; and Louis Harris, "Polls: An Insight," *Newsweek*, November 11, 1968, p. 34.

4. Charles Roche to LBJ, October 22, 1968, Box 3, White House Office Files (WHOF) of Charles Roche, Lyndon Baines Johnson Presidential Library (LBJ Library); Voter Opinion on Campaign Issues, Box 9, Research Files, 1968 Campaign Papers, Humphrey MSS; Minnesota Historical Society (MHS).

5. Panzer to LBJ, October 28, 1968, Box 26, Ex PL/Nixon, Richard, White House Subject Files (WHSF), LBJ Library.

6. "Narrow Victory, Wide Problems," *Time*, November 15, 1968, p. 19; "Nixon's Hard-Won Chance to Lead," *Time*, November 15, 1968, pp. 24–25; George Reedy to LBJ, October 5, 1968, Box 26, Ex PL/Nixon, Richard, WHSF, LBJ Library; Theodore H. White, *The Making of the President 1968* (New York: Atheneum, 1969), p. 467; Gerald Hursh to Orville Freeman, September 27, 1968, Box 16, Citizens for Humphrey Files, 1968 Campaign Papers, Humphrey MSS, MHS.

7. "Wallace and His Folks," *Newsweek*, September 16, 1968, p. 25.

8. Panzer to LBJ, September 16, 1968, Box 27, Ex PL/Wallace, George, WHSF, LBJ Library; "Why They Want Him," *Time*, October 18, 1968, p. 19.

9. Jonathan Rieder, *Canarsie: The Italians and Jews of Brooklyn against Liberalism* (Cambridge: Harvard University Press, 1985), p. 243.

10. The Wallace campaign song (to the tune of "The Battle Hymn of the Republic") was: "He stands up for law and order, / The policeman on the beat. / He will make it safe to once again / Walk safely on the street. / He'll uproot the seeds of treason, / He'll restore the courts of law, / So justice can prevail. / Won't you stand up with George Wallace! (repeated three times) / So all men can be free!" Chester, Hodgson, and Page, *An American Melodrama*, p. 651. See also "Wallace and His Folks," *Newsweek*, September 16, 1968, p. 26; and Liva Baker, *Miranda: Crime, Law, and Politics* (New York: Atheneum, 1983), p. 243.

11. Stephan Lesher, *George Wallace: American Populist* (Reading, Massachusetts: Addison-Wesley, 1994), pp. 405–406; Dan T. Carter, *The Politics of Rage: George Wallace, The Origins of the New Conservatism, and the Transformation of American Politics* (New York: Simon and Schuster, 1995), pp. 305–306. See also "Wallace's Army: The Coalition of Frustration," *Time*, October 18, 1968, p. 16.

12. Marshall Frady, *Wallace* (New York: World Publishing Co., 1968), pp. 8–9; Carter, *The Politics of Rage*, pp. 366–367; "Wallace and His Folks," *Newsweek*, September 16, 1968, p. 27; Chester, Hodgson, and Page, *An American Melodrama*, p. 283; "Wallace: The Unspoken Issue," *Newsweek*, November 4, 1968, p. 36.

13. Among Wallace supporters, men outnumbered women 8 to 1. Panzer to LBJ, October 22, 1968, Box 27, Ex PL/Wallace, George, WHSF, LBJ Library; Gerald Hursh to Doug Bennet, John Stewart, October 23, 1968, Box 16, Citizens for Hum-

phrey Files, 1968 Campaign Papers, Humphrey MSS, MHS. See also "Wallace: The Unspoken Issue," *Newsweek*, November 4, 1968, p. 36; and "How Dr. Gallup Sees the Campaign Homestretch," *U.S. News & World Report*, November 4, 1968, p. 40. For a description of several of LeMay's gaffes, see Carter, *The Politics of Rage*, pp. 359, 361.

14. Campaign Policy Committee Minutes, September 18, 1968, Box 1, Personal Political Files (PPF), 1968 Campaign Papers, Humphrey MSS, MHS; Gerald Hursh to Doug Bennet, John Stewart, October 23, 1968, Box 16, Citizens for Humphrey Files, 1968 Campaign Papers, Humphrey MSS, MHS; Lesher, *George Wallace*, p. 413.

15. COPE pumped out more than 10 million mailings, spent almost $10 million, and on election day alone mobilized more than 65,000 volunteers—after using almost 20,000 workers at phone banks and another 58,000 for canvassing homes during the fall. In all, the AFL-CIO registered 4.5 million new voters. Carl Solberg, *Hubert Humphrey: A Biography* (New York: Norton, 1984), pp. 388–389.

16. Carter, *The Politics of Rage*, p. 352; White, *The Making of the President 1968*, p. 426. Campaign Policy Committee Minutes, September 25, 1968, Box 1, PPF, 1968 Campaign Papers, Humphrey MSS, MHS; "Wallace's Army: The Coalition of Frustration," *Time*, October 18, 1968, pp. 16, 18–19.

17. John P. Roche to LBJ, June 6, 1967, Box 76, PL/Name Political Affairs, WHSF, LBJ Library; Dutton to Joe Napolitan, September 9, 1968, Box 2, Democratic National Committee Files: O'Brien, 1968 Campaign Papers, Humphrey MSS, MHS; O'Brien to LBJ, October 8, 1968, Box 43, WHOF of Joseph Califano, LBJ Library.

18. According to a recent biographer, Nixon made an "overt quest to appropriate the issue from Wallace." Lesher, *George Wallace*, pp. 403, 414. See also Carter, *The Politics of Rage*, pp. 328, 364.

19. Interview with Murphy Martin of WFAA-TV in Dallas, October 13, 1968, PPS 208 (1968).175.1 (1), Speech Files, PCP, Richard M. Nixon Library (RMN Library).

20. Carter, *The Politics of Rage*, p. 313.

21. Lesher, *George Wallace*, p. 399.

22. Rieder, *Canarsie*, p. 174; and "Wallace: The Unspoken Issue," *Newsweek*, November 4, 1968, p. 35.

23. "The truth is that for many Americans George Wallace is telling it like it is," concluded John Hart, a reporter. "He is accurately describing a vision of America that is widespread enough to threaten the tranquility of the two major parties." *CBS Evening News*, August 12, 1968, Television News Archive (TNA). Charles Murphy said it was unclear whether Wallace was a hero or demagogue. What he offered his supporters was a consistent message, a "litany of hope to these people, a litany of hate to others. But the message is winning converts, it's getting across. And the crest of this movement is yet to come." *ABC News*, September 12, 1968, TNA.

24. *ABC News*, September 18, 1968, TNA.

25. See Lesher, *George Wallace*, p. 422; Frady, *Wallace*, p. 137; Carter, *The Politics of Rage*, pp. 345, 348; and Michael Kazin, *The Populist Persuasion: An American History* (New York: Basic Books, 1995), pp. 30–31.

26. Lesher, *George Wallace*, pp. 427–428; "Wallace's Army: The Coalition of Frustration," *Time*, October 18, 1968, p. 16; Carter, *The Politics of Rage*, p. 316; and "Wallace and His Folks," *Newsweek*, September 16, 1968, p. 28.

27. See Robert G. Sherrill, "George Wallace: 'Running for God,'" *Nation*, May 8, 1967, p. 591 and Robert B. Semple Jr., "Negroes in Poll Ask For More Police," *New York Times*, September 9, 1966, pp. 1, 54.

28. *CBS Evening News*, October 21, 1968, TNA.

29. "Wallace's Army: The Coalition of Frustration," *Time*, October 18, 1968, p. 15; Louis Harris, "Polls: An Insight," *Newsweek*, November 11, 1968, p. 34; "The Anatomy of the Vote," *Newsweek*, November 11, 1968, pp. 35–36.

30. Kevin Phillips, *The Emerging Republican Majority* (Garden City, New York: Doubleday, 1970), pp. 79, 170–174, 352; Rieder, *Canarsie*, p. 243.

31. Carter, *The Politics of Rage*, p. 369; Lesher, *George Wallace*, p. 428.

32. Panzer to LBJ, September 6, 1968, Box 28, Ex JL 3, WHSF, LBJ Library.

33. Confidential minutes, September 18, 1968, Box 1, PPF, 1968 Campaign Papers, Humphrey MSS, MHS.

34. "It is very important to understand that the demand for increased action on crime prevention and the maintenance of law and order is not a covert demand for anti-Negro action," Kirkpatrick informed Freeman. "The demand is spread through all segments of the population." Confidential minutes, September 27, 1968, Box 1, PPF, 1968 Campaign Papers, Humphrey MSS, MHS; Kirkpatrick to Freeman, October 4, 1968, Box 1, PPF, 1968 Campaign Papers, Humphrey MSS, MHS.

35. James Rowe to HHH, July 31, 1968, Box 1, PPF, 1968 Campaign Papers, Humphrey MSS, MHS; "A Survey of the Race for President," Box 15, Citizens for Humphrey Files, 1968 Campaign Papers, Humphrey MSS, MHS.

36. *Issues and Answers*, July 7, 1968, Box 30, Speech Text Files (STF), 1968 Campaign Papers, Humphrey MSS, MHS.

37. In 16 states worth a total of 317 electoral votes, blacks were a decisive factor. Timothy N. Thurber, *Hubert H. Humphrey and the African American Freedom Struggle* (New York: Columbia University Press, 1999), p. 204.

38. Similarly, Humphrey supporters believed by a margin of 57 to 32 percent that ending poverty was essential for the restoration of "law and order." Among blacks, the margin was 71 to 21 percent; among Jews, it was 68 to 22 percent. Voter Opinion on Campaign Issues, Box 9, Research Files, 1968 Campaign Papers, Humphrey MSS, MHS.

39. Speech to National Press Club, June 20, 1968, Box 29, STF, 1968 Campaign Papers, Humphrey MSS, MHS; Patricia Harris to Humphrey, June 27, 1968, attached to Humphrey to Harris, July 15, 1968, Box 2, Research Files, 1968 Campaign Papers, Humphrey MSS, MHS.

40. "Crime and Law Enforcement—Draft," n.d., Box 1331, Research Files, Vice-Presidential Papers (VPP), Humphrey MSS, MHS; David Williams to Ted Van Dyk and Doug Bennet, September 13, 1968, Box 2, Research Files, 1968 Campaign Papers, Humphrey MSS, MHS; David Ginsburg to Humphrey, September 10, 1968, Box 1, PPF, 1968 Campaign Papers, Humphrey MSS, MHS.

41. *CBS Evening News*, October 21, 1968, TNA; Confidential minutes, September 25, 1968, Box 1, PPF, 1968 Campaign Papers, Humphrey MSS, MHS; "The Overshadowing Issue," *Time*, August 2, 1968, p. 11. See also Humphrey to American Legion Convention, September 11, 1968, Box 31, STF, 1968 Campaign Papers, Humphrey MSS, MHS; and Humphrey to AME Churches, May 2, 1968, Box 28, STF, 1968 Campaign Papers, Humphrey MSS, MHS.

42. Interview in Washington, June 30, 1968, Box 29, STF, 1968 Campaign Papers, Humphrey MSS, MHS; "Law, Order and Justice" for Nation's Business, August 1968, Box 2, Research Files, 1968 Campaign Papers, Humphrey MSS, MHS; Humphrey to John Stewart, June 8, 1968, Box 2, Research Files, 1968 Campaign Papers, Humphrey MSS, MHS.

43. Interview with Pittsburgh-area college newspaper editors, *WTAE-TV*, September 13, 1968, Box 31, STF, 1968 Campaign Papers, Humphrey MSS, MHS; Interview on *KDKA-TV*, September 14, 1968, Box 31, STF, 1968 Campaign Papers, Humphrey MSS, MHS; "Crime and Law Enforcement—Draft", n.d., Box 1331, Research Files, VPP, Humphrey MSS, MHS; Speech in Louisville, Kentucky, September 20, 1968, Box 31, STF, 1968 Campaign Papers, Humphrey MSS, MHS; "Issues and Answers," August 11, 1968, Box 30, STF, 1968 Campaign Papers, Humphrey MSS, MHS.

44. Interview in Washington, June 30, 1968, Box 29, STF, 1968 Campaign Papers, Humphrey MSS, MHS; Address to AME Churches, May 2, 1968, Box 28, STF, 1968 Campaign Papers, Humphrey MSS, MHS; Address to AME Zion Church, Detroit, May 14, 1968, Box 29, STF, 1968 Campaign Papers, Humphrey MSS, MHS; Remarks to New Jersey Citizens for Humphrey, August 15, 1968, Box 30, STF, 1968 Campaign Papers, Humphrey MSS, MHS.

45. Humphrey to Freeman, September 18, 1968, Box 1, PPF, 1968 Campaign Papers, Humphrey MSS, MHS; Orville Freeman OH, interview by T. H. Baker, February 14, 1969, LBJ Library.

46. Remarks at John Jay College of Criminal Justice, October 11, 1968, Box 32, STF, 1968 Campaign Papers, Humphrey MSS, MHS; Speech to 33rd Annual Convention of Catholic War Veterans, August 7, 1968, Box 30, STF, 1968 Campaign Papers, Humphrey MSS, MHS; Remarks to American Legion Convention, September 11, 1968, Box 31, STF, 1968 Campaign Papers, Humphrey MSS, MHS; Bill Welsh to Al Spivak, September 16, 1968, Box 1, Democratic National Committee Files: Staff, 1968 Campaign Papers, Humphrey MSS, MHS.

47. Interview with *WLAC-TV* in Nashville, October 1, 1968, Box 32, STF, 1968 Campaign Papers, Humphrey MSS, MHS; Humphrey to Ramsey Clark, September 6, 1968, Box 96, Ramsey Clark MSS, LBJ Library.

48. The seven states with the highest crime rates all had Republican governors. By comparison, the five states with the lowest crime rates all had Democratic governors. Wallace's Alabama was ranked first in murders per capita. Agnew's Maryland was ranked first in violent crimes per capita. Doug Bennet to Humphrey, n.d., Box 2, Research Files, 1968 Campaign Papers, Humphrey MSS, MHS; Remarks to American Legion Convention, September 11, 1968, Box 31, STF, 1968 Campaign Papers, Humphrey MSS, MHS.

49. Why Johnson remained so loyal to Clark is unclear since the president often stated openly that the attorney general was "the worst appointment he ever made." Ben Wattenberg, interview with author, December 19, 1997. One official believes that it was because the president liked Tom Clark (Ramsey's father), felt guilty about engineering his resignation from the Supreme Court (to clear a seat for Thurgood Marshall), and therefore was not going to fire his son. Nicholas Katzenbach, interview with author, March 6, 1998.

50. Califano had to sneak because Johnson was extremely annoyed that he had leaked several legislative ideas to the Humphrey campaign. Joseph A. Califano, Jr., *The Triumph and the Tragedy of Lyndon Johnson: The White House Years* (New York: Simon and Schuster, 1991), p. 326. "It was interesting how detached we were [from the campaign]," recalled an assistant. "One [reason was] that the president said we should be detached, with good reason. Presidents tend to do this. They want their place in history. And there was always a certain tension between Johnson and Humphrey." He added that, "We were worn out too. Everyone was exhausted." Matthew Nimetz, interview with author, July 17, 1995. For proposed edits, see Califano to John Stewart, October 9, 1968, Box 43, WHOF of Joseph Califano, LBJ Library.

51. David Cohen and Mike Naftalin to John Stewart and Doug Bennet, October 9, 1968, Box 2, Research Files, 1968 Campaign Papers, Humphrey MSS, MHS. See also Robert Nathan to John Stewart, October 9, 1968, Box 8, Research Files, 1968 Campaign Papers, Humphrey MSS, MHS.

52. Television address on Law and Order, October 12, 1968, Box 32, STF, 1968 Campaign Papers, Humphrey MSS, MHS.

53. Nixon outspent Humphrey by almost two to one on television as well as more than four to one on radio and two to one in newspapers. Kathleen Hall Jamieson, *Packaging the Presidency: A History and Criticism of Presidential Campaign Advertising* (New York: Oxford University Press, 1984), pp. 233–236.

54. "Marshall Plan," Humphrey Campaign, 1968, Political Commercial Archive of the University of Oklahoma, Norman, Oklahoma (PCA); "The Loser: A Near Run Thing," *Time*, November 15, 1968, p. 33.

55. Gerald Hursh to Orville Freeman, September 24, 1968, Box 16, Citizens for Humphrey Files, 1968 Campaign Papers, Humphrey MSS, MHS.

56. Gerald Hursh to Orville Freeman, October 2, 1968, Box 16, Citizens for Humphrey Files, 1968 Campaign Papers, Humphrey MSS, MHS; Gerald Hursh to Doug Bennet, October 21, 1968, Box 16, Citizens for Humphrey Files, 1968

Campaign Papers, Humphrey MSS, MHS; Bill Connell to Humphrey, October 26, 1968, Box 16, Citizens for Humphrey Files, 1968 Campaign Papers, Humphrey MSS, MHS; Gerald Hursh to Doug Bennet, John Stewart, October 23, 1968, Box 16, Citizens for Humphrey Files, 1968 Campaign Papers, Humphrey MSS, MHS.

57. Humphrey to Larry O'Brien, October 21, 1968, Box 1, PPF, 1968 Campaign Papers, Humphrey MSS, MHS.

58. Remarks at St. Paul's Cathedral, Los Angeles, October 24, 1968, Box 33, STF, 1968 Campaign Papers, Humphrey MSS, MHS; "Meet the Press," October 27, 1968, Box 33, STF, 1968 Campaign Papers, Humphrey MSS, MHS; John Martin to Humphrey, October 30, 1968, attached to remarks for Rockford Airport Rally, November 1, 1968, Box 33, STF, 1968 Campaign Papers, Humphrey MSS, MHS.

59. Remarks in Levittown, November 3, 1968, Box 33, STF, 1968 Campaign Papers, Humphrey MSS, MHS.

60. Humphrey won an overwhelming majority of the black vote—but his percentage was below what Johnson had received. "The Shape of the Vote," *Time*, November 15, 1968, p. 21; "The Anatomy of the Vote," *Newsweek*, November 11, 1968, pp. 35–36.

61. *NBC Nightly News*, September 6, 1968, TNA.

62. "They are not racists or sick; they are not guilty of the crime that plagues the land," said Nixon of the "silent majority." Presidential Nomination Acceptance Speech, 8/8/68, PPS 208 (1968).58.11.2, Speech Files, RMN Library.

63. Garment to Nixon, April 15, 1968, Box 3, Series I, RMN Library; Radio address, May 8, 1968, Box 76, Record Group 15—Gubernatorial Press Office, Rockefeller MSS, Rockefeller Archive Center (RAC). In 1968, 70 percent of voters lived outside large cities, divided evenly between suburbs and small towns or farms. "Where Voters Live—Mostly Outside Cities," *U.S. News & World Report*, November 4, 1968, p. 43.

64. RMN Position Book, Box 3, Series I, RMN Library; Kevin Phillips, n.d., Box 8, Series II, RMN Library; Pittsburgh press conference, September 8, 1968, PPS 208 (1968).75 (1), Speech Files, RMN Library; Press Conference, Disneyland Hotel, September 17, 1968, PPS 208 (1968).102, Speech Files, RMN Library; and "Face the Nation," October 27, 1968, Box 33, STF, 1968 Campaign Papers, Humphrey MSS, MHS.

65. John Sears to Nixon, September 9, 1968, Box 21, Series II, RMN Library. See also William Casey to Nixon, September 6, 1968, Box 3, Series II, RMN Library.

66. "Order and Justice Under Law," September 29, 1968, Box 20, Ramsey Clark MSS, LBJ Library.

67. Ibid.

68. *Face the Nation*, October 27, 1968, Box 33, STF, 1968 Campaign Papers, Humphrey MSS, MHS.

69. "Order and Justice Under Law," September 29, 1968, Box 20, Ramsey Clark MSS, LBJ Library; Interview, *WAVE-TV* in Louisville, September 26, 1968, PPS

208 (1968).126, Speech Files, RMN Library; Q&A program in California, July 16, 1968, PPS 208 (1968).49, Speech Files, RMN Library; Press Conference, Disneyland Hotel in Anaheim, September 17, 1968, PPS 208 (1968).102, Speech Files, RMN Library; Press Conference of Ramsey Clark, August 14, 1968, Box 117, Ramsey Clark MSS, LBJ Library; *NBC Nightly News*, August 14, 1968, TNA; *NBC News*, October 16, 1968, TNA.

70. Press Conference of Ramsey Clark, August 14, 1968, Box 117, Ramsey Clark MSS, LBJ Library.

71. "Order and Justice Under Law," September 29, 1968, Box 20, Ramsey Clark MSS, LBJ Library; Buchanan to Nixon, September 7, 1966, Box 18, Research Files, RMN Library; Press Conference, Disneyland Hotel in Anaheim, September 17, 1968, PPS 208 (1968).102, Speech Files, RMN Library.

72. "Order and Justice Under Law," September 29, 1968, Box 20, Ramsey Clark MSS, LBJ Library; Liva Baker, *Miranda: Crime, Law, and Politics* (New York: Atheneum, 1983), p. 248.

73. "Order and Justice Under Law," September 29, 1968, Box 20, Ramsey Clark MSS, LBJ Library; Statement, October 10, 1968, PPS 208 (1968).169, Speech Files, RMN Library; Question and Answer program in California, July 16, 1968, PPS 208 (1968).49, Speech Files, RMN Library; Press Conference in Pittsburgh, September 8, 1968, PPS 208 (1968).75 (1), Speech Files, RMN Library.

74. Ray Price to Nixon, June 29, 1968, Box 18, Series II, RMN Library; Garment to Nixon, April 15, 1968, Box 3, Series I, RMN Library; Price to Nixon, July 27, 1967, PPS 500.10–5, Research Files, RMN Library.

75. "Nixon's Hard-Won Chance to Lead," *Time*, November 15, 1968, p. 23.

76. Three years earlier, William Safire had written that "about the last thing in this world Dick Nixon will stand still for is an attempt by some of the Madison Avenue crowd to re-do his 'image.'" Safire to Peter Flanigan, April 19, 1965, Box 20, Series II, RMN Library. But Nixon was desperate and, according to one journalist, he first had admen choose the image he should project and then permitted them to remake him in that image. However, a leading scholar of campaign advertising has accused McGinniss of "selective amnesia" and the misuse of sources, even those he provides in his appendix. See Joe McGinniss, *The Selling of the President 1968* (New York: Trident Press, 1969), p. 193 and appendix; and Jamieson, *Packaging the Presidency*, pp. 262–269.

77. "Nixon's Hard-Won Chance to Lead," *Time*, November 15, 1968, p. 23.

78. Haldeman to Nixon, June 20, 1967, Box 9, Series II, RMN Library; Haldeman to Robert Ellsworth, December 8, 1967, Box 9, Series II, RMN Library. By 1984, the Reagan campaign had mastered the principles outlined by Haldeman. See Lou Cannon, *President Reagan: The Role of a Lifetime* (New York: Simon & Schuster, 1991), chapter 17.

79. Ironically, Haldeman told Nixon that he didn't need TV, that if he just mentioned law and order six times in every speech he would win easily. McGinniss, *The Selling of the President 1968*, pp. 63, 81.

80. "Wrong Road," Nixon Campaign, 1968, PCA.

81. Presidential Nomination Acceptance Speech, August 8, 1968, PPS 208 (1968).58.11.2, Speech Files, RMN Library; "Woman," Nixon campaign commercial, 1968, Political Advertisement, 1954–1984 (1984), compiled by Marshall Reese, available from Electronic Arts Intermix, Inc., New York; "Crime," Nixon Campaign, 1968, PCA; "Order," Nixon campaign commercial, 1968, Anthology of Political Commercials, The Museum of Television and Radio, New York.

82. "Woman," Nixon campaign commercial, 1968, Political Advertisement, 1954–1984 (1984), compiled by Marshall Reese, available from Electronic Arts Intermix, Inc., New York.

83. "Crime," Nixon Campaign, 1968, PCA; "Order," Nixon campaign commercial, 1968, Anthology of Political Commercials, The Museum of Television and Radio, New York. McGinniss, *The Selling of the President 1968*, pp. 88–89.

84. Chester, Hodgson, and Page, *An American Melodrama*, pp. 762–763.

85. "Narrow Victory, Wide Problems," *Time*, November 15, 1968, p. 20; "The Way the Voting Went—And Why," *U.S. News & World Report*, November 18, 1968, pp. 40, 42; "Nixon's Hard-Won Chance to Lead," *Time*, November 15, 1968, p. 22.

86. Ibid. See also Thurber, *Hubert H. Humphrey and the African American Freedom Struggle*, p. 219.

EPILOGUE

1. "The Troubled American," *Newsweek*, October 6, 1969, p. 30.

2. Nixon statement, June 22, 1968, PPS 208 (1968).37, Speech Files, Richard M. Nixon Library (RMN Library).

3. The bill would also expand the federal government's wiretapping authority and impose mandatory-minimum sentencing guidelines on federal judges.

4. Nixon to Haldeman, May 25, 1970, Box 2, President's Personal File, White House Special Files (WHSF), National Archives (NA).

5. James T. Patterson, *Grand Expectations: The U.S., 1945–1974* (New York: Oxford University Press, 1996), pp. 736–737.

6. Charles Colson to Nixon, November 16, 1970, Office Files of H.R. Haldeman, Box 342, WHSF, NA.

7. Nixon to Haldeman, December 1, 1970, Box 2, President's Personal File, WHSF, NA.

8. As usual, the record is complicated and controversial, even if one assumes the data are accurate. On the one hand, the *total* crime rate (against persons and property) rose by almost 30 percent from 1969 to 1971. On the other hand, it fell by 3 percent in 1972—the first decrease in 17 years—as most of the nation's largest cities reported substantial declines. The *violent* crime rate, however, increased steadily until 1976. In Washington, meanwhile, the *violent* crime rate rose by almost 10 percent in 1971, then fell in 1972 and 1973 before climbing again in 1974 and 1975.

Uniform Crime Reports (UCR), Bureau of Justice Crime Statistics (http://www.ojp.usdoj.gov/bjs/welcome.html).

9. Jack W. Germond and Jules Witcover, *Blue Smoke and Mirrors: How Reagan Won and Why Carter Lost the Election of 1980* (New York: Viking Press, 1981), p. 381.

10. William Berman, *America's Right Turn: From Nixon to Clinton* (Baltimore: The Johns Hopkins University Press, 1994), p. 114.

11. Liva Baker, *Miranda: Crime, Law, and Politics* (New York: Atheneum, 1983), pp. 309–310; Richard M. Scammon and Ben J. Wattenberg, *The Real Majority* (New York: Coward, McCann, 1970), pp. 230–238.

12. Wallace Turner, "Crime Is Top Issue in Races on Coast," *The New York Times*, August 31, 1981, p. A11; Todd Purdum, "Rose Bird, Once California's Chief Justice, Is Dead at 63," *The New York Times*, December 6, 1999, p. B18.

13. Tom Smith, Liberal and Conservative Trends in the United States Since World War II, GSS Social Change Report No. 29 (Chicago: National Opinion Research Center, 1989). See also Alan Wolfe, *One Nation, After All* (New York: Penguin Putnam, 1998), p. 120.

14. David C. Anderson, *Crime and the Politics of Hysteria: How the Willie Horton Story Changed American Justice* (New York: Random House, 1995), pp. 206–257.

15. Anderson, *Crime and the Politics of Hysteria*, pp. 213, 215, 226, 229.

16. Martin Walker, *The President We Deserve: Bill Clinton: His Rise, Falls, and Comebacks* (New York: Crown Publishers, 1996), p. 19.

17. Ben J. Wattenberg, *Values Matter Most: How Democrats or Republicans or a Third Party Can Win and Renew the American Way of Life* (New York: Regnery, 1996), p. 156. See also David Johnston and Tim Weiner, "Seizing the Crime Issue, Clinton Blurs Party Lines," *The New York Times*, August 1, 1996, p. A1.

18 "Crime Bill: What Passed," *USA Today*, August 29, 1994, p. 5A.

19. Sidney Blumenthal, "Crime Pays," *The New Yorker*, May 9, 1994, pp. 42–44.

20. Jim Dwyer, "A Reborn City," *The New York Times*, December 31, 2001, p. A1.

21. Randall Kennedy, *Race, Crime, and the Law* (New York: Pantheon Books, 1997), p. 15; Alfred Blumstein and Joel Wallman, eds., *The Crime Drop in America* (Cambridge University Press, 2000), pp. 3, 13; Warren E. Leary, "Violent Crime Continues to Decline," *The New York Times*, August 28, 2000, p. A10.

22. Blumstein and Wallman, eds., *The Crime Drop in America*, passim; Lawrie Mifflin, "Crime Falls, But Not on TV," *The New York Times*, July 6, 1997, p. E3; Laurie Goodstein, "Death Penalty Falls from Favor as Some Lose Confidence in Its Fairness," *The New York Times*, June 17, 2001, p. A14.

23. Thomas L. Friedman, "Blair for President," *The New York Times*, December 18, 2002, p. A33.

Bibliography

MANUSCRIPT AND DOCUMENTS COLLECTIONS

Arizona Historical Foundation, University of Arizona, Tempe, Arizona (AHF), Barry M. Goldwater Papers (Goldwater MSS)
——1964 Presidential Campaign Files (PCF)
——Microform Reels (MR)
——Preliminary Inventory—Goldwater Political
——Series W (Unprocessed) Files
The Bancroft Library, University of California, Berkeley (Bancroft Library), Oral History Collection
Eugene C. Barker Center for American History, University of Texas at Austin (Barker Center), Barry Goldwater Collection (BGC)
Hoover Institution Archives, Stanford University, Palo Alto, California (Hoover Institution)
——John Ehrlichman Papers (Ehrlichman MSS)
——Denison Kitchel Papers (Kitchel MSS)
——Ronald Reagan Papers (Reagan MSS)
Lyndon Baines Johnson Presidential Library, University of Texas at Austin (LBJ Library)
——Administrative Histories
——Diary Backup
——Cabinet Papers
——Democratic National Committee File (DNC)
——Legislation
——Federal Records

——Handwriting File
——Legislative Background (LB)
——Name Files
——National Security Files (NSF)
——Office Files of John Macy (OFM)
——Office Files of the President (OFP)
——Oral Histories (OH)
——Statements File (SF)
——Task Force Reports (TFR)
——Tom Johnson's Notes of Meetings (TJN)
——White House Confidential Files (WHCF)
——White House Famous Names (WHFN)
——White House Office Files (WHOF)
——White House Press Office (WHPO)
——White House Social Files (WHSF)
——White House Subject Files (WHSF)
John F. Kennedy Presidential Library, Boston, Massachusetts (JFK Library)
——Oral Histories (OH)
——President's Office Files (POF)
——White House Central Subject Files (WHCSF)
——Robert F. Kennedy Papers (RFK MSS)
——1968 Presidential Campaign Papers (PCP)
——Attorney General's Papers (AGP)
——U.S. Senate Papers
Library of Congress, Washington, D.C. (LOC)
——Emanuel Celler Papers (Celler MSS)
——National Urban League Papers (NUL Papers), Parts II and III
——National Association for the Advancement of Colored People Papers (NAACP Papers): Administrative File (III); Administrative File (IV); Branch Files (III); Branch Files (IV); Legal Department (III); Legal Department (IV); Printed Matter (III); Printed Matter (IV)
——A. Philip Randolph Papers (Randolph MSS)
——Joseph Rauh Papers (Rauh MSS)
——Earl Warren Papers (Warren MSS)
George Meany Memorial Archives, Silver Spring, Maryland (GMMA), AFL-CIO Papers
——Committee on Political Education Research Division Files (COPE Papers)
——Department of Legislation
——Minutes of Executive Council Meetings
Minnesota Historical Society, St. Paul, Minnesota (MHS), Hubert H. Humphrey Papers (Humphrey MSS)
——Vice-Presidential Papers (VPP)

——1968 Campaign Papers: Candidate Files; Citizens for Humphrey Files; Democratic National Committee Files: O'Brien; Democratic National Committee Files: Staff; Personal Political Files (PPF); Research Files (RF); Speech Text Files (STF)

The Museum of Television and Radio, New York, New York, Anthology of Political Commercials

National Archives, Washington, D.C. (NA), Nixon Collection

——White House Special Files (WHSF)

——White House Central Files (WHCF)

New York Municipal Reference Library, New York (NYMRL), John W. Lindsay Papers (Lindsay MSS)

——Confidential Subject Files

——Correspondence Files

——Departmental Correspondence

——Subject Files

Political Commercial Archive of the University of Oklahoma, Norman, Oklahoma (PCA)

Richard M. Nixon Library, Yorba Linda, California (RMN Library), 1968 Presidential Campaign Papers (PCP)

——Speech Files

——Research Files

——Series I and II

Rockefeller Archive Center, Tarrytown, NY (RAC), Nelson A. Rockefeller Papers (Rockefeller MSS)

——Record Group 15—Gubernatorial Series

——Record Group 15—Gubernatorial Speeches

——Record Group 15—Gubernatorial Office Records

Southern Historical Collection, University of North Carolina, Chapel Hill, North Carolina (SHC), Senator Sam J. Ervin, Jr. Papers (Ervin MSS)

Television News Archive, Vanderbilt University, Knoxville, Tennessee (TNA)

PERSONAL INTERVIEWS AND CORRESPONDENCE

Califano, Joseph, August 8, 1995.

Cater, Douglass, July 13, 1995.

Cutler, Lloyd, September 21, 1995.

Gaither, James, September 25, 1995.

Goldwater, Barry to author, July 12, 1994.

Katzenbach, Nicholas, March 6 1998.

Nimetz, Matthew, July 17, 1995.

Schlei, Norbert, July 6, 1995.

Vorenberg, James, July 18, 1995.
Wattenberg, Ben, December 19, 1997.
White, Lee, March 16, 1998.
Yarmolinsky, Adam, July 19, 1995.

NEWSPAPERS AND PERIODICALS

Nation
National Review
Newsweek
New Republic
New York Times
Time
U.S. News & World Report
Washington Post

PUBLISHED SOURCES

Aaron, Henry J. *Politics and the Professors: The Great Society in Perspective*. Washington, D.C.: Brookings Institution, 1978.

Abbott, David W., Louis H. Gold, and Edward T. Rogowsky. *Police, Politics, and Race: The New York City Referendum on Civilian Review*. Cambridge, Massachusetts: American Jewish Committee and the Joint Center for Urban Studies of Massachusetts Institute of Technology and Harvard, 1969.

Ambrose, Stephen E. *Nixon: The Triumph of a Politician 1962–1972*. New York: Simon and Schuster, 1989.

Anderson, David C. *Crime and The Politics of Hysteria: How the Willie Horton Story Changed American Justice*. New York: Random House, 1995.

Anderson, Totton J. and Eugene C. Lee. "The 1966 Election in California." *Western Political Quarterly* 20 (June 1967): 535–552.

Andrew, John A. III. *The Other Side of the Sixties: Young Americans for Freedom and the Rise of Conservative Politics*. New Brunswick: Rutgers University Press, 1997.

Baker, Liva. *Miranda: Crime, Law, and Politics*. New York: Atheneum Press, 1983.

Bass, Jack and Walter de Vries. *The Transformation of Southern Politics: Social Change and Political Consequences since 1945*. New York: New American Library, 1976.

Belknap, Michal R. *Federal Law and Southern Order: Racial Violence and Constitutional Conflict in the Post-Brown South*. Athens: University of Georgia Press, 1987.

Bell, Daniel. *The End of Ideology: On the Exhaustion of Political Ideas in the Fifties*. Glencoe, Illinois: The Free Press, 1960.

Bernstein, Irving. *Guns or Butter: The Presidency of Lyndon Johnson*. New York: Oxford University Press, 1996.

Beschloss, Michael R. *Taking Charge: The Johnson White House Tapes, 1963–1964*. New York: Simon & Schuster, 1997.

Biles, Roger. *Richard J. Daley: Politics, Race, and the Governing of Chicago*. DeKalb: Northern Illinois University Press, 1995.

Biondi, Martha. *To Stand and Fight: The Struggle for Civil Rights in Postwar New York City*. Cambridge: Harvard University Press, 2003.

Blumenthal, Sidney. *Pledging Allegiance: The Last Campaign of the Cold War*. New York: HarperCollins, 1990.

Bornet, Vaughan Davis. *The Presidency of Lyndon B. Johnson*. Lawrence: University Press of Kansas, 1983.

Brauer, Carl M. "Kennedy, Johnson, and the War on Poverty." *Journal of American History* 69 (June 1982): 98–119.

Brennan, Mary C. *Turning Right in the Sixties: The Conservative Capture of the GOP*. Chapel Hill: University of North Carolina Press, 1995.

Brink, William and Louis Harris. *Black and White*. New York: Simon and Schuster, 1967.

Brinkley, Alan. *Voices of Protest: Huey Long, Father Coughlin & the Great Depression*. New York: Vintage Books, 1982.

Brown, Edmund G. *Reagan and Reality: The Two Californias*. New York: Praeger Publishers, 1970.

Burnham, David. *Above the Law*. New York: Scribner, 1996.

Butterfield, Fox. *All God's Children: The Bosket Family and the American Tradition of Violence*. New York: Alfred A. Knopf, 1995.

Button, James W. *Black Violence: Political Impact of the 1960s Riots*. Princeton: Princeton University Press, 1978.

Califano, Joseph A. Jr. *The Triumph and the Tragedy of Lyndon Johnson: The White House Years*. New York: Simon and Schuster, 1991.

Canfield, James Lewis. *A Case of Third Party Activism: The George Wallace Campaign Worker and the American Independent Party*. Lanham, Maryland: University Press of America, 1984.

Cannon, Lou. *President Reagan: The Role of a Lifetime*. New York: Simon & Schuster, 1991.

Cannato, Vincent. *The Ungovernable City: John Lindsay and His Struggle to Save New York*. New York: Basic Books, 2001.

Carlson, Jody. *George C. Wallace and the Politics of Powerlessness: The Wallace Campaigns for the Presidency, 1964–1976*. New Brunswick, New Jersey: Transaction Books, 1981.

Carmichael, Stokely and Charles V. Hamilton. *Black Power: The Politics of Liberation in America*. New York: Random House, 1967.

Carson, Clayborne. *In Struggle: SNCC and the Black Awakening of the 1960s*. Cambridge: Harvard University Press, 1981.

Carter, Dan T. *The Politics of Rage: George Wallace, The Origins of the New Conservatism, and the Transformation of American Politics*. New York: Simon and Schuster, 1995.

Caute, David. *The Year of the Barricades: A Journey through 1968*. New York: Harper and Row, 1988.

Center for Research on Criminal Justice. *The Iron Fist and the Velvet Glove: An Analysis of the U.S. Police*. San Francisco: Garrett Press, 1975.

Chafe, William H. *Never Stop Running: Allard Lowenstein and the Struggle to Save American Liberalism*. New York: Basic Books, 1993.

Chalmers, David. *And the Crooked Places Made Straight: The Struggle for Social Change in the 1960s*. Baltimore: The Johns Hopkins University Press, 1991.

Chester, Lewis, Godfrey Hodgson, and Bruce Page. *An American Melodrama: The Presidential Campaign of 1968*. New York: Viking, 1969.

Chevigny, Paul. *Police Power: Police Abuses in New York City*. New York: Pantheon, 1969.

Christian, George. *The President Steps Down*. New York: Macmillan, 1970.

Clark, Ramsey. *Crime in America*. New York: Simon and Schuster, 1970.

Cleaver, Eldridge. *Soul On Ice*. New York: Dell, 1968.

Cloward, Richard A. and Lloyd E. Ohlin. *Delinquency and Opportunity: A Theory of Delinquent Gangs*. Glencoe, Illinois: The Free Press, 1960.

Cloward, Richard A. and Frances Fox Piven. *Regulating the Poor: The Functions of Public Welfare*. New York: Random House, 1971.

——. *The Politics of Turmoil*. New York: Pantheon, 1974.

Colburn, David R. *Racial Change and Community Crisis: St. Augustine, Florida, 1877–1980*. New York: Columbia University Press, 1985.

Coles, Robert. "Race and Crime Control." In *Race, Crime, and Justice*, eds. Charles E. Reasons and Jack L. Kuykendall. Pacific Palisades: Goodyear Publishing Company, 1972.

——. *The Middle Americans: Proud and Uncertain*. Boston: Little, Brown, 1971.

Collins, Robert M. "The Economic Crisis of 1968 and the Waning of the 'American Century.'" *American Historical Review* 101 (April 1996): 396–422.

Conkin, Paul. *Big Daddy from the Pedernales: Lyndon Johnson*. Boston: Twayne, 1986.

Conklin, John E. *The Impact of Crime*. New York: Macmillan, 1975.

Conot, Robert. *Rivers of Blood, Years of Darkness*. New York: Bantam Books, 1967.

Cox, Archibald. *Crisis at Columbia*. New York: Vintage, 1968.

——. *The Warren Court*. Cambridge: Harvard University Press, 1968.

Cray, Ed. *Chief Justice: A Biography of Earl Warren*. New York: Simon and Schuster, 1997.

——. *The Enemy in the Streets: Police Malpractice in America*. New York: Anchor Books, 1972.

Cronin, Thomas E., Tania Z. Cronin, and Michael F. Milakovich. *U.S. v. Crime in the Streets*. Bloomington: University of Indiana Press, 1981.

Cummins, Eric. *The Rise and Fall of California's Radical Prison Movement*. Stanford: Stanford University Press, 1994.

Dallek, Matthew. *The Right Moment: Ronald Reagan's First Victory and the Decisive Turning Point in American Politics*. New York: The Free Press, 2000.

Dallek, Robert. *Flawed Giant: Lyndon Johnson and His Times, 1961–1973*. New York: Oxford University Press, 1998.

——. *Lone Star Rising: Lyndon Johnson and His Times 1908–1960*. New York: Oxford University Press, 1991.

Davis, Angela. *If They Come in the Morning*. New York: Third Press, 1971.

Davis, Mike. *City of Quartz: Excavating the Future in Los Angeles*. New York: Vintage Books, 1992.

DeLoach, Cartha 'Deke.' *Hoover's FBI: The Inside Story by Hoover's Trusted Lieutenant*. Washington: Regnery, 1995.

Divine, Robert A. *Exploring the Johnson Years*. Austin: University of Texas Press, 1981.

Douglas, Jack D., ed. *Crime and Justice in American Society*. New York: Bobbs-Merrill, 1971.

Draper, Alan. *A Rope of Sand: The AFL-CIO Committee on Political Education, 1955–1967*. New York: Praeger, 1989.

Dulaney, Marvin W. *Black Police in America*. Bloomington: University of Indiana Press, 1996.

Edsall, Thomas Byrne with Mary D. Edsall. *Chain Reaction: The Impact of Race, Rights, and Taxes on American Politics*. New York: Norton, 1991.

Edwards, Lee. *Goldwater: The Man Who Made a Revolution*. Washington: Regnery, 1995.

Ehrlichman, John. *Witness to Power: The Nixon Years*. New York: Pocket Books, 1982.

Eliff, John T. *Crime, Dissent, and the Attorney General: The Justice Department in the 1960s*. Beverly Hills, California: Sage, 1971.

Epstein, Edward J. *Agency of Fear: Opiates and Political Power in America*. New York: Putnam's, 1977.

Erskine, Hazel. "The Polls: Demonstrations and Riots," *Public Opinion Quarterly* 31 (Winter 1967–68): 668–682.

Ervin, Sam. *Preserving the Constitution*. Charlottesville, Virginia: The Michie Co., 1984.

Evans, Rowland Jr. and Robert Novak. *Lyndon B. Johnson: The Exercise of Power*. New York: New American Library, 1966.

——. *Nixon in the White House: The Frustration of Power*. New York: Vintage Books, 1972.

Farber. David. *Chicago '68*. Chicago: University of Chicago Press, 1988.

Feeley, Malcolm M. and Austin D. Sarat. *The Policy Dilemma: Federal Crime Policy and the Law Enforcement Assistance Administration, 1968-1978*. Minneapolis: University of Minnesota Press, 1980.

Fine, Benjamin. *1,000,000 Delinquents*. New York: The World Publishing Company, 1955.

Fine, Sidney. *Violence in the Model City: The Cavanagh Administration, Race Relations, and the Detroit Riot of 1967*. Ann Arbor: The University of Michigan Press, 1989.

Fogelson, Robert M. "White on Black: A Critique of the McCone Commission Report on the Los Angeles Riots." *Political Science Quarterly* 82 (September 1967): 337–367.

——. *Violence as Protest*. New York: Doubleday, 1971.

——. "Review Symposium." *American Political Science Review* 63 (December 1969): 1269–1275.

Formisano, Ronald P. *Boston Against Busing: Race, Class, and Ethnicity*. Chapel Hill: University of North Carolina Press, 1991.

Frady, Marshall. *Wallace*. New York: World Publishing Co., 1968.

Free, Lloyd A. and Hadley Cantril. *The Political Beliefs of Americans: A Study of Public Opinion*. New Brunswick, New Jersey: Rutgers University Press, 1967.

Friedman, Lawrence M. "The Social and Political Context of the War on Poverty: An Overview." *A Decade of Federal Antipoverty Programs: Achievements, Failures, and Lessons*, ed. Robert H. Haveman. New York: Academic Press, 1977.

——. *Crime and Punishment in American History*. New York: Basic Books, 1993.

Gammage, Allen Z. and Stanley L. Sachs. *Police Unions*. Springfield, Illinois: Charles C. Thomas, 1972.

Garofalo, James. *Public Opinion About Crime: The Attitudes of Victims and Non-Victims in Selected Cities*. Washington, D.C.: National Criminal Justice Information and Statistics Service, 1977.

Gates, Daryl F. with Diane K. Shah. *Chief: My Life in the LAPD*. New York: Bantam Books, 1992.

Geis, Gilbert. "Statistics Concerning Race and Crime." *Crime and Delinquency* (April 1965). In *Race, Crime, and Justice*, eds. Charles E. Reasons and Jack L. Kuykendall. Pacific Palisades: Goodyear Publishing Co., Inc., 1972.

Genovese, Michael A. "Richard M. Nixon and the Politicization of Justice." In *Watergate and Afterward: The Legacy of Richard M. Nixon*, eds. Leon Friedman and William F. Levantrosser. Westport, Connecticut: Greenwood Press, 1992.

——. *The Nixon Presidency: Power and Politics in Turbulent Times*. Westport, Connecticut: Greenwood Press, 1990.

Gilbert, James. *A Cycle of Outrage: America's Reaction to the Juvenile Delinquent in the 1950s*. New York: Oxford University Press, 1986.

Gitlin, Todd. *The Sixties: Years of Hope, Days of Rage*. New York: Bantam Books, 1987.

Glendon, Mary Ann. *Rights Talk: The Impoverishment of Political Discourse*. New York: The Free Press, 1991.

Goldberg, Robert Alan. *Barry Goldwater*. New Haven: Yale University Press, 1995.

Goldwater, Barry M. *With No Apologies: The Personal and Political Memoirs of United States Senator Barry M. Goldwater*. New York: Morrow, 1979.
——. *The Conscience of a Conservative*. New York: Hillman Books, 1960.
Goodwin, Richard N. *Remembering America: A Voice from the Sixties*. Boston: Little, Brown, 1988.
Goulden, Joseph C. "The Cops Hit the Jackpot." In *Policing America*, eds. Anthony Platt and Lynn Cooper. Englewood Cliffs, New Jersey: Prentice Hall, 1974.
Governor's Commission on the Los Angeles Riots. "Violence in the City—An End or a Beginning?" In *The Politics of Riot Commissions, 1917–1970*, ed. Anthony M. Platt. New York: Macmillan, 1971.
Greene, John Robert. *The Limits of Power: The Nixon and Ford Administrations*. Bloomington: University of Indiana Press, 1992.
Griffith, Robert. "Dwight D. Eisenhower and the Corporate Commonwealth." *American Historical Review* 87 (February 1982): 87–122.
Graham, Hugh Davis. "The Ambiguous Legacy of American Presidential Commissions." *The Public Historian* 7 (Spring 1985): 5–25.
——. "On Riots and Riot Commissions: Civil Disorders in the 1960s." *The Public Historian* 2 (Summer 1980): 7–27.
——. "The Paradox of American Violence." In *Violence in America: Historical & Comparative Perspectives*, eds. Hugh Davis Graham and Ted Robert Gurr. Beverly Hills: Sage Publications, 1979.
Halberstam, David. *The Powers That Be*. New York: Knopf, 1979.
Haldeman, H.R. *The Haldeman Diaries*. New York: Putnam's, 1994.
Hall, Stuart A. *Policing the Crisis: Mugging, the State, and Law and Order*. New York: Holmes & Meier, 1978.
Hamby, Alonzo L. *Liberalism and Its Challengers: From F.D.R. to Bush*. Paperback edition. New York: Oxford University Press, 1992.
Harrington, Michael. *The Other America: Poverty in the United States*. New York: Macmillan, 1962.
Harris, Richard. *The Fear of Crime*. New York: Praeger, 1968.
——. *Justice: The Crisis of Law, Order, and Freedom in America*. New York: Dutton, 1970.
Hawes, Joseph M., ed. *Law and Order in American History*. Port Washington, New York: Kennikat Press, 1979.
Hayden, Tom. *Rebellion in Newark: Official Violence and Ghetto Response*. New York: Random House, 1967.
Heath, Jim. *Decade of Disillusionment: The Kennedy-Johnson Years*. Bloomington: Indiana University Press, 1975.
Hess, Karl. *In a Cause that Will Triumph: The Goldwater Campaign and the Future of Conservatism*. Garden City, New York: Doubleday, 1967.
Horne, Gerald. *Fire This Time: The Watts Uprising and the 1960s*. Charlottesville: University of Virginia Press, 1995.

Jackson, Kenneth T. *Crabgrass Frontier: The Suburbanization of the United States*. New York: Oxford University Press, 1985.

Jackson, Thomas F. "The State, the Movement, and the Urban Poor: The War on Poverty and Political Mobilization in the 1960s." In *The "Underclass" Debate*, ed. Michael B. Katz. Princeton: Princeton University Press, 1993.

Jacobs, Paul. *Prelude to Riot: A View of Urban America from the Bottom*. New York: Random House, 1966.

——. "The McCone Commission." In *The Politics of Riot Commissions, 1917–1970*, ed. Anthony M. Platt. New York: Macmillan, 1971.

Jamieson, Kathleen Hall. *Packaging the Presidency: A History and Criticism of Presidential Campaign Advertising*. New York: Oxford University Press, 1984.

Jeffries, John C. *Justice Lewis F. Powell, Jr.* New York: Scribner's, 1994.

Johnson, David R. *American Law Enforcement: A History*. Wheeling, Illinois: Forum Press, 1981.

Johnson, Lyndon Baines. *The Vantage Point: Perspectives of the Presidency, 1963–1969*. New York: Holt, Rinehart and Winston, 1971.

——. *Public Papers of the Presidents of the United States: Lyndon B. Johnson, 1963–1964*. 2 vols. Washington, D.C.: U.S. Government Printing Office, 1965.

——. *Public Papers of the Presidents of the United States: Lyndon B. Johnson, 1965*. 2 vols. Washington, D.C.: U.S. Government Printing Office, 1966.

——. *Public Papers of the Presidents of the United States: Lyndon B. Johnson, 1966*. 2 vols. Washington, D.C.: U.S. Government Printing Office, 1967.

——. *Public Papers of the Presidents of the United States: Lyndon B. Johnson, 1967*. 2 vols. Washington, D.C.: U.S. Government Printing Office, 1968.

——. *Public Papers of the Presidents of the United States: Lyndon B. Johnson, 1968*. 2 vols. Washington, D.C.: U.S. Government Printing Office, 1969.

Kahn, Roger. *The Battle for Morningside Heights*. New York: Morrow, 1970.

Kalman, Laura. *Abe Fortas: A Biography*. New Haven: Yale University Press, 1990.

Katz, Michael B. *The Undeserving Poor: From the War on Poverty to the War on Welfare*. New York: Pantheon Books, 1989.

Katznelson, Ira. *City Trenches: Urban Politics and the Patterning of Class in the United States*. New York: Pantheon Books, 1981.

Kazin, Michael. *The Populist Persuasion: An American History*. New York: Basic Books, 1995.

Kearns, Doris. *Lyndon Johnson and the American Dream*. New York: Harper and Row, 1976.

Kelley, Robin D.G. "The Black Poor and the Politics of Opposition in a New South City, 1929-1970." In *The "Underclass" Debate*, ed. Michael B. Katz. Princeton: Princeton University Press, 1993.

Kennedy, John F. *Public Papers of the Presidents of the United States: John F. Kennedy, 1961*. Washington, D.C.: U.S. Government Printing Office, 1962.

——. *Public Papers of the Presidents of the United States: John F. Kennedy, 1963*. Washington, D.C.: U.S. Government Printing Office, 1964.

Kennedy, Randall. *Race, Crime, and the Law*. New York: Pantheon Books, 1997.

Kessel, John H. *The Goldwater Coalition: Republican Strategies in 1964*. New York: Bobbs-Merrill, 1968.

Klare, Michael T. "Bringing It Back: Planning for the City." In *Policing America*, eds. Anthony Platt and Lynn Cooper. Englewood Cliffs, New Jersey: Prentice Hall, 1974.

——. "Policing the Empire." In *Policing America*, eds. Anthony Platt and Lynn Cooper. Englewood Cliffs, New Jersey: Prentice Hall, 1974.

Klein, Woody. *Lindsay's Promise: The Dream that Failed*. London: Macmillan, 1970.

Kleindienst, Richard. *Justice: The Memoirs of an Attorney General*. Ottawa, Illinois: Jameson Books, 1985.

Killian, Lewis M. *The Impossible Revolution?* New York: Random House, 1968.

Klinkner, Philip. *The Losing Parties*. New Haven: Yale University Press, 1994.

Knapp, Daniel and Kenneth Polk. *Scouting the War on Poverty: Reform in the Kennedy Administration*. Lexington, Massachusetts: Heath/Lexington Books, 1971.

Kopkind, Andrew. "White on Black: The Riot Commission and the Rhetoric of Reform." In *The Politics of Riot Commissions, 1917–1970*, ed. Anthony M. Platt. New York: Macmillan, 1971.

Kutler, Stanley I. *The Wars of Watergate: The Last Crisis of Richard Nixon*. New York: Knopf, 1990.

Ladd, Everett Carl. *Transformations of the American Party System: Coalitions from the New Deal to the 1970s*. New York: Norton, 1975.

Lait, Jack and Lee Mortimer. *U.S.A. Confidential*. New York: Crown, 1952.

Lardner, James. *Crusader: The Hell-Raising Police Career of Detective David Durk*. New York: Random House, 1996.

Lasser, William. *The Limits of Judicial Power: The Supreme Court in American Politics*. Chapel Hill: University of North Carolina Press, 1988.

Leinen, Stephen. *Black Police, White Society*. New York: New York University Press, 1984.

Lemann, Nicholas. *The Promised Land: The Great Black Migration and How It Changed America*. New York: Knopf, 1991.

Lesher, Stephan. *George Wallace: American Populist*. Reading, Massachusetts: Addison-Wesley Publishing Co., 1994.

Levy, Peter B. *Civil War on Race Street: The Civil Rights Movement in Cambridge, Maryland*. University of Florida Press, 2003.

Lipsky, Michael and David J. Olson. *Commission Politics: The Processing of Racial Crisis in America*. New Brunswick, New Jersey: Transaction Books, 1977.

Lukas, J. Anthony. *Nightmare: The Underside of the Nixon Years*. New York: Bantam, 1976.

Mailer, Norman. *Miami and the Siege of Chicago: An Informal History of the Republican and Democratic Conventions of 1968*. New York: Bantam Books, 1969.

Matusow, Allen J. *The Unraveling of America: A History of Liberalism in the 1960s*. New York: Harper and Row, 1984.

McGirr, Lisa. *Suburban Warriors: The Origins of the New American Right*. Princeton: Princeton University Press, 2001.

McGinniss, Joe. *The Selling of the President 1968*. New York: Trident Press, 1969.

Miller, James. *"Democracy Is In the Streets": From Port Huron to the Siege of Chicago*. New York: Simon & Schuster, 1987.

Moore, John E. "Controlling Delinquency: Executive, Congressional, and Juvenile, 1961-1964." In *Congress and Urban Problems*, ed. Frederic N. Cleaveland. Washington: The Brookings Institution, 1969.

Moore, William H. *The Kefauver Committee and the Politics of Crime*. Columbia: University of Missouri Press, 1974.

Morris, Roger. *Richard Milhous Nixon: The Rise of an American Politician*. New York: Holt, 1990.

Moynihan, Daniel Patrick. *Maximum Feasible Misunderstanding: Community Action in the War on Poverty*. New York: The Free Press, 1969.

Murphy, Bruce Allen. *Fortas: The Rise and Ruin of a Justice*. New York: Morrow, 1988.

Murphy, Patrick V. and Thomas Plate. *Commissioner: A View from the Top of American Law Enforcement*. New York: Simon and Schuster, 1977.

Musto, David. *The American Disease: Origins of Narcotics Control*. New Haven, Connecticut: Yale University Press, 1973.

Navasky, Victor S. *Kennedy Justice*. New York: Atheneum, 1971.

Nicholas, Alex. *Black in Blue: A Study of the Negro Policeman*. New York: Appleton-Century Crofts, 1969.

Niederhoffer, Arthur. *Behind the Shield: The Police in Urban Society*. New York: Doubleday , 1967.

Nixon, Richard M. *RN: The Memoirs of Richard Nixon*. New York: Grosset and Dunlap, 1978.

Novak, Robert D. *The Agony of the GOP 1964*. New York: Macmillan, 1965.

O'Brien, David M. *Storm Center: The Supreme Court in American Politics*. New York: Norton, 1986.

O'Connor, Alice. "Community Action, Urban Reform, and the Fight Against Poverty." *Journal of Urban History* 22 (July 1996): 586–625.

O'Neill, William L. *Coming Apart: An Informal History of America in the 1960s*. New York: Random House, 1971.

O'Reilly, Kenneth. *"Racial Matters": The FBI's Secret File on Black America, 1960-1972*. New York: The Free Press, 1989.

——. "The FBI and the Politics of the Riots, 1964–1968." *Journal of American History* 75 (June 1988): 94–98.

Oshinsky, David. "*Worse Than Slavery*": *Parchman Farm and the Ordeal of Jim Crow Justice*. New York: The Free Press, 1996.

Parmenter, Tom. "Breakdown of Law and Order." *Trans-Action* 4 (September 1967): 13–22.

Parmet, Herbert S. *Richard Nixon and His America*. Boston: Little, Brown, 1990.

Patterson, James T. *America's Struggle Against Poverty, 1900–1980*. Cambridge: Harvard University Press, 1981.

——. *Grand Expectations: The U.S., 1945-1974*. New York: Oxford University Press, 1996.

Perlstein, Rick. *Before the Storm: Barry Goldwater and the Unmaking of the American Consensus*. New York: Hill and Wang, 2001.

Phillips, Kevin. *The Emerging Republican Majority*. Garden City, New York: Doubleday, 1970.

Pinto, Vince. "Weapons for the Homefront." In *Policing America*, eds. Anthony Platt and Lynn Cooper. Englewood Cliffs, New Jersey: Prentice Hall, 1974.

Pollack, Jack Harrison. *Earl Warren: The Judge Who Changed America*. Englewood Cliffs, New Jersey: Prentice-Hall, 1979.

Powers, Richard Gid. *Secrecy and Power: The Life of J. Edgar Hoover*. New York: The Free Press, 1987.

President's Commission on Law Enforcement and the Administration of Justice. *The Challenge of Crime in a Free Society*. Washington, D.C.: U.S. Government Printing Office, 1967.

——. *Crime and Its Impact—An Assessment*. Washington, D.C.: U.S. Government Printing Office, 1967.

Price, Ray. *With Nixon*. New York: Viking, 1977.

Quinney, Richard. *Criminology: Analysis and Critique of Crime in America*. Boston: Little, Brown, 1975.

Reasons, Charles E. *Race, Crime, and Justice*. Pacific Palisades, California: Goodyear, 1972.

Report of the National Advisory Commission on Civil Disorders. New York: Bantam Books, 1968.

Reedy, George E. *The Twilight of the Presidency*. New York: World, 1970.

Rieder, Jonathan. *Canarsie: The Italians and Jews of Brooklyn Against Liberalism*. Cambridge: Harvard University Press, 1985.

Rogin, Michael. "Wallace and the Middle Class: The White Backlash in Wisconsin." *Public Opinion Quarterly* 30 (Spring 1966): 98–109.

——. *Political Change in California: Critical Elections and Social Movements, 1890–1966*. Westport, Connecticut: Greenwood Press, 1970.

Ruchelman, Leonard. *Police Politics: A Comparative Study of Three Cities*. Cambridge: Ballinger Publishing Company, 1974.

Safire, William. *Before the Fall: An Inside View of the Pre-Watergate White House*. Garden City, New York: Doubleday, 1975.

Scammon, Richard M. and Ben J. Wattenberg. *The Real Majority*. New York: Coward, McCann, and Geoghegan, 1970.

Scheingold, Stuart A. *The Politics of Street Crime: Criminal Process and Cultural Obsession*. Philadelphia: Temple University Press, 1991.

——. *The Politics of Law and Order: Street Crime and Public Policy*. New York: Longman, 1984.

Schell, Jonathan. *The Time of Illusion: A Historical and Reflective Account of the Nixon Era*. New York: Vintage Books, 1975.

Scher, Richard K. *Politics in the New South: Republicanism, Race, and Leadership in the Twentieth Century*. New York: Paragon House, 1992.

Schlesinger, Arthur. *Robert Kennedy and His Times*. Paperback edition. New York: Ballantine Books, 1978.

Schoenwald, Jonathan. *A Time for Choosing: The Rise of Modern American Conservatism*. New York: Oxford University Press, 2001.

Schulz, Dorothy Moses. *From Social Worker to Crimefighter: Women in United States Municipal Policing*. Westport, Connecticut: Praeger, 1995.

Schuparra, Kurt. *Triumph of the Right: The Rise of the California Conservative Movement, 1945–1966*. New York: M.E. Sharpe, 1998.

Schwartz, Bernard. *Super Chief: Earl Warren and His Supreme Court*. New York: New York: New York University Press, 1983.

Self, Robert O. *American Babylon: Race and the Struggle for Postwar Oakland*. Princeton: Princeton University Press, 2003.

Shadegg, Stephen. *What Happened to Goldwater?* New York: Holt, Rinehart and Winston, 1965.

Shakur, Sanyika (a.k.a. Monster Kody Scott). *Monster: The Autobiography of an L.A. Gang Member*. New York: The Atlantic Monthly Press, 1993.

Sidey, Hugh. *A Very Personal Presidency: Lyndon Johnson in the White House*. New York: Atheneum, 1968.

Silberman, Charles E. *Criminal Violence, Criminal Justice*. New York: Random House, 1978.

Silver, Allan. "The Demand for Order in Domestic Society: Themes in the History of Urban Crime, Riot and Police." In *The Police: Six Sociological Essays*, ed. David J. Bordua. New York: Wiley, 1967.

Simon, David. *Homicide: A Year on the Killing Streets*. Paperback edition. New York: Ballantine, 1992.

Simon, James F. *In His Own Image: The Supreme Court in Richard Nixon's America*. New York: McKay, 1973.

Skolnick, Jerome H. *Justice Without Trial: Law Enforcement in Democratic Society*. New York: Wiley, 1967.

——. *The Politics of Protest*. New York: Simon & Schuster, 1969.

Solberg, Carl. *Hubert Humphrey: A Biography*. New York: Norton, 1984.

Sorin, Gerald. *The Nurturing Neighborhood: The Brownsville Boys Club and Jewish Community in Urban America, 1940-1990*. New York: New York University Press, 1990.

Stinchcombe, Arthur L. *Crime and Punishment—Changing Attitudes in America*. San Francisco: Jossey-Bass Publishers, 1980.

Sundquist, James L., ed. *On Fighting Poverty: Perspectives From Experience*. New York: Basic Books, 1969.

——. *Politics and Policy: The Eisenhower, Kennedy, and Johnson Years*. Washington: The Brookings Institution, 1968.

Thurber, Timothy N. *Hubert H. Humphrey and the African American Freedom Struggle*. New York: Columbia University Press, 1999.

Turner, William W. *The Police Establishment*. New York: Putnam's, 1968.

Tuttle, William M., Jr. *"Daddy's Gone to War": The Second World War in the Lives of America's Children*. New York: Oxford University Press, 1993.

Unger, Irwin. *Turning Point: 1968*. New York: Scribner's, 1988.

Valenti, Jack. *A Very Human President*. New York: Norton, 1975.

Viteritti, Joseph P. *Police, Politics, and Pluralism in New York City: A Comparative Case Study*. Beverly Hills: Sage Publications, 1973.

Walker, Daniel. *Rights in Conflict: "The Chicago Police Riot."* New York: The New American Library, 1968.

Walker, Samuel. *Popular Justice: A History of American Criminal Justice*. New York: Oxford University Press, 1980.

Wallace, George C. *Stand Up for America*. Garden City, New York: Doubleday, 1976.

Warn, Keith L. "System Engineering Approach to Law Enforcement." In *Law Enforcement Science and Technology: Proceedings of the 1st National Symposium on LE Science and Technology*, ed. S.A.Yefsky. Chicago: Thompson Book Company, 1967.

Webb, Lee Webb. "Repression—A New 'Growth Industry.'" In *Policing America*, eds. Anthony Platt and Lynn Cooper. Englewood Cliffs, New Jersey: Prentice Hall, 1974.

White, F. Clifton. *Suite 3505: The Story of the Draft Goldwater Movement*. New Rochelle: Arlington House, 1967.

White, Theodore H. *The Making of the President 1964*. New York: Atheneum, 1965.

——. *The Making of the President 1968*. New York: Atheneum, 1969.

——. *The Making of the President 1972*. New York: Bantam Books, 1973.

Wicker, Tom. *A Time to Die*. New York: Ballantine, 1976.

Wildavsky, Aaron. "The Empty-Head Blues: Black Rebellion and White Reaction." *The Public Interest* 11 (Spring 1968): 3–16.

Wilkins, Roger. *A Man's Life: An Autobiography*. New York: Simon and Schuster, 1982.

Wills, Garry. *The Second Civil War*. New York: New American Library, 1968.
——. *Nixon Agonistes*. Boston: Houghton Mifflin, 1970.
Wilson, James Q. *Thinking About Crime*. Paperback edition. New York: Vintage, 1985.
——. "Crime in the Streets." *The Public Interest* 5 (Fall 1966): 26–35. In *Law and Order in a Democratic Society*, eds. Marvin R. Summers and Thomas E. Barth. Columbus, Ohio: Charles E. Merrill Publishing, Co., 1970.
Wilson, Jerry V. *Police Report: A View of Law Enforcement*. Boston: Little, Brown, 1975.
Witcover, Jules. *1968: The Year the Dream Died*. New York: Warner Books, 1997.
Wolanin, Thomas R. *Presidential Advisory Commissions: Truman to Nixon*. Madison: University of Wisconsin Press, 1975.
Wolfgang, Marvin E. *Crime and Race: Conceptions and Misconceptions*. New York: Institute of Human Relations Press, 1970.
Wolfgang, Marvin and Franco Ferracuti. *The Subculture of Violence*. New York: University Press, 1967.
Wolman, Harold L. "Policy Form in the Institutional Presidency: The Johnson Task Forces." In *The Presidential Advisory System*, eds. Thomas E. Cronin and Sanford D. Greenberg. New York: Harper and Row, 1969.
Woodiwiss, Michael. *Crime, Crusades, and Corruption: Prohibitions in the U.S., 1900–1987*. Totowa, New Jersey: Barnes and Noble Books, 1988.
Zarefsky, David. *President Johnson's War on Poverty: Rhetoric and History*. Tuscaloosa: University of Alabama Press, 1986.

UNPUBLISHED SOURCES

Calder, James D. "Presidents and Crime Control: Some Limitations on Executive Policy Making." Ph.D. diss., Claremont, 1978.
Cowan, Ruth. "The New York City Civilian Review Board Referendum of November 1966: A Study in Mass Politics." Ph.D. diss., New York University, 1970.
Gifford, James Priest. "The Political Relations of the PBA in the City of New York, 1946–1969." Ph.D. diss., Columbia University, 1970.
Mahoney, Barry. "The Politics of the Safe Streets Act, 1965-1973." Ph.D. diss., Columbia University, 1976.
McGirr, Lisa. "Suburban Warriors: Grass-Roots Conservatism in the 1960s." Ph.D. diss., Columbia University, 1995.
Scruggs, Donald. "LBJ and the National Commission on Civil Disorders (The Kerner Commission): A Study of the Johnson Domestic Policy Making System." Ph.D. diss., University of Oklahoma, 1980.
Sugrue, Thomas J. "The Origins of the Urban Crisis: Race, Industrial Decline, and Housing in Detroit, 1940-1960." Ph.D. diss., Harvard University, 1992.

Walrath, Christine. "The Impact of Racial Rioting on Crime in the United States: 1960–1991." Ph.D. diss., University of Maryland—Baltimore, 1993.
Windler, Charles W. "The 1964 Wisconsin Presidential Primary." Ph.D. diss., Florida State University, 1983.

Index

COLUMBIA STUDIES IN CONTEMPORARY AMERICAN HISTORY

Alan Brinkley, General Editor

Lawrence S. Wittner, *Rebels Against War: The American Peace Movement, 1941–196* 1969

Davis R. B. Ross, *Preparing for Ulysses: Politics and Veterans During World War II* 1969

John Lewis Gaddis, *The United States and the Origins of the Cold War, 1941–1947* 1972

George C. Herring, Jr., *Aid to Russia, 1941–1946: Strategy, Diplomacy, the Origins of the Cold War* 1973

Alonzo L. Hamby, *Beyond the New Deal: Harry S. Truman and American Liberalism* 1973

Richard M. Fried, *Men Against McCarthy* 1976

Steven F. Lawson, *Black Ballots: Voting Rights in the South, 1944–1969* 1976

Carl M. Brauer, *John F. Kennedy and the Second Reconstruction* 1977

Maeva Marcus, *Truman and the Steel Seizure Case: The Limits of Presidential Power* 1977

Morton Sosna, *In Search of the Silent South: Southern Liberals and the Race Issue* 1977

Robert M. Collins, *The Business Response to Keynes, 1929–1964* 1981

Robert M. Hathaway, *Ambiguous Partnership: Britain and America, 1944–1947* 1981

Leonard Dinnerstein, *America and the Survivors of the Holocaust* 1982

Lawrence S. Wittner, *American Intervention in Greece, 1943–1949* 1982

Nancy Bernkopf Tucker, *Patterns in the Dust: Chinese-American Relations and the Recognition Controversy, 1949–1950* 1983

Catherine A. Barnes, *Journey from Jim Crow: The Desegregation of Southern Transit* 1983

Steven F. Lawson, *In Pursuit of Power: Southern Blacks and Electoral Politics, 1965–1982* 1985

David R. Colburn, *Racial Change and Community Crisis: St. Augustine, Florida, 1877–1980* 1985
Henry William Brands, *Cold Warriors: Eisenhower's Generation and the Making of American Foreign Policy* 1988
Marc S. Gallicchio, *The Cold War Begins in Asia: American East Asian Policy and the Fall of the Japanese Empire.* 1988
Melanie Billings-Yun, *Decision Against War: Eisenhower and Dien Bien Phu* 1988
Walter L. Hixson, *George F. Kennan: Cold War Iconoclast* 1989
Robert D. Schulzinger, *Henry Kissinger: Doctor of Diplomacy* 1989
Henry William Brands, *The Specter of Neutralism: The United States and the Emergence of the Third World, 1947–1960* 1989
Mitchell K. Hall, *Because of Their Faith: CALCAV and Religious Opposition to the Vietnam War* 1990
David L. Anderson, *Trapped By Success: The Eisenhower Administration and Vietnam, 1953–1961* 1991
Steven M. Gillon, *The Democrats' Dilemma: Walter F. Mondale and the Liberal Legacy* 1992
Wyatt C. Wells, *Economist in an Uncertain World: Arthur F. Burns and the Federal Reserve, 1970–1978* 1994
Stuart Svonkin, *Jews Against Prejudice: American Jews and the Fight for Civil Liberties* 1997
Doug Rossinow, *The Politics of Authenticity: Liberalism, Christianity, and the New Left in America* 1998
Campbell Craig, *Destroying the Village: Eisenhower and Thermonuclear War* 1998
Brett Gary, *The Nervous Liberals: Propaganda Anxieties from World War I to the Cold War* 1999
Andrea Friedman, *Prurient Interests: Gender, Democracy, and Obscenity in New York City: 1909–1945* 2000
Eric Rauchway, *The Refuge of Affections: Family and American Reform Politics, 1900–1920* 2000
Robert C. Cottrell, *Roger Nash Baldwin and the American Civil Liberties Union* 2000
Wyatt Wells, *Antitrust and the Formation of the Postwar World* 2002
Cyrus Veeser, *A World Safe for Capitalism: Dollar Diplomacy and America's Rise to Global Power* 2002
Michael Janeway, *The Fall of the House of Roosevelt: Brokers of Ideas and Power from FDR to LBJ* 2004
Jonathan Bell, *The Liberal State on Trial: The Cold War and American Politics in the Truman Years* 2004